BEIJING OPERA COSTUMES

BEIJING

OPERA COSTUMES

THE VISUAL COMMUNICATION
OF CHARACTER AND CULTURE

Alexandra B. Bonds

HAWAI'I   UNIVERSITY OF HAWAI'I PRESS | HONOLULU

Library of Congress Cataloging-in-Publication Data

Bonds, Alexandra B.

Beijing opera costumes : the visual communication of
character and culture / Alexandra B. Bonds.

    p.   cm.

Includes bibliographical references and index.

ISBN 978-0-8248-2956-8 (hardcover : alk. paper)

1. Opera — Production and direction — China —
Beijing. 2. Costume — China — Beijing.

3. Opera — China — Beijing.   I. Title.

MT955.B63 2008

792.502'60951 — dc22   2007043309

Publication of this book has been assisted with funding
from the Chiang Ching-kuo Foundation for International
Scholarly Exchange and the School of Hawaiian, Asian,
and Pacific Studies, University of Hawai'i

Designed by April Leidig-Higgins

Printed by Kings Times Printing Press, LTD

CONTENTS

LIST OF TABLES

Tables are located following the text in chapter eight.

PREFACE

In 1960 the noted scholar of Chinese performance, A. C. Scott, wrote in his book *Chinese Costume in Transition* that "to treat stage costume in any detail requires a book in itself . . . ."[*] His words inspired me to compose the first book written in English dedicated to the exploration of this beautiful and expressive aspect of the art of traditional Jingju (capital drama), commonly known as Beijing opera, and I am grateful to Mr. Scott for his seminal research of the topic, as well as his challenge. He was the first of many people who stimulated and assisted me in the creation of this work. While in Taipei, Taiwan, on a teaching Fulbright Fellowship in 1990–1991, I mentioned my interest in traditional Jingju costumes, and one of my colleagues told me that the main goal of those costumes was to identify the role for the audience. As a costume designer myself, this statement set off a chain reaction in my brain, because identification of the character is a principal goal in Euro-American costume design as well. I wondered how these two distinct images of dress could follow different paths to end up in the same place. Eighteen years of research later, I am still fascinated by the universal desire to imbue dress with the expression of character and the unique approaches to that end taken by each culture. During my research in Beijing, a Jingju colleague, Professor Li Wencai, explained, "When we give performances abroad, the martial arts and the costumes are the most attractive elements to our audiences. When our foreign colleagues see the costumes, they are amazed." I anticipate that you, too, will be amazed by the dazzling beauty of these costume creations, as well as the depth of meaning ascribed to the brilliant colors and intricate ornamentations.

In writing this book, I have used standard Chinese terms where the words are specific to the theatre or historical context and have included English translations in the text the first time each word is used in a chapter, as well as in the glossary. When the Chinese word is merely the name of a garment, and translates directly to English, then I employ the English word after introducing the Chinese. I have written the terms using *pinyin*, the official romanization system used in the People's Republic of China. For the sake of consistency, all non-*pinyin* romanization has been converted to *pinyin*, except for titles and authors of Chinese works published in western languages and in self-chosen English titles of Chinese organizations. The form of Chinese theatre focused on in this book has been known by many names throughout its history, and has been referred to in English as Peking opera or, more recently, Beijing opera. The Chinese name for this performance style in the People's Republic of China has been standardized as Jingju (capital drama), and that is how I refer to it. Further discussion of this issue can be found in

[*] Scott, *Chinese Costume in Transition*, 58.

the Introduction and Chapter One. The ancient word for costumes, *xingtou*, was seen in print as early as the Jin period (220–420). *Xing* means all of the clothes and *tou* refers to headdresses; together, *xingtou* encompasses everything in connection with costuming. In the early twentieth century, when modern Chinese began to replace the classical language, *fuzhuang* (putting on clothes), a generic term for all clothing, daily wear and costumes, joined *xingtou* as a word used for Jingju costumes. Because the translations for both words essentially parallel the English, this book uses the word costumes.

I conducted research at the Academy for Traditional Chinese Opera (Zhongguo Xiqu Xueyuan) in Beijing, as the first foreigner to go there specifically for the study of costume arts. The Academy of Traditional Chinese Opera is the only institute offering university-level training in Jingju in China, and it is considered a major center for the style. There, I attended classes, dress rehearsals, and performances; conducted interviews; and arranged tutorials in costume theory and practice. I attended performances by the two major Jingju troupes in Beijing, the National Jingju Company (Zhongguo Jingju Yuan) and the Beijing Jingju Company (Beijing Jingju Yuan), as well as by other troupes in Beijing and Taipei. The color photographs used in the text were taken during the performances. I traveled to Hebei province to the Donggaokou Embroidery Factory to observe the embroidery and construction process of the costumes. My research has also taken me to the Department of Theatre and Dance at the University of Hawai'i at Manoa, the foremost department for the study of Jingju in the English-speaking world. The Jingju tradition there is taught by Dr. Elizabeth Wichmann-Walczak, who studied in Nanjing with Madame Shen Xiaomei, the youngest personal disciple of Mei Lanfang (1894–1961), who was one of the greatest performers of female roles in the twentieth century. Madame Shen is a leading practitioner of the Mei *pai*

(style of performance). I observed the dressing and makeup process during dress rehearsals and performances at Manoa and prepared the pattern drafts and embroidery photographs from their costume collection. These two institutions form the foundation of my field research. While in Taipei, Beijing, and Honolulu, I attended over sixty Jingju performances, including full-length plays and evenings of scenes. Unless otherwise noted, the examples in the text are from my personal observations of these performances. In addition, I have examined books in English by both western and Chinese authors, and bilingual assistants have translated books in Chinese for me.

I would like to acknowledge the many organizations that offered support for the creation of this book. The United States Institute for Theatre Technology (USITT) has twice honored me with the Herbert D. Greggs Award for research excellence and with a generous fellowship that supported eighteen months of research, including two trips to Beijing. The Commissioners' Fund of USITT provided support for color photographs. This book would not have been possible without the encouragement and generosity of both the organization and the members of USITT. The University of Oregon has provided support through two research awards, a Summer Research Award to study in the Jingju costume collection of the Department of Theatre and Dance at the University of Hawai'i, Manoa, and a Humanities Center Research Award providing release time and a secluded office for ten weeks. In addition, a contribution for printing costs came from the Humanities Center. The Dean's Office of the College of Arts and Sciences at the University of Oregon recognized my work with a Richard Bray Award that provided funding for additional travel to Beijing, and subvention support. Another source of inspiration and photographs was the Qing dynasty collection of imperial robes of the Jordan Schnitzer Museum of Art, University of Oregon.

The following people have been unsparing in the

sharing of their knowledge and time. Fan Yiqi, my personal Rosetta stone, was tireless in pursuing research details and explicating the intricacies of the culture of Jingju. He also identified the characters and actors in the images. At the University of Hawaiʻi, Dr. Elizabeth Wichmann-Walczak, Professor Sandra Finney, Linda Yara, and Hannah Schauer opened doors to their knowledge and costume storage for me. Shanti Markstrom transformed my pattern drafts into the beautiful drawings used in the book. *Theatre Design and Technology* editor, David Rodger, and graphic designer Deborah Hazlett published my first articles and encouraged me to complete my study with a book. Both Elizabeth Wichmann-Walczak and Dr. David Rolston, University of Michigan, were exceptionally generous in reviewing my manuscript. I would also like to express my gratitude to my copy editor, Margaret Black, and the designers and staff of the University of Hawaiʻi Press for their guidance and expertise in shaping my initial inspiration into this exquisite volume.

Many people acted as resources and exchanged ideas, including Hattie Mae Nixon, Dale Gluckman, Vicki Vanecek-Young, Christine Sundt, Professor Charles Lachman, Beth Christensen, Jean Nattinger, and Zhang Weidong. Wang Weiwei and Guo Dongmei helped with additional research details. Others opened their costume collections for research and photographs, including Zhu Wengui, Wang Zhengying, and Yang Naiqing of the Beijing Xicheng Community Recreation Center. My research sample of embroidery is based on their collections, along with the holdings of the University of Hawaiʻi and the Academy of Traditional Chinese Opera.

As my command of Chinese is insufficient for conducting in-depth research, I have sought assistance from a host of invaluable translators: Katrin Zimmermann, whose language abilities are consummate, Fan Xing, and Megan Evans, all three of whom translated for me in Beijing. Written works were translated by Fan Yiqi, Chiati Liu, Daniel Baird, Nathan Hilgendorf, Xiang Kuiyao, and Sun Mei and Tian Chenshan translated Tan Yuanjie's *Zhongguo jingju fuzhuang tupu (An illustrated guide to costume in Jingju)*. Many actors patiently allowed me to photograph their makeup preparations while I was at the Academy of Traditional Chinese Opera: Wang Liang Liang, Jiao Jing Ge, Liu Kui Kui, Li Yanyan, and Yin Dongjun, and the entire cast of *Judge Bao and the Case of Qin Xianglian* from the Department of Theatre and Dance at the University of Hawaiʻi.

I am especially grateful to Chai Lixing, the Dean of Foreign Students, for arranging my classes with the knowledgeable and experienced teachers at Academy of Traditional Chinese Opera: Li Wencai, Head of the Acting Department, Li Shuo, Liu Xiaoqing, Ma Jing, Tan Yuanjie, Wang Shiying, Wu Wenxue, Yin Yongming, Zhang Jing and Zhang Yiyuan. I also studied with Zhao Zhenbang and Zou Zhiqiang in Beijing at the Affiliated Middle School for Traditional Chinese Opera (Zhongguo Xiqu Xueyuan Fushu Zhongxue). The precepts of Jingju costumes are open to individual interpretation, as it is a mutable art form. When sources have not been in agreement, I have endeavored to find a common ground. While every effort has been made to assure accuracy, any errors and deficiencies are mine.

INTRODUCTION

More than 300 forms of indigenous theatre entertainment incorporating song and music have evolved in China. The different forms of *xiqu* (music-drama), commonly translated as Chinese opera, were developed and performed in specific regions throughout the country. Jingju (capital drama), known in the west as Peking/Beijing opera, is based in Beijing and is the most widespread and influential of the theatre forms, having been the nationally dominant form of indigenous theatre for over one hundred years. Variously called *pihuang*, for the principal modes of music, Jingxi (capital theatre) and Guoju (national drama), the name Jingju emerged in the nineteenth century and has been widely used since 1949. Jingju fuses song, speech, dance, music, and acrobatics simultaneously into an integrated performance. Jingju today is presented in three types: traditional, newly written historical, and contemporary. This book focuses on the costumes used in traditional Jingju as currently performed in the late twentieth and early twenty-first centuries. Photographic examples from newly written historical dramas have been incorporated when the costumes match those used for traditional Jingju performances.

This book represents my understanding and interpretation of traditional Jingju costumes based on my own research, the teachings of my Chinese professors, and a life's work in the study and practice of Euro-American costume design. Writing from the perspective of the outsider, my viewpoint can both enhance and inhibit the findings. My knowledge and talents in the field of costuming give me a foundation for research and analysis of clothing of other periods and cultures. My practice as a designer enables me to identify and explore the issues of importance to the study of dress. With this experience, I can identify and explicate aspects of traditional Jingju dress that have not been previously articulated. However, not being Chinese, I lack the innate understanding of the field that comes from inhabiting the way of life. To address this shortcoming, I have embraced all aspects of Chinese culture in the preparation of this material: the history of dress, textiles, embroidery, design, and symbolism, to name a few. Cultural context informs the choices made in theatrical clothing in both east and west, so I have applied the methodology for costume design analysis that I have adopted in my own context to the structure of this study.

The discipline of costumes in traditional Jingju is vast and infinitely complex. To effectively cover the range of materials, I employed some selectivity. In limiting discussion to performances of traditional Jingju plays in the contemporary period, I have concentrated on establishing current aesthetic principles and usage patterns of the costumes and on uncovering the relationship between the existing costumes and their imperial precedents. Therefore the historical precedents of traditional Jingju practices, the evolution of individual costumes, or the descriptions of imperial garments are included only when the information elucidates the current use or image of a traditional Jingju costume. The costumes are not intended to replicate past garments, and the historical examples in fact prove the inherent theatricality of the stage versions. Reforms that have been made in existing costumes and the development of new pieces are included when they add to the understanding of the costume description. Costumes from other regional forms of *xiqu*, such as Cantonese (Yueju) and Taiwanese *(gezai xi)* have not been addressed.

This book presents a comprehensive reference for traditional Jingju costumes. Chapter One introduces a brief history of Jingju and description of the staging precepts, which provides a context for the costumes. The theoretical basis presented in Chapter Two contains the underlying principles of costumes and their selection for the roles. Analysis of the design components of form, color, and ornamentation occurs in Chapters Three, Four, and Five. Tan Yuanjie told me in a personal communication on May 29, 2002, that three techniques can be employed for explaining the system of costuming for traditional Jingju. Several books from China sort the costumes by their form and then relate the different colors and pattern of that form to the characters. A second approach delineates the costumes by story, providing a "costume plot" that lists the garments and accessories needed for each character in a play. The third system organizes the material by the character. This book includes examples of all three approaches, discussing the individual costumes in Chapter Six, the format of the costume plot, and the typical wardrobe of the role types in Chapter Eight. Chapter Seven covers makeup, hair, and headdresses to complete the image. Technical aspects are examined through the patterning and construction practices in Chapter Three, the application of makeup in Chapter Seven, and the dressing process in Chapter Eight. The combination of theoretical and practical information about the costumes will enable the reader to envision the garments in both a cultural context and performance construct. A glossary of Chinese words follows the text, along with a dictionary introducing many of the characters discussed. All photographs in this book are by the author or reproduced by permission from the Jordan Schnitzer Museum of Art, University of Oregon, The Nelson-Atkins Museum of Art, and Elizabeth Wichmann-Walczak.

ABBREVIATIONS

Performances were documented in Beijing, Taipei, and Manoa. In the interest of brevity, the names of the troupes have been abbreviated as follows:

ATCO Academy for Traditional Chinese Opera (Zhongguo Xiqu Xueyuan), Beijing, China.

AMSTCO The Affiliated Middle School for Traditional Chinese Opera (Zhongguo Xiqu Xueyuan Fushu Zhongxue), Beijing, China

BIBOAP Beijing International Beijing Opera Amateur Performance (Beijing Guoji Jingju Piaoyou Yanchanghui), Beijing, China

BJC Beijing Jingju Company (Beijing Jingju Yuan), Beijing, China

BTAS Beijing Theatre Arts School (Beijing Xiqu Xuexiao), Beijing, China

DTD, UHM Department of Theatre and Dance, University of Hawai'i, Manoa

JPBOC Jiangsu Province Beijing Opera Company (Jiangsu Sheng Jingju Yuan), Shanghai, China.

NFDAAPOT National Fu-hsing Dramatic Arts Academy Peking Opera Troupe (Fuxing Jutuan), Taipei, Taiwan.

NJC National Jingju Company (Zhongguo Jingju Yuan), Beijing, China

NKKCOC National Kuo Kuang Chinese Opera Company (Guo Guang Jutuan), Taipei, Taiwan.

PRSCJ Performances of Recommended Stars of Chinese Jingju (Zhongguo Jingju zhi xing tuijian yanchu), Beijing, China

DYNASTIES

Western Zhou: 1100 BC–771 BC

Eastern Zhou: 770 BC–221 BC
   Spring and Autumn: 770 BC–475 BC
   Warring States: 475 BC–221 BC

Qin: 221 BC–207 BC

Han: 206 BC–220 AD

Wei and Jin: 220–420

Southern and Northern: 420–589

Sui: 589–618

Tang: 618–907

Song: 960–1279
   Northern Song: 960–1127
   Southern Song: 1127–1279

Yuan: 1279–1368

Ming: 1368–1644

Qing: 1644–1911

BEIJING OPERA COSTUMES

The World of Traditional Jingju

1

The roots of Jingju and music-dramas reach far back into the history of China, for as early as the Zhou dynasty (1100–221 BC), records of ritual dance exist. Dancing was used in ceremonies and festive events, and was often embellished with spoken words and musical accompaniment. The integration of these performance elements found in ancient dance continues on as the essence of Chinese indigenous theatre. Succeeding dynasties saw the addition of other significant components of performance that contributed to the foundations of traditional Jingju. During the Tang dynasty (618–907), considered a pinnacle of classical arts, taste, and style in Chinese history, the Pear Orchard Academy for music and drama training was formed under Emperor Xuanzong (r. 712–756) (also known as Minghuang), and for this act he has long been considered one of the early patrons of theatrical performing arts. Although the focus of the Academy was to cultivate entertainers, primarily musicians, from among the women and children of the palace, the conservatory is generally acknowledged as having contributed to the development of theatre.[1] The Song dynasty (960–1279) saw the rise of *nanxi* (southern drama), which found popularity in the Southern Song court in Hangzhou.[2] The division of characters into role categories developed during this period, including the ancestors of the four main roles used in contemporary Jingju: the *sheng* (standard male characters), the *dan* (female characters), the *jing* (larger-than-life comic or villain characters), and the *chou* (smaller-than-life comic characters). A fully recognized theatre form, *zaju* (lit. "variety drama"), emerged during and was patronized by the Mongol Yuan dynasty (1271–1368). The Mongols initially abolished the civil service exams, which by the Song had become the main avenue to governmental positions. As a consequence, prospective candidates who were well versed in classical literature and the writing of poetry no longer had an outlet for their talents. Instead, many scholars think, these individuals turned to playwriting, thereby contributing a key aspect, the plays themselves, to complete the theatrical form, in what some consider the Golden Age of Chinese dramatic literature.

With the establishment of the Ming dynasty (1368–1644), China was once again ruled by the ethnic Han majority. *Zaju* began to be written by literati and performed at court, as well as receiving popular support. With the input of literati playwrights, *nanxi,* the fairly crude earliest form of southern drama, developed into the more refined and elaborate *chuanqi* (lit. "transmit the strange"), and also won the patronage of the court. These plays were performed according to a variety of local musical systems that competed with each other. The sixteenth century saw the development of Kunqu (lit. "songs of Kunshan"). Based on a local tradition but borrowing elements from outside that tradition, Kunqu emerged as the national, classical dramatic form, patronized by the court and most literati. Credit for the development of its musical system is given to Wei Liang-fu (c.1522–1573), a musician and performer. Beautiful melodies and classical language were combined with graceful movements to create the Kunqu performance style. The literary element was also a key component in Kunqu, and the plays were valued for the quality of the writing in addition to being a basis for performance. Liang Chenyu (c. 1520–1594) was the first successful Kunqu playwright, and as the form grew in popularity, scholars became more involved in playwriting than ever before. Also during the Ming dynasty, the system of painting faces, using patterns and colors to express the character, flourished, and this contributed yet another aspect of performance that has descended to contemporary Jingju.

During the Qing dynasty (1644–1911), the Qianlong emperor, who reigned from 1736–1796, was an admirer of theatre performance. When his eightieth birthday was celebrated in 1790, performing companies from nearby provinces gathered in the capital city of Beijing to participate in the festivities and pay homage to the emperor. The best of the troupes from Anhui province enjoyed great success in the capital, so other troupes performing in the Anhui style came to Beijing as well, where they interacted with performers from other regions, particularly Hubei and Shanxi. The combination of their talents and regional styles, along with the traditions of Kunqu, the aristocratic Ming theatre, formed the basis for a new theatre form, that of Beijing. The emerging form was called *pihuang,* a combination of the names for the two principal modes of music incorporated into the new style, *xipi,* a modal system from Hubei province, and *erhuang,* a modal system from Anhui province. As the form developed and spread to other cities, a new name, Jingxi (capital theatre), came into use in the latter half of the nineteenth century. The strength of the new form came from absorbing the best aspects of existing forms and the melding of all that had come before. Hence, in addition to being the celebration

of the emperor's birthday, 1790 is considered by some as the birth of the theatrical form now called Jingju.

Once established in the late eighteenth century, Beijing's own regional theatre form continued to develop and flourish. The emphasis on poetry and scholar-beauty romances in the Kunqu style was challenged with an increase in the Jingju tradition's employment of martial and popular literature. *The Romance of the Three Kingdoms (Sanguo yanyi)* is one source often drawn upon for play material. This great epic, attributed to Luo Guanzhong, (c. 1330–1400), concerns the struggle for power from the end of the Han (c. 206 BC–220 AD) through the Three Kingdoms period (220–280). The new subject matter changed the dramatic focus to male characters and incorporated the use of acrobatics to portray the battles, further shifting the form's emphasis from literary to performative.

Jingju reached its peak in the first half of the twentieth century, when it was enhanced by the emergence of some of China's best actors, notably Mei Lanfang (1894–1961), a superb player of female roles. He contributed to the spreading awareness of the form by touring other countries. Performances declined during the Japanese invasions of China, but were revitalized after the Communist revolution in 1949, and the name Jingju was devised. After mid-century, the practice of men playing women's roles diminished, and women began to perform more frequently in Jingju. During the Cultural Revolution, Jingju was transformed into model revolutionary opera, with a repertoire limited to plays that supported the Party line, and the sumptuous costumes were replaced by Mao suits and peasant dress. Restored to its original scope in the 1980s, Jingju continues to evolve as a living form of theatre, with performances of traditional, newly written historical, and contemporary plays. Combining the heritage of a millennium of *xiqu* (music-drama) development and absorbing the admirable aspects from eighteenth- and nineteenth-century forms in the years since the emperor's birthday in 1790, Jingju has become the leading form of *xiqu* in China.[3]

Role Types

Every character in a Jingju play is assigned to a role type according to the character's important personality traits and the circumstances in the play. The four major role types continue to be *sheng, dan, jing* (painted-face characters), and *chou* (lit. "ugly," clown characters), though the descriptions of the latter two have evolved since the Song dynasty. The role types contain subdivisions for age and performance skills. In performance, each role projects an ideal through distinct techniques of movement and vocal quality, as well as specific standards of hair, makeup, and dress. However, the use of role types does not imply that the characters are stereotypes. Both intelligent and foolish characters appear within the role subdivisions, and conversely, a court official can be assigned to a *sheng, jing,* or *chou* role, depending on the nature of his character. The assignment of the role types is determined by what the characters in each category have in common, while at the same time room is left for a variety of personalities.

Sheng. The *sheng* roles are generally the dignified and decent men, with a range of personal characteristics and status. Within the *sheng* roles are two major subdivisions by age, *laosheng* (mature men) and *xiaosheng* (young men), and another subdivision for warriors, *wusheng* (martial men). Many *laosheng* are scholars and statesmen, often members of the court or heads of households. Their social status may also be lower, but if so, they are still intrinsically deserving of respect. Many of the plays with a *laosheng* in the principal role involve the *laosheng* remaining composed while performing difficult, but noble tasks in the face of adversity. *Laosheng* usually wear long *pi* (formal robes) or *mang* (court robes) with water sleeves *(shuixiu)*, white silk extensions

to the cuff of the garment sleeve, high-topped, high-soled boots *(houdi xue)*, and fabric headdresses. They wear skin-toned makeup, with the addition of peach color around the eyes and between the brows. Their eyes and brows are accented with black liner. *Laosheng* are further distinguished by a long, thin, three-part beard called a *sanliu ran*. Their performance skills focus on song, speech, and dance-acting (Fig. 1.1). A subcategory of *laosheng* is *wulaosheng*, older men who are generals and have fighting skills. The older fighters have the same makeup as their scholarly counterparts, but they usually wear the *kao* (armor) instead of robes, and metal filigree war helmets *(kui)* instead of fabric-covered hats. They add combat skills to their *laosheng* training (Fig. 1.2).

The *xiaosheng* are generally under thirty and unmarried or recently married. *Xiaosheng* are subdivided into two categories, the *wenxiaosheng* (civil *xiaosheng*, sometimes shortened to *xiaosheng*), who are the princes, scholars, dandies, and lovers, and the *wuxiaosheng* (sometimes shortened to *wusheng*), who are valiant young generals. The *wenxiaosheng* often wear soft *xuezi* (informal robes) in pastel colors, embroidered with flowers, and with water sleeves, simple headdresses, and high-soled boots. Their skills include song, speech, and dance-acting (Fig. 1.3). The *wuxiaosheng* generally wear *kao*, high-soled boots, and often have long feathers *(lingzi)* attached to their silver or gold filigree helmets (Fig. 1.4). They add combat training to their skills. To show their youth, the *xiaosheng* roles have paler makeup than the *laosheng* characters, with cherry-blossom cheeks of red rouge from above the brow to mid-cheek and between the brows. Their eyes are rimmed with black lines, and their eyebrows are reinforced with black as well. The *xiaosheng* are also beardless.

The *wusheng* are the fighting male roles. Two subdivisions in this category are named for the costumes that they wear. The *changkao wusheng* (long-armor martial men) are high-ranking younger warriors who also wear

FIGURE 1.1. The *laosheng* roles are mature men who are scholars and statesmen. The court robe of a *laosheng* is a *mang* with round dragons, and the headdress is a *zhongsha* (loyal hat) with a *fuma taozi,* a hat ornament to indicate he is an imperial son-in-law, and feathers to show his military function. *Silang Visits His Mother (Silang tan mu).* Character: Yang Silang, actor: Du Peng. BJC, Beijing, China. October 7, 2001.

kao, helmets, and high-soled boots. They focus on combat skills, particularly with prop weapons, but are also trained in song and speech (Fig. 1.5). The *duanda wusheng* (quick-fighting or short-clothing fighting males) play individual fighters, or disenfranchised bandits and criminals. They can also be supernatural characters that engage in combat. The *duanda wusheng* often wear *kuaiyi* (lit. "fast clothes") or *baoyi* (lit. "leopard/panther" or "embracing" clothes, hero's clothes). Thin-soled ankle boots *(baodi xue)* are worn to enable the performance of martial arts sequences, which include hand-to-hand combat and acrobatics (Fig. 1.6). The basic makeup for these two roles resembles that for the *laosheng,* with the skin-toned face. In addition, between their brows, the

FIGURE 1.2. Mature standard males who are also military men are *wulaosheng*. This *wulaosheng* is dressed in a combination of *mang* over *kao* to indicate he is reviewing his troops. His beard is a *cansan* (gray three-part beard). *A Sorrow that Transcends Life and Death (Sheng si hen)*. Character: Zong Ze, actor: Ye Jinyuan. BJC, Beijing, China. July 30, 2000.

wusheng have an arrowhead shape of rouge pointing upwards. Like the *xiaosheng,* they appear without the beards.

Dan. The *dan*, or female, roles have four main subdivisions: *laodan* (mature women), *qingyi* (lit. "black clothing," young to middle-aged women), *huadan*, (lit. "flower" women, lively young women), and *wudan* (military women). The *laodan* are the elderly women, generally dignified and ranging in social position from dowager empresses to poor grandmothers. Their age is often indicated by a walking staff, bent posture, and limited movement, yet they speak and sing in a hearty natural voice. Their faces are practically unadorned, and they wear gray to white hair in a small bun on the

FIGURE 1.3. *Wenxiaosheng* play youthful scholars, princes, and lovers. Their daily wear is often a pastel *hua xuezi*, with floral embroidery. The hat pictured is a *Xu Xian jin,* a smaller version of the *yawei jin* (duck-tailed hat), specifically for this role, with a piece of white jade *(maozheng)* in front to indicate his youth. The performer wears the typical *xiaosheng* makeup, with an arc of rouge between his brows. *The Broken Bridge (Duan qiao).* Character: Xu Xian, actor: Song Jie. BJC, Beijing, China. July 2, 2000.

crown of the head, wrapped in a simple scarf. They wear knee-length robes in blended colors, with water sleeves, *chenqun* (lit. "inside skirts"), and *fuzi lü* (lit. "good fortune" shoes) with a slight lift (Fig. 1.7).

The *qingyi* roles are decorous women, young to middle-aged, who have been raised to behave within the social norm. The name of the role comes from a black robe with blue bands of trim that women in this role often wear when their fortunes have turned for the worse (Fig. 6.18). The characters are empresses and noble women, filial daughters, faithful wives, or lovers in distress, usually because of a dire complication that is resolved by the end of the play. Their training features song, often plaintive arias, speech in a falsetto voice, and dance-acting. They project demure deportment with downcast eyes and delicate manners. The

FIGURE 1.4. Young military generals, *wuxiaosheng*, usually are dressed in *kao*, worn here with the *zijin guan* (lit. "purple gold headdress"). The pink and white makeup features an arc shape on the forehead. *Mu Guiying Takes Command (Mu Guiying gua shuai)*. Character: Yang Wenguang, actor: Zeng Baoyu. BJC, Beijing, China. July 16, 2000.

FIGURE 1.5. The *changkao wusheng,* high-ranking young warriors, wear the *kao,* seen here with a *zhajin ezi* (lit. "tied cloth" helmet and diadem). This role's makeup includes a wedge shape between the brows and a natural-colored face. *Yandang Mountain (Yandang shan).* Character: Meng Haigong, actor: Li Shiyou. BJC, Beijing, China. September 9, 2001.

FIGURE 1.6. Individual fighters are called *duanda wusheng* (see figure to left) and may wear *baoyi* (hero's clothes) with a *ruan luomao* (soft beret). The makeup calls for a wedge shape between the brows. The figure on the right is a *wuchou,* a comic martial fighter, in *hua kuaiyi* (flowered "fast clothes"). Though the stage is fully lit, the actors pantomime darkness. *Fight at Crossroads Inn (Sancha kou).* Character, left: Ren Tanghui, actor: Yin Dongjun; character, right: Liu Lihua, actor: Liu Yao. ATCO, Beijing, China. June 2, 2002.

qingyi makeup resembles that of their suitors, the *wenxiaosheng,* with a pale face enhanced with cherry-blossom rouge from the eyebrows fading out over the cheeks. The female roles do not have rouge between the brows. The eyes are emphasized with black liner, and the brows are drawn rising up towards the temples. They often wear *nüpi* (women's formal robes) that are knee length, in pastel colors, embroidered with pretty floral compositions, and with water sleeves. A long "one hundred pleats skirt" *(baizhe qun)* and flat shoes *(caixie)* complete the ensemble. Their complicated hairstyles are elaborately dressed with jewels or covered with ornately decorated headdresses (Fig. 1.8).

The *huadan* are the flirtatious, roguish, energetic young women in comic and lighthearted roles. In contrast to the *qingyi,* the *huadan* use a vivacious demeanor,

FIGURE 1.7. *Laodan,* the elderly women's roles, are often attired in *nüpi* in maroon or olive green. The roundels indicate a dignified character. The skirt has fewer pleats than the one for *qingyi.* Their makeup is skin-toned, with little embellishment, and the hair is *zongfa* (lit. "palm fiber hair"), dressed with a *leizi* (black velvet strip with pearl) and scarf. *Hongniang (Hongniang).* Character: Madam Cui, actor: Zhang Jing. NJC, Beijing, China. October 5, 2001.

with an upturned face and playful movements that go beyond the boundaries of social decorum. Their skills are focused on speech, dance-acting, and hand gestures. The *huadan,* when playing commoners, often wear a short jacket *(ao)* that does not have water sleeves, with either a pleated skirt or trousers *(kuzi)* and flat shoes. While their makeup is the same as the *qingyi,* their hair may have slightly less rich jewelry. *Huadan* are nicely dressed despite their lower status (Fig. 1.9).

The roles for martial women are called *wudan,* and within that category are the *daoma dan* ("sword and horse" martial women). The hair and makeup for martial women resembles that of the other young female characters. The *wudan* correspond to the *duanda wu-*

FIGURE 1.8. Young to middle-aged women are *qingyi*, with pink and white makeup and sometimes the *datou* (complete hair), seen here with imitation kingfisher feather ornaments. In this example, the character is married and wearing a *nüpi* over a *xuezi* (informal robe), with a center-front closing. A brooch decorates the neckline of the inner garment. The white fabric at her wrists is the water sleeves, skillfully folded by flicking her hands. *Mu Guiying Takes Command (Mu Guiying gua shuai)*. Character: Mu Guiying, actor: Dong Yuanyuan. BJC, Beijing, China. July 16, 2000.

sheng, and usually wear a similar short costume, a *zhan'ao zhanqun* (martial jacket, skirt, and trousers), but with the addition of skirt flaps, and flat ankle boots called small "barbarian" boots *(xiao manxue)*. The choice of costume is related to the combat needs of the scene, as *wudan* may also wear other combat dress. *Wudan* are generally independent combatants, trained in acrobatics and hand-to-hand combat, often fighting as many as four men at once with sticks and swords (Fig. 1.10). *Daoma dan* can wear *nükao* (female armor), which creates a more formidable figure, enhanced with flower and phoenix embroidery and additional streamers, and a filigree helmet with long feathers attached. The combat specialty of the *daoma dan* parallels that of

FIGURE 1.9. The *huadan* roles are vivacious women of lower status. In this example, she wears a jacket and trousers with a small apron and is pantomiming breaking her sewing thread in her teeth. Her hairstyle is the *datou*, with jewels framing the forehead and rhinestones around the rest of her head. *Picking Up the Jade Bracelet (Shi yuzhuo).* Character: Sun Yujiao, actor: unidentified. Independent players, Beijing, China. September 8, 2001.

FIGURE 1.10. *Wudan* specialize in martial acrobatics and are often dressed for combat in the *zhan'ao zhan qun* (martial jacket and trousers), but they add a skirt to the jacket and trousers style worn by male soldiers. This character's headdress is the *qixing ezi* (seven-star diadem), with a symbol on top to indicate that she is a spirit of the drought. This character wears feathers and foxtails on her headdress because she is not a human. *The Magic Cistern (Ju da gang)*. Character: Wang Daniang, actor: Huang Hua. ATCO, Beijing, China. June 1, 2002.

the *changkao* version of the *wusheng*, as both wear long armor and focus on swords and lances in their battles, which are often on horseback (Fig. 1.11).

An additional subcategory for women's roles was developed in the twentieth century by Mei Lanfang and other *dan* actors. Called *huashan* (lit. "flower shirt"), this role combined qualities from at least two of the four *dan* role types for young women, the *qingyi*, *hua-dan*, *daoma dan*, and *wudan*. The break with tradition enabled the *dan* actors to combine performance skills and thereby create more complex renditions of characters. The *huashan* wear costumes suited to the nature of their roles, including new costumes that Mei specifically designed for these characters. The concept of crossing over role-type boundaries continues, though the term *huashan* is less common now.

FIGURE 1.11. Women warriors who specialize in song and combat are *daoma dan*. They are usually dressed in the *nükao,* which is distinguished from the male version by multicolored streamers hanging from the waist. The headdress is a *qixing ezi,* and her makeup conforms to the pink and white style for young women. *The Ruse of the Bamboo Forest (Zhulin ji).* Character: Liu Jinding, actor: Pan Yuejiao. ATCO, Beijing, China. May 31, 2002.

Jing. The *jing* roles are also referred to as *hualian* ("flower" face) because of the patterns in their makeup. These characters are distinguished from the *sheng* roles in that they are men of great strength with formidable physical or mental powers and are much bolder onstage than the stately scholars. The characters in the *jing* role type range from fierce warriors, upright judges, and trustworthy officials to evil administrators and bandits.

Supernatural beings also appear in this category. *Jing* can be identified immediately in performance by their facial paint, which is often applied in complex patterns and vivid colors. Though the Chinese social norm prefers that one's inner nature be concealed, the *jing* wear their personalities on their faces. Through precise conventional patterns, the unique facial design for each character conveys information about their inner feel-

FIGURE 1.12. The *jing* roles, bold men of great strength, range from fierce warriors to court administrators. Their character is revealed through their painted-face makeup, in this case, the white color indicates his treachery. This *jing* is wearing a red *mang* and *xiangsha* (prime minister's hat). *The Gathering of Heroes (Qunying hui)*. Character: Cao Cao, actor: Luo Changde. BJC, Beijing, China. July 23, 2000.

ings and morals. The heightened facial impact is balanced by a broad padded vest *(pang'ao)*, a long, thick beard, and high-soled boots, creating overall a larger-than-life visual image to match the power of the characters in this role (Fig. 1.12). The singing voice is equally commanding, with greater force than the other roles. Actors selected for this role are generally of stocky build with a broad face, but the costume and makeup can make actors appear that way if the individuals themselves are not of that scale naturally.

Within the *jing* category are three main subdivisions. The principal roles are played by the *zhengjing* (primary *jing*), or *da hualian* (big painted face), also referred to as *heitou* (lit. "black head," after the black face makeup of one of the characters, Judge Bao) or *tongchui* ("copper hammer," after a scepter held by a character in this category). The *fujing* (supporting *jing*) or *jiazi hualian* (posture painted face) perform secondary characters whose portrayal requires speaking and acting skills, and the *wujing* (military *jing*) or *shuaida hua* (fighting painted face) act as fighting men. The *zhengjing* characters are the statesmen and generals whose roles feature strong singing skills. They usually wear *mang* with large writhing dragons embroidered above deep crashing waves at the hem (Fig. 1.12). The *fujing* feature acting skills and are dressed like the principal *jing* roles. The *wujing* are the martial painted-face roles. Like the *sheng* roles, this category is divided into *changkao,* for those who wear *kao,* and *duanda* for the more active fighters in the simpler martial arts clothing that includes the *kuaiyi.* The boundaries of costume distinction for the *jing* characters are blurred, since they often appear in a range of locations and situations requiring different dress. For this reason, in this text the single category of *jing* will be used for identifying the clothing of painted-face roles.

Chou. The *chou,* or comic, roles include foolish magistrates, nagging women, and servants. The characters are generally humorous and optimistic. No social status or rank is implied; emperors and beggars can be classified in the *chou* category if their personality deserves it. The word *chou* is written with the same simplified Chinese character as the word ugly, making the two homophones. This convergence is visualized in their makeup, which features a white patch over the nose and eyes that is intended to make the face look weak and dim-witted. The white block of makeup causes these characters to sometimes be called *doufu* or "bean-curd" face. *Chou* are also called *xiao hualian* (little painted face) for their small area of makeup. They may also wear beards that are short and oddly shaped. The *chou* are released from the traditional ideal of character portrayal to the extent that they can ad lib and address the audience directly. Their skills include speech and dance-acting. Because of their reduced level of dignity, they

FIGURE 1.13. The civil *chou* roles, called *wenchou,* include foolish court officials, such as this one wearing a *guanyi* (official's robe) and *zhongsha* (loyal hat). His beard is a *chousan* (three-part *chou* beard). The process of applying this makeup is illustrated in Figs. 7.17–18. *A Visit to the Family Grave (Xiao shangfen).* Character: Liu Lujing, actor: Jiao Jingge. ATCO, Beijing, China. May 31, 2002.

rarely play the leading character, but instead provide the comic moments.

The *chou* roles are divided into three subcategories: *wenchou* (civil *chou,* sometimes shortened to *chou*), *wuchou* (martial *chou*), and *caidan* (female *chou,* also called *choudan*). The *wenchou* roles in court scenes are the imprudent officials (Fig. 1.13). They wear the same kind of costumes as their *sheng* colleagues of the same status, but because their characters are flawed, the *chou* wear

FIGURE 1.14. Comic women's characters are played by male actors as *caidan*. Here, the makeup is a caricature of the *qingyi* for this ugly stepsister. *The Phoenix Returns to Its Nest (Feng huan chao)*. Character: Cheng Xueyan, actor: Zhu Jinhua. BJC, Beijing, China. July 9, 2000.

dress in the same style *kuaiyi* as other hand combatants or in a special version, the *hua kuaiyi* (flowered "fast clothes"), and thin-soled ankle boots (Fig. 1.6). Undignified women, ugly stepsisters, and some matchmakers fall into the role of *caidan*. Instead of the white patch, the makeup for the *caidan* roles parodies the delicate polish of the *qingyi* face or the dignity of the *laodan*, depending on the age of the *caidan* character. (Fig. 1.14). The younger *caidan* wear comic versions of the *qingyi* robes, in unusual colors, with skirts that may be too long. Their movements mock the graceful elegance of genuine *qingyi* characters. The older *caidan* may wear *caipo ao* (colorful old women's jackets) that are oversized and boxy, and trousers that are too short (Fig. 6.41).

Supporting Roles. Since little scenery is used in the performance of traditional plays, the stage is often set with human scenery instead. Every courtroom will have a lineup of attendants, who are arranged four to a group for ordinary officials, six for nobles, and eight or more for emperors. The groups may be *longtao* (a nonspeaking entourage), formerly called *liuhang* (lit. "flowing-role type," nonspeaking attendants), or *gongnü* (female palace maids), and they are arranged symmetrically on the stage, flanking the center chair and table that depict the throne (Fig. 2.1). The fighting supporting roles are played by *wuhang* (soldiers), who are well trained in the acrobatic combat techniques (Fig. 1.15). Domestic maids are *shinü* (women who take orders). *Za* (unimportant roles) actors portray additional supernumeraries.[4]

Plays

Traditional Jingju plays are for the most part anonymous. Rather than works of great literature penned by famous playwrights, the plays, based on existing stories, have generally evolved through performances and the actors' collaborations. The plays present a mere framework for the performance, and as such have fewer words than standard western scripts. Onstage, the writ-

a costume shorter than the ideal, the color may be out of the accepted range, and their embroidery may be less decorous. *Wenchou* can also play servants, woodcutters, boatmen, waiters, and other working-class men. For these roles they are dressed in some of the simplest costumes in traditional Jingju, unembroidered silk or cotton robes tucked up to reveal their trousers and gaiters *(bangtui)* underneath (Fig. 6.37). The *wuchou* are also comic martial characters, who are usually quite resourceful and clever with their counterattacks. They

ten play becomes enriched with movement and vocal stylizations that convey the essence of the story in non-verbal terms. The number of plays for traditional Jingju is estimated to be as high as 4,000 or 5,000. Of these, around 480 are still in performance.

The stories tend to focus on higher-status characters, although a breadth of social positions is included in both principal and minor roles. The themes depict traditional life and values, particularly the Confucian concepts of justice and righteousness in behavior and outcome, romantic love in a family context, loyalty to emperor and country, filial piety and family respect, and brotherly love. Confucianism also influences the outcome of the dramas, as good is rewarded and evil is punished. There are few real tragedies; most plays include some humor and usually have a happy ending, at least in Confucian terms. Precepts of Buddhism and Daoism are also included in the stories, blended onstage as they were in daily life in China.[5]

Legends, mythology, popular historical novels, and romances from ancient China are primary resources for the Jingju plays. As many of the accounts are well-known components of Chinese culture, most audience members are familiar with the story lines. They come to the performances to see these well-loved individuals from their heritage come alive onstage and to appreciate the actors' ability to portray their favorite characters.

Three works of historical fiction comprise major sources of material for traditional Jingju plays, *The Romance of the Three Kingdoms, Outlaws of the Marsh (Shuihu zhuan),* and *Journey to the West (Xiyou ji). The Romance of the Three Kingdoms* tells of the struggle between the Wei, Shu, and Wu kingdoms from the end of the Han dynasty in 220 until 280, the closing of the Three Kingdoms era. A sworn brotherhood of heroes, Liu Bei, Guan Yu, and Zhang Fei, tries valiantly, but fails, to overcome the ruthless warlord, Cao Cao. Around ninety plays have evolved from the Three Kingdoms stories, including *The Gathering of Heroes (Qun-*

FIGURE 1.15. Soldiers are played by *wuhang,* trained in combat and acrobatics, and dressed in *bingyi* (soldier's clothes). The headdress in this example is a *toubu* and *ezi* (scarf and diadem). *Yandang Mountain (Yandang shan).* Character: soldier of Meng Haigong, actor: unidentified. BJC, Beijing, China. September 9. 2001.

ying hui), The Ruse of the Empty City (Kongcheng ji), and *The City of Baidi (Baidi cheng).* Another epic, *Outlaws of the Marsh,* attributed to Shi Nai'an (c. 1290–1365), additionally known as *The Water Margin,* was also written in the fourteenth century about events of 200 years earlier in the late Northern Song dynasty. A group of outlaws has rejected the culture of corrupt officials and banded together to form a Robin Hood-like society, in which they act gallantly, according to the rules of chivalry. *Journey to the West,* a book by Wu Cheng'en (c. 1500–

FIGURE I.16. The Monkey King, Sun Wukong, is a character from literature whose stories have transferred to the stage. His makeup is a pictogram of monkey features, and a scattered pattern of whorls and wavy lines represents his fur on his costume. *Causing an Uproar in the Dragon King's Palace (Nao longgong)*. Character: Sun Wukong, actor: unidentified. Independent players. Beijing, China. September 8, 2001.

c. 1582), recounts the adventures of Sun Wukong, the Monkey King, as he joins the monk Xuanzhuang in his travels from China to India to collect the sutras of Buddhism and bring them back to China. Many episodes of the monkey's adventures have been made into staged versions, to the delight of audiences (Fig. 1.16).

One of the most famous folktales to become a traditional Jingju play is *The Legend of the White Snake (Baishe zhuan)*. Bai Suzhen is a magical snake who transforms to human form to live among the mortals (Fig. 1.17). She marries and has a child, but is relentlessly pursued by a monk, Fahai, who insists that she cannot remain within his realm.

The great historical epics and legends have sometimes

FIGURE 1.17. Bai Suzhen, the White Snake, is a snake in human form. When pregnant, she wears the *yaobao* (lit. "bloated" skirt) high on the chest. Her headdress is a *xiao ezi* (small diadem). *The Broken Bridge (Duan qiao)*. Character: Bai Suzhen, actor: Yan Guixiang. BJC, Beijing, China. July 2, 2000.

been adapted into more than one play as their stories are often too long to perform as a single presentation, and each chapter recounts a distinct event. These sources form a significant portion of the traditional Jingju repertoire, and therefore many of the major characters appear in several story segments, which are separate performances, and therefore gain increased recognition and appreciation from audiences.

In addition to the traditional plays that have been passed down for generations, modern plays began to be written in the 1930s and continued on after the founding of the People's Republic of China.[6] The twentieth-century plays consist of two styles, newly written historical dramas that re-envision past events and often embody current political thought, and contemporary dramas that are performed in an updated performance style in modern dress. This volume references some modern productions when the costumes are the same as for traditional Jingju.

Traditional Jingju plays are loosely divided into two categories, civil plays *(wenxi)*, featuring domestic scenes, and martial plays *(wuxi)*, focusing on battles and heroic struggles. The heritage of this division can be traced as early as the Zhou dynasty, when the dancing style was divided into these two forms, with the civil dances described as elegant and graceful, and the military performances as more forceful and featuring dancing with weapons.[7] The categories are not rigid or exclusive, and both types of action can appear in one play. The civil and martial designations indicate the primary features of a scene, describing both the content and the role types to perform in the scene.

Civil plays focus on stories about seeking justice and domestic life, as well as love affairs between talented scholars, *xiaosheng*, and beautiful maidens, *qingyi*. A *huadan*, as a matchmaker, or a *chou* playing a dim-witted servant often needs to solve an intrigue to assure that the lovers come together in the end. Civil plays can also feature a *laosheng* character defending the future of the country in a court intrigue where nobility and loyalty are the essential virtues. Others contain stories of strong women who resist dire situations that test their character. The performance style emphasizes song, speech, and dance-acting. Melodic accompaniment for the song and dance sections usually features the *jinghu* (two-stringed spike fiddle), but flutes or other instruments can sometimes be used. The costumes for civil scenes are generally civilian clothing, elegant soft robes in blended colors, with floral and geometric embroidered patterns.

Martial scenes depict the struggles between rival states, warriors, or bandits, and often come from *Three Kingdoms* and *Outlaws of the Marsh* sources. The plots entail military intrigue, revenge, and strategy, with the noble characters frequently prevailing because of their superior strength of character and intelligence. The content of the performance shifts to the martial arts and acrobatics, and the roles featured are the *jing*, as generals, along with *wusheng* and *wudan*. Percussion accompaniment is central to these scenes, and the stage is often completely empty to allow space for the battles. In the martial portions of a play, the costumes tend to be the stiff and voluminous formal robes worn at court and the different forms of armor and soldiers' uniforms used for military engagements. The colors are stronger than they are for civilian clothing, with dragons and other powerful beasts decorating the costumes.

Visual Components

Stage. Early Chinese stages were set up in teahouses or temple courtyards, and featured a thrust stage with areas on three sides for viewing. In this configuration, the stage was a raised square with a canopy above, supported with decorated pillars. A balustrade encircled the stage at the base of the pillars. An embroidered curtain with square openings on the right and left for entrances and exits was hung on the back wall. The audience level on the floor was arranged with tea tables, which were reserved for men. An upper level contained boxes where the female audience members could sit. Refreshments were served before and during the performance.

The emperors of the Qing dynasty were particular fans of *xiqu* performances, and there were several theatres built in the Forbidden City (Zijin Cheng), including the Belvedere of Flowing Music (Changyin Ge), constructed in 1776. Still extant, this structure takes the teahouse arrangement to another level, adding two more floors of stages above the first. The carved and beautifully painted thrust stage is surrounded by an open courtyard and a two-story viewing building. According to a sign in the courtyard of the theatre, the three-story stage in the Forbidden City was used for extravagant performances which "called for Buddhist worthies and Taoist [sic] immortals swarming over the three stages, moving in and out of the normal entrances and exits as well as ceiling openings and floor wells." The emperor and empress watched the performance from the two-story building opposite the stage, and the ministers were seated on the sides. The Summer Palace (Yihe Yuan) also has a theatre, called The Garden of Virtue and Harmony (Dehe Yuan) where the Dowager Empress Cixi (1835–1908) watched performances (Fig. 1.18).

Some of the original teahouse-style theatres still exist in Beijing, such as the Huguang Native-place Association (Huguang Huiguan), but much of traditional Jingju is currently performed on a proscenium stage, where the walls of the stage house separate the actors from the audience. In some of the proscenium theatres, there are two sections in the house, with traditional tea tables in the front and rows of auditorium-style seating behind and in the balcony. Although the performance has been transferred to a western-style building, in the theatres with table seating, much of the teahouse atmosphere remains.

In the proscenium theatres, a house curtain marks the beginning and end of each performance. A second curtain upstage of the house curtain masks the minimal changes of scenery. A third curtain parallel to the proscenium line covers the upstage wall, and it may be plain or have a design on it. Standard masking drapes are used at the top and sides of the stage. The floor is covered by a rug, either a Chinese carpet with a single central pattern and border, or a solid-color one. The carpet is usually a pale gold or neutral green color. As the language used in traditional Jingju plays is somewhat antiquated, as well as stylized in presentation, most performances are supplemented with Chinese subtitles on either side of the stage, particularly during the sung

FIGURE 1.18. The Garden of Virtue and Harmony in the Summer Palace has a three-story stage surrounded by a courtyard designed for Jingju performances.

elements. The musicians are not considered part of the visual picture. They are rarely costumed and are only partially visible to the audience as they are seated on the stage left side of the acting area, just inside the edge of the opened house curtain.

Settings. The settings are characterized by simplicity and flexibility, in contrast to the elaborate costumes and makeup. The title of the play or the dialogue often expresses the location, and the costumes of the characters project their position and wealth, so the scenery is relieved of these responsibilities. Complex depictions of

FIGURE 1.19. Two chairs and a table can represent a variety of interior scenes. The *jing* character on the left is wearing a *kai chang* (official's informal robe), with large, opposing lions embroidered on the surface, and the *laosheng* on the right has on a *mang. Reconciliation of the Prime Minister and the General (Jiang xiang he)*. Character, left: Lian Po, actor: Yang Chi. Character, right: Yu Qing, actor: Han Shengcun. BJC, Beijing, China. July 2, 2000.

time and place are not a featured element of the traditional Jingju stage, and what needs to be known about the environment is established in the minds of the spectators by the actors' art. With its roots in small touring companies, the minimalist approach to the scenic elements was a practical matter as well. Nominal scenery may also be a result of the original stage formation, with a thrust stage and audience on three sides, where any large pieces of scenery would obstruct the view of part of the audience. A table and two chairs comprise the principal pieces of furniture onstage (Fig. 1.19). They are simply designed and are concealed with embroidered satin covers, the color of the covers contributing to the identification of the location. Yellow is the traditional color for the emperor; therefore yellow covers on the furniture indicate the palace. Red is commonly used for officials, and olive green may be used in the home of an older character, as that color is associated with age. An absence of embroidery on the covers indicates the relative poverty of the owners. The furniture can also be transformed by placement. A central table flanked by two chairs indicates a private home where is it possible to have a conversation. A chair behind the table turns the setting into an official location. The addition of ranks of attendants on either side of the furniture raises the site to a throne room. A chair placed on top of the table denotes either a higher-ranking location or transformation of the scene into a mountain, ship, or bridge. A single chair on the side of the stage becomes a precipice from which suicides can jump. For battle scenes, the stage is generally cleared completely, so that the entire surface becomes open for martial displays and acrobatics.

Set pieces have been introduced into the repertoire when a location cannot be depicted by the furniture alone. Some take the familiar forms of stage scenery made of muslin and wood. Painted to create an illusion of the item they represent, they may be only a fragment of the piece portrayed. A painted stone wall indicates a fortress or city wall, a rock may designate a battlefield, and the addition of a decorated screen transforms the stage to a study. The nuptial bed for a wedding scene is fabricated by suspending a pair of red curtains from pole supports fastened to the chairs (Fig. 1.20). The use of banners, either hung from the flies or carried by attendants, presents a palace or other ceremonial location. Soldiers carry flags onstage to stand for other troops, one flag said to represent 1,000 marching soldiers and 10,000 mounted soldiers. Square flags with water imagery on them are used to indicate a battle at sea, while flags with flames mean fire, and black flames represent wind. In some productions, elaborate settings in full stage proportions have been designed, particularly in Shanghai versions of Jingju, but extensive settings for

traditional plays are still the exception. When the set needs to be shifted, stagehands draw the central curtain to conceal their work. The actors can proceed with the scene in front of the curtain, which is then removed once the transformation is completed. While the performers move with consummate skill, the elevated style does not apply to the stagehands. In China, they are not dressed to be a part of the performance and are usually not seen, though in Taiwan, the prop men are still visible and dressed in long dark robes.

Props. Props are often incorporated to aid with the depiction of objects too large to bring onstage. The piece becomes a symbol for the whole. A boatman carries an oar to represent his boat as well (Fig. 6.62). An attendant carries two flags with wheels on them to become both the sedan chair and the driver (Table 6.32.B and 6.32.N; Table 6 is located in Chapter Eight, and references to the illustrations found in that table will henceforth follow this format). When horses are needed for travel or battle, a riding crop *(mabian)* decorated with tassels represents the horse (Fig. 6.27). A square block of wood wrapped in a yellow scarf stands for the official seal of the emperor, and a round block in a red scarf signifies a severed head. For a banquet, cups for wine or tea are brought on without any food or liquid. Drinking from a cup becomes symbolic for eating the entire meal. For battle scenes, a variety of props, such as swords, sticks, axes, and halberds, represent the tools of war.

Pantomime. Most items of the structural environment, including doorways and windows, are not represented onstage at all. In cases when these objects are needed for stage action, the actor pantomimes their presence. Traditional Chinese doorways were built with a center opening and a raised threshold. In the performance of a traditional Jingju play, to pass through a door, the actor mimes sliding open the latch, opening the double doors, and stepping over the threshold. Sewing occurs without needle or thread, the performer using the motions of drawing out the thread, threading it

FIGURE 1.20. A wedding takes place in front of a nuptial bed created with chairs and curtains. *The Phoenix Returns to Its Nest (Feng huan chao)*. Character, left: Mu Juyi, actor: Liu Yuechun. Character, right: Cheng Xue'e, actor: Li Hongmei. BJC, Beijing, China. July 9, 2000.

through the needle, and taking stitches (Fig. 1.9). Watching someone eat is considered unpleasant, so the actors pantomime these acts, covering their mouths with their sleeves to conceal ingestion (Fig. 2.8). In addition to indicating absent objects, pantomime expresses actions. Sitting at a table with the head resting on the hand depicts sleep. Since real tears would destroy the carefully applied makeup and distort the singing voice, lifting the sleeve to the corners of the eyes portrays crying.

Staging. Formalized staging movement patterns are utilized throughout the traditional repertoire. Actors usually enter on stage right and come partway downstage to announce who and where they are. When the scene is completed, they exit stage left. After everyone has left the stage at the end of a scene, the next people who enter are generally in another location. Onstage, an emphasis on symmetry and balance occurs both in the placement of scenery and the positioning of actors in static scenes. In formal processions preceding a scene in a palace, two or four pairs of attendants enter from stage right, often carrying banners. They proceed in a straight line to the downstage center point of the stage, then divide and circle around to their symmetrical positions on either side of the throne. In general, curved lines are preferred over straight in movements for the body through space. When two armies prepare for battle, they circle each other in parade formation before beginning combat. The battle itself involves circular moves in both duel and battalion configurations. On a smaller scale, most gestures follow the curvilinear pattern as well. Another staging technique uses *liangxiang* (lit. "to strike a pose"), dynamic pauses in the movement to display the inner nature of a character's essence or state of being.

Lighting. Early Jingju was performed in the daytime without artificial lighting, and lighting was added initially for the musicians. After the turn of the twentieth century, evening performances came into being. Lighting was introduced to help the audience see the players, an innovation that contributed to the elaboration of the costumes. Traditional Jingju plays are now normally performed under fully illuminated white lights, without blackouts or changes of lighting between scenes. If color were used in the general illumination, it could interfere with the wide range of colors in the costumes. In some performances, colored lights project onto a cyclorama, creating an evening scene with deep blue, for example; bringing prop lanterns onto a fully lit stage may also imply night. When visibility is crucial to the scene, the actors may pantomime darkness while under full illumination. One famous play, *Fight at Crossroads Inn (Sancha kou)*, has an entire scene where two characters perform an elaborate battle while pantomiming darkness under full stage lighting (Fig. 1.6).

Costumes

Historical Background. Ancient China was known as "the land of impeccable attire."[8] Clothing has long been a sign of personal significance throughout the cultures of the world, and the people of ancient China developed this precept into an exacting art. From the early times of the more than 5,000-year history of the country, the Chinese people believed that personal clothing and adornment were indicative of being cultured and civilized.[9] In a land where attire was given this degree of importance, dress also became a way to identify people, an outward expression of one's place in society. A system of assigning clothes to distinguish members of the court was formalized into sumptuary laws as early as the Zhou period. Developing throughout the rest of China's history, clothing differentiations distinguished status, rank, and position in society through the assignment of embroidered symbols, significant colors, and specific garments. Traditional theatre evolving in this rank- and clothing-conscious context logically absorbed a design language that emphasized clothing for the identity of characters.

Though traditional Jingju costumes appear to replicate historical dress, the two forms are quite distinct entities for several reasons, both historical and practical. To begin with, early theatre emerged from ritual dances where period authenticity was not an issue. When stories were added to the dance, the concept of historicity was disregarded again in favor of movement and characterization. From these early roots, the significance of historical recreation did not evolve as an important factor in stage depictions. In the Song dynasty, actors wore clothing from everyday life, but by the Yuan and Ming dynasties, specific costumes were made for performances. At this time another distinction between real life and theatre costumes evolved from regulations that prohibited actors from wearing certain garments.

Many of the emblems on imperial and court clothing held great significance and were therefore forbidden to those who had not earned the right to wear them. As a result, theatre performers did not generally have access to cast off upper-class clothing to use onstage. Nor could the actors duplicate imperial symbols on the costumes they made. With some aspects of current clothing disallowed, the design of costumes necessarily avoided realistic representation. The performances were often staged outside in open venues, so the colors, decorations, and height were often exaggerated to increase visibility, though it would not have been advisable for theatrical dress to surpass the elegance of the contents of the emperor's wardrobe. By the Ming era, a majority of the costumes were already conventionalized into distinct theatrical versions, though a small proportion still resembled contemporary dress.[10]

In the eighteenth and nineteenth centuries, costumes from other types of performances were once again a source of ideas for theatrical dress. When Jingju evolved from a synthesis of local performance forms, the best costumes from each regional form were also integrated into the range of costumes used. Kunqu costumes particularly, as well as some aspects of Kunqu performance, influenced the characteristics of the later Jingju style, and the nature of the costumes used for Kunqu and Jingju still overlap in contemporary performance.

The early troupes were not wealthy, and the costumes were costly, so the precedent developed for reusing costumes for many characters and for many years. This necessity may have given rise to the assignment of certain costumes for certain roles. In early performance situations, with limited lighting and visibility, this practice also helped to clearly identify the characters, for repeated exposure to certain costumes would help the audience recognize them. Evidence indicates that the system of storing the costumes in trunks by their type had arisen by Ming times, signifying that regulations

for characters to wear the same types of costumes had developed by that time as well.[11]

During the Qing era, when the Manchus seized power from the majority Han, Manchu dress was required for all who attended court and official functions. Sumptuary laws did not affect dress in private life, however, and as a consequence the Han population continued to wear the style of clothing they had worn in the Ming dynasty, particularly the Han women. The mixing in everyday life of clothing from different regions and different time periods further contributed to the blending of costumes styles onstage. Items of Manchu dress were introduced into the costume repertoire towards the end of the Qing dynasty, and dress of differing eras is still mixed anachronistically in performance. The current range of costumes can be roughly divided by source into three parts, with approximately equal numbers coming from the Ming and earlier dynasties, the Qing dynasty, and theatrical invention. In terms of usage, however, the Ming and earlier styles, and the theatrically based garments appear onstage far more frequently than garments from the Qing dynasty. In examining the costumes of traditional Jingju at the beginning of the twenty-first century, the two key distinctions from imperial dress are that Jingju has added the dimension of theatrical style, and as a living art form it has continued to evolve since the end of imperial influence.

Costume imagery was most positively advanced during three periods in history. The first was during the reigns of Kangxi (1662–1722) and his grandson, the Qianlong emperor, under whom the initial spark for Jingju ignited. The second period of advancement was under Dowager Empress Cixi, a strong patron of theatre performances.[12] Cixi invited famous actors from the city to perform within the palace, rewarding them with money or even official rank for their services. Because the imperial family supported Jingju, its popularity spread, along with the production of the garments for the stage.[13] Centers for the creation of costumes emerged in Nanjing, Hangzhou, and Suzhou, and costumes continue to be embroidered and assembled in these and other locations today. After the fall of the last dynasty in 1911, the imperial edicts pertaining to costumes no longer had significance, which made possible increased invention in the creation of costumes. Brighter colors and bolder embroidery patterns developed during this third fertile era. The 1920s and 1930s saw more advances in costume design because of Mei Lanfang, who heightened the visual image of women by redesigning the costumes and hairstyles for many of his favorite roles in his own new plays.

Tracing this line of evolution demonstrates that even conventionalized garments change over time. Photographs of Jingju performances from the first half of the twentieth century illustrate that fairly recent costumes differ considerably from the current style. For example, the size and density of the embroidery has simplified, and the forms of some costumes have changed. The costumes continue to evolve within the pattern of the performance aesthetic.

The Four Major Costumes. In current usage, there are four garment types that comprise the greater part of the Jingju wardrobe for traditional plays, *mang* (Fig. 1.1), *pi* (Fig. 1.7), *kao* (Figs. 1.4 and 1.5), and *xuezi* (Fig. 1.3). These four garments are worn for specific occasions by both male and female roles, and the word *nü* (woman) added before each garment word indicates the gender of the wearer; *nümang, nüpi, nükao,* and *nüxuezi.* The limited variety of forms reflects the small range of garments also found in the daily life of the Chinese people. In both cases, different choices in fabric, hue, and decoration in the making of the garments establishes the rank of the person or the role type of the character who wears them. The visual variations in costumes now project six levels of character identification: male/female,

youth/age, civilian/military, upper/lower status, rich/poor and Han/ethnic. For fabric distinctions, upper- and middle-status characters wear silk garments, while the lowest of servants dress in cotton. Color differences display rank, status, and age, while the ornamentation communicates gender, wealth, status, rank, and profession. Each garment can be created in an infinite variety of renditions, with different combinations of color and pattern, making a richly extensive vocabulary of dress. This language of clothing forms the foundation for the further examination of costumes in this book.

Aesthetic Principles

The traditional Jingju world is shaped by three aesthetic principles: synthesis, stylization, and convention. Through synthesis, "song and speech in performance occur simultaneously with the dance-like movement of the performer; dance-acting and combat are interwoven on the stage with melodic and/or percussive accompaniment."[14] The synthesis between the actors' movements and the costumes forms a significant component of the performance style. With its roots in dance, virtually every piece of clothing has been purposefully developed to assist and emphasize movement. The water sleeves, the beards, and the headdress feathers become extensions and enhancements of the actor's body. Manipulating these costume pieces effortlessly for emotional expression becomes a central aspect of the actor's performance.

In performance, "stylization refers to the divergence between the behaviors of daily life and their presentation onstage, that is, the representation of those behaviors in performance, within a particular style. In Beijing opera, stylization is considered to be the act of raising and refining *(tilian)* the behaviors of daily life, with an aim of making them beautiful. . . ."[15] Just as the performers create a stylization of reality, the same holds true for the costumes. The stylization in costumes moves away from reality through the absence of three elements: time, place, and season. Rather than carefully recreating the images of the distinct dynasties, the costumes are a pastiche of periods blended with sheer theatricality. Anachronisms occur both within and among the individual costumes. Though the costumes may appear to be imperial dress, in actuality, they are far from historical replications. The construct of time further disintegrates with the repeated usage of costumes. All plays, regardless of their time period, are presented with the same selection of costumes, and through these stylized costumes, time occurs both simultaneously and without chronology.

References to location and season are also absent from the styles of traditional Jingju costumes. Although the stories in traditional Jingju plays take place in a variety of places, the costumes do not reflect the regional dress of each ethnic group. The only distinction made in this regard is that the majority Han people in the plays are dressed in Han-style costumes that resemble Ming and earlier dress, while all minorities are dressed in the same garments of Qing dynasty origin, regardless of their location or ethnicity (Fig. 6.5). While Qing imperial dress was divided into two seasons, with differing fabrics, and the days for changing from winter to summer and back again were strictly determined by imperial edict, the seasons are not depicted in traditional Jingju garments. These precepts of costuming are further elaborated in Chapter Two.

The third aesthetic principle, convention, is "an aspect of stylization: conventions are also a departure from daily reality. But conventions are more specialized: they include specific practices to which fairly precise meanings have been ascribed by tradition. The use of a particular convention sign serves to signal its ascribed meaning to the audience."[16] Rather than projecting information about the external environment of

time, place, and season, the costumes instead express role types. In the development of a shared language for the costumes, two significant aspects have emerged: the costumes have been limited to a small number of standard forms that can achieve greater variety through color and ornamentation, and the costumes are designated with characteristics that visually communicate the given circumstances of the role types, creating a repeating and recognizable image for the audience. To accommodate the costume conventions, each troupe now develops a standard stock of garments to cover their repertoire of traditional plays, and their wardrobe person meticulously learns which costumes are required for each performance of a given play.

Beauty

The ultimate aim of the integration of synthesis, stylization, and convention is to realize the Jingju definition of beauty. The movement, for both the body in space and the body parts in isolation, reflects the Chinese admiration for the perfection of the circle. A sense of effortlessness in the execution of movement is a second admired value. The actors must be in command of their technique throughout their performance; they must find their notes with ease, perform their movements effortlessly, and manipulate their costumes with the utmost grace and agility. The costumes, headdresses, and makeup provide a visually attractive image that is enhanced by the beauty of the carefully curved gestures of home and court and the precision acrobatics of the martial artists. Destitute characters wear plain, but not dirty costumes; lower-status women have fewer but still elegant adornments in their hair; and distressed characters wear their garments askew rather than torn. The overlaying of beauty reduces the contrasts among characters, creating a distinct visual language to portray the range of personalities in society. The actor within the costume, on the other hand, has many tools within the conventionalized style to represent aspects of personality that may not be visible in the dress. Nothing can occur, however, that might deviate from the prescribed pattern or completeness of the performance, thereby taking away from the perfection to which the presentation aspires.

In the world of Jingju, the actor is the central element in the performance. The actor's accomplishment in mastering the challenging performance style forms the key to audience enjoyment of the theatrical event. Because of the focus on the actor, costume becomes the foremost visual aspect. Building on the incomparable sumptuousness of the clothing of the Chinese imperial court, the costumes in traditional Jingju have reached a magnificence of textile expression and beauty in their own right. Fashioned from brilliantly colored silk fabrics and lavishly hand-embroidered with multicolored and metallic threads in exquisite floral and faunal ornamentation, each costume projects an image of unmatched elegance. When the figures attired in this brilliant dress are viewed in combination with their elaborately evocative face painting and glittering rhinestone-bejeweled and pearled headdresses, the combination creates an image of breathtaking beauty. In a cultural context where fine textiles and adornment have long been admired, the costumes used today for the performance of traditional Jingju plays can now easily compete with the past grandeur of the courts, exemplifying the pinnacle of Chinese stage costume. The following chapters will explore the art of the costumes in both theory and practice to offer a comprehensive view of the function of the costumes in the performance of traditional Jingju.

The World of Traditional Jingju Costumes

2

An elaborate system of telegraphing character through the visual image has developed for modern Jingju costumes, which uses prescribed garments with specific symbolism in color and decoration. During the 200 years that Jingju has evolved, garments and colors have been chosen to define the most appropriate image for each character in each play. The choices result from the combined input of the dressers, the performers, and the responses of the audiences, rather than from the imagination of a specific costume designer. Through selection of the most desirable articles of clothing from several dynasties and their modification to suit theatrical needs, the choices have gradually developed into a pattern of visual language that now serves as the design aesthetic. Though the sources are quite varied, the overall look has become unified by standardization of the clothing through simplicity of cut, clarity and intensity of color, and the scale and amount of ornamentation. The combinations of the costumes onstage are selected to convey not only the individual characters, but to produce the most beautiful stage picture possible (Fig. 2.1).

Costumes and Roles

The unique system of traditional Jingju costumes, as expressed through the precepts of stylized conventionalized dress, was introduced in Chapter One. The costumes have developed to represent roles; the dynasty,

season, and region are not represented through clothing. China has both extensive lands and a long history, and the stories in Jingju plays cover the length and breadth of the country and its past. Identifying each region and time period in every play could be a very complicated issue. Instead, the costumes that have evolved for traditional Jingju focus on the distinctions among the role types and accommodate this vast region and time in a single conventionalized style. The information about the character communicated by the costumes focuses on the characters' physical characteristics and personal circumstances, but nothing in the costume communicates the time period, the geographic location, or the weather. In other words, a significant component of the most notable aspects of traditional Jingju dress include what is *not* revealed, a quality that reflects the traditional Chinese preference of indirect expression and innuendo.

The characters in traditional Jingju are divided into four major role types: *sheng* (standard male), *dan* (female), *jing* (painted face or formidable male), and *chou* (clown). The role types and subtypes have been detailed in Chapter One. Within the conventionalized nature of traditional Jingju, just as each role's subsets have recognizable identities, so, too, each has a distinctive visual image, from choice of the headdress and makeup, through their dress, to their shoes. The rules for the attire of each role type and the styles of clothing have

FIGURE 2.1. The costumes are unified by simple forms with beautiful colors and embroidery. The acting ensemble is arranged for a formal court setting, with sets of eunuchs and *gongnü* (female palace maids) flanking the throne. *Defending the State (Da bao guo)*. NJC, Beijing, China. October 5, 2001.

become relatively fixed. To achieve these standardized identities, the costumes for each role type are selected from a specific range of clothes, and all characters within that role type are dressed from this same assortment of garments. Within the garments used for a given role type, the choice of clothes further reflects the role subtype, defining age, position, or disposition. Then the garments may also indicate the nature of the individual character, the characteristics of that individual's personality, and the given circumstances. The determination of the wardrobe becomes more refined with each progression of character delineation. Therefore, members of a role subtype will wear the same general style of

costume, and a named character within a role subtype could wear virtually identical garments in productions of the same play by different companies.

For example, *sheng* roles generally wear the *xuezi* (informal robe), *pi* (formal robe), or *mang* (court robe). Their version of these robes are distinct from the same type of robes when worn by the other male characters, *jing* and *chou*. Within the *sheng* range of garments, the *xiaosheng* (young men) will wear specific versions of these pieces that fall within the conventions of the style of the young man's role. Their garments will all share the characteristics of color and ornamentation for younger men. Therefore, a *xiaosheng* looks essentially

FIGURE 2.2. Lü Bu's pink *mang* informs the audience of his romantic nature. He wears a *zijin guan* (lit. "purple gold headdress") on his head. *Lü Bu Shoots an Arrow (Yuanmen she ji)*. Character: Lü Bu, actor: Jiang Qihu. NJC, Beijing, China. April 29, 1996.

explain the next level of identification, the similarities of the same character in different productions. In a performance of *Lü Bu and Diaochan (Lü Bu yu Diaochan)* produced by the National Jingju Company (Beijing, China. April 27, 1996), Lü Bu appeared in a pink *mang*, a color indicating that he is young, handsome, and romantic (Fig. 2.2). Further research reveals that Lü Bu is often dressed in pink. In Lu Qing's *Peking Opera Stardom, Celebrating 200 Years of Peking Opera*, he is depicted in the same play in a similar pink *mang*.[1] Lü Bu also appears in other plays wearing pink, although his garment changes depending on the circumstances. In a performance of *Lü Bu Shoots an Arrow (Yuanmen she ji)*, (NJC, Beijing, China. April 29, 1996), he wore a similar pink *mang* and later changed to a *jianyi* (archer's garment), and it retained the pink color (Fig. 6.26).

The patterns of dressing are not inflexible, however. Other factors may be considered when selecting the costumes for each character, including the actor's interpretation of the role and the availability of garments. Lü Bu also appears dressed in white garments, which are often worn by young warriors, as he did in a performance of the same play by the Beijing Jingju Company (Beijing Jingju Yuan) on July 15, 2000. In this case, the choice of white emphasized his admirable attributes as a young general rather than his amorous aspects, associated with the color pink. In general, the type of garment, established by the cut, remains the same from production to production and scene to scene, while the color and embroidery may be more mutable, as long as these elements are within the range determined for a given role type or subtype (see Table 6.22.B and 6.22.N for another example of pink for a *xiaosheng*). Conversely, because there are a limited number of garments, the same robe will be worn by different characters as long as the color and the surface pattern are correct for the role type. The pink *mang* worn by Lü Bu can be worn by other handsome young men, but not by *laosheng* (mature male); they never wear pink. The white *mang* that Lü

the same in every traditional Jingju performance, and he is distinct from a *laosheng*. The *hua xuezi* (flowered *xuezi*) they wear falls from the shoulders, laps over to the right side, and has floral embroidery around the collar and on the left side of the hem. Their pale makeup has a dusting of light pink around the eyes and between their brows. Because they are young, they do not wear beards. A headdress conceals their hair, and they wear thick-soled boots *(houdi xue)* (Fig. 6.12).

Lü Bu, a dashing young general and *xiaosheng* role in the Three Kingdoms saga, can be used as an example to

Bu wears, however, can also be worn by a *laosheng*, as white generally represents loyalty, and is not associated with age. Color is not the only predetermined aspect of costumes for specific characters. In some cases, the amount and style of the embroidery is also consistent for a given character. The *sheng*-style *mang* worn by Lü Bu will have sedate round dragon designs repeated ten times over the surface. On the other hand, a *mang* worn by a *jing* character will have fewer and larger dragons that stretch over the entire surface from shoulder to hem (Fig. 6.2).

Identity through Costumes

Beyond identifying the role types, the costumes also convey information about the specific circumstances of the characters. There are six pairs of identifying characteristics projected by traditional Jingju costumes: male/female, youth/age, upper/lower status, rich/poor, military/civilian, and Han/minority. In addition to these identifiers that describe the role, the costumes may provide other information about dramatic circumstances, including the event in the scene, such as a wedding or funeral, the character's relationship to others in the story, the character's mood, and his or her importance in the play.

Male and Female. The sex and age of characters are clearly projected through their costumes. While the garment vocabulary for male and female roles overlaps, the costumes clearly indicate the sex of the role by form and decoration, among other characteristics. Men's robes are full length, while women's generally come to the knee, and are worn over a pleated skirt. Some garments for women are distinguished by adding pieces to the men's version. The *nükao* (female armor) has layers of streamers in the lower half (Fig. 1.11), and a divided skirt is added to the martial men's jacket and trouser garments to make the combination suitable for the martial women (Fig. 1.10). The embroidery on men's and women's martial garments also differs; men's clothing often has fierce beasts such as tigers and dragons, while women's garments often are decorated with flowers and phoenixes. Color does not generally contribute to distinguishing male and female garments, although male court and martial garments generally are embroidered with greater amounts of golden thread. Gender is also distinguished by makeup and headdress designs. Though the young *sheng* and *dan* characters share the lightened face with pink cheeks, the *sheng* have an arc or arrowhead between their brows. Younger women's roles generally have elaborately styled hair, with beautiful rhinestone and floral decorations, while men wear either fabric caps or metal filigree helmets that conceal their hair.

Youth and Age. Age is projected by all three components of the costume: the form, color, and surface ornamentation. *Xiaosheng* wear the full-length crossover *hua xuezi* most commonly at home, while *laosheng* wear the full-length *pi* with the center front closing. *Qingyi* (young to middle-aged women) wear the center front closing *nüxuezi* (woman's informal robe), while the crossover style of *nüxuezi* is worn by their older counterparts, the *laodan* (mature women). Sometimes the *laodan* will wear their skirt over the *nüxuezi*, making an even more pronounced difference in the silhouette. At court, male characters who wear red robes in their youth and middle age change to maroon as they age. Young empresses dress in either yellow or red, while dowager empresses appear in either an orange or olive-green *nümang* (female court robe). Youthful civilian roles wear pastel colors, such as lake blue and pink. By contrast, their parents wear maroon, olive green, and neutral colors. The free-form sprays of flowers on the robes of youths are replaced by more controlled roundels of flowers, symmetrically placed, on robes of their parents (Fig. 2.3).

Older married men and women often dress in identically colored and patterned robes of different lengths (Fig. 6.7), unlike their younger counterparts, who wear

FIGURE 2.3. Age is differentiated by color and pattern. The garments of young people, as in the *nüxuezi* for this *qingyi*, are often pastel, with free-form floral embroidery, and mature characters such as this *laodan* usually wear an olive-green or maroon *nüpi*, with roundel patterns. *The Phoenix Returns to Its Nest (Feng huan chao)*. Character, left: Cheng Xue'e, actor: Li Hongmei. Character, right: Madam Cheng, actor: Lü Xin. NJC, Beijing, China. October 3, 2001.

complementary garments. The skirts of wealthy *qingyi* have multicolored embroidery, which changes to gold for high-status *laodan*. Age also appears in the makeup, with younger faces painted pink and white, and older roles having a skin-toned color. Although young unmarried men generally do not wear beards, young married men do, and as they age, the color changes from black to gray to white. For older female characters in the *laodan* roles, gray or white hair wrapped in a scarf designates their age.

Upper and Lower Status. Status, wealth, occupation and nationality are often registered in dress. Every traditional Jingju play has characters of differing social status. The costumes clearly establish the social hierarchy, from the emperor and aristocrats in their *mang*, to the attendants attired in matching livery, the *longtao yi* (attendant robe) (Table 6.33.B and 6.33.N). Generals dress in the elaborate *yingkao* (hard or complete armor) (Fig. 6.9), while their foot soldiers appear in simple *bingyi* (soldiers' clothes) (Fig. 1.15), a jacket and trousers set. Both the voluminous robes worn at court and the multipieced armored suits present a massive and commanding presence compared with the more natural silhouettes of the lower-status characters. In private scenes, a higher-status man dresses in the *pi* or an embroidered *xuezi*. A lower-status male will likely wear a plain *xuezi*, as do servants and children. A *qingyi* usually wears a "one hundred pleats" skirt *(baizhe qun)* and a *nüpi* (woman's formal robe) with elegant water sleeves *(shuixiu)* (Fig. 6.8), whereas a *huadan* (lit. "flower" woman, lively young woman) may dress in a fitted jacket with straight sleeves and either a skirt or trousers (Figs. 1.9 and 6.40). The thickness of the sole of the shoe also contributes to the hierarchy of the costume. Where servants and women wear flat-soled shoes, generals and officers of the court wear elevated boots, with a depth of one to four inches depending on their status (Fig. 1.2). Higher-ranking roles also wear more elaborate headdresses, with gold filigree, pearls, festive pompoms, and long pheasant feathers *(lingzi)*. Color contributes to status; yellow can be worn only by the emperor and his family (Fig. 4.3), and the other pure colors, red, green, white, and black, appear more often on important characters in official positions. Blended colors, on the other hand, are worn more frequently for domestic scenes. Servants and workmen commonly wear the neutral colors, which have the least status (Fig. 6.36). The amount of embroidery also reflects the position of a character, and the *mang* worn for court and the *kao* used for generals are two of the most elaborately ornamented costumes in the repertoire. Gold couching (thick metallic threads sewn on top of the fabric) is lavishly applied to these garments, while multicolored threads appear on the clothing for domestic scenes. Servants and workers have unadorned costumes.

Rich and Poor. Social status is not always tied to wealth, for many plays feature high-status men or women who are down on their luck. These currently disadvantaged characters wear garments with a cut similar to that of the wealthy, but without the beauty of color or intensity of ornamentation. Formerly well-off men may wear a plain *xuezi* in a drab color or a black *xuezi,* either plain or with minimal embroidery (Table 6.19.B and 6.19.N). The deserted *qingyi* wears a plain center-front-opening *xuezi,* traditionally in black with blue borders. Her hair will be ornamented with simple silver pins, instead of the elaborate rhinestones worn by women of wealth (Fig. 6.18). When well-off characters have an even more significant downturn in fortune, a beleaguered scholar, for example, they wear the *fugui yi,* ironically called the garment of wealth and nobility because the characters, though currently impoverished, usually return to their previous position by the end of the play. The *fugui yi* is a black silk *xuezi*-style robe, with multicolored silk patches carefully arranged on the surface (Fig. 6.20). No matter how destitute a character may be, the overall necessity of beauty dominates the design process, and no peasant or misfortunate appears ragged or dirty. Those who are always poor also have specific costumes, in tea colors or indigo blue, and sometimes made from cotton rather than silk (Figs. 6.16 and 6.28). The difference in the drape of the fabric contributes to variances in form, as the soft unembroidered costumes hang limply. The characters who retain their wealth and position wear a range of ceremonial and informal dress appropriate for their elevated position, the *mang, pi,* or *xuezi.* The *mang* often has splendid gold couching reinforcing the wealth of the wearer and making the garment stand away from the body (Fig. 1.1). The other upper-status clothes are made in pure or blended colors, with colored embroidery in complex patterns.

Civil and Military. Costume and headdresses express civil and military appointments. The typical general in a combat situation dresses in the *yingkao,* intricately embroidered with geometric and animal imagery, with four flags strapped to the back, and a metal filigree helmet decorated with pompoms and pearls (Fig. 1.4). Soldiers wear uniform *bingyi,* with matching headdresses (Figs. 6.34 and 6.35). By contrast, civilians wear domestic clothing, the *pi* and the *xuezi,* often with floral patterns, and soft or stiffened fabric hats (Fig. 6.12). In addition to garments indicating occupation, the delineation of rank through clothing has always been important in Chinese society. Generations and dynasties of rulers carefully dictated the color and decoration of the clothing to be worn by different ranks of both military and civil officers of the court, so everyone understood the standing of their compatriots at first glance. Special robes with rank badges indicated an officer's standing, with his rank designated by the creature on the badge, birds for scholars and beasts for military men. The clothing strictures of the historical edicts have become somewhat extraneous in the courts portrayed in traditional Jingju plays. Jingju civil officers wear the *guanyi* (officials' robe) with rank badges depicting birds, but the birds are most often cranes, which signifies the first degree, and this seems to imply that the specific bird signifying a given rank is no longer essential. Military officials rarely appear in the *guanyi* robe onstage, so robes with beasts representing the military ranks are uncommon. Rank is portrayed only to the degree necessary to make the point (Fig. 6.22). The colors of the traditional Jingju *guanyi* are red and maroon for those of higher rank and blue for the lower ranks (Figs. 4.6 and 6.22). Black *guanyi* can be worn by men outside the system of rank. This particular sequence of colors is a traditional Jingju invention and not reflective of court standards.

FIGURE 2.4. Daizhan Gongzhu, left, is a princess of a northern dynasty dressed in a Manchu-derived costume of the Qing dynasty, while Madam Wang, right, as the wife of a Tang dynasty prime minister, wears clothing reflecting her Han heritage. *The Red-Maned Fiery Steed (Hongzong liema)*. Character, left: Daizhan Gongzhu, actor: unknown. Character, right: Madam Wang, actor: Zhai Mo. BJC, Beijing, China. October 6, 2001.

Han and Minority. The sixth pair of identifiers indicates whether a character comes from Han or minority heritage. While one of the overall precepts of traditional Jingju costumes is that they do not specify region, they do distinguish Han Chinese from all other ethnicities. The Han people are the majority in China, and despite many centuries of outsider rule, the Han managed to retain their national characteristics in dress. Most costumes utilized in traditional Jingju are based on the

Han styles that prevailed even into the Manchu rule of the Qing dynasty (1644–1911). The characteristics of Han dress include tubular-shaped sleeves, a straight or slightly trapezoidal-shaped body, and a center-front or asymmetrical closing to the right. Towards the end of the Qing dynasty, Manchu-style clothing began to be absorbed into the traditional Jingju costume vocabulary. Some Qing garments, including the *jianyi*, with its distinctive horseshoe-shaped sleeves, and the *magua* (riding jacket), a short, straight-bodied garment with straight sleeves, became standard dress for both Han and minority characters onstage (Fig. 6.30). When the same *jianyi* is worn with a *bufu* (coat with a badge) and *nuanmao* (warm hat), both from Qing court dress, the combination implies an officer of a foreign court (Fig. 6.53). Some characters are distinguished as being non-Han by the addition of two long white foxtails to the back of their headdresses, a reference to the barbarian habit of wearing fur (Fig. 7.40). The change in clothing for female minority characters is more all-encompassing, as they have a completely different wardrobe based on the full-length garment worn by Manchu women in the Qing dynasty, the *qimang* (Manchu robe) for court, and the *qipao* (Manchu gown) for informal scenes. These are worn with the *qitou* (Manchu hair) styled into the distinctive *liangba tou* ("two pieces of hair") or "archway" shape on top of the head. (*Qi* is a colloquial term for Manchu. It refers to their use of banners in their military battalions). In the play *The Red-Maned Fiery Steed (Hongzong liema),* Daizhan Gongzhu wears a *qimang* and *liangbatou,* as she is a princess of a northern dynasty (Fig. 2.4).

With so much information about the character telegraphed by the costume, one may wonder about the lack of suspense and revelation in performance. The costume imagery and the role type make it clear from the beginning who is the hero and who will prevail in the story. Most Chinese audience members are quite familiar with the plots of the plays, as the stories are integral to their literature and history. A synopsis of the play is also included in the program, for anyone needing it. The audience comes to the theatre to appreciate the talent and execution skills of the specific actors performing that day, not to be amazed or enlightened by the outcome of the play.

Absence of Time Period

Though the costumes clearly define the roles, they do not indicate the time period, a characteristic that supports the standardized look for each role type. The same stock of costumes can be used whether the play takes place in the Han dynasty (206 BC–220 AD) or the Tang (618–907). By looking more closely at the historical evolution of dress, the feasibility of this blending becomes more evident. Chinese political history has included dynasties ruled by several different ethnic groups. Some of these diverse rulers recognized the importance of establishing an official dress to identify both the dynasty and the hierarchy of the court. For example, during the reign of the Qianlong emperor, from 1736–1795 in the Qing dynasty, the Board of Ritual published an illustrated book of sumptuary laws, *The Illustrated Precedents for the Ritual Paraphernalia of the Imperial Court* (*Huangchao liqi tushi*). The book described in great detail the style of dress required of court officials.[2] The preface of the catalog, purportedly written by the Qianlong emperor himself, also pointed out how previous foreign dynasties of the Northern Wei, the Liao, the Jin, and the Mongol had abandoned their traditional clothing in favor of Chinese robes. Within one generation they had lost their sense of ethnic identity, and Qianlong believed as a consequence their dynasties came to an end.[3]

As the new dynasties would often absorb and modify only slightly the clothing of the previous rulers, clothing introduced in an early dynasty might continue for several subsequent dynasties with only minor changes.

In addition, once the clothing rules of the individual dynasties were established, the visual image of dress changed very little during the course of the dynasty. The Ming dynasty, for example, lasted for 276 years from 1368–1644, and the imperial clothing was largely unaltered over that period of time. The slow cycle of change in China provides a much narrower range of historical dress from which to choose as well as garments that span many centuries. Seen from this perspective, combining periods seamlessly onstage becomes less complicated.

Though the imperial courts recognized the significance of dynastic visual identity, traditional Jingju clothing has bypassed this distinction in historical dress. When the performers appear onstage together, they may be standing side by side wearing costumes from different periods. In *The Red-Maned Fiery Steed,* the northern princess dresses in Qing dynasty dress, while the wife of the Tang dynasty prime minister wears the Han style *nümang* (Fig. 2.4). The *xuezi*, worn onstage for informal wear, came from a garment from ancient times that continued to be worn through other periods, while the *jianyi* developed from a full-length gown with horseshoe cuffs typical of the Qing dynasty. Both are now used as common articles of dress for traditional Jingju characters and are frequently worn concurrently onstage. A single garment may also be a blend from different periods. For example, the precursor to the *mang* was a formal court robe that started in the Tang dynasty, but the version worn onstage more closely resembles the Ming cut. The style of the dragon and wave patterns embroidered on the surface, however, is based in the Qing dynasty formats.[4]

Absence of Season

The costumes do not indicate season or changes in climate. During the Qing dynasty, members of the court had winter and summer versions of their clothes. The winter clothes were quite heavy, often lined with furs for additional protection from cold. In summer, the clothing changed to lighter-weight silks and gauzes, although several layers of clothing would still be worn. The Chinese believed that there was order and symmetry in the laws of nature and a rhythm to the seasons. By imitating these processes in their dress, they hoped to live in harmony with the forces that caused the seasons to change from one to another. Therefore, the Board of Ritual would decide when clothing should be changed from winter to summer wear, and the day was announced by imperial edict.[5] But weather rituals are superfluous in the world of traditional Jingju. The stock costumes are made without reference to the effects of temperature. The play itself establishes the climate, from the well-known story or from lines spoken by the performers. Performers may add a cloak to indicate traveling from one town to the next, but they will not wear the cloak merely to protect themselves from the bitter cold of the winters in Beijing (Fig. 6.59).

Absence of Region

The population of China has fifty-six ethnic groups, each with a distinctive fashion of dress, but the range of regional distinctions does not appear onstage in the traditional Jingju. While the specific geographical region of China is not identified by the costumes, the costumes do distinguish the Han or ethnic Chinese from "foreigners" in the context of the play, as described in the identifiers above. All Han people in every play are dressed in the same fashion, and all foreigners, regardless of origin, are dressed in the standard "foreigner" costume. As some of the conventions for theatrical dress were established during the Ming dynasty, the last dynasty of the majority Han people to rule, their clothing style contributes to the bulk of costumes used in traditional Jingju. The Manchu ruled during the last dynasty, the Qing, and their costumes became the basis for "foreigners" towards the end of that dynasty. Prior to the introduction of Qing dynasty dress for ethnic

minorities, it is not known how or if distinctions were made in dress for the non-Han roles.[6]

Dramatic Circumstances

Locale and Occasion. Though the geographic region is not indicated through the costumes, the clothing does communicate the more immediate locale and the event to some extent. Costumes can signal if a character appears at court, at work, at home, or on the battlefield. Scholars wear a *xuezi* while in their study with their books and calligraphy, but they change either to their *guanyi* or *mang* for a court appointment, as their position allows. For military men, the dress at court can also be a *mang* or *kao*, which may be worn without flags for an appearance in court, but with flags when they are prepared for battle. Events can also be signified by color. As red is the color of happiness and auspicious events, a bride and groom appear in red robes and headdresses for a wedding onstage, just as they would in life in China (Fig. 1.20). White indicates mourning, and in *The City of Baidi (Baidi cheng)* the opening scene is stunning, with the entire cast in white robes grieving the death of the sworn brothers of the hero, Liu Bei (Fig. 2.5).

Character Relationships. Characters have a role that they perform within the context of the play, relationships with other characters, and a specific function in the plot. Character relationships are generally evident in traditional Jingju. Because of all the other information already telegraphed about age, occupation, status, and role type, the audience can discern the daughter and the mother, the lover of the daughter, the warrior and his army, the servant of the emperor, and so on. As the clothing identifies the character so completely, it also indicates what their interaction will be with the other roles.

Character Mood. For the most part, decorum dictates that the mood of the character seldom becomes a major component when considering the selection of

FIGURE 2.5. *The City of Baidi* opens with a scene of mourning, with the entire cast and setting in white. *The City of Baidi (Baidi cheng).* Character, left: Liu Bei, actor: Zhang Jianguo. Character, center: Guan Xing, actor: Yu Lei. NJC, Beijing, China. September 30, 2001.

traditional Jingju dress. The conquered warrior may remove parts of his garments to show his defeat. He may appear in only the *kaotui* (leg flaps) of his armor over a *jianyi*, with his headdress removed, revealing his hair (Fig. 8.2). In madness or distress, the character may wear the garment on only one arm, and a tendril of hair may be dislodged (Fig. 8.3). Altering how an existing garment is worn retains the precept of beauty and increases the visual vocabulary without the need to provide additional costumes. In times of great distress, however, abandoned wives and defeated heroes may change to another costume to reflect their altered disposition (Fig. 6.18).

Character Significance. The costume can sometimes tell the audience the importance of the character. Generally, importance comes with rank and status, but occasionally a play may feature a lower-status character in a principal role. A *huadan* wears the same type of garments whether she plays the minor role of best friend and confidant, or the central character, such as Hongniang, a matchmaker and the title character in *Hongniang*. However, depending on the actor's interpretation, she may wear a better-quality version of the expected costume and more elaborate embroidery or with the addition of beading (Fig. 2.6).

Genre and Scale. At least one dramatic aspect of

FIGURE 2.6. A *huadan* may add a beaded collar when playing a principal role. She wears the *guzhuang* style clothing, with fitted waist, along with the *guzhuang tou*, the corresponding form of hairstyle. *Hongniang (Hongniang)*. Character: Hongniang, actor: Guan Bo. NJC, Beijing, China. July 31, 2000.

the play is not specifically projected by the costumes. The genre of traditional Jingju cannot be perceived from the particular costumes worn, as the same stock of garments is used for civil comedies, love stories, and military battles. However, the type of play may be evident by the preponderance of a certain type of costume, such as *xuezi* and *pi* in a civil story, and *kao* in a martial play. In addition, the scale of the costumes does not alter depending on the size of the theatre in traditional Jingju; rather, the blocks of fabric color combined with

the details of embroidery allow for appreciation at any distance.

The information that Jingju costumes project about physical characteristics, given circumstances, and dramatic context is not equally balanced. The physical life of the character and their immediate surroundings receive emphasis, whereas the clues for the environment and dramatic context are subtler. Clothing establishes the basic elements of the character and the story, while much of the rest of the dramatic action belongs to the actor and the play. However, the conventions of dress are significant for their ability to project the chosen character concepts to the audience. Because of this attribute, an old saying pertaining to Jingju costumes declares it is better to don a worn costume than the wrong costume (*ning chuan po, bu chuan cuo*).

Selection Process

The choices that have been made about what costumes to use are challenging to delineate and categorize, as the motivation behind the repetition of convention sometimes appears random. Some costumes are virtually direct copies of historical garments, while others are theatricalized. Though the characters wear the correct garments for their position, the images on their garments do not necessarily accurately reflect their specific ranks. Young lovers are designated to wear floral decorations on their garments, but the specific language of flowers is not followed. The choices are determined by what is considered essential for communication of the characters to the audience. Because the plots of the plays are familiar to most Chinese audiences, the precise moment in time is communicated by the story line rather than the costumes. As long as the audience can determine whether a character is an officer or a civilian, and the general status of the character is evident, the specific rank within these two categories is irrelevant. Floral sprays are a symbol for youth and romance, and their presence implies enough information about those who wear them, without needing the details that designated flowers can portray. The costumes have developed to send clearly whatever message is needed to advance the story, and the remaining details have diminished for stage purposes. The blend of specific and generic levels of communication in the imagery also allows the costumes to be worn by a number of characters within the role types assigned to a given garment. As with the earlier forms from which Jingju evolved, the costumes were never intended to be a measure of historical customs or an accurate reflection of reality. While many of the costumes onstage can be traced to garments of historical dress throughout Chinese history, very few appear onstage unaltered from their original form. On the other hand, the deviations can, in some cases, be so slight that the costumes can be mistaken for their real-life counterparts. And in any case, the costumes can be appreciated for capturing the essence of the former grandeur of the imperial court, although anachronism and inaccuracy are subjugated to theatrical tastes and needs. As traditional Jingju is an art form and not a museum, this form of artistic license can be exercised. The rules of both traditional Jingju costume and imperial dress are applied to serve the art form rather than to restrict it, and are merely a framework for the artistry of performance. The costumes create an alternate existence that appears to be real in the theatrical context; they are a reflection of historical clothing, but created to serve the purposes of the stage.

Costumes and Movement

Throughout the history of traditional Jingju, the evolution and enhancement of dress and acting style have mutually influenced each other. The actors primarily developed the costumes, and the reforms they initiated were intended to improve the actor's art. The style of the costuming was refined so that virtually every element of the garments supported and enlarged the performance and expression of the actor, making their feelings and intentions more visible to the spectators. While the actor's face is the main area for expression, the full body and the garments are considered a second face with an image large enough to carry expressions to the farther reaches of the audience. As clothing conceals the actors except for their hands and faces, body movements are all perceived through the fabric of dress. Where fitted clothing is intended to articulate the beauty of the body, the flowing garments worn by traditional Jingju actors reveal the beauty of movement and posture.[7] With the actors' careful manipulation, the clothing becomes an extension of the body where each piece of the costume can contribute to the grace of motion and expression of character. Two aspects of conventionalization merge on the actor, standardized costumes and predetermined movement patterns, as the gesture patterns can not exist without the repeated use of conventionalized garments. While the costumes support the actor's performance, they also predetermine a standard of excellence and conformity to the style. Expertise and effortlessness in wearing and gesturing in the costume is an essential element in creating the overall beauty desired in performance.

In the same way that the costumes specify the characters, the individual garments predetermine movement techniques. The long, full robes of court demand a dignified, slow gait, as the shorter garments for clowns and servants imply a more casual bearing. In addition to the overall movement patterns, many different elements of clothing have established techniques associated with them for specific gestures. Costume pieces with specific movements include, among others, the water sleeves, the beards, and the feathers on the headdresses. With these pieces, each movement of the costume becomes a contributor to the actor's total art. The training of each actor includes the intricate language of costume expression through movement, so that the actions are well in-items, therefore, becomes a natural extension of that actor's performance. Some of the gestures are stylizations and refinements of the movements that came about from actual people wearing such clothes prior to the twentieth century, while others came from the dance heritage. By incorporating the clothing actions into expressions of emotion, the gestures shift from a utilitarian realm to one of expression.[8]

Water Sleeves. The water sleeves exemplify the symbiotic relationship between the actor and the costume. Water sleeves are white silk extensions attached to the sleeves of garments of upper-status male and female roles. The handling of the sleeves develops throughout the training process, and elegant sleeve movements are the sign of an accomplished performer. The extended sleeves evolved from ancient dance costumes and have long been considered essential to the elegance of the dancer. Many of the arm and hand gestures of the *qingyi* can be traced to the styles of movement from these older dance forms.[9] Other movements may have come from courtly life, where long and wide sleeves were the norm for hundreds of years. In performance, the movements of the hands are extended from the natural through the conventions of style. The hands are used almost continually throughout speech and song, the actions coordinating with and emphasizing the meanings of the text. As with movement through space, arm and hand movements are based on curved lines. To point to an object, for example, the actor starts the hand movement in the opposite direction from the object and then curves the hand around in a graceful arc to arrive at the object. With each gesture, the water sleeves add emphasis to the hands, drawing attention through both the contrasting white color and the flow of the fabric. The sleeves can embellish inner feelings that might not project from facial expressions, simply because they make each arm movement physically larger and clearer. Water sleeves also are utilized in more customary ways as well, to dab the eyes when crying or to cover the face for

FIGURE 2.7. Students practice in rehearsal garments to integrate their movements with the costumes. Student, ATCO, Beijing, China.

tegrated into the performances. Cotton rehearsal garments, often made by the students for themselves, are used during the arduous training process so that the actors are well familiar with the pieces long before the performances (Fig. 2.7). As an actor trains for a specific range of roles, each needs learn to use only a narrow spectrum of clothing. The wearing and use of those few

FIGURE 2.8. Actors may cover their faces with their water sleeve to eat or speak privately. *Hongniang (Hongniang)*. Character, far left: Hongniang, actor: Guan Bo. Character, left: Cui Yingying, actor: Tang Hexiang. NJC, Beijing, China. July 31, 2000.

modesty when eating or laughing, as showing the teeth is unrefined (Fig. 2.8). When the sleeves are in repose, they are folded in accordion pleats on the forearm, the more skillful performers accomplishing this placement with a few effortless flicks of the wrist.

Feathers. Of all the minute and magnificent movements that the costumes augment, perhaps the two most significant pieces of Chinese theatrical dress are the water sleeves mentioned above and the six-foot-long pheasant feathers on the headdresses. The pheasant-feather extensions on the military helmets of generals vividly combine beauty and expression. The feathers formerly were reserved for foreign characters, but now they appear on the headdresses of many heroes and heroines. The pair of feathers attached to each side of the headdress is not merely an attractive addition, it also emphatically draws attention to the wearer through both line and movement. As with the water sleeves, feather movements enlarge the gestures and emotions of the wearer. For example, rotating the head in circles, with the feathers tracing the pattern in the air, expands a sense of anger. Shaking the head back and forth quickly,

causing the feathers to quiver and undulate, adds to extreme frustration. Biting crossed feathers in the mouth heightens the appearance of aggressive feelings (Fig. 2.9). A particular skilled gesture with the plumes occurs in *Lü Bu and Diaochan* when Lü Bu is lured into flirting with Diaochan. He listens to her intently until he is ready to make his advance. Manipulating one feather using only head movements, he caresses her cheek with the tip and then gallantly withdraws it to show his esteem for her (BJC, Beijing, China. July 15, 2000).

Hair and Headdresses. Headdresses are decorated with several articulated ornaments to enable small movements. Spring-mounted pearls and woolly pompoms frame the face, and long tassels hang from either side of some of the helmets and crowns. The *shamao* (lit. "gauze hat," an official's hat), a category of hats, have a pair of wings *(chi)* attached to the back on springs; they project horizontally to the sides, creating movement with the slightest shift of the head. Women's headdresses are composed of many rhinestone pins, often with spring-mounted elements and beaded fringe. The extraneous movement of the many small parts creates a fluttering,

FIGURE 2.9. Feathers on the headdress, here a *zijin guan,* can be used to heighten the expression of emotions. *The Gathering of Heroes (Qunying hui).* Character: Zhou Yu, actor: Li Hongtu. BJC, Beijing, China. July 23, 2000.

the characters, the beards are used for expression. Beards are smoothed, lifted, and swung around to broaden various emotions. Beards are often stroked upon entering a room, symbolic of checking the appearance, while patting a beard with an open palm indicates a character considering a problem.[10] When crying, the beard can be used to dab the eyes dry.

Garments and Accessories. Specific garments and their accessories provide additional individual movement techniques. To increase his scale, a general in a *kao,* when first appearing onstage, may strike a pose, holding his two *kaotui* (leg flaps) at right angles to his body (Fig. 2.11). Subjects bowing to the emperor will make their obeisance appear grander by lifting and spreading the hems of their garments before kneeling in front of the throne. This gesture, of course, also makes it easier to stand at the end of the ceremony. The stiffened jade belts *(yudai)* worn with the *mang* and the *guanyi* add size to the figure as they are considerably larger than the circumference of the waist and hang suspended away from it. To reinforce the dignity of the character, an actor will place his hands on the side front sections of the jade belt with his elbows jutting out. In this expanded pose, they are prepared to listen to court edicts and procedures (Fig. 1.1).

Some soldiers wear a firm wide sash *(luandai)* tied tightly around the waist, with the two tasseled ends falling down the center front (Fig. 4.7). In battle, the ends of the sash may be dashingly kicked up to the hand, tucked into the sash or tossed over one shoulder, to get them out of the way.

In the battle sequences, the most powerful and prestigious characters are dressed in the *yingkao,* with four flags strapped to the back. The *yingkao* is made of many independent fabric panels that hang flat in repose, adding bulk and majesty to the roles, and when these segments flair tempestuously in the heat of combat, they add to the sense of energy and urgency on the battlefield. The battles are choreographed with repeating cir-

glittering effect that adds to the overall elegance of the stage picture.

Hairpieces can also be objects inspiring movement. Characters who have suffered defeat or humiliation and are in a state of distress wear the *shuaifa* (lit. "to toss the hair") hairstyle, with a ponytail on a three-inch post affixed to the top of the crown. When pushed to their limit, these characters kneel on one knee, remove their headdresses, and rotate their heads in a circle causing the hair to swing in a wide arc around them, in an expression of extreme despair (Fig. 2.10).

Beards. Long beards are worn by most *laosheng* and *jing* roles. In addition to adding age and distinction to

FIGURE 2.10. The *shuaifa* (lit. "to toss the hair," a ponytail) indicates a character in distress. *Li Yaxian (Li Yaxian)*. Character: Zheng Yuanhe, actor: Liu Yuechun. BJC, Beijing, China. May 26, 2002.

cular movements, ensuring that the double apron panels and hip segments swing out from the legs, and the flags and their streamers fly around the head and shoulders, along with the feathers mounted on the helmet. This theatrical version of armor does not seem to limit the movement capabilities of actors in any way, as generals in full armor can leap into the air, land in splits, kick their feet above their heads, and execute back flips, despite the bulk of the costume and the bamboo frame supporting the flags on their backs.

In contrast, the costumes for the *wuhang* (acrobatic soldiers) are simplified to accommodate their more intense acrobatic movement. The trousers are cut with fullness in the legs, hips, and waist that is folded to fit in the center front and tied with a cord. The simple geometric shape of the trousers allows for the aggressive flips and leaps, yet the trousers also do not fall off.

The jackets are cut without shaping in the armscye, or shaped armhole, as there is no seam between the sleeve and the torso, yet the performers have full rotation in their arms. Additional ornamentations worn by the soldiers, such as matching neckpieces, may be secured in place by tabs tucked in under a tight belt (Fig. 2.12).

When characters enter a room or change position, they adjust their garments. The movement usually is symbolic rather than sartorial, and, as such, employs only a partial motion. For example, a *qingyi* will stroke only the top part of her hair, or a *xiaosheng* will partially straighten his water sleeves. The aesthetic principle is to indicate just enough of the gesture to express the idea; a full action is considered excessive. The movements have been abbreviated to indicate the adjustment without taking too much focus.[11]

Walking. The different roles have distinctive walk-

FIGURE 2.11. A warrior holds out the *kaotui* (leg flaps) of his *kao* to look more imposing. *Turning Aside the Iron Carts (Tiao huache).* Character: Gao Chong, actor: Zhou Long. ATCO, Beijing, China. June 2, 2002.

FIGURE 2.12. Tabs from the collar piece reach to the belt to secure additional pieces for *wuhang* (acrobatic soldiers). The embroidered designs of treasures on their costumes are lucky emblems to indicate that they are divinities, as do their red silk scarves with rosettes. *The Magic Cistern (Ju dagang)*. Characters: Heavenly Soldiers, actors: unidentified. ATCO, Beijing, China. June 1, 2002.

ing techniques suitable to their types, and the footwear relates to these patterns. *Laosheng, xiaosheng,* and *jing* characters wear tall boots with high soles. The front of the platform is cut back at an angle to make forward motion more feasible. The walking style entails lifting each foot up and to the front of the body with the leg straight and then rocking forward to shift the weight. The back foot then progresses along the ground to meet the extended foot, before the sequence repeats for another step. Women for the most part wear flat-soled shoes. They walk with a gliding motion, taking tiny steps, with one foot barely ahead of the other, in imitation of the historical manner of feminine demeanor. The actor and troupe leader Wei Changsheng (1744–1802) introduced a technique for imitating the look and movement of bound feet, called *caiqiao* (lit. "stepping on stilts"). A device was used to support the wearer on tiptoe, similar to the *en pointe* position in ballet, though that practice has generally fallen into disuse. There were two versions of the stilts, pieces of wood that were strapped to the feet, *ruanqiao* (soft stilts) and *yingqiao* (hard stilts), the latter being much more challenging to master. Women's pleated skirts are also of note in creating the proper walk. The ideal method of walking entails not disturbing or rippling the pleats, as was desirable in imperial times.[12]

When a reform was initiated in the clothing styles, such as the innovations introduced by Mei Lanfang, there often needed to be a consequent reform in the movement patterns. The position of a hand on the hip that may have been flattering in one garment could be uncomplimentary in a new version. Along the same lines, when women began playing the female roles more often after the middle of the twentieth century, as they were real women and no longer imitating women, the movement patterns changed accordingly. Gradually, with practice and experimentation, a new visual language developed based on female movement by females. The symbiotic relationship between the actors and their costumes adds to the continuing growth and enrichment of the traditional Jingju style.

Costume Sources

The conventionalized costumes eliminate the need for a costume designer, and as a result, dressers generally manage traditional Jingju costumes. The wardrobe personnel for each troupe maintain a stockroom of conventionalized costumes from which they select the costumes for each performance. The stock of costumes normally contains a selection of garments for each role. If additional costumes are needed, the wardrobe person or another knowledgeable member of the troupe will order the costumes from a factory or purchase them at a store. For made-to-order costumes, the wardrobe person determines which characters will wear the new costumes, selects appropriate colors for the fabric and embroidery threads, along with the details of the images to be embroidered, and then places an order. With this system, many of the costumes are one-of-a-kind. Alternatively, costumes may be purchased directly from shops. In Beijing, an enclave of costumes shops is clustered around an alley south of Zhushi kou. The costumes available here range from low to higher-quality garments.

The significance of the system of traditional Jingju costume lies in the interlocking characteristics of the function of dress: to project the character, but not the environment, and to support the actor in expression of the character through movement. Every aspect of a costume has been decided by the needs of the story and the actor, causing a complex language of visual communication to develop in order to serve these purposes. In costumes of the traditional Jingju, what is not evident in the costumes is just as important as what is visualized. By abandoning a meticulously created reality from the start, and avoiding references to specific periods, seasons, and regions, the costumes, as well as the other aspects of traditional Jingju, present an alternate reality unique to the Chinese stage. This reality is framed by the beauty created by the extravagantly colored and embellished costumes, symbolic of character and the Chinese culture. The audience is invited into a world where the visual language of clothes plays an equal part with the spoken word.

The Form and Historical Roots of Costumes

When classifying traditional Jingju costumes, the Chinese use a system of "outer" and "inner" elements to describe the visual impact. The outer describes the overall image, primarily the silhouette, which is rather simple, yet it indicates all six of the identifiers: the person's status, gender, wealth, nationality, age, and whether they are military or civilian. The inner image is created by the combination of color and design on the surface of the costume. The composition of these elements reveals more information about the specific character, his or her personality, and his or her relationship to other characters, as well as elaborating on the six identifiers. The outer and inner characteristics work together to create impressions for the audience.

The form of the costumes is composed of geometric shapes, which are essentially rectangular or trapezoidal. Garments are constructed to maintain the geometry of the pattern pieces, without gathers or drapery. Garments with more complicated cutting usually are based on the same shapes and embellished by the addition of flat tabs and panels, with either straight or curved edges. The one deviation from this flatness is the women's skirt, which is pleated. When the garments are worn, the form is varied by having the costume hang either in flat sections from shoulder to hem, or stretch tightly around the body, held in place with a sash. With few exceptions, the shape of the clothing conforms to the natural body shape. The geometry of the cut also simplifies working with a stock of costumes. As the fit of each garment to the body is not precise, a single garment may be used by most of the performers who play a given role type.

Historical Background

Traditional Jingju costumes evolved from both historical clothing and costumes of previous performance styles, each contributing distinct images onstage. The relationship between historical and stage forms of dress evolved by happenstance rather than plan. Without a designer to shape and fashion garments according to character and theatrical intent, the costumes evolved through the spontaneous inventions of actors and practitioners. Connections between reality and theatricality can be made now through the advantageous lens of hindsight.

Throughout the history of imperial China, Han rule alternated with that of non-Han invaders, and the leaders of each succeeding Han dynasty chose to return to the designs of earlier Han forms of dress. Cross-cultural influences in clothing existed in the intervening periods, when invaders took over the rule of the country and established their own form of clothing. As a result, a range of ethnic and period clothing styles were worn at any given period in time. In the Qing dynasty (1644–1911), for example, official clothing was regulated, and all in attendance at court were required to dress in the Manchu style of the rulers, regardless of their ethnic-

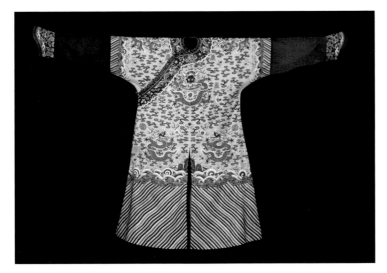

FIGURE 3.1. The Qing dynasty *jifu* has the cut of a Manchu garment and an embroidery pattern of dragons and waves developed by the Han, as can be seen in this adolescent emperor's semiformal coat. Photograph courtesy of the Jordan Schnitzer Museum of Art, University of Oregon, Murray Warner Collection of Oriental Art; acquired 1909, Peking, MWCh45.4.

FIGURE 3.2. The stage version of the court robe, the *mang,* is made in the form of a Han robe with wide sleeves, but uses a Qing dynasty version of the original Han pattern of ornamentation. From the author's collection.

ity. However, dress at home was not under court edict, and the majority Han people continued to wear their own style of clothing for private functions. In addition to dress from different ethnicities and eras being worn simultaneously, hybrid clothing developed from the interplay of cultures in the country, which resulted in historical garments that combined Han characteristics with those of other tribes. The Qing dragon robe *(longpao,* later renamed *jifu,* lit. "auspicious coat"), is an example; it has the cut of a Manchu garment with the decoration of Han Chinese cosmology (Fig. 3.1).[1] Onstage, a similar blending of cultures occurs in the *mang* (court robe) costume, which has the cut of a Ming dynasty (1368–1644), or Han, robe, and a Qing dynasty Manchu version of Han surface ornamentation (Fig. 3.2).[2] The environment of dress that intermingled real life models combined with nonrealistic influences inherited from dance and other theatrical forms has contributed to the current interpretation of clothing on the traditional Jingju stage. Rather than being out of harmony by combining costumes of different times and places, the Jingju costumed image may be considered a logical theatrical interpretation of the larger Chinese cultural context.

The costumes in traditional Jingju can be loosely ascribed to three sources: Han-style clothing from the Ming and earlier times, Manchu clothing of the Qing dynasty, and theatrically invented garments. In actuality, most, if not all, costumes have been transformed in some way from their original historical appearance, making theatrical style a significant component of all of the costume imagery. The following sections detail the three sources and offer examples of costumes that may be attributed to each category.

In Asia, three distinct traditions evolved for the production of clothing. In India, Malaysia, and other countries in Southeastern Asia through the islands of the archipelagos, clothing derived from woven and uncut cloth that was wrapped around the body in a sari or sarong fashion that involved minimal sewing. The garment was essentially created each time it was worn by being draped around the wearer. From Southern China to Japan and Korea, clothing again derived from woven cloth, but the peoples in these areas added seaming and minimal cutting to minimize waste of the lengths of fabric. The resulting clothing was based on large rectangular blocks for the body and sleeves. The third tradition of clothing production developed in Northern China, Manchuria, and Mongolia. In this region, body coverings were created from the hides of local animals, using shapes that fit well on the prepared skins, but these forms did not transfer to a layout on fabric without producing waste in the scraps. Clothing of this type fit more closely to the body and arms, recreating the shape of the animal on the human form.[3] The latter two of these tra-

ditions figured prominently in the evolution of garments in Chinese history and therefore in the development of costuming on the stage.

Cloth-Based Sources of Clothing

The weaving and geometric cutting tradition was the basic method for clothing production of the Han people in China. Weaving began as early as the second millennium BC as evidenced by the findings of silk and hemp fragments dated to that era.[4] Early weaving techniques using a narrow backstrap loom did not produce fabric wide enough to cover the body.[5] The width of the cloth therefore determined the nature of the assembly of the garments. From the Zhou dynasty (1100–221 BC) the basic Han form of dress consisted of a robe *(pao)* and trousers *(kuzi)* made from this narrow cloth.[6]

Han garments throughout the dynasties either met at the center front or overlapped to the right. Two techniques were used to provide the extra width in the front to create the overlap, adding fabric symmetrically to each side, or adding different width pieces to each front panel.[7] The lap was generally a diagonal straight line from the shoulder across the body towards the opposite underarm, with a slight curve on the lower edge to fit around the body. The neck and lap opening was finished with a wide collar band. Another version met at the center front in a V-neck, and then the lap was squared off to the right and dropped straight to the hem. Loom widths increased from only 20 inches in the Han dynasty (206 BC–220 AD) to 27 inches in the Ming dynasty.[8] Though the fabric width had increased, the construction techniques were unaffected, and similar robes continued to be worn by the Han through the Qing dynasty.

Cloth was a precious commodity, as it took time to process and produce. Silk was admired not only for clothing, but also as a reward for service to the emperor. Owning cloth symbolized wealth and one's position in society, so it was essential that the garments made from cloth continue to minimize waste and maximize the effect of cloth on the body. With this fundamental approach to textiles, Han garments did grow in both volume and in number of layers.[9] Though initially the fabric was not to be wasted by being cut and left out of the garment, large measures of fabric were used to make each of the robes, and the Han garments eventually did develop into a trapezoidal shape.

Han Garments and Traditional Jingju Costumes

Dragon Robe and *Mang*. Garments of the Ming court, the last Han dynasty, consisted of voluminous robes with large sleeves. The dragon robe (*longpao)* was first recorded in the Tang dynasty (618–907) and used for informal wear during the Ming dynasty. The body of the garment was slightly trapezoidal in shape, with side vents to the underarm seams. Extensions *(bai)* were added to the vents to create a flap that wrapped from the side front over the back. The front had a crossover closing to the right, with a round neck and a convex curve from the side of the neck to the underarm seam, a shape first used in the Tang dynasty.[10] The volume of the dragon robe was enhanced by hoop-shaped jade ornamented belts (*yudai)* that encircled the robe. The sleeves were both wide and long, because covering the hands was considered proper in Chinese etiquette. The mass of the garments created an imposing image that was reinforced by the slow and elegant movement style of the court rituals.[11]

This cut of garment recurs today on the traditional Jingju stage in the *mang* worn by the emperors and the highest-level members of the court. The form of the stage version appears to be quite close to that of the original, for it shares the rounded neckline and curved crossover front lap, and the open side seams with extensions that lap over the back. The sleeves are long, with a slight flare, and water sleeves *(shuixiu),* a theatrical addition, extend from the hems (Figs. 3.2, 1.1, and Appendix 1.1).

Official Robe and *Guanyi*. Civil and military officers of the Ming court wore the official's robe, emblazoned with a rank badge to indicate their position. The nine levels of rank were indicated by different creatures depicted on the badges at the front and back of the chest. From this garment emerged the stage version, the *guanyi* (official's robe). The robe appears onstage worn primarily by the civil officers. The size and shape of the badge have been altered from the Ming versions to a square that resembles the Qing rank badges. Depiction of the specific ranks of characters is not practiced onstage. The form of the *guanyi* is essentially the same as that for the *mang* (Fig. 6.22, Appendix 1.1).

***Beizi* and *Pi*.** The *beizi* (long robe) originated in the Song dynasty (960–1279), and was worn by men and women. Originally, the sleeves were fuller, but in the Ming period, the sleeves became tubular. The neckline and opening of the center front of the early *beizi* had a band finishing the edges to the hem, but gradually a contrasting neckband encircled the neck and stopped at mid-chest, where there was a closing. The body of the garment was essentially straight, with vents at the side seams. The *beizi* transferred to traditional Jingju usage in the form of the *nüpi* (woman's formal robe) and the *pi* (men's formal robe). The tubular sleeves of the *pi/nüpi* are longer than wrist length, to which the water sleeves are added, and the hem comes to the knee for women and the ankle for men. The body of the *nüpi* retains straight sides and vents, but the men's *pi* has flared side seams with vents (Fig. 6.7, Appendix 1.2–1.3).

***Jiaoling pao* and *Xuezi*.** The historical *jiaoling pao* (long robe with crossover closing), with its crossover closing to the right, was widely worn as early as the Zhou period. The *jiaoling pao* was made from two lengths of cloth starting at the back hem, continuing over the shoulders and down to the front hems. They were seamed together at the center back and under the arms, often leaving vents on the lower side seams. Two additional pieces of fabric were added at the shoulders to form sleeves. The front of the *jiaoling pao* was left open, and it could have been tied or belted at the waist. As the form of the *jiaoling pao* evolved, other pieces could be added to increase the width at the sides or to create an overlap in the front.[12] The neckline eventually was finished with a wide, straight collar band, the sleeves were full, and this practical garment could be worn for a variety of purposes. The historical *jiaoling pao* became the *xuezi* (informal robe) in traditional Jingju usage, and is widely worn as informal clothing. The stage version has narrower tubular sleeves that are longer than the wrists and have water sleeves added. The closing is asymmetrical, with the right side falling straight from the shoulder and neck intersection and the left crossing over to be tied under the right arm. The body of the *xuezi* is slightly trapezoidal, and the side seams are vented. Male characters wear a full-length *xuezi*, while the *nüxuezi* (woman's informal robe) is knee-length (Fig. 6.16, Appendix 1.4). There are two forms for women, both called *nüxuezi,* one with a cross-over closing that matches the men's version and another with a center-front closing (Fig. 6.18, Appendix 1.5). The *xuezi* is easily the most versatile stage garment, as it can be worn by all four major role types. Through changes in fabric and ornamentation, the *xuezi* appears on servants, scholars, clowns, young women, and mature women. One of the earliest garments in Chinese clothing history, it continues to dress a significant part of the population of traditional Jingju performances.

Baoyi. The *baoyi* ("leopard/panther" or "embracing" clothes; that is, tight, hero's clothes) is related to Ming dynasty dress because the jacket has the straight crossover closing of the *xuezi* and is secured with ties. The tapered sleeves are closed with frogs, which is evidence of Qing influence. A double layer of pleated fabric attached to the hem of the jacket is a theatrical addition

called "moving water" *(zoushui).* The trousers are conventional (Fig. 6.31, Appendix 1.6–1.7).

Trousers. Trousers *(kuzi)* date from the Bronze Age in China. Initially, separate leggings, probably made of leather, were worn by the northern tribes to provide protection while riding horseback. Tubular fabric loin coverings were gradually joined to the leggings to create true trousers. During the Warring States period (475–221 BC), a king of the Zhao state, now in Shanxi province, required his mounted warriors to wear trousers, thereby changing the dress of generations of Chinese.[13] The cutting patterns for these fabric trousers evolved to include more shaping, such as gussets or a diagonal seam in the crotch, a shape that continues in stage usage. The waist is not fitted, but rather comes straight up from the width at the hip. The waistband is made of a different fabric, likely a cotton, and is folded across the front of the body to fit and then tied with a cord (Fig. 6.61). The cotton fabric, selected to prevent slipping, is then folded over the cord. There are ties at the ankles as well. The shaping allows for the full range of movement needed in an active life, onstage and off (Fig. 4.7, Appendix 1.7).

Skirt. The Chinese skirt *(qunzi)*, or paired aprons, appeared in Han clothing as early as the Song dynasty, apparently also absorbed from nomadic neighbors. The skirt was made of two panels that lapped center front and back, with the openings between the sections that enabled horseback riding. An extant example of a Chinese skirt from the Song dynasty found in Huang Shen's tomb in Fuzhou, Fujian province, shows a wraparound style with flat and pleated sections, and a wide waistband with ties.[14] The historical version has straight panels in the front and back, with pleated sections on either side, much like the skirt worn in traditional Jingju today (Fig. 6.8). The waistband is cotton and is tied around the waist with strings. One of the common clothing combinations worn by Ming dynasty women consisted of a center-front-opening, knee-length robe worn over a pleated skirt, and this combination is reflected onstage with the *nüpi* or *nüxuezi* and skirt (Appendix 1.8). Different sizes and depths of pleats are employed to distinguish the skirts for the different role types.

The *mang, pi,* and *xuezi* comprise three of the four principal costumes worn by most traditional Jingju characters. The greatest difference among these three garments is in the shape of the neckline. The round neckline with curved closing on the *mang* and *guanyi* is considered to be the highest level of closing. The center-front closing of the *pi* is next in rank, and the straight crossover closing on the *xuezi* has the lowest status.[15] While the sources of garments divide almost evenly among Han, Manchu, and theatrical roots, in actual usage, more characters appear in these three garments than any others, giving the overall stage impression a predominantly Han look.

Hide-Based Sources of Clothing

Manchu garments entered the Chinese realm with the establishment of the Qing dynasty in 1644. The roots of the hide-based tradition of Northern China are described earlier, and although the clothing was now made from fabric, the endemic animal shape was still reflected in the cloth clothing. The typical garments were based on the northern robe and trousers tradition, but with its hide origins, the Manchu-style robe evolved into a leaner version, that fit more closely to the body than Han clothing did. The lower part of the garments had some flare, reflecting the natural contours of the animal skin, and allowed for ease of movement. The crossover piece for the front lap on the robe was shaped in an S-curve from the neck to the underarm, an indication of the irregular shape of animal skins rather than the straighter line used for cloth garments by the Han.[16] While the robes took on the straight shoulder

line accomplished from a fold in the fabric when made of cloth, the vests continued to have sloping shoulder lines and curved armholes, instead of the straight lines used for fabric garments made from the geometric cut.

In addition to the impact that materials had on the development of Manchu clothing, their nomadic lifestyle contributed to their choices in creating garments. Much of their active life was spent riding horseback. Therefore, the upper garments had crossover closings in the front, creating a double layer to break the chill of the wind. The jackets were sealed with toggles and loops for a secure closure. The sleeves were cut narrow to the wrist, with hoof-shaped cuffs that could be folded down over the hands for further protection from the cold. The robes were vented in the front and back so that the skirts would split comfortably over the back of the horse. Although earlier invaders had worn garments that crossed to the left, the Manchu garments lapped to the right, the same as the Chinese. Neither the Han nor the ethnic minorities distinguished male and female garments by the direction of the closing.

Manchu Garments and Traditional Jingju Costumes

Jifu and *Jianyi.* The full cut of the Ming dynasty robes was the antithesis of the aesthetics of the Qing courtiers, who preferred the narrower clothing of their nomadic heritage. Therefore the Qing version of the Ming's dragon robe reflected the hide-based form and nomadic roots with narrow sleeves, tight horseshoe cuffs, and center-front and back openings in the skirt. Renamed *jifu* by the Manchu, it was worn belted closely to the body for semiformal events. When it was made of cloth, the *jifu* followed the Han tradition of cutting the garments in a single piece on each side from the front to the back hem, without a shoulder seam. Another piece of fabric was added to the front to create the overlap,

FIGURE 3.3. The cut of the *jianyi* costume resembles the Qing dynasty *jifu* (Fig. 3.1) and is worn by both Han and minority characters. From the author's collection.

and the *jifu* was closed with toggles and loops. The lower sleeves were fashioned from a fabric different from the body of the garment, a reflection of the evolution from layered nomadic clothing into a single unit (Fig. 3.1).

The *jifu* is closely imitated onstage by the *jianyi* (archer's robe), although the contrasting lower sleeves of the *jifu* do not generally appear on the *jianyi*. (A rare example of this characteristic can be seen in Fig. 5.1.) The *jianyi* is also worn with a small separate collar (*shanjian*). Like its historical predecessor, the *jianyi* is worn belted. Though it is rare for Qing-style garments to be assigned to Han characters, the *jianyi* has crossed over into wider usage and is worn by both Han and minority characters (Figs. 3.3, 6.26–28, and Appendix 1.9).

Bufu. After 1759, members of the imperial court were required to wear a *bufu* (coat with a badge) over their *jifu* for official appearances.[17] The *bufu* was the Qing dynasty replacement for the Ming official's robe with rank badges. The narrower *bufu* was based on a geometric cut, with a straight body just longer than knee length.

It had three-quarter-length sleeves, a round neckline, a center-front closing, and vents on the sides. The narrower torso of the garment meant that the rank badges *(buzi)* on the front and back were smaller as well. This same combination appears onstage as the *bufu,* with the same name, and it is worn over the *jianyi.* The stage *bufu* is virtually identical to its historical forerunner, making it possible for actual *bufu* to be used onstage. When the *jianyi* and *bufu* are worn in combination, the garments signify "foreign" dress, and they are designated for officers of minority courts onstage (Fig. 6.53) The cut of the *bufu* resembles the *magua* (see below), but it is longer (Appendix 1.10).

Magua. For informal events in the past, a plainer robe might have been worn with a shorter surcoat, the *magua* (lit. "horse jacket"). The cut of the historical *magua* is similar to the *bufu*, but the *magua* has full-length tubular sleeves and a hip-length full-cut torso, and it lacks the rank badges. The historical *magua* transferred to the stage as a costume of the same name, and this riding jacket is worn in combination with the *jianyi* by military men of both Han and minority origin when traveling or arriving at court (Fig. 6.30, Appendix 1.10).

Jacket and Trousers. The jacket and trousers (*kuaiyi*, lit. "fast clothes") from history can be seen onstage as the *kuaiyi* for nonofficial martial characters and the *bingyi* for regimental soldiers. Both use the S-curve and frog closing of the Qing-style garments. The sleeves are fitted and closed at the wrist with frogs, another Qing characteristic. The trousers are the traditional cut (Figs. 6.31–35, Appendix 1.7 and 1.11).

Vests. In casual dress, the Manchu vests (*kanjian*) for both men and women utilized the sloping shoulder and rounded armholes that had developed from hide-based garments. The vests were made with a variety of front closings and an optional standing collar. The vests worn onstage retain the slanted shoulder seam and curved armholes and are worn in a variety of styles and lengths by a wide range of characters, Han and minority (Fig. 6.62, Appendix 1.12).

Dragon Robe and *Qimang*. Some clothing styles of Manchu women were adopted directly for stage use towards the end of the Qing dynasty. The Manchu garments for women are easily identified onstage as their robes are full length, while the Han-based robes are knee length and worn with a pleated skirt, a distinction that was also the case during the Qing dynasty.

The Manchu woman's dragon robe *(longpao)* was a trapezoidal-shaped, full-length robe. The side seams were left open quite high on the thigh. The neck was round, with an S-curved closing to the right. The sleeves were tubular, yet they still had wide horseshoe-shaped cuffs at the hem. The stage *qimang* (Manchu court robe) reflects the form of the historical dragon robe and seems identical except for the sleeve cuffs, which are now applied in the turn-back position. The edges of the necklines and front closings of both garments are treated with a border of contrasting fabric, further augmented with strips of patterned trim. The use of these borders and the turn-back cuffs are another example of cross-cultural influence, as these are Han styles that were adopted by the Manchu.[18] Borders were added to garments early in the history of Han clothing, initially to increase the life of the garment, but they gradually became more decorative, with many contrasting layers.[19] During the Qing dynasty, all garments were worn with separate collars underneath to keep the silk outer garments clean. The collar that was worn with the dragon robe had a standing band with a small rounded collar, and this unit was attached to a dickie worn inside the robe. The *qimang* is worn with a collar *(lingyi)* as well. When worn onstage, the *qimang* indicates imperial females of the minorities in ceremonial situations (Fig. 6.5, Appendix 1.13).

***Qipao*.** The *qipao* (Manchu gown) was a slimmer full-length gown with a standing band collar attached to the neck of the dress and tubular sleeves. Onstage in scenes of daily life, minority women characters wear a costume version of this garment called by the same name. The neck, closings, side vents, sleeves, and hems are decorated with two bands of contrasting fabric, usually in two colors, and the surface is embroidered with flowers and butterflies (Fig. 6.52). A more fitted version of the *qipao*, with tapering sleeves and side seams curved to shape to the body, developed after the end of the Qing dynasty, and it also appears onstage. The Qing dynasty *qipao* that inspired the stage version is also the precursor to the popular body-hugging *qipao* still worn today by Chinese and western women alike (Appendix 1.14).

Theatrically Based Clothing

In addition to the costumes derived from historical clothing, innovative designs were developed by modifying existing costumes or creating original garments. The changes came about because of theatrical need and aesthetics, when clothing from reality was inadequate in meeting theatrical desires. Most often, it is actors wishing to improve the performance of their characters through artistic or practical changes in dress who have developed these new costumes. The invented costumes reflect the cultural context in tandem with the creativity of the developers, and they blend seamlessly with the other costumes as part of the stage picture.

Nümang. Imperial women did not have a robe for court wear until the Qing dynasty. The women's stage *nümang* (woman's court dress) developed from the traditional Jingju version of the male *mang*.[20] There are two knee-length versions of the *nümang*. One has straight sides and hem resembling the men's *mang* (Fig, 6.3, and a shorter version of Appendix 1.1). The other has an additional contrasting border with a wavy, undulating edge around the sides, hem, and sleeve cuffs, a traditional Jingju invention that appears on other created costumes. As with other high-ranking garments, the *nümang* has water sleeves (Fig. 6.4, Appendix 1.15).

Kao. Kao (armor) is among the most spectacular of the theatrical innovations and only modestly draws from historical precedents. Early Chinese armor was made of metal and leather, and used an overlapping fish-scale pattern of separate pieces to protect the body. As armor developed, it appears that surface ornamentation was as important as protection, and some highly decorated suits of armor were made primarily for ceremonial purposes. In the Tang, Song, and Ming dynasties, segmented flaps with animal heads could cover the shoulder areas. The fitted torsos and apron panels had several layers, with an array of colors and patterns on them (Fig. 3.4). In the Qing dynasty, both the silhouette and surface of the armor changed. The armor was constructed in two major pieces. The upper portion reflected the shape of court garments, with tapering sleeves, turned back cuffs, and trapezoidal torso. The lower piece consisted of full-length flaps covering the front of the legs and around to the sides. The center front of the flaps was vented, and the back left uncovered for horseback riding (Fig. 3.5).

FIGURE 3.4. The statues outside the Ming tombs wear segmented armor with shapes and ornamentation similar to stage armor. Dingling, imperial tomb of the Wanli emperor (1573–1620).

Traces of both historical forms are blended with pure invention for the stage armor worn by traditional Jingju generals. The theatrical armor consists of a tabard with sleeves, separate leg flaps, underarm pieces, a collar, and four flags. The use of segmented pieces carries over from the historical models, with separate flaps in the shoulder area that are still sometimes decorated with animal heads, underarm segments, and layered panels over the legs. Two aprons of staggered length comprise the front and the back of the tabard, and the two separate panels *(kaotui)* are worn tied around the waist to

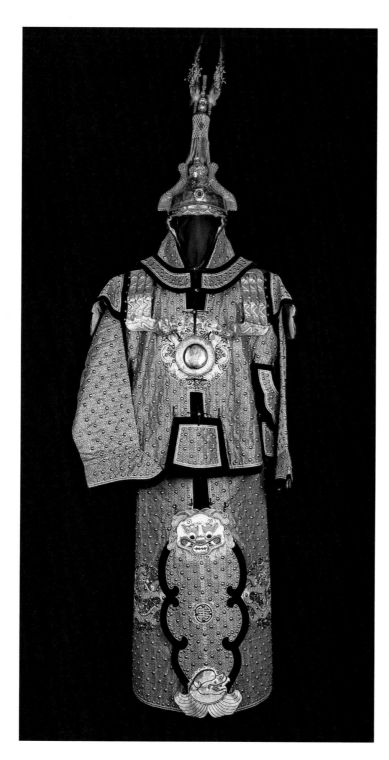

FIGURE 3.5. A Manchu palace guard's ceremonial armor made from silk fabric, decorated with couched gold-wrapped thread and multicolored silk floss. The use of gold couching transferred to theatrical armor. Photograph courtesy of the Jordan Schnitzer Museum of Art, University of Oregon, Murray Warner Collection of Oriental Art, MWCh64:1 a-e.

hang on the sides. The greatest differences between the historical and stage designs include the broad, padded belt *(kaodu)* in the front, the addition of a separate collar, and the use of four flags *(kaoqi)* on the upper back. The padded belt and flags contribute significantly to the scale and volume of the armored figure onstage and were no doubt added with the theatrical impact in mind (Fig. 6.9, Appendix 1.16). Two additional layers of streamers in the skirt area ornament the *nükao* (women's armor), as well as a wider cloud collar *(yunjian)*, and deep fringe around the edges of all the segments (Fig. 6.10, Appendix 1.17).

Gailiang kao and *Gailiang nükao.* The *gailiang kao* (reformed armor) more closely resembles the armor of history, but it is considered a theatrical invention as the design can be traced to a specific actor, Zhou Xinfang (1895–1975, stage name Qiling Tong, lit. "seven-year-old boy," that is, a prodigy), who developed it as an alternative to the *kao* when a quick change was needed.[21] Worn by both male and female combatants, the *gailiang kao* or *gailiang nükao* have layers of panels over both the torso and the legs. The cloud collar and shoulder flaps with tapering sleeves resemble the *kao* design, but in these garments, they are combined with a fitted torso and a wide, fitted fabric belt. A shaped peplum flap covers the area from the waist to the hips, and a variety of layered and shaped panels are arranged around the legs. The edges of the panels are fringed. The *gailiang kao* and *gailiang nükao* are worn by members of a military retinue for off-battlefield skirmishes (Fig. 6.11, Appendix 1.18).

Zhan'ao zhanqun. The *zhan'ao zhanqun* (martial jacket and skirt) is a traditional Jingju-developed costume for female fighters of lower rank. A divided skirt augments the jacket and trousers worn by male fighters. The jacket has a center-front closing and is worn cinched at the waist, creating a peplum over the hips. The center front of the skirt panels is open, with the lower edges

curving away to the sides, and the back panels overlap and are open at the center back to allow for acrobatic maneuvers (Fig. 1.10, Appendix 1.19).

Kai chang. Another garment of theatrical origin is the *kai chang* (informal open robe) worn by military and governmental men in their private quarters. As such, the *kai chang* is halfway between a *mang* worn at court and a *xuezi* worn in private by nonofficial characters. The form for the *kai chang* is indeed a hybrid of these two garments, with the back of the body, the extensions that cross from the front over the back, and the sleeves with water sleeve additions following the cut of the *mang.* The front of the garment has the straight crossover lap with a wide neckband that is characteristic of the *xuezi.* The hems of the *kai chang* have an undulating edge, reinforced by a wavy band of fabric of the same or contrasting color. In some examples, the band virtually circumnavigates the front of the *kai chang*, reaching around the neckline, down the side front edge, across the hem, and up the opposite side. The same effect is repeated on the hem of the inner extension and back hems. With the exception of the hem, the bands are straight-edged (Figs. 1.19, 6.21, Appendix 1.20).

Bagua yi. The *bagua yi*, with its eight trigrams on the surface, is a garment for characters who have magical abilities related to Daoism. The cut is similar to the *kai chang*, with the addition of a flat, attached belt and two hanging tabs in the front. The *bagua yi* is further distinguished by the fact that the curved shapes on the hem continue up the side openings. These added bands are made of contrasting color fabric. Additional bands are sewn on the bottoms of the sleeves with wavy upper edges and straight hems, to which the water sleeves are attached (Fig. 6.43, Appendix 1.21).

Eunuch Robes. The round-neck court robe for eunuchs *(yuanling taijian yi)* represents a stage version of court dress worn specifically by eunuchs. It does not have a true counterpart in historical clothing because eunuchs wore essentially the same clothing as others. The round neckline and curved overlap closing are shaped similarly to the *mang*. The sleeves are tubular with water sleeve additions. A horizontal seam at the lowered waistline has two separate skirt panels pleated into it, with an overlap on the left side, a feature unique to this garment. Knotted fringe is set into the lower edge of the contrasting waistband. The neck, side closing, and hems also have a border of the same contrasting color fabric, which is also used to create six roundels that are applied to the robe, one at the front and back of the chest and two each on the front and back of the skirt panels (Fig. 6.24, Appendix 1.22). A second style of eunuch robe is the crossover closing eunuch robe *(xieling taijian yi)*; its body and ornamentation are the same as the round neck version, and it has a closing similar to the *xuezi*.

Gongzhuang. As with the other invented costumes, elements of the *gongzhuang* (palace garment) resemble dress from life, but the combination of its characteristics makes it unique. The *gongzhuang* is comprised of a geometric torso, with a separate cloud collar and two or three layers of streamers over a pleated skirt. A matching number of apron layers are affixed on the center front and back of the dress. The sleeves are longer than the wrists and have either three layers of water sleeves, in pink, blue, and white, or plain white ones. The seven wavy stripes of multicolored fabrics on the sleeves reflect the use of banded trim on unofficial jackets, and the skirt streamers suggest the decorations brides wore over their skirts.[22] The potential heritage of the garment is further asserted by John Vollmer, who explains, "the link between empress and bride at least in the late imperial period is emphatic," and he further speculates that the *gongzhuang* garment may have originated in the theatre, perhaps in court dance entertainments and then influenced the dress of the court, rather than the other way around.[23] The implication is that the gar-

ment crossed over among theatre costumes, brides, and empresses to become a costume worn by high-ranking princesses and concubines onstage, often for dancing (Figs. 3.6, 6.29, and Appendix 1.23).

Mei Lanfang Designs. Mei Lanfang, the most famous actor of women's roles in the twentieth century, was also a major contributor to the development of theatrical costumes. He initiated the performance of new plays, in which he dressed in garments that had been carefully researched and designed from historical models.[24] Though his designs were based on ancient styles, they resembled a modern silhouette as well. Unlike the voluminous stately gowns in stage usage, Mei presented more streamlined garments, fitted at the waist to enhance the dance movements. His designs share certain characteristics, including a slim jacket and pleated skirt, with contrasting color pieces. The jackets have tubular sleeves, with or without the water sleeves, and are worn tucked into the skirts and finished with a wide belt. The skirts have fewer pleats than the typical skirt worn by the *qingyi* roles. A collar or bib and short skirt panels attached to a wide waistband, all with fringed edges, complete the ensemble (Fig. 6.59).

Form and Conventions of Usage

As the forms of the garments translate loosely from history to the stage, such is also the case with conventions of wear. The dynasties' system of strict rules governing what clothing one wore continues to be applied to stage characters, whose dress must follow theatrical rules. The garments and the rules differ, but the impact of sumptuary laws in life resonates with the assignment of costumes onstage. Costumes are designated for characters according to their status, as well as the event, as was the case under imperial rule.

Similar to historical clothing, traditional Jingju garments also come in a limited number of forms that are

FIGURE 3.6. The *gongzhuang* is one of the most complicated costumes in cut, color, and ornamentation. The sleeves have multicolored bands that match the colors of the streamers attached at the waist, and the surface is richly enhanced by appliqués. From the collection of James Young, Honolulu, Hawai'i.

infinitely varied by color and ornamentation. One example of this trait are the trousers worn by every character onstage, male or female. The trousers for demure young ladies are embroidered with bands around the hem, while the embroidered designs on foot soldiers' trousers is scattered on the surface, and the *sheng* roles often wear plain-colored trousers *(caiku)*. Though the shapes of the garments repeat, through diverse combinations of fabrics, colors, and embroidery, the same type of garment can serve a wider range of the population.

As it was considered inappropriate for the shape of the body to be evident inside the clothing, the Chinese robes were generally loose fitting.[25] The same can be said for most traditional Jingju clothes worn by characters of higher status; their garments generally fall straight from the shoulder. The volume of the garment also speaks to the wearer's wealth, as greater amounts of fabric and more layers speak to the wearer's place in society. While the emperor, his courtiers, and generals conceal themselves within layers of robes or elaborately layered armor, the stage distinguishes lower-status characters or military roles by dressing them in fewer pieces or costumes that are stretched tightly around the body and secured with a sash, reducing their comparative scale.

Patterning and Cut of Costumes

Patterns for the costumes reveal they are made from basic geometric shapes, rectangular or trapezoidal, in a fashion similar to their historical counterparts. The cut of garments for men and women is essentially the same in the garment styles that are shared by both sexes, although women's garments are smaller than the men's, as well as shorter. Most garments are cut in one size for each type of costume, as most actors conform to a given size range, though exceptions may be made for actors who are different heights. The proportions of the garments appear to carry over from garment to garment, with similar angles for the trapezoidal shape in the body and comparable circumferences in the tubular sleeves. For example, the circumference of the chest of men's full-length robes measures from about 44 inches to 48 inches, and they flare to an average of 72 inches at the hem.[26] The additional length for the sleeve is attached in a straight, unshaped seam that falls below the natural shoulder line. The sleeves tend to be cut in squares, although some garments have a sleeve design that tapers either inward or outward. The circumference of the tubular sleeves is from around 22 inches to 24 inches. The shape of the curve where the side seams meet the underarm seams of the sleeve remains the same on all the garments, accomplishing the almost right-angle shift with a curve that falls within a two-inch square. The sleeves reach to the wrist unless the garments have water sleeves, in which case the garment sleeve is longer to add grace to the sleeve when folded on the lower arm. The water sleeves equal the width of the garment sleeves and come in two lengths, approximately 14 inches for men's garments and 25 inches for the female characters, who employ the sleeves much more in their expressions. The water sleeves are constructed with the woven selvage on the lower edge to avoid the bulk of a hem, and this makes them easier to control.

Garments close either at the center front or crossover to the right for both men and women. The wrap of the right-closing garments takes several shapes, as described above. The absence of shoulder seams requires that either the underlap or overlap be added to the garment. The underlap is usually pieced to the right side of the garment in a seam that can be concealed by the collar band, so that there is no seam visible on the front of the garment. The underwrap often drops straight down from the intersection of the neck and shoulder points, creating an asymmetrical closing. When a collar band is applied onto this neckline as in the *xuezi*, it is likewise asymmetrically shaped, with the underwrap side straight and a slight curve starting at the right shoulder point. A convex curved lap appears on the *mang* and the *guanyi*, to name two garment types. The curve starts at the rounded neck and arcs to the underarm seam. Again, the underlap is pieced onto the garment, with the seam barely concealed by the overlap, which is finished with a facing and tied at the ends of the wrap curve. The underlap stops slightly short of the center front rather than continuing to the opposite side, creating another unbalanced closing, although in this case the difference in shape is not visible.

The Manchu-style closing, with the S-curved overlap, is constructed in the same way, generally without a seam in the center front and with the underwrap attached to the right side along the same cut line as the overwrap. Other lap shapes are used on some of the short vests, including the *pipa* closing, named after the musical instrument it resembles. This Qing-based style goes straight to the right of the center-front neck point, drops down over the bust point, and then cuts to the left to the center front of the waist, where it turns downward again, creating a vent in the center front. Vests have retained the tapering shoulder seam and rounded armholes of the Manchu style.

The underlaps on the robes are shorter at the hem towards their inner edge so that they are not visible under the overlap, with the exception of the *jianyi*. Because the *jianyi* is sometimes worn with the outer flap lifted up and the underlap is revealed, the hem lengths are identical. To compensate for the geometric cut of the trapezoidal robes, the hems are curved up on the side seams so that they hang level when worn. The backs are usually about an inch longer than the front, and most robes are slit on the side seams.

The *jianyi*, being a Qing-based form, has some other distinctions in the cut. As it was developed for horse-back riding, it is divided in the center front and back, rather than on the sides as with other garments. Sometimes the *jianyi* has a seam in these locations to accommodate the vent. If the overlap is pieced on instead of the underwrap, as with some *jianyi,* the overlap is simply attached at the center-front seam. The sleeves are joined to the body in a straight seam around the bicep and taper to the wrist. A separate flared cuff is attached at the wrist. The cuff is curved around the outer edge, with the weight of the curve to the back of the garment. A gusset is sometimes inserted under the arm to allow for the acrobatics of the performers who wear this kind of garment.

A bias binding wide enough to create a facing on the inside edge, or a standing band collar, commonly referred to as a Mandarin collar, may be used to finish the rounded necklines. A slight curve is cut in the standing band collar to allow it to fit closely to the neck. Both the long, wide collar band on the straight-style crossover closings and the Mandarin collar are stiffened with interfacing and sometimes rice glue is applied to the fabric as well.

Garments are closed primarily with ties or frogs. Tying closures continue to be used on garments that are linked to the Han heritage, including the *mang,* the *pi,* and the *xuezi,* while frog closings are used on garments that emerged from the tribal traditions, such as the *jianyi, magua,* vests, and jackets. An odd number of toggles and loops is thought to be lucky for center-front

closings, as can be seen on the *magua.*[27] The closures are made from fabric that matches the bias edgings. The ties for fastening garments are tapered to be narrow at the garment end and flared at the end of the tie, and they end in an arrow shape. Skirts and trousers are tied to the waist using a string that is not sewn to the garment. The hems of the trousers have attached ties for cinching the trousers underneath the booties. On some garments, such as the *gongzhuang,* a modern Velcro fastener has replaced the traditional forms of closure.

Theatrically invented costumes build on the geometric forms and are further embellished by the addition of flat tabs and panels, with either straight or curved edges. These additional, shaped pieces often repeat from garment to garment. The women's *nükao* uses the same basic shapes as the men's, on a smaller scale and with the addition of a double layer of skirt streamers. Both of the *kao* have a similarly curved edge on the upper sleeve flap attached at the shoulder, and this is left open under the arm for facility of movement, while the lower sleeve is seamed closed and fastened with frogs. The cut of the *gailiang kao* allows for more variety than other garments, particularly in the decorative shapes of the peplum and the leg panels. Cut like a vest, the torso has sloping shoulders and rounded armscyes, yet the sleeve cap and lower sleeve resemble the sleeve pieces of the *kao.* The *kai chang, bagua yi,* and wavy-edged version of the *nükao* use the same dimensions for the undulations in the wavy edges on the hem. The streamers on the *gongzhuang* reflect the shapes of the tabs used in the *nükao.* A distinctive arabesque shape called a *ruyi tou* ("may things be as you wish") occurs in the same form in several garments on necklines and at the top of side vents (Fig. 5.4 and Appendix 1.3). The repetition of the decorative elements serves to unify the form among the costumes (see the notes to Appendix 1).

Construction

The techniques for making garments, and subsequently for constructing costumes, were likely passed from one generation to the next through "observation, oral direction and hands-on practice."[28] A level of consistency in construction practices in costumes examined from several locations implies industry-wide standards. I observed specific construction and embroidery techniques at the Donggaokou Embroidery Factory in Hebei province. The factory is a compound of one-story, simply appointed brick buildings. The embroidery and construction process takes place in four rooms: the first for cutting the fabric into large pieces and marking the embroidery designs, the second for storage and selection of the colors of floss, the third with frames for the embroidery, and the fourth, which is a sewing room.

In the patterning room, a large table is used to prepare the fabric for embroidery. When I visited the factory, the workers were marking a *mang* for execution. With the wider fabric manufactured by modern looms, the center-front and back seams have been eliminated in many garments. When the fabric purchased is wider than the garment pattern, the workers at the factory tear it to a narrower width prior to marking out the embroidery and grid lines. The fabric is usually prepared to the width of the garment at the hem, and that width determines where the armscye seams are placed. This technique continues the tradition of historical garment construction, and helps serve the desire to create even longer sleeves for ceremonial attire.[29]

The torn fabric is placed on the table, and the center line, some grid lines, and maximum boundaries are chalked onto the fabric, but the actual seam lines of the garment are not applied until after the piece is embroidered. This technique for marking the fabric reflects historical garment production that also used the chalked plumb lines to block out the shape of the gar-

FIGURE 3.7. Guidelines for the embroidery are transferred from the paper pattern to the fabric with white pigment. Donggaokou Embroidery Factory in Hebei Province.

ment.[30] Next, the embroidery motifs are drawn on the fabric (Fig. 3.7). After the silk for the top of the *mang* has been marked, the costume makers prepare canvas for use in the lower part of the *mang* to support the dense gold couched embroidery located there. The pattern drafters dampen the canvas with water and iron it for preshrinking before the figures are transferred. For the embroidered images on both sections of the *mang,* pieces of transfer paper are pre-marked with the designs and pricked with tiny holes. A stock of templates for the basic motifs is kept on hand for reuse, although designers can create new designs when requested. They line up the transfer paper with the grid lines and hold it in place with weights. Then they rub a pad filled with white liquid pigment onto the surface of the pattern to transfer the design to the fabric. After the design is transferred, the fabric is moved to the embroidery room for workers to begin the embroidery. (The embroidery process is discussed in Chapter 5.)

Once the embroidery is completed, the pieces are transferred to the sewing room for assembly. Brown paper patterns for the garments are kept in this room.

FIGURE 3.8. A seamstress applies rice paste to the seam allowances to stiffen them before stitching. Donggaokou Embroidery Factory in Hebei Province.

The seam lines are chalked onto the embroidered pieces, the excess fabric is trimmed away, and the seam allowances are stiffened with a rice paste from the edge of the fabric to the seam line (Fig. 3.8). The construction of garments is straightforward for the most part because of the simple geometric shapes. Two essential sewing techniques demonstrate the basic elements of construction, one for the main garment and one for the decorative pieces and collars. The *xuezi* and *pi* are examples of the simplicity of sewing techniques for the body of the garment. The sleeve pieces are first machine stitched to the main body of the garment, and the lining assembled in the same way. Then the lining is attached to the main garment at the center front from below the collar to the hems, across the hems, and up the side vents and the sleeve hems. The garment is then folded, with the two layers of the outer fabric right sides together and the two layers of the lining right sides together, aligned along the side seams with the fronts inside the backs, and the ends of the sleeves in a long tube. A single seam closes each side of the garment, and then it is turned right side out through the neck hole. The entire garment is now finished with clean edges and no facings, and all the seam allowances are folded towards the back half of the garment. With the main body of the garment assembled, the neck edge is finished with the collar piece. The water sleeves are hand-stitched in place after the garment is completed.

The collars, as well as the decorative panels on the more complex garments, are edged with a bias border (made from strips cut at a 45-degree angle from the straight of grain). The Han clothing tradition included finishing the edges of garments with bias bindings. At first, the bias strips were used as reinforcement and to prevent raveling, but later contrasting colors were used, and the binding became a decorative element.[31] The same is now true of traditional Jingju costumes, where most of the bias edgings are also decorative (Fig. 3.9). A stiffening glue is brushed onto the bias strips before sewing them in place. The pieces to be bound do not have a seam allowance. The bindings that are decorative borders are sewn to the face fabric 3/16 of an inch inside of the edge, and then pressed to the outer edge of the garment, where they are caught in the seam that also attaches the lining. This technique is employed for stitching the bias edges around the decorative pieces and flaps of the *gongzhuang* and *kao*, for example. When the bias binding is used in the neck hole, there is no seam allowance on the neck hole, and the inner edge of the binding functions as a facing instead. Some garments, including the *mang* and *guanyi*, have an extra piece of cording inserted into the bias edging to create a piping that adds dimension to the neckline. The corded neckline detail carries over from the Ming dynasty.[32]

The standing collars are stiffened with an interfacing and glue. In some cases the collars and the neck edges are both completely finished, and then the collar is stitched to the neckline of the garment, while other examples indicate that the collar was applied in the conventional way, with the raw edges of the neckline concealed between the layers of the collar. Many of the curved decorative pieces and borders in contrasting colors are clean-finished on the inner edge and machine-stitched to the garment along the inner edge of the binding. The linings in the smaller panels and streamers of the *nükao* and *gongzhuang* are hand-stitched in place. The collar on the jacket of the *zhan'ao zhanqun*

FIGURE 3.9. The edges of collars and shaped pieces are finished with a bias binding, often in a contrasting color. *Nükao* from the collection of James Young, Honolulu, Hawai'i.

can be finished in another way. The binding is stitched only onto the neck edge of the collar, and then the collar is attached to the neck of the garment. A single strip of bias-cut fabric is then machine-stitched around the front edges of the garment and collar, and around the top edge of the collar in a continuous seam.

Long robes are usually slit on the side seams, and the performer's movement can include lifting the gar- ment to deliberately expose the lining. The linings are contrasting colors, generally light blue, yellow, or white, so most garments are clean-finished, and facings are used only on the neck edges. The linings are sometimes basted to the center front and back of the long robes, and for additional support, the linings may be basted in place around the embroidered borders. The trousers are the only unlined costumes.

When a garment requires a firmer silhouette than might be achieved by a soft silk fabric, there are several techniques used to modify the way that the fabric falls. The linings for the softer garments are usually silk taffeta, which provides a slightly stiffer line for the garments. The *mang* needs a firmer silhouette to add to the dignity of the garment. In addition to the canvas used in the lower section of the robe, the *mang* may be lined with a coarse loosely woven fabric, to further enhance the rigid volume of the garment, while also helping to absorb perspiration. Some of the *guanyi* and the *jianyi* have muslin linings in the upper part of the garment and silk taffeta in the lower part where the lining is visible.

The collar bands may have a cotton lining that serves the dual function of making the collar more firm and providing a surface that can be cleaned of makeup. Other areas, like the floating panels inside the *kao*, are supplemented with a layer of paper that is glued to the back of the face fabric. The most rigid piece of all the costumes is the front waistband of the *kao*, which is stiffened with cardboard and padding. This also provides a greater dimensionality because it permits the waistband and the lower part of the costume to stand away from the actor's body, creating added girth.

In the case of the *mang* and the *guanyi*, the side seams of the front pieces have added extensions. The garments are clean-finished around the hems, openings, and back vents, leaving the front side seams open. The extension is then attached by placing it between the right sides of the lining and face fabrics and stitching a single seam. The underarm seam can be finished with a serger machine that sews the seam and simultaneously overcasts the edge. When the serger is used, it can attach all four layers of face fabric and lining at once, a rare example of modern technology being interjected into the traditional construction process.

For garments with gussets, such as the *jianyi*, the gussets are made with two pieces, one each attached to the front and the back. The garment edges are pressed under on all sides, and the gusset is topstitched in place separately to the face fabric and the lining. Then a single seam attaching the two pieces of face fabric and two pieces of lining is stitched from the wrist to the hem. On some Qing-based examples of costumes, including the *jianyi*, the S-shaped curve of the underwrap is pressed under and topstitched onto the garment, rather than sewing the two pieces in the standard format with right sides together.

The skirts are made from two identical panels that are lined, turned right side out, and sewn to a single cotton waistband with an overlap in the back. They are knife-pleated away from the centers, meeting in an inverted box pleat on the sides. The pleats are flared slightly, rather than following the grain of the fabric. After the pleats have been set, they are hand-basted from behind to hold the shape. The basting threads are a permanent part of the skirt, making a honeycomb pattern in the pleats when they spread open.

Fabrics

China's long love affair with beautiful fabrics caused the culture to develop from its earliest times a high level of technical skills in the crafting of textiles. Techniques for silk production, weaving, and dyeing, as well as embroidery, all emerged in China thousands of years ago. The production of silk fabrics was among the first of China's contributions to the evolution of fine textile arts. According to the legend described in Confucius's *Book of Odes*, silk was discovered around 2700 BC by the Princess Leizu of the Xiling clan, wife of Emperor Huangdi. While drinking tea under a mulberry tree, a cocoon fell into her cup. "She started to play with the tiny gray ball, and was amazed to find it contained a delicate thread of extraordinary texture."[33] Romantic as this tale may sound, sericulture seems actually to have been widely developed prior to that date. An ivory cup, dating from at least 4000 BC, has a silkworm design carved on it, and a woven silk textile fragment has been dated around 3500 BC.[34] The discovery that later made Chinese silk superior to that from other locations was the realization that if the worm was bred in captivity and the chrysalis killed before it pierced the thread of the cocoon, the prized long filament would remain unbroken, creating a sleeker, more lustrous fabric.[35] Throughout imperial China, silk, hemp, and cotton were the three main fibers used to produce clothing, with silk being used predominantly for the upper classes.[36] During the Ming dynasty, the cities known for producing silks were Nanjing, Suzhou, and Hangzhou.

With a surface that will be modified by extensive embroidery, the selection of fabrics employed in traditional Jingju costumes is fairly limited. Silk fabrics in solid colors with a lustrous satin or matte crepe finish are used for the garments of all the higher-status characters. In one example studied at the University of Hawai'i, the lining had separated from the face fabric, revealing that the fabric was a charmeuse, a silk fabric with satin sheen on one side and matte on the reverse, which indicated the possibility that many of the silk garments could be constructed from this one fabric by using both surfaces. In a few cases, for soft garments, a monochromatic jac-quard silk is used. The woven design is small scale, usually an overall geometric pattern, and it would not read significantly to the audience. For some of the military costumes, a heavier weight of silk satin may be used. The water sleeves are silk broadcloth to give them the body needed for manipulation by the performer. Cotton is used for some of the garments of lower-status characters and for the waistbands of the skirts and trousers.

The form of garments bridges the transition from historical dress to stage costumes, drawing from both real life and theatrical vision to create a unique world in performance. The silhouette of the garments is essential for identifying the role, indicating the character, and to some extent, the immediate locale. The form of the costume also establishes the foundation for the other components of design, the color and the texture. The loose, simple forms of the costumes provide an uninterrupted canvas for the extensive but carefully controlled range of colors and the prescribed embroidery designs. The aspects of design find a balance between the understatement of the form and the bold colors and intricate patterns displayed on the surface.

At first glance the vibrant colors of the fabrics on the traditional Jingju stage may appear to be random and unrestrained, yet a complex system of color meanings for the garments and the roles controls the stage picture. While the silhouette of the garment represents the primary indication of the role type, the color of the fabric projects information about the specific character. To achieve this aim, the costume color selections are relatively fixed for many of the characters. The hues of the embroidery are drawn from a similar, though wider range of colors as the fabrics, and patterns of color combinations are repeated frequently. Aesthetics and traditional customs, rather than symbolism, determine the mixture of embroidery colors to be applied to the different fabric colors.

History of Color Symbolism

In his book *Five Colors of the Universe*, John Vollmer describes the Chinese perception of the universe through yin and yang, the positive and negative forces of universal existence, and how this is also viewed as the interplay between complementary aspects. The axes of yin and yang have an impact on all things within the universe, with yin representing the qualities of the earth and moon, darkness, and female attributes, and yang referring to the traits of heaven and the sun, lightness, and male attributes. The interaction between these two aspects was elaborated into the five-phases system,

wherein the five phases, or elements, of earth, fire, water, metal, and wood, correspond to the five cardinal directions in the Chinese compass, which adds "center" to north, south, east, and west to make five points. Each direction links to a color and may be associated with an emblematic totem or season. Yellow, as the center of the universe, is associated with the earth and the Chinese empire. Because of its vital significance in cosmology, a version of yellow was the color chosen to represent the imperial family. Red connects with the direction of south, which is represented by fire and a great scarlet crow with three legs. A color of vast energy, red correlates with happiness and good luck and therefore is worn for weddings, births, and other family celebrations. The color black relates to the north, and connects with water, a tortoise surrounded by a snake *(xuanwu)*, and winter. White is associated with the west and metal. Autumn is the season for white, and the white tiger is the emblematic animal for this color. The metal component of white connects to the blade of a knife, which can kill, so white also represents death. White is also linked to old age and decline and is therefore worn for mourning. In this context, white becomes an unlucky color. The last of the five colors is *qing,* which in Chinese can indicate both blue and green, with green being dominant in this context. Green represents the east and wood, as well as spring and youth, and green dragons are the corresponding animal emblem.[1] The cultural beliefs associated with color were additionally manifested through clothing regulations, with colors being assigned by rank and status and expressing the wearer's age, as well as relating the garments to the environment and season and placing them in the order of the universe.[2]

The art of dyeing naturally developed along with the creation of textiles. The making of silk can be traced to before 3500 BC, and China had dye workshops for coloring those fabrics as early as 3000 BC. The five dominant colors for fabrics were blue, yellow, red, white, and black, all derived from natural fibers or dyes.[3] These five colors corresponded with the color-mixing system of primaries, the basic units of color, as well as the Chinese conceptualization of the world, given the mutability of blue and green. Color distribution by status arose from the process of dyeing the cloth. In the Warring States period (475–221 BC), colors were divided into two major categories, the pure and the blended. The pure colors were the five dominant colors, and mixing of the pure colors created the blended ones. The blended range included green, a bright red, jade green, purple, and another shade of yellow. Upper-class nobles and officials were allowed to wear the pure colors, while the blended colors were the only ones available to the lower classes. The use of colors was carefully monitored in this early period, and no breach of the color code was tolerated.[4] This early precedent for connecting social standing to color designations established a pattern that continued throughout Chinese history, although the specific colors assigned to each status were subject to change with different dynasties.

In the Ming dynasty (1368–1644), the chosen color for the emperor was yellow. By the Qing period (1644–1911), the colors for the heirs, wives, and concubines were carefully assigned by rank and relationship to the emperor, with each dressed in varying hues of yellow, from greenish yellow to apricot and brown. Anyone outside of the royal circle was forbidden to wear these specific colors pertaining to yellow. In addition to yellow, the emperors of the Qing dynasty also wore other designated colors in the performance of annual rituals.

The officers of the court were assigned robe colors according to their rank. The system of using color to distinguish court officials began in early times and became more refined during the Tang dynasty. Many alterations occurred in the colors throughout the Tang and subsequent dynasties, but the range from highest to lowest rank generally included purple, pink, green, and blue. In the Ming dynasty, officials' robes changed to a color range of more pure colors, with the first through fourth ranks dressed in red, the fifth through seventh ranks assigned to blue, and the eighth and ninth ranks in green.[5] The Qing dynasty limited the colors of officials' robes to blue and black.

Colors for private use by the nobility were not under imperial control and a multiplicity of colors developed for informal garments. Women's clothing in the Song dynasty came in lovely soft colors, such as light blue, lavender, and silvery gray.[6] By the Ming dynasty, textile creators had developed a vast range of colors, making life behind the scenes at court splendidly colorful. The trend continued into the Qing dynasty, when hundreds of colors were added to textile production. The methodology for dyeing with natural materials progressed to the point where "there were so many different colours that it was 'difficult to find names for them all.'"[7] The Dowager Empress Cixi (1835–1908) was particularly fond of shades of blue and lilac, as she felt they were more flattering to her coloring.[8]

While the court was robed both formally and informally in a variety of attractive colors and expensive fabrics, commoners throughout history were limited in the range of colors and textiles they could wear. Even though the forms of their garments were similar to those of the court, the lower class was clearly distinguished by color, as well as quality of fabric. The garments of the lower classes ranged from natural browns, beiges, and off-whites, to shades of blue from indigo dyes, colors that were inexpensive to produce. Rather than silk, their clothing was made from more humble fibers, such as cotton or hemp.

Clothing color associations also arose outside of imperial regulations and were based on social patterns and customs for family celebrations and rituals. Red, as the color of happiness, became the preferred color for weddings and family occasions. White was the color for mourning for everyone beneath the imperial family, who were mourned in black. Although colors were not specifically codified for age groups, a natural pattern developed of attractive bright or pastel colors for youth and more neutral colors for the aged.

These influential precepts of colors translated to traditional Jingju costumes. The regulations and symbolism behind the costumes for the stage may indeed even surpass those for the court, for they have the additional purpose of communicating the inner life of the characters to the audience. Using a vocabulary shared in all performances, the colors express power, rank and status, location and age, as can be seen in the historical precedents. In addition to establishing a character's place in society, the colors also project personal aspects of personality, including loyalty, bravery, or deception.

Upper and Lower Colors

The colors for traditional Jingju costumes are divided into a system of upper five *(shang wuse)* and lower five *(xia wuse)* colors. The upper colors are red *(hong)*, green *(lü)*, yellow *(huang)*, white *(bai)*, and black *(hei)*, which correspond with the colors of the five directions. As the upper colors are the purest, and considered the finest in historical terms, they appear on garments of nobles and officials at court in their formal dress and on generals, and commonly appear more on male and leading characters. Their designation as "upper colors," however,

refers to their frequency of use onstage, rather than exclusively to status. The sequence of the colors also indicates the order in which they are stored, rather than rank. The hues of the lower colors vary somewhat, but they can generally be listed as purple *(zi)*, pink *(fen)*, blue *(lan)*, lake blue *(hulan)*, which is similar to sky blue or turquoise, and bronze or olive green *(qiuxiang, fragrant autumn)*. The purple color *zi* resembles maroon in the western sense and will be called maroon for clarity. The lower colors are generally worn in informal scenes, much as they were in the past, though maroon and blue can be used for court, as well. As most of the lower colors are not primaries, they also have more variation in execution. Several pastel versions of blue fall into the lake-blue category, such as aqua and turquoise, and beige and mustard can also be ascribed to bronze/ olive green. In addition to their historical and cosmic meanings, the colors attributed to the upper and lower categories contain another layer of connotations for personality traits.

Though the five upper and five lower colors are the principal colors that are drawn on when constructing costumes, no colors are forbidden onstage. Those that fall outside the ten tend not to be used as much simply because of the preference for "talking colors" that project a stronger meaning. A third category contains other colors that appear onstage, the complicated or mixed colors *(zase)* including orange, gray, and brown. All of the colors in this category have to be mixed using two, three, or more colors. While every color has a meaning, the colors in this group have the least significant meaning as well as the lowest position in the hierarchy.[9] Neutralized fabric colors are rare on the dress of the principals because of the desire for meaningful, as well as attractive colors. Instead, light browns and beiges, called tea colors *(cha)*, are used for the costumes of servants, workers, and the elderly. Gray, off-white, and other neutral colors appear on monks, as they do in actuality.

Meanings of the Upper Five Colors

A vast range of meanings can be expressed by a single color. A red *mang* (court robe) has different significance depending on its embroidery patterns and different connotations from a red *pi* (formal robe). Where colors have multiple messages, the color needs to be viewed in context with the other aspects of the garment's form and texture, along with the character's makeup and headdress, and the specific character and scene for the meaning to become more evident. The following sections describe some of the typical applications of color meanings.

Red. Red carries the favorable associations of respect, honor, and loyalty connected with essentially good characters. Red *mang* are often worn at court by the high-ranking nobles and principal statesmen who are the steadfast subjects of the emperor, and second in rank only to the emperor (Fig. 4.1). Red also appears at court when worn by the highest-ranking officials, who are attired in red *guanyi* (official robe) (Fig. 6.22). Red can reflect passion at different levels, for it is worn by executioners and criminals, and represents the deprivation of life (Figs. 6.38 and 6.39). Men of power, intensity, and status who are not necessarily on the side of good can also appear in red garments. In contrast, the *nü-mang* (female court robe) (Fig. 6.4), *gongzhuang* (palace garment) (Fig. 6.29), and the *nükao* (female armor) (Fig. 6.10) are often constructed from red fabrics because red is considered the most beautiful of the colors. Since red was worn for weddings in real life, red also appears onstage for marital unions (Fig. 1.20) and can be worn by matchmakers, such as the principal character in *Hongniang* (Fig. 2.6).

Green. Green indicates a high-ranking or military function for the wearer and is worn by generals on and off the battlefield and civil officials in charge of military affairs (Fig. 4.2). Green may also be worn by princes or regents. A slightly sharper color of green appears on the *xuezi* (informal robe) worn by *chou* (clowns), and with

a shift in color, the meaning changes to indicate low-minded and petty characters who may have fraudulent ambitions (Fig. 6.15 and Table 6.6.b). Another color of green in the skirt *(chenqun)* on an older woman indicates the worthiness of old age and maturity (Fig. 6.3).

Yellow. Only the emperor, members of the imperial family, and their retinues can wear a specific hue of yellow, and this color choice comes from the historical designation of yellow for royalty (Fig. 4.3). Although yellow represents the most powerful color, it is listed as third and placed in the storage trunks third so that the garments do not "get a swelled head." Characters with wisdom, who are worthy of respect, who can solve problems cleverly and outwit their adversaries, may wear other shades of yellow. Sun Wukong, the Monkey King, wears yellow because he has been appointed a saint of heaven and a Buddha of triumph, and the color of heavenly saints is yellow (Fig. 1.16).

White. White garments can be used for men who have grace, charm, and loyalty to their country. Both *xiaosheng* (young men) and *laosheng* (mature men) are seen in white *mang* and white *kao* (armor) (Figs. 1.2 and 1.4). White garments can also be used to show the youth of female characters, as *qingyi* (young to middle-aged woman) can wear white *nüpi* (woman's formal robe) and all of them wear white pleated skirts *(baizhe qun)* with their other garments (Figs. 6.4 and 6.8). A pleated white "bloated" skirt *(yaobao)* worn over the other garments indicates a sickly or pregnant wearer (Fig. 1.17). The tradition of wearing white for mourning has transferred to stage usage. Characters in mourning may appear with a simple strip of white fabric draped over their heads, under their headdresses, or they may dress completely in white (Figs. 2.5 and 4.4).

Black. A black *mang* represents characters who enforce laws and penalties, and who are straightforward, brave, honest, and upright (Fig. 4.5). Outside of court wear, black garments take on many other meanings that are quite opposed to the elevated significance of

FIGURE 4.1. A red *mang* is worn by honorable and loyal men, usually upper-ranking nobles and significant statesmen. The headdress of this *laosheng* character is a *gailiang xiangdiao* (reformed decorated prime minister's hat). *Reconciliation of the Prime Minister and the General (Jiang xiang he).* Character: Lin Xiangru, actor: Tan Xiaozeng. BJC, Beijing, China. July 2, 2000.

court. For *qingyi*, a black center-front-closing *nüxuezi* (woman's informal robe) indicates poverty that may have been brought about through the loss of husband or family. The color was originally called *qing* (dark or black), a hue unique to Chinese culture that falls somewhere between blue, green, and black; it is the shade of the night sky just as it turns dark. The word *qing* combined with *yi* (clothing) evolved to give the characters who wore such colors their role name, *qingyi* (lit. "black clothing") (Fig. 6.18). *Xiaosheng* who have not yet passed their exams dress in black *xuezi,* considered one of the lowest garments, because their financial resources are precarious (Table 6.19.B and 6.19.N). Servants wear black, from the heads of household to waiters (Table

FIGURE 4.2. A military advisor to the king may be dressed in a green *mang,* as with this character, who is in charge of military personnel. The white collar and water sleeves create a border around the costume color, separating it from the face and hands. This *laosheng* wears a *zhongsha* (loyal hat). *Reconciliation of the Prime Minister and the General (Jiang xiang he).* Character: Yu Qing, actor: Han Shengcun. BJC, Beijing, China. July 2, 2000.

FIGURE 4.3. A specific hue of yellow is reserved for the emperor, a *laosheng* in this example, and his immediate family. The crown is a king's hat *(wang-mao)*. *Women Generals of the Yang Family (Yangmen nüjiang)*. Character: Song Renzong, actor: Li Wenlin. NJC, Beijing, China. October 3, 2001.

FIGURE 4.4. Mu Guiying mourns for her husband by wearing all-white armor with a white rosette on the chest. The blue embroidery on white fabric creates a strong contrast of dark on light. Her headdress is a *qixing ezi* (seven-star diadem). *Women Generals of the Yang Family (Yangmen nüjiang).* Character: Mu Guiying, actor: Deng Min. NJC, Beijing, China. October 3, 2001.

6.3.B and 6.3.N). Stealthy fighters who are illegal or mysterious and want to escape recognition also wear black (Fig. 6.32).

Meanings of the Lower Five Colors

The lower five colors are used in some of the official garments listed above, as well as in informal, domestic clothing. While two of the lower colors appear in court regularly, the others are more for informal wear and, as such, carry less significant meanings.

Maroon. Maroon is used for the upper ranks in the *guanyi,* and *laosheng* wearing this garment are generally noble and forgiving (Fig. 4.6). Maroon *pi/nüpi* suggest an older age and the respect that goes with that status (Fig. 6.7). A *mang* in maroon is more likely to be worn by a *jing* role, to indicate high-ranking and dominating characters. When there are too many characters assigned to wear red in a scene, one or more may be shifted to maroon without changing the meaning.

Pink. Pink indicates youth in traditional Jingju. A pink costume on a *xiaosheng* indicates he is young,

FIGURE 4.5. A black *mang* worn by Judge Bao indicates that he reinforces the laws with upright honesty. The gold couching creates a strong light color on the dark background of his black *mang*. He often wears the *xiangsha* (prime minister's hat) with this *mang*. The makeup design for Judge Bao is *zhenglian* (whole face), with a crescent moon on the forehead and ladle-shaped eyebrows, and his beard is a *man rankou* (long, full beard). *The Beating of the Dragon Robe (Da longpao).* Character: Bao Zheng, actor: unidentified. NJC, Beijing, China. October 9, 2001.

FIGURE 4.6. A maroon *guanyi* represents the higher ranks at court. This *laosheng* wears a *zhongsha*, commonly paired with the *guanyi*. *The Gathering of Heroes (Qunying hui)*. Character: Lu Su, actor: Tan Xiaozeng. BJC, Beijing, China. July 23, 2000.

handsome, and romantically inclined (Figs. 4.7, 2.2, and Table 6.22.B). Young *qingyi* often wear *nüpi* in delicate pink, and it is the second most common color of the *nükao*.

Blue. The third of the lower colors is a royal blue. A blue *mang* signifies high status and may be assigned to virtuous characters who are calm and firm. Another use for a blue *mang* is for characters with military duties in

charge of justice and punishment (Fig. 4.8). Extremely brave and fierce warriors wear blue *kao*. Blue also carries a significance of rank, with a blue *guanyi* being worn by those in the lowest ranks. Blue relates to youth in the cosmic order, but both youthful and loyal court officers and generals can be dressed in blue-trimmed white garments. In domestic situations, mature couples may be dressed in matching blue *pi*. Blue and green, because of their close association in Chinese color theory, are parallel in their meanings onstage, with blue garments being a slightly less powerful version of green ones. When more than one character onstage needs to wear green, the lesser one may be switched to blue. Unembroidered blue satin *jianyi* (archer's robes) appear on lowly soldiers or servants (Table 6.32.B and 6.32.N), and cotton garments in blue colors similar to the indigo dyes used in real life, are worn by merchants and servants (Fig. 6.28).

Lake Blue. Lake blue is utilized for youthful roles, both male and female. The *xiaosheng* wearing *xuezi* in one of these lighter blues are considered scholarly, elegant, and handsome young men, and their *qingyi* lovers are quietly demure in their lake blue *nüpi*. These blues most often occur in clothing worn at home, rather than at court (Fig. 4.9).

Olive Green. The fifth of the lower colors translates variously as olive green, bronze, gray, brown, beige, and copper, and are all part of a range of colors that are used to represent elderly characters in traditional Jingju. At court, both men and women of rank can wear an olive-green or beige *mang* (Figs. 4.10 and 6.3). Matching olive-green *pi* may be worn in private situations by an older couple of higher status (Table 6.1.N b and 6.29.N b), while lower-status mature characters may be dressed in plain *xuezi* in olive green or any of the other drab colors (Fig. 6.16).

Some colors outside the basic ten can have a meaning ascribed to them by connecting them with similar colors. For example, a range of pastels, including lavender

FIGURE 4.7. A pink *jianyi* indicates a youthful and handsome warrior. Here it is cinched at the waist with a wide, firm sash and has cords tied around the chest. The headdress is a *zijin guan*, also worn by young noblemen. This example is wearing high-soled, high-topped boots and red trousers. *The Eight Mallets (Ba da chui)*. Character: Lu Wenlong, actor: Xin Xiaoming. ATCO, Beijing, China. June 1, 2002.

FIGURE 4.8. For this character the blue *mang* represents his office in a capital court. The *jiansha* (sharp or pointed *shamao*-style headdress) indicates his treachery and cruelty, which is also indicated by his *youbai zhenglian* (shiny, oil-based makeup in the whole face design). *Xie Yaohuan (Xie Yaohuan)*. Character: Lai Junchen, actor: Shu Tong. ATCO, Beijing, China. May 31, 2002.

FIGURE 4.9. *(Right)* A *xiaosheng* wearing a lake-blue *hua xuezi* is considered an elegant and handsome scholar. Here he also wears a *qiaoliang jin* (bridge hat). *Hongniang (Hongniang)*. Character: Zhang Jun, actor: Song Xiaochuan. NJC, Beijing, China. July 31, 2000.

and pale green, is often worn by younger characters and project the same impression as lake blue (Table 6.10–13.B and 6.10–13.N). Characters who appear in more than one garment in a play sometimes have both in the same color, particularly for official functions. A general in a green *mang* at court may change to green *kao* to go to battle. If an official character appears in more than one play, he or she may wear the same color in subsequent appearances. A character's clothing color may also come from their name or from the literature written about

them. For example, a person with the family name of Huang, meaning yellow, may be dressed in yellow costumes, though not the imperial yellow, and the White Snake, Bai Suzhen, wears only white (Fig. 1.17).

Color Combinations by Role Type

The distribution of garment colors follows regular combinations within the role types, with some roles more likely to wear certain colors. The following sections describe the dominant, but by no means exclusive, colors of costumes by role type.

Laosheng. *Laosheng* usually wear upper colors because they are generally scholars, officials, and advisors to the throne. Their *mang* and *kao* are most often red, white, or green (Figs. 1.2, 4.1, and Table 6.2.B). For older *laosheng*, the *mang* may be olive green or beige (Table 6.2.N). When traveling, *laosheng* may to wear a red *jianyi* (archer's robe) with a black *magua* (riding jacket) (Fig. 6.30). *Laosheng* in official positions tend to wear the *guanyi* of the higher ranks, in either red or maroon, although supporting *laosheng* characters are also seen in blue (Figs. 4.6 and 6.22). When a civil *laosheng* dresses for noncourt events, he wears a maroon, olive-green, or blue *pi*, colors of maturity and respect (Figs. 6.7, 7.35, Table 6.1.B and 6.1.N a and b). Military characters in private quarters can be dressed in a *kai chang* in white or red (Fig. 6.21). A *laosheng* character in a position of lesser status or wealth may be dressed in a plain *xuezi* in a neutral beige or brown, blue, olive green, or black (Figs. 6.16 and 6.17).

Xiaosheng. *Xiaosheng* wear the same colors of *mang* as the older men: white, red and green, with the addition of pink, a frequent choice (Figs. 2.2, 2.9, 6.1, Table 6.22.B and 6.22.N). Most *xiaosheng* who have a rank at court wear the red *guanyi*. A *hua xuezi* in lake blue, lavender, or pink is the most common garment for *xiaosheng* to wear outside of court, when they are well-to-do scholars (Figs. 1.3 and 4.9). If they have yet to pass their

FIGURE 4.10. Olive green indicates older characters, as with this *laosheng* wearing a *mang*. *The City of Baidi (Baidi cheng)*. Character: Zhuge Jin, actor: unidentified. NJC, Beijing, China. September 30, 2001.

exams or if their fortunes have failed, then they wear a black *xuezi*, either with a white contrasting neckband or a matching neckband, and either plain or with minimal embroidery (Table 6.19.B and 6.19.N). *Xiaosheng* rarely wear a *pi,* but when they do, their *pi* comes in either yellow for the character of emperor or red for a wedding or achieving the position of top scholar in the examinations (Fig. 1.20 and Table 6.23.B and 6.23.N).

Wuxiaosheng, Wusheng. When dressed in *kao, wuxiaosheng* (martial young men) and *wusheng* (martial men) are frequently clad in white (Fig. 1.4) Their *kao* often have blue borders around the white garments. These young generals may also wear the *kao* in red and green (Fig. 6.9). When military young men are in private quarters, their *kai chang* are generally white or red. They may also wear a version of the *xuezi* made of white satin (Fig. 7.34).

Laodan. At court, *laodan* wear *nümang* in yellow, orange, or olive green (Fig. 6.3). The *nüpi* for *laodan* often comes in olive green, blue, or maroon, but it can be brown or dark green as well. If they are still married and appear onstage simultaneously with their husbands, their *pi* garments usually match those of their husbands (Fig. 6.7, Table 6.1.B and 6.29.B., 6.1.N b and 6.29.N b). *Laodan* in lower circumstances will wear the crossover closing *nüxuezi* in olive green, gray, brown, maroon, or off-white if they are particularly destitute (Figs. 6.16 and 6.19).

Qingyi. When at court, *qingyi* wear versions of the *nümang* usually in either red or yellow, depending on their position (Fig. 6.4). They may also wear a *gongzhuang* with a red bodice and multicolored streamers (Fig. 6.29). In domestic scenes, *qingyi* are most likely to appear in *nüpi* in colors similar to those worn by *xiaosheng.* Their *nüpi* come in lake blue, pink, white, and yellow, to name a few of the colors (Fig. 6.8 and Table 6.10–12.B and 6.10–12.N). After marriage in a red *nüpi,* the *qingyi* colors shift to a darker range, often a deep blue or maroon (Fig. 1.8). When they wear the *nüxuezi,*

they use the center-front-opening version distinct to female characters (Table 6.13.B and 6.13.N). The range of colors reflects the pastel range of the *nüpi,* unless the *qingyi* has lost her position and money, in which case, she wears a black *nüxuezi* with a blue border (Fig. 6.18). In more recent performances, this garment has taken on some colors and can be a gray-blue or green, with contrasting border.

Huadan (**Lively young women**). *Huadan* usually have white, pink, or blue jackets and skirts *(aoqun)* (Fig. 6.40), which they sometimes wear with darker vests or collar-and-peplum combinations, or a combination of pastel jacket and trousers *(aoku),* with a contrasting apron *(fandan)* (Fig. 1.9).

Daoma dan. When *daoma dan* ("sword and horse" women warriors) go to battle, their *nükao* are most often red or pink, with multicolored streamers (Fig. 6.10), but when many women are onstage in armor simultaneously, as in *Women Generals of the Yang Family (Yang men nü jiang),* the *nükao* comes in a spectacular array of pastel colors (National Jingju Company, October 3, 2001). If wearing *gailiang kao* (reformed armor), the garments are often blue (Fig. 6.11).

Wudan. For the *wudan* (martial women) in the *zhan'ao zhanqun* (martial jacket and trousers), the colors are most often red, blue, or white (Fig. 1.10).

Jing. The *jing* wear intense colors to match their bold personalities and to contrast with their face color. At court, they usually wear *mang* in red, green, black, maroon, or blue (Figs. 1.12, 4.5 and 4.8). When dressed in *kao* for battle, the *jing* roles appear quite often in black, red, green, blue, and orange (Figs. 7.6, 7.10). Military *jing* usually travel in the *magua,* usually black, often over a blue or maroon *jianyi.* In personal quarters, *jing* often appear in the *kai chang* in red, green, black, or maroon (Fig. 1.19). They rarely wear the *pi,* and if they wear a *xuezi,* it may indicate lower status or defeat and can be a dark or neutral color (Fig, 6.14).

Chou. The *chou* seldom have the eminence or personality required for the wearing of the higher status and rank garments. On the rare occasion that they do appear in a *mang*, often when they are playing the character of a eunuch, they are dressed in green or olive green. *Chou* playing eunuchs are also dressed in the *taijian yi* (eunuch robe) in yellow, red, maroon, blue, and green (Fig. 6.24). *Chou* also can portray crafty court officials, commonly wearing a *guanyi* in red or blue (Fig. 1.13). When *chou* travel as officials, they may wear the *magua*, usually in black, but sometimes in yellow or orange, with the *jianyi*, often made of red fabric. *Chou* warriors are of lower rank than that necessary to wear the *kao*. Instead, they appear in versions of the *bingyi* (soldiers' clothing) or *hua kuaiyi* (flowered "fast clothes) in bright or dark colors depending on the nature of the character (Figs. 1.6 and 6.33). A *chou* rarely wears a *pi*, but if he is playing an emperor or royal relative, a possibility when the character is foolish or corrupt, the *chou* may wear a yellow *pi* (Table 6.4.B and 6.4.N). The *chou* also wears a red *pi* when he marries (Table 6.7.B.and 6.7.N). *Chou* of status often appear in the *hua xuezi*. The most common color of the *xuezi* they wear is a green that diverges from the green worn by honest and loyal characters (Fig. 6.15 and Table 6.6 B). *Chou* perform servant roles dressed in plain black, blue, or brown garments (Figs. 6.28 and 6.37).

Aesthetics of Color Composition

The Chinese love of vibrant colors and striking juxtapositions applies to the clothing worn onstage. Colors that would normally not be combined in daily life are featured side by side onstage, with bold and breathtaking results. Any given play will most likely display much of the available vocabulary of color from the upper and lower system, as there will be characters from a variety of roles, positions, and dispositions onstage during the telling of the story. The attractiveness of these combinations can be attributed to interlocking factors of aesthetics, including unity, harmony, and balance.

Fabric Colors. By establishing a specific palette from which all the garments are made, the color range is limited to hues that have been determined to be effective together onstage. Within the wide span of full intensity to pastel colors, the majority of the hues are clear, lacking neutralization through the addition of a complementary color. The exceptions are the olive greens used for the elderly and the beiges and grays for the poor. By having this clarity in common, even though a wide range of hues appears onstage, a unity emerges. In addition, most of the garments consist of a single color in the fabric, resulting in large areas of color broken only by the embroidered decorations. The use of one major color per garment simplifies the overall image, creating another form of unity. Each large block of color is often bordered by white edges that frame the figure and divide the colors among all the characters. At the neck, a white collar *(huling)* separates the garments from the face, while the white water sleeves *(shuixiu)* highlight the hands (Figs. 4.1–3). For male characters, the boots have visible thick, white soles to create a border on the base of the image (Figs. 4.5 and 4.7). Young women have white skirts that create a border on the lower portion of their garments (Figs. 6.4 and 6.8). The white frame creates focal points on the areas where the actors will express themselves, at the face, hands, and feet. The strong contrast of bright white against the large areas of pure colors heightens the visual clarity.

The strong contrasts of the intense colors find another unity by attiring groups of related characters, including palace maids, dancers, and attendants, in costumes of the same color. In this way, when extras are onstage, agreement comes from the common color of the costumes. Attendants flank the table of a person of status, in colors suited to the rank of the central character, thus replacing the need for additional furniture to dress the stage (Fig. 2.1). Each army wears a common color, with opposing sides wearing contrasting colors (Figs. 1.15 and 6.35, both from *Yandang Mountain (Yandang shan).*

BJC, Beijing, China. September 9. 2001). The colors of the armies' costumes are generally determined by the color of their leader.

The relationship among the colors of costumes on-stage is to some extent predetermined by the conventions of each character, whose colors may be dictated by tradition. The dresser has a measure of control of the overall image through the selection of specific colors when a range is possible, though. For example, in choosing from the available pastels, harmony can be achieved in the dress of young lovers by dressing them in colors that are complementary, and female servants may wear clothing that looks appealing with that of their mistresses. If there are too many characters onstage in the same color, then the dresser may choose to switch the color of the lesser characters for a better balance. In addition to color conventions for the outer garments, there are general rules concerning inner garments as well; *laosheng* usually wear red trousers, and *xiaosheng* often wear light blue or pastel ones, for example. But while tradition predetermines many decisions about the principal colors of garments, the colors of the embroidery on the costumes are not a factor in selecting garments for specific characters.

Colors in the Embroidery. The embroidery colors in traditional Jingju costumes are selected by those who make the garments or those who request the costumes, and their choices are based on intuition, knowledge of past garments, and established aesthetics. The concentrated colors of the fabrics are carefully mitigated by selection of embroidery colors that complement the fabric color. Using a degree system based on the arrangement of colors on the color wheel, pleasing color combinations have been predetermined for each kind of garment in each color. Threads are applied in several combinations: metallic only (Fig. 2.11), metallic with color accents (Figs. 5.5 and 5.9), monochromatic, monochromatic with metallic accents (Fig. 5.11), and combinations of two to multiple colors with metallic

outlines (Fig. 5. 7). A second principle for the selection of embroidery colors comes from the importance of contrast between the figure and ground colors, either light on dark or dark on light, to assure maximum visibility from a distance. The contrast is augmented by the third principle, the introduction of outlines to separate the colors, heightening their individual clarity. Applying these three principles, as elaborated in the following section, creates repeating combinations of color usage, so that costumes of the same color and form generally have the same color combinations on the surface.

Degree System for Fabric and Embroidery Floss Colors. While the colors of the garments are divided into the upper and lower colors, embroidery colors are based on the color wheel. Complementary colors are opposites on the wheel, or 180 degrees apart (Fig. 4.11). This combination is deemed to be the most striking of contrasts, one that combines a primary and a secondary color. The red/green dyad and the orange/blue dyad are used on *mang* and *kao*. As gold equates with yellow, and so-called purple appears as maroon, then maroon garments finished with golden couching, a common pairing, can also be considered as a part of this degree category. Within the degree system, either the surface or the embroidery or both can be lightened to a pastel for another range of combinations. A lavender robe with pale yellow flowers employs 180 degrees. Colors that are just off of the primaries also are contained in this category; for example, a teal blue-green garment with red-orange embroidery, a common choice, can also be considered a 180-degree color combination.

Colors separated by a third of the wheel, or 120 degrees, create a contrast with less impact. Color combinations in this category include red and yellow, yellow and blue, and blue and red in the primary colors. These combinations are often applied to the *mang* and the *kao*. Pastel variations of these combinations are used, putting together pink and soft yellow and pink and pale blue on the domestic clothing. Generally, pastel versions

FIGURE 4.11. A contrast of light embroidery on a dark fabric makes the pattern more visible to the audience. The combination of red and green represents 180 degrees of color separation. The paired dragons are playing with a flaming orb or pearl above the mountains and waves. *Kao* from the collection of the ATCO.

of the colors are used when the secondary colors are put together in 120-degree combinations, peach with pale green, light green and lavender, lavender and peach, and pink with blue on floral garments (Fig. 4.12).

The third category in the degree system, 90 degrees, is for colors that are adjacent on the color wheel, which correspond with the analogous range. Combinations in this group that are regularly used include yellow and green, green and blue in full intensity, blue and lavender, and lavender and pink in the pastel range. As with the other color combinations, the saturated versions appear on court and battle garments, while the paler ones

are generally used on the less powerful costumes worn at home (Fig. 4.13).

Though the 180-degree difference is the most admired for intensity, the 120-degree difference appears more frequently. The degree system naturally combines warm and cool colors in the 180-degree combination, and four of the six 120-degree combinations, with that tension giving the garments an energetic surface. The color combinations of the degree system are used as guidelines when embroidering the garments, but they are not employed when the dresser selects the costumes for the characters.

FIGURE 4.12. Pink fabric with blue embroidery illustrates 120 degrees of separation in the colors. Dark embroidery on a light background is another form of contrast. To heighten the contrast, the darker shades are placed on the outer edges of the petals when embroidering light flowers on pale fabrics. The flowers are outlined in silver metallic threads, and the branches are accented with maroon wooly threads. *Nüpi* from the collection of DTD, UHM, Manoa, Hawai'i

Light and Dark Contrast. In selecting the colors of the embroidery, the contrast between the figure and the ground becomes another of the primary considerations. For the maximum effect, colors are selected based on their value, the amount of lightness or darkness, a tech-

nique that was also employed in Qing-dynasty dragon robes.[10] In almost all the garments the difference between the colors of the fabric and the embroidery floss is quite pronounced. The contrast permits the embroidered images to be seen from a distance and for them to contribute to the overall texture of the stage costume picture. The contrast is created with either light colors on a dark ground or dark colors on a light fabric. On garments with saturated colors, red, green, black, maroon, and blue, the ornamentation is usually applied with gold couching, which makes a highlight on a darker foundation (Fig. 4.11). These combinations are found on *mang*, *kao*, *kai chang*, and *jianyi*, all garments worn by the most powerful men in the plays. The mid-range-value colors of the domestic garments, the *pi* and *xuezi*, usually have lighter colors of embroidery on them, lessening the contrast. For floral patterns, the sequence of the shading on the petals is selected to create the greatest contrast between the edges of flowers and the garment color. When the fabric is a mid-tone or darker intensity, the darkest tone of the petals appears on the inside of the flower, and the lightest at the edge, creating a high contrast between the flower and the background (Fig. 5.3). With paler fabric, this gradation is reversed, and the darkest tone of the petal appears at the edge (Fig. 4.12).

Contrast increases for powerful characters and lessens for some examples of both youth and age. The greatest dark on light contrast appears on the white garments with dark blue embroidery on the *mang*, *kao*, and *kai chang* worn by military characters (Fig. 4.4). Conversely, the golden couching on a black *mang* or *kao* creates the highest contrast of light on dark (Fig. 4.5). Lesser contrast appears on the costumes of young and old characters. One common garment for elderly characters, the olive-green *pi*, often has gold or silver embroidery with aqua or blue accents. As these are analogous colors, the subtle contrast suggests age through faded intensity (Fig. 4.13).

Outlines. Strong color contrasts between the embroidery and the fabric are used frequently to create a bold statement. To manage the contrasts, a third, neutral color appears between them, moderating the contrast and creating a more harmonious effect. Gold or silver threads are most often selected for such borders, as they are perceived to match all colors (Fig. 5.8). The border melts the contrast, canceling out the clash of the colors while creating a shining edge to highlight the figures. A Chinese adage says red and green do not go together except in traditional Jingju costumes, where they are separated by gold. Black or maroon threads are also used to divide colors, and they are particularly effective for separating adjacent areas of metallics or two pastel colors (Fig. 4.12). The use of borders around objects which have the same intensity as the foundation color comes from historical precedents.[11]

Fabric and Embroidery Floss Colors

Unity occurs in the visual image by using like colors of embroidery on the same colors of fabric to make garments of the same form that are worn in similar situations. In contrast, the same color fabric will have different colors of embroidery when made into different kinds of garments. For example, when a red fabric is constructed into court or battle garments worn by nobles and generals, then gold is the predominant color for the applied decoration, making visual the wealth and power of the characters. But when red is used for costumes worn by women warriors, princesses, concubines, brides, and grooms, the embroiderer uses multicolored threads to communicate beauty and elegance. One constant carries over in the colors employed for the leaves on flowered garments: leaves are most often stitched in

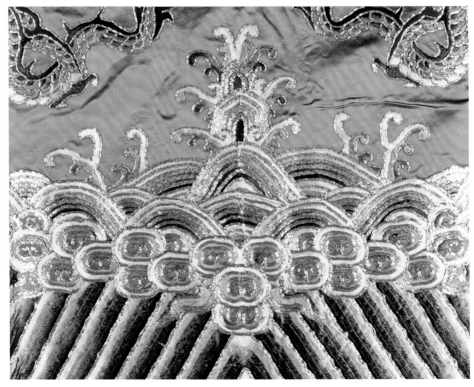

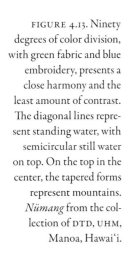

FIGURE 4.13. Ninety degrees of color division, with green fabric and blue embroidery, presents a close harmony and the least amount of contrast. The diagonal lines represent standing water, with semicircular still water on top. On the top in the center, the tapered forms represent mountains. *Nümang* from the collection of DTD, UHM, Manoa, Hawai'i.

shades of a teal blue-green, creating a subtle harmony across the range of costumes. Blue appears to be considered a most beautiful and compatible color for embroidery, as it is the most common color applied, used either alone in three shades *(sanlan)* or combined with metallics. The following examples of color distribution on the four major garments provide a representative model for how fabrics and embroidery flosses are allocated.

Mang. The red *mang* for men usually has gold or blue embroidery or a combination of the two (Fig. 1.1). Accent colors, including blue, gray, or white, are worked into the design. Green *mang* are almost consistently couched in gold threads with accents of red, maroon, or gray (Table 6.2.B). *Mang* made of yellow fabric tend to have blue embroidery, with accents of red, black, and gray (Fig. 4.3). Gold is often worked into the waves on these robes. White *mang* most often have blue embroidery, some with gold worked in as well (Fig. 2.9). Gray and red are common accent colors in this combination. Black *mang* are couched predominantly with gold threads, with green and red details (Fig. 4.5). *Mang* in maroon fabric are almost exclusively couched with gold threads, using voids in the pattern and allowing the maroon to show through to create the shapes. Blue *mang* are decorated with gold threads with accents of red added to distinguish the figures (Fig. 4.8). Blue embroidery floss is the most common color on the pink *mang*, with other colors including lavender and green used in the waves, clouds, and lucky symbols (Fig. 2.2 and Table 6.22.B). The *mang* does not come in lake blue, the fourth of the lower colors. Olive-green *mang* generally are embroidered with tints and shades of blue floss, with white and red accents and gold in the waves (Table 6.2.N).

Pi. Pi for *xiaosheng* are made in only two colors. Red *pi* are worn for weddings and to celebrate achieving number one scholar status. They are embroidered with roundels of flowers in several pastel colors, including blue, green, pink, and lavender, with areas of gold worked into the design (Fig. 1.20). Yellow *pi* are worn by emperors and are usually decorated with blue or multicolored dragons and sometimes with waves. Maroon, dark blue, and olive-green *pi* are worn by *laosheng*, and they generally have roundel patterns in gold or gold and silver (Fig. 6.7). Blue or maroon can be worked into these patterns for additional contrast and interest. The *laosheng* tend to wear garments with metallic embroidery even in informal situations, where the *xiaosheng* shift to more colorful robes outside of court.

Kao. The man's *kao* may have contrasting fabric borders as well as embroidery colors. The borders may be limited to bands around the flag and padded belt or they may encompass all the pieces. Border colors usually correspond with the dominant embroidery color beyond the gold couching. Like the *mang* embroidery, the *kao* are primarily couched in gold, with colors used for accents to bring out the features of the images. Red *kao* usually have gold couching with blue accents or vice versa. Green, lavender, black, or teal may also be used as accent colors only. The green *kao*, like the green *mang*, is usually finished with gold threads and red accents (Fig. 4.11). Yellow *kao* are quite rare, but they would tend to have gold embroidery and contrasting blue borders of fabric. White *kao* have blue, gray, or black embroidery, with either gold or silver couching (Fig. 1.4). Silver couching on a white *kao* can indicate mourning. Kao constructed in black fabric have gold couched figures with red and green accents (Fig. 7.10). Maroon *kao*, like the maroon *mang*, have solid gold or silver couching, without accent colors. Blue *kao* are couched in gold or silver (Fig. 2.11). Pink, lake-blue, and olive-green *kao* for male roles are rare, if they exist at all. If they did, their embroidery would be multicolored. Outside of the ten upper and lower colors, orange *kao* are common, and they are decorated with either complementary blue embroidery or gold couching or both (Fig. 7.6).

Xuezi. Xiaosheng appear in soft crepe *hua xuezi*, made from a range of pastel colors with contrasting pastel flowers on the collar and left hem. The embroidery colors include pink, peach, yellow, aqua, blue, and lavender. On the teal and aqua garments, most combinations include a tangerine or peach color to create the 180-degree contrast (Fig. 1.3). Brightly colored *xuezi* in cerise and green, among others, are worn by the *chou* and decorated with a scattered pattern of flowers or lucky symbols in multicolored embroidery flosses (Fig. 6.15). In addition to the crepe *xuezi*, military men wear another version, made of satin. The satin *xuezi* come primarily in the intense colors of red, green, blue, and white. These garments are usually decorated with a single color, often gold for the first three and blue for the white version (Fig. 6.13). Of the remaining upper and lower colors, yellow rarely appears on a *xuezi*, and maroon, blue, and olive green are generally undecorated.

Nümang. The women's *nümang* with the wavy border has exquisite multicolored embroidery, combining a spectrum of colors in the feathers of the phoenix and sometimes using those colors for the water in the waves (Fig. 6.4). In some examples, a gold couched diaper grid appears on the main body and sleeves of the garment (Fig. 5.7). With red or yellow being used for the main body of the garment, the borders are blue or teal. The colors embroidered on the border are often more subdued and use a range of gray to black or silver and gold. The straight-edged *nümang* worn by the *laodan* characters comes in yellow, orange, or olive green. The yellow *nümang* follow the pattern established in the men's yellow *mang*, using blue as the dominant color. The orange *nümang* also have blue embroidery. Olive-green *nümang* have a combination of blue, gold, and silver worked into the dragons and waves (Figs. 4.13 and 6.3).

Nüpi. Women's *nüpi* come in a number of the upper and lower colors. Red *nüpi* are used exclusively for weddings and festive scenes. Often the embroidery on the bride and groom's costumes matches in both pattern and color, with multicolored pastels and gold being the most used colors for these garments (Fig. 1.20). Green

occasionally appears as a deep forest green on women's *nüpi*, along with teal, both decorated with pastel flowers, often pink or peach, creating the 180 degrees of contrast. The intensity of the colors of the flowers on these darker fabrics can be deeper than that for the pastels (Table 6.10.B). Yellow, white, pink, and lake blue, as lighter ground colors, have less intensely colored flowers, but it is still enough to create the desired contrast (Fig. 6.8). Pink, peach, yellow, aqua, blue, and lavender are used in combinations of one, two, and three for the flowers on all of these garments. Maroon, blue, and olive-green *nüpi* are worn by the older female roles. These garments have metallic embroidery primarily, with accents in blue, aqua, or maroon, often in designs identical to their male counterparts (Fig. 1.7).

Nükao. Even more brilliantly colored is the women's *nükao*, one of the few costumes to have several colors of fabric in the foundation of the garment. With up to five colors of streamers in the skirt area and horizontal bands on the sleeves, the basic *nükao* resembles a phoenix. Red is the most common of foundation fabric colors, being placed on the chest, upper arms, waist piece, and central aprons. The figures on the *nükao* are generally phoenixes and flowers, embroidered in pastel pink, aqua, lavender, yellow, and peach, among others. Different colors of embroidery are then used to ornament the different hues of fabric around the costume, creating a richly colored surface (Figs. 1.11 and 6.10). As pink is pale, the embroidery floss colors for a pink *nükao* are usually darker, and in the blue and the red range. Other colors of *nükao* have the same variety of colors in the streamers and embroidery, all selected to complement the base fabric color. A white *nükao*, worn for mourning, has a more limited range of blue and lavender embroidery (Fig. 4.4).

Nüxuezi. The center-front-opening version of the female *nüxuezi* may have embroidery on it, while the crossover one does not. The conventions of color usage on the *nüxuezi* are similar to those for the *nüpi*, although the *nüxuezi* generally has fewer colors combined on the surface. The *nüxuezi*, a less important garment than the *nüpi*, is usually worn under the *nüpi*, or as an outer garment by palace maidens. A colored *nüxuezi*, commonly blue or lavender, may have one color for the flowers, with green leaves, or it can be in the monochrome group with flowers and leaves of the same color (Table 6.13.B and 6.13.N).

Lining Colors

As the linings of the garments frequently are exposed during movement, those colors also contribute to the overall impact of color onstage. Some garments have generic lining colors that are used for all pieces no matter what the exterior, while others have linings that are selected for the color of the garment. The *mang* are generally lined in a yellow, coarsely woven fabric that adds both body and color to the garment. Male and female *pi* and *xuezi* are most often lined in pale blue, although white is becoming common. The *kao*, which are involved in the most vigorous movements, have linings selected to enhance the overall color of the garment. When they enter the stage, characters wearing the male *kao* armor often stop and pose, with the legs flaps held out to increase their size, thereby revealing the contrasting color of the lining within (Fig. 2.11).

The rules for color in stage dress are possibly more extensive and complicated than those that existed in real life, for the entire population of characters in performance comes under the regulations, not just the select members of the court. The colors onstage are based on those of actual garments, with some heightening of intensity and contrast for greater projection to the audience. The theatrical need for audiences to know about the characters when they come onstage has deepened the levels of meaning regarding colors to include psychological characteristics along with circumstances such as age and wealth. The blocks of color are larger in the traditional Jingju versions because the embroidery is less dense and the stitched figures are greater in scale. As a result, a much brighter, clearer picture appears onstage than would have been seen in court. In the context of the staging and the acting, the colors on the costumed characters are not perceived in a vacuum, but rather as an enrichment of the other forms of communication.

While every nationality has distinct ideas about the use of color, some color connotations are universal. Although cultures may not share the identical color language, we all sense how color relates to the world around us, and many of our impressions of color come from the elements and the seasons, as did the color system for Chinese culture that was absorbed by traditional Jingju dress. The color meanings in traditional Jingju are both based on the universal and have much to communicate about the Chinese view of the world, as well as the characters in performance.

The Aesthetics and Meanings of the Embroidered Imagery

The interaction of the color of the garments with the subjects and arrangement of the embroidery on the surface embodies the "inner" aspects of the costumes, not the minute details found in the type of stitch or the species of flower. The impact of the whole conveys the intent of the costume. The contents and placement of the surface designs follow predetermined patterns for each garment and role, within the flexibility allowed by the traditions. The subjects are drawn from the Chinese language of symbols, although as theatre and as an art form, the designs on traditional Jingju costumes move beyond the heritage of the court.

Embroidery in Chinese History

Along with the processes of textile production, the Chinese developed several methods for creating designs on the surface of the fabrics. In the Warring States period (476 BC– 221 BC), looms for weaving damask-patterned fabrics were first developed and by the Tang dynasty (618–907), they were quite advanced. In actuality, the Jacquard loom for weaving brocades, patented by Joseph Marie Jacquard in 1804 in France, was based on the Chinese weaving technology.[1] As well as brocades, tapestry weaving was also highly advanced in the Tang dynasty. In tapestry weaving, different colored weft threads, rather than passing the width of the loom, are woven back and forth only in the area required to create the design. The fabric produced from this technique was called *kesi* (carved or cut silk) because it appeared that the threads have been cut.[2] Along with woven fabrication, painting processes such as block printing, resist dyeing, and gilding developed as textile-enhancing techniques.

Embroidery was a fourth technique developed for textile embellishment. Silk threads are particularly conducive to creating excellent embroidery, and the art of stitched designs developed in China along with the evolution of the use of silk fabrics.[3] Virtually all of the textile cultural artifacts of the early dynasties were embroidered.[4] Among the earliest evidences of embroidery are imprints in the patina of two bronzes of the Shang dynasty (1558–1051 BC). The bronzes were wrapped in fabric, and as the fabric deteriorated, it made an impression clear enough to distinguish the threads and chain stitch of the embroidery. Tomb textiles from the Han dynasty (206 BC–220 AD) contain several embroidery stitches that are still used, including the stem stitch and the knot stitch.[5] The satin stitch flourished during the Tang dynasty, as well as the process of couching, which at this time used threads wrapped in gold metal.[6]

The fiber arts thrived in the Song dynasty (960–1279), as variations of the satin stitch emerged and innovative technology, including metal needles, improved the quality of needlework. Another significant development of the Song era was the merging of embroidery designs with the art of painting, for embroiderers in search of innovative subject matter began stitching duplicates of famous paintings.[7] The techniques of satin stitching in these examples of purely ornamental embroidery "became an art form in its own right, distinguished from embroidery for more practical uses," adding a new level to artistry in thread.[8] The Yuan rulers (1279–1368) were particularly interested in the use of gold threads in embroidery.[9] During the Qing dynasty (1644–1911), embroidery production developed on a larger scale with a wider range of colors. Considered a fine art, embroiderers were recognized as honored professionals.[10] Embroidered textiles have long been highly valued in China, not only for dress, but also for interior decorations, court rituals, and treasured gifts.

Initially, theatre costumes were painted because the troupes were not allowed to use quality fabrics or techniques, there being a political need to distinguish between performance and real life. In the early Ming dynasty (1368–1644), as the economy flourished, the art of embroidery became more widespread, and many young girls, even peasants, learned how to make the stitches. As embroidery became more common, it was more feasible for embroidery to be used on costumes.[11] In the Qing dynasty, when traditional Jingju formed, most imperial formal and informal items of clothing were made from brocade, tapestry, or embroidered fabrics. Traditional Jingju costumes did not absorb all of these techniques because brocades and tapestries were costly and more exclusive. Embroidery required the least technology, and as a result, the costumes of traditional Jingju still use embroidery almost exclusively for multicolored effects. Occasional examples of painted costumes do occur, however (Fig. 5.1).

Extant examples of traditional Jingju costumes from the eighteenth and nineteenth centuries show how the

FIGURE 5.1. A rare example of a painted costume appearing with embroidered costumes, this *jianyi* also has seldom used lower sleeves of a contrasting fabric, a trait of the historical precursor, the *jifu*. The separate collar and bib in gold brocade is worn on the outside. The headdress is the *nuanmao* (warm hat) of Qing dynasty origin. *Silang Visits his Mother (Silang tan mu)*. Character: Guojiu (older relative of the princess), actor: Lang Shilin. BJC, Beijing, China. October 7, 2001.

surfaces of theatrical costumes were embroidered and treated with rich details. The Metropolitan Museum of Art collection contains an eighteenth-century theatrical costume for a warrior that is decorated with separate panels, flanges, and appliquéd shapes embroidered in satin stitches. In describing this piece, Jean Mailey remarks that "the imperial theatre must have claimed the talents of the best of the imperial costumers and embroiderers...."[12] Today, in postrevolutionary China, the art of embroidery has dwindled because demand from the imperial court is lacking. With the exception of garments made for tourists, theatrical costumes are virtually the only garments still made with hand embroidery. Fortunately, both for traditional Jingju and for the art of embroidery, the long tradition of this skill has not entirely died out.

Several ancient embroidery techniques, minute satin stitches, golden threads, and the styles of Chinese paintings, are currently employed in contemporary Jingju costumes. On the other hand, contemporary traditional Jingju embroidery can be distinguished from earlier needlework by its enhanced colors and larger motifs that are employed for a heightened aesthetic onstage. As the costumes used in traditional Jingju are based on a limited number of garments with conventionalized forms, variety is achieved in the visual imagery through surface design. These embroidered elements also distinguish each garment and make it specific to a role type.

Embroidery Techniques

Fabrics in traditional Jingju costumes are selected from solid color silks with a satin or crepe surface. Three factors describe the stitching techniques of embroidery: the choice of colors, the thread type and thickness, and the kind of stitches that are used. The colors for the embroidery come from a range similar to those of the fabrics: red, green, yellow, white, black, maroon, pink, blue, lake blue, and olive green. The full range of values

of the colors occurs, from the palest tints to the darkest shades for modeling, but a color that has been mixed with its complement or otherwise neutralized rarely occurs. By adhering to this convention, the palette remains harmonious in spite of the spread of hues across the spectrum.

For imperial dress, Qing records indicate that the silk embroidery for a court robe would have taken one person sixteen days to draw the pattern, thirteen months to complete the gold work, and one year and four months to embroider the silk sections of the design.[13] The costumes of traditional Jingju are elaborately embellished, but with a larger scale of the ornamentation less densely arranged than court garments. In addition, the stitches are also larger and the accuracy of the stitches less meticulous. While it takes less than two years to complete a traditional Jingju costume, the embroidery still represents a time-consuming and painstaking process. With several embroiderers assigned to a garment, an order for a new costume can be filled in about one month, depending on the size of the stitches requested and the amount of embroidery in the design.

I observed the embroidery and construction processes at the Donggaokou Embroidery Factory in Hebei Province. It was a common practice, and still is, for the embroidery to be done in factories in the countryside as the process is labor-intensive and wages are lower outside the big cities. Embroiderers spend nine to ten hours a day, seven days a week at their jobs. Some work at the factory in the room with the embroidery frames, while others work at home. At the time I was there, the Donggaokou factory employed about 200 people, and both men and women were engaged to do the stitching. The designs to be embroidered on a garment are marked on the fabric and stitched prior to construction of the costume. After stretching the marked fabric pieces on the frame, the side edges were rolled in so that only a small portion of the pattern is visible at a time. The smaller size makes it easy to reach all the areas to be worked.

The embroiderers work the areas of color created by the satin stitch first. They complete all the areas designated for a color on the small visible area and then move on to the next color. Once the colored design is finished, they then couch metallic threads around the figures. When the visible area is completed, they cover the reverse side with glue to hold the shape, the finished embroidery is protected by paper, and they roll the frame to reveal the next area to be worked.

Embroidery Colors. The selection of colors for the embroidery begins with the member of the troupe or the performer who is making the order. He or she discusses the colors with the factory representative, and they make decisions based on tradition and aesthetics, experience and practice, and working from photos of previous garments. The collaborators also endeavor to imply through the color and designs the character's personality and to determine the right combination for best visibility. Every costume is likely to be unique, even though it adheres to conventions for the roles and the garment. Once the selection of colors has been agreed upon, the embroiderers often determine the location of each color as they stitch, since placement of the colors is not indicated on the fabric like a paint-by-number canvas. Some pieces may have paper stickers indicating thread color at strategic points on the fabric. Several people may work on a single garment, so clear communication about color location becomes crucial. The use of color in embroidery and how it relates to the fabric color is discussed in Chapter Four.

Embroidery Threads. The embroidery threads are generally a multistranded silk, left untwisted for maximum reflection. The embroiderers separate the desired number of strands from a hank of untwisted silk that is precut into manageable lengths. In addition to the silk floss used for filling in the images, most designs are outlined with a metallic thread. This thread consists of a thick core wrapped with very thin strips of gold or silver metallic foil. A third kind of thread with a woolly texture can be used for outlining when a stronger thread or a colored line is desired.

Embroidery Stitches. The majority of the designs are worked in a satin stitch or one of its variations. The satin stitch consists of a series of parallel stitches used to fill in an area. The stitches are so close together that they conceal the base fabric. For best results, the stitches are worked through and around the fabric so that the pattern develops on both sides, rather than back and forth across the face of the fabric. By moving in this circular pattern, the stitches can be closer together without unstitching each other. The double thickness created by this technique also gives the stitches more dimensionality (Fig. 5.2). Satin stitches are applied in rows, with each row being about ¼ inches to 3/8 inches wide. The direction of the stitches usually follows the contour of the object. Depending on the nature of the design, the petals of a flower can be stitched in either vertical, straight rows or a concentric curved pattern of equal-length stitches that is called the layered short-straight stitch. A long-and-short stitch may be used when shades of a color are needed to model an area such as the flower's petals (Fig. 5.3).[14] Varying the length of the stitches as the color shifts creates a more diffuse transition. Single long stitches, called the pine-needle stitch, are used for the centers of some flowers, such as cherry blossoms, to indicate the stamens. In addition, the Chinese knot or seed stitch can be worked into flowers to represent the grains of pollen (Fig. 5.4). To create this stitch, the thread is wrapped around the needle one or more times before the needle is inserted into the fabric. The wrapped thread forms small loops on the surface of the fabric.

Once the satin stitch has been used to fill in the areas of the design, most of the embroidered motifs are outlined with gold or silver metallic thread in a technique called couching. Rather than piercing the fabric with this thicker thread, one or two strands are placed on the surface of the fabric and stitched in place with a second-

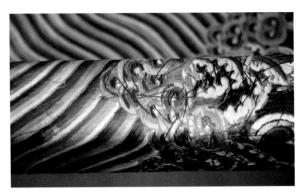

FIGURE 5.2. The back of the embroidery shows how the stitches are complete on both sides of the fabric. Donggaokou Embroidery Factory in Hebei Province, China.

FIGURE 5.3. The long-and-short stitch used in some of the petals of this peony creates a soft blend of colors. An outline of black woolly thread strengthens the color contrast. Woman's vest from the collection of DTD, UHM, Manoa, Hawai'i.

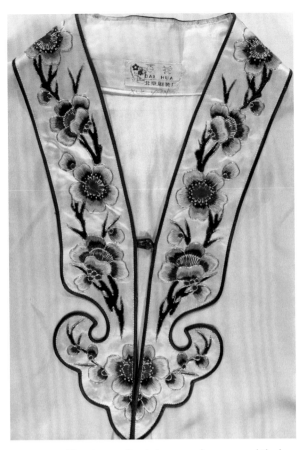

FIGURE 5.4. The pine-needle stitch creates the centers, while the Chinese knot appears as pollen in these cherry blossoms. The end of the collar band is finished in the *ruyi tou* arabesque, which is shaped like a sacred fungus. *Nüpi* from the collection of DTD, UHM, Manoa, Hawai'i.

ary thread (Figs. 4.11, 5.5, and 5.6). The lighter-weight thread loops around the metallic thread at ¼-inch intervals. The secondary thread can be either a neutral color or a more vivid one to increase the strength of the outline. When the color of both the garment and the embroidered image is pale, a third color of thread may be used instead of the metallic thread to outline the forms and increase the contrast (Fig. 5.3). The couching may also be used to fill in entire areas to create a particularly rich effect. In this instance, the couching is outlined with an even heavier woolly thread in a darker color to give shape to the forms. Colored satin stitches appear on garments for females and scholars to indicate their elegant manners, while the costumes of court and military characters have more metallic couching for a bolder effect.

Similar embroidery techniques, including color palette, thread type, and kind of stitch, are generally used

FIGURE 5.5. Gold couching richly ornaments the surface of court and military costumes. The dragon on the lower apron indicates that this character is a warrior for the emperor. The motif at the base of the inner piece is a lion's head on a fish body. The borders are made up of a stylized water pattern. *Kao* from the collection of Zhu Wengui, Beijing, China.

for all embroidered costumes in traditional Jingju, creating a unity of style across the range of dress. The placement and composition of the designs on the surface and the subjects of the embroidery distinguish garments. In addition, each type of garment has its own characteristic

FIGURE 5.6. The gold threads are couched onto the fabric using a lighter-weight thread to secure them on the surface. Donggaokou Embroidery Factory in Hebei Province, China.

style of ornamentation, which may be specified for each role type. The density of the patterns and the amount of metallic thread further identify the roles. These qualities make possible an infinite variety of surface design within the system of clothing, and they help communicate the role to the audience.

Composition

To describe the aesthetic components of the embroidery, traditional Jingju costumes can be loosely divided into three groups: civil, court, and military. Each category has a distinct composition or placement for the embroidered augmentation. Civil clothing includes the *pi* (formal robe) with a center-front closing, worn full length by men and knee length over a skirt *(qunzi)* for women, and the *xuezi* (informal robe). The *pi, xuezi,* and skirt are decorated primarily with floral arrangements, or, in the case of the *pi,* alternatively with roundels containing calligraphy or lucky objects. Dress for court, including the *mang* (court robe) and *guanyi* (official robe), is embroidered with nature, animal, and bird imagery, each following a set convention. Military wear, the *kao* (armor) and the *gailiang kao* (reformed armor), has an ornate combination of geometric and animal imagery on the surface.

Traditional Jingju garments have had their own evolution distinct from the dress at court, and they often combine the styles of historical periods with purely theatrical designs. However, comparing them with the system of embroidery used in later Qing dynasty (1644–1911) dress, as described by Vollmer in *Decoding Dragons,* the embroidery patterns in traditional Jingju dress share many characteristics with those used in the Qing period. Therefore, Vollmer's system of analyzing Qing ornamentation can be applied in a meaningful way to traditional Jingju dress. The embroidered objects, Vollmer notes, were not stitched indiscriminately, but were selected and placed on the garment according to prescribed patterns.[15] Vollmer organizes the embroidery in Qing dynasty imperial dress according to two components, composition and imagery. He further divides the composition of ornament on Qing garments into four categories: bordered, dispersed, consolidated, and integrated.[16]

Borders. Borders are contrasting color fabrics that are applied onto the edges of garments. Many costume items such as the *xuezi* and *pi* have contrasting fabric used for the neckband. Conventional borders are used around the edges of the cloud collars *(yunjian)*, on some designs of the *kao* (Fig. 1.4), and on the women's garments derived from the Qing dynasty, to name a few. The Qing garments are distinct, as they have more borders, covering the neckline and crossover closing, the sleeve hems, and the side slits and hems (Fig. 6.52). They also have an additional narrower contrasting trim that follows the inner edge of the border. When used, borders are either plain or embroidered with a motif different from the rest of the garment and are further set off by a bias band, often a third color, around the edge. When the border ends in the middle of a garment, such as the bottom of the neckband on a *nüpi* (woman's formal robe), the border may be finished with a distinctive arabesque shape that is almost identical on all garments (Fig. 5.4). The design is called a *ruyi tou* ("may things

be as you wish"). The arabesque evolved from an early cloud symbol, or the sacred fungus *(lingzhi)*, and can be seen on many historical garments as well.

Dispersed Patterns. Dispersed patterns are distributed in either a grid or a scattered scheme. The grid scheme has an overall interlocking geometric pattern, also called a diaper pattern. The diaper pattern may be used on a *nümang* (women's court robe) or the bodice of the *gongzhuang* (palace garment), for example. The entire surface of the court robe may be couched in a diagonal netting pattern, with ornaments at each intersection (Fig. 5.7). The scattered composition, a design pattern that first appeared in the Song era, distributes motifs evenly across the surface of the garment. The costume for Sun Wukong, the Monkey King, has a scattered pattern that alternates two types of hair design, wavy lines in sets of three and whorls, hair in circles, embroidered in black with gold couching (Fig. 1.16). Soldiers who perform the acrobatics of battle may be dressed in the martial jacket and trousers *(bingyi)* with a scattered pattern of animals or lucky charms (Fig. 6.35). Scattered patterns, either floral or symbolic, also appear on the *hua xuezi* worn by *chou* (clown) characters. In this case the random pattern indicates the character's foolishness (Fig. 6.15 and Table 6.5.B and 6.6.B).

Consolidated Patterns. Consolidated designs have four different manifestations, with arrangements of circles, single squares, yokes, and bands. The circular motifs occur in several forms on traditional Jingju costumes. Considered the most perfect shape, the circle was originally reserved for the imperial family, but now it appears on the costumes of other higher-ranking characters as well. The content as well as the shape determine the status of the wearer. Round dragon motifs are worn by the highest-ranking *sheng* (standard male), including the emperor and high court officials (Figs 1.1 and 6.1). Round phoenixes are embroidered on the garments of some of the royal women (Fig. 5.7). As early as the Tang dynasty, round flowered patterns appeared on garments.

FIGURE 5.7. A diaper pattern creates an interlocking grid on the surface surrounding a round phoenix motif, rendered in multiple hues. *Nümang* from the collection of James Young, Honolulu, Hawai'i.

In traditional Jingju, similar round flower patterns are worn by *laosheng* (mature men) and married women, either *qingyi* (young or middle-aged women) or *laodan* (mature women), in civil scenes. The prototypical round pattern repeats eight circles embroidered in a mixture of geometric patterns and flowers, dragons, or phoenixes. The round designs are placed on the robe with one at the center front and back at chest height, two at the knees in the front and back, and two on the sleeves (Figs. 1.7 and 6.7). Square motifs are suitable for civil and military officers, so the square-shaped *buzi* (rank badge) appear on the front and back of the *guanyi* (Figs. 5.8 and 6.22).

Yokes in Qing garments are identified as areas embroidered in the shape of a yoke on a garment without an actual yoke seam. Yokes are a less common decoration in Jingju, but do occur in a few instances. For example, the black *mang* often worn by Judge Bao frequently has a ring of circular ornaments stitched around the shoulders and tops of the arms in a yoke shape (Figs. 4.5 and 5.9). This use of the yoke pattern comes from the Qiu school of *jing* performers, founded in the mid-twentieth century by Qiu Shengrong (1915–1971), and the costumes for all of their official characters wear this pattern of embroidery. For women's dress, such a shoulder emphasis is accomplished with the addition of a cloud collar, an elaborately embroidered capelet with a standing band collar that is worn with the *nümang*, *nükao* (female armor), and *gongzhuang* (Figs. 6.4, 6.10,

FIGURE 5.8. The square *buzi* (rank badge) appears on the *guanyi* and indicates the wearer's rank. *Guanyi* from the collection of DTD, UHM, Manoa, Hawai'i.

and 6.29). This collar, with its curved edges and knotted fringe, is an item of Han dress traditions that continued into the twentieth century.[17] The consolidated category also includes bands of embroidery. Embroidered bands appear on the women's skirt at the hem and around the front and back panels (Fig. 5.10). The *nüxuezi* (women's informal robe) with the center-front closing also may have embroidered bands down the center-front opening, around the hem, and up the side slits and the hem of the sleeves.

Integrated Compositions. Integrated compositions combine motifs over the entire surface of the garment in a unified theme. Where Qing court garments use celestial, terrestrial, and panoramic vistas for this category, traditional Jingju costumes draw primarily from the terrestrial motif used on the historical garment known as a dragon robe *(longpao*, later renamed *jifu)*. This garment was viewed as a representation of the universe, and its distinctive embroidery pattern has been transferred to the *mang* for stage usage in court scenes. The components of terrestrial composition that the imperial and

theatrical garments share include the hem areas decorated with parallel diagonal straight or wavy lines representing standing water *(lishui)*, topped by concentric semicircles representing still water *(woshui)*. Emerging from the water, at the four axes of the robes, are trapezoidal mountains representing the four cardinal points on the compass (Fig. 4.13). Originally, the mountains were dominant, but gradually the depth of the waves increased to cover the lower part of the robe to the knees, and the mountains decreased in size. Dragons and clouds decorate the remainder of the surface to complete the terrestrial theme (Fig. 5.11). Two significant differences in the embroidery occur between the historical and stage garments. In imperial dress, originally only the emperor could wear a garment with a five-clawed dragon *(long)*. It was not suitable for costumes to copy the emperor's symbol, so the theatrical version of this garment originally had a four-clawed dragon *(mang)* on it. Such embroidery was also worn by nobles. The written character *mang* is now the word for python, and the Jingju robe derives its name from this creature. Since

FIGURE 5.9. *Jing* performers of the Qiu school wear a distinctive yoke pattern embroidered around the neck of their *mang*. The upper two dragons are playing with a pearl, or flaming orb. Below the waves are ancient smooth-style dragons without scales. From the collection of Zhu Wengui, Beijing, China.

FIGURE 5.10. Embroidered bands of trim encircle the edges of the center panels on the skirt. Skirt from the collection of DTD, UHM, Manoa, Hawai'i.

FIGURE 5.11. This five-clawed dragon in a circular motif is surrounded by clouds and lucky objects, a lotus on the left and goldfish on the right. *Qimang* from the collection of James Young, Honolulu, Hawai'i.

China no longer has an emperor, the *mang* robe often has a five-clawed dragon, but it is still called a *mang*, and hence the translation to court robe rather than dragon robe. The second distinction comes with the twelve symbols of imperial power that are scattered into the composition of the historical dragon robe. Because these symbols were also reserved exclusively for the emperor's use, the surface of the *mang* in traditional Jingju employs the eight emblems of Daoism, Buddhism, or Confucianism instead. The meaning and usage of these ornaments will be discussed in the following section, on emblematic imagery.

Floral Fragments. Along with these categories of embroidered compositions, another motif, the floral fragment in free form, occurs in stage usage. Flowers are a dominant image in traditional Jingju dress, and their arrangement on the fabric surface does not appear in the categories delineated by Vollmer, most likely because they were used on informal dress, and rather than adhering to a single principle of composition, the floral fragment appears in a variety of locations. In the

composition formula often seen in Song Academy floral paintings, the placement of the subject creates a balance between positive and negative space in floral compositions. Most arrangements will include more space above the subject than below, as the unornamented area above links to heaven and that below to the earth, and the floral subject, being of the earth, connects earth to heaven.[18] Two-thirds of the surface is generally left blank to focus on the essential simplicity of the image, and most of the subject of the picture is confined to the lower segment of a diagonally divided picture space (Fig. 5.12).[19] The pattern of placement from the paintings is reflected in many of the floral fragments on costumes (Fig. 5.13). Asymmetry logically represents the essence of nature, being a more dynamic reflection of the natural growth of plants. While the individual motifs are asymmetrical, a design can be reversed and repeated on the two front panels of a *nüpi*, creating an overall symmetry from asymmetrical designs (Table 6.10-12.B). The area of the field, or the garment piece, determines the size and number of the flowers. Odd numbers of blooms

FIGURE 5.12. This Song dynasty painting illustrates the similarities between the painting style and that of embroidered floral subjects. *Fighting Birds on a Branch of Camellia* by Tou-ch'iao. Photograph courtesy of The Nelson-Atkins Museum of Art, Kansas City, Missouri (Purchase: Nelson Trust 49–13).

FIGURE 5.13. Depictions of flowers such as these chrysanthemums are stylized in an asymmetrical composition with multicolored blossoms. *Nüpi* from the collection of DTD, UHM, Manoa, Hawai'i.

are considered more auspicious than even numbers, and flowers in different stages of growth are incorporated to add to the natural effect. A single curving stalk of five flowers 3 to 4 inches in diameter can be arranged into a balanced composition on the back of a *nüpi*. On the *xuezi*, the surface provides a larger area for decoration and voids. For young scholars, the flower fragments are placed on their *hua xuezi* on the left side of the hem and the right side of the chest, around the asymmetrical closing (Fig. 6.12 and Table 6.21.B).

Imagery

The early written form of the Chinese language was based on pictorial images. Many of the written characters evolved from symbolic drawings of the concepts of the words. In the same way, the images employed in dress were selected for their associative values and were intended to have a function beyond beauty. Traditional

Jingju costumes absorbed some of the symbolic meanings connected with the subject matter of the images. Though the costumes are not meticulously recreated from information in imperial edicts concerning dress, many of the basic concepts of cultural symbolism are still honored. For example, civilian costumes generally have floral and bird imagery, while animals are used for military men, as was the case in history. The conventions of dress are mutable within role type, but not across role categories. As theatrical garments can be used for a variety of characters within the role type, the garments are embroidered with generic flowers or rank symbols suitable for the range of men and women who may wear them. In addition, while most of the imagery comes from nature, the objects are idealized and stylized. Lions and tigers are depicted in a codified style and appear alongside of fanciful composites, such as the dragon and phoenix. Just as some of the animals are invented, the flowers are subject to the artist's creativity as well. Some flowers are recognizable blooms, while others are generic.

A comparison between the images of imperial dress and those of traditional Jingju costumes reveals the imagery overlaps to the same extent that the compositions described above are linked. Within the system of imagery of Qing dynasty clothing, Vollmer delineates six separate types: floral, faunal, figural, imperial, scenic, and emblematic.[20] Traditional Jingju costumes primarily utilize four of these categories: floral, faunal, imperial, and emblematic. Floral images indicate the harmonious existence between humans and nature, and often represent wishes of abundance and success in many areas of life. Faunal images include both animals and birds, which often carry symbolic connotations. Imperial imagery appears on court dress and includes a dragon, placed within a cosmic landscape. The emblematic category contains three groups of eight meaningful objects related to Daoism, Buddhism, and Confucianism. Their placement on a garment evokes social success or good fortune. Emblematic images also include the rebus, a distinctive punning device unique to the Chinese language.[21]

Floral Imagery. In Chinese culture, women's informal garments were commonly embroidered, where, apart from dragon robes, Chinese men rarely wore embroidered clothes. Roundel patterns, butterflies, floral and fruiting sprays, and garden vignettes were reserved for women's dress.[22] By contrast, in the traditions of Jingju costumes, men in several role types frequently wear garments with embroidered images. Floral designs are most likely to occur on informal dress, including the garments worn by many of the characters at home and at noncourt functions, the *xuezi*, *pi*, and skirt.

The blossoming of the arts in the Song dynasty, when painting became the most popular of art forms and was practiced by scholars as well as professional artists, influenced the style of floral decorations in informal dress. A new style of painting emerged that reinterpreted the natural world. Chinese art historians customarily divide these paintings into three large subject categories, figures, landscape and flowers, and animals. Centuries later, of these three, floral and animal subjects came to be the most used in traditional Jingju costumes. In Northern and Southern Song academic flower and bird painting, the common components in style were manifested in "careful realism, studied selective presentation and genuine affection lavished upon the small and colorful things of the garden."[23] The gentlemanly art of painting was highly esteemed by the Chinese, as was the art of embroidery, and these two arts began to influence each other, for both shared an interest in a stylized depiction of flowers and animals. Painters and embroiderers began reproducing each other's works, and the aesthetic of Chinese brush painting blended with that of embroidery. Many exquisitely embroidered works of art extant from this period are indistinguishable from their painted counterparts without close viewing. This interrelationship of the two arts resulted in several shared characteristics: a typical stylized essence of the subject, the presence of line, outline, and shading (but the absence of shadow), the control of space, and the selection of color. By focusing on modeling the form with these techniques, the limitations of two-dimensional art, flatness, lack of depth, and linearity, were shifted to a benefit.[24] These characteristics have traversed time and can also be identified in current traditional Jingju costume embroidery.

The brush artist sought to depict an object in essence rather than in actuality, using artistic shorthand to create a stylized image that would draw the viewer into the composition to complete it in the imagination. To create a flower composition for example, a painter would not take painting tools to the garden to work from an actual flower, but would render it from memory or from his experience of the flower. The artist would paint not what the eye saw, but what the mind knew.[25] Floral subjects were usually depicted in fragments, so that the composition appeared to be seen from a close point of view. Rather than depicting an entire bush, the painter created a branch with several blossoms to represent a microcosm of the plant's entire existence (Fig. 5.12).[26] An important aspect of the mastery of Chinese painting was to develop a facility for handling the brush to create specifically admired strokes. Artists learned to execute the traditional style by painting the same object repeatedly, often from an example of their master, thereby gaining control over the technique and the stylized image of the subject. From this convention, over time, likenesses were refined and perfected, and became accepted as the ideal representations.[27] Similarly, in traditional Jingju costume embroidery, while each chrysanthemum, for example, is unique, it will always be executed within a distinct, accepted style. The stylization is not limited to one version of the chrysanthemum, but all mums will be rendered in conventional styles that have evolved for that flower. They are generally depicted with the petals spread apart and distinctly rendered, often with half of the petals going up and the other half going down (Fig. 5.13). This aspect of stylization embodies the nature of traditional Jingju performance and other arts of China, where individual artists of each succeeding generation build on the existing tradition, adding their personal spirit to the continuum.

Early painting was closely aligned with the art of calligraphy. The elegance of brush stroke admired in calligraphy influenced the painters and the embroidery artists. Graceful line and outline were key components of brush painting and were often used to define shapes. In tradi-

tional Jingju costumes today, very few floral motifs are depicted without the edges outlined in metallic or dark-colored threads. On stage, the addition of the outline around all the floral forms gives them clarity, increasing their visibility from a distance (Figs. 5.3 and 5.13).

Chinese painting style emphasizes a technique of loading the brush with two tones of color for effective shading.[28] The areas painted with strokes from this technique have a graceful combination of shades, creating a smooth blend from dark to light. Flower petals and leaves are painted with this stroke, giving a heightened sense of dimensionality through the chiaroscuro effect of light and dark on the petals. Paintings from the Song dynasty appear to be the first to elevate this elegant shading to a high art. The stitchers of embroidery adopted this technique, and it remains a vital component in the embroidery of costumes. Flowers usually have a minimum of three or as many as five tints of embroidery floss shading each petal and two or three shading each leaf. The stitches are carefully blended to create an imperceptible shift between the colors (Fig. 5.3). The direction of the stitches affects the reflective quality of the threads, giving added dimensionality to the design.[29] While the shading on the individual petals is paramount, the flower itself casts no shadow. All embroidered objects are depicted floating in a void, with no shadows to ground them. In addition, the angle of light is not evident. The petals are dark in the center and light on the outside edge, regardless of the direction in which they are facing. The exception to this pattern occurs with a pale color of fabric. In this case, the outside edges of the flower will be the darker to provide contrast with the background color (Fig. 4.12).

Initially, Chinese artists chose to rely primarily on more subdued colors in their paintings. While some embroidered paintings are quite subtle, brilliant colors can also be seen in examples from the Song dynasty on. One possible explanation for this shift may be the gradual introduction of brightly colored fabrics as a ground for the embroideries and costumes, including peacock greens and blues, Chinese red, and cerise. In the case of traditional Jingju costumes, the brighter colors of thread are needed in the embroidery not only to contrast with the some of the intense colors of the garments, but also to project the designs to the audience. The vivid colors are also joined in unique combinations on individual garments. A single stalk may contain flowers of different colors, with as many as three hues being quite common (Fig. 5.13). A specific flower can also be rendered in a variety of colors that are not limited by the natural colors of that flower. The most popular colors for flowers seem to be reds, including peach, cerise, and pink, as well as purple, blue, and yellow. Leaves tend to be in the blue-green range, although some examples have a more leaf-green color. The graceful, elegant overall effect of the stylization and color of the flowers in informal dress creates a sense of tranquility for the domestic scenes.

In addition to the artistic elements of the decorations, many flowers contain symbolic and auspicious messages. Flowers represent the four seasons: the plum blossom for winter, peonies or orchids for spring, the lotus for summer, and the chrysanthemum for autumn. As there are no seasons indicated in traditional Jingju, the seasonal meanings of the flowers are not used, but each flower conveys other messages, as well. Plum blossoms stand for resistance and the will to live because they bloom in the winter. Peonies, with their bold beauty and commanding size, carry meanings of wealth and advancement. They are variously assigned meanings of brightness and masculinity, love and feminine beauty, and as an omen of good fortune (Fig. 5.3).[30] The lotus, in a concept that comes from Buddhism, represents purity and nobility, as its white blossoms emerge unsullied from the mud. The chrysanthemum appears quite often, being valued for its variety and richness of color. It is regarded as the national flower and the symbol of noble personalities, gentility, fellowship, and longevity (Fig. 5.13).[31] In addition to these four, roses, which appear regularly on young women's robes, are a symbol of eternal youth and lasting springtime.[32] Principal characters sometimes have characteristics specifically communicated through the flowers on their robes, but because the costumes are interchanged among characters within a role type, for most characters the flowers are merely ornamentation indicating gentility.

Faunal Imagery. In Chinese culture, specific animals carried desired qualities and were embroidered onto items of clothing to endow the wearer with those attributes. For example, the tiger, embodying courage and fierceness, appears on the garments of a warrior. In other cases, the creatures convey wishes for a good life, as with the crane, which has come to symbolize longevity. Symbols for behavioral characteristics are assigned specifically to either men or women, but animals representing social wishes can appear on the dress of either gender. The faunal language on women's clothes is less complicated than that on men's garments because floral imagery predominates on women's garments.

Animal imagery appears on the male garments including the *guanyi*, *bufu* (coat with a badge), *kao*, and *kai chang* (informal official robe). The *guanyi* resembles the garment of rank developed from the Ming dynasty tradition and is now worn by traditional Jingju officials of the court. A long robe with an asymmetrical closing, the historical garment was relatively free from ornament except for the *buzi* that were placed on the center of the chest and back. The rulers from the Mongol tribes of the Yuan dynasty (1271–1368) had worn square decorations woven into their robes, although these ornaments were not associated with rank, but the *buzi* were instituted as insignia badges in 1391, in the Ming dynasty.[33] As the circular shape, often manifested in dragons and phoenixes, was employed primarily for the royal family, the square form of these badges became emblematic for the court officers.[34] While the right to wear a rank badge was bestowed by the emperor, recipients had to provide the badge themselves, and hence a tradition developed of having the badges made separately from the garment and stitched on. Since the officers were likely to have aspirations for a higher rank, the symbol indicating the rank was often embroidered on a separate, interchangeable piece as well. There were two categories of rank: civil for scholars and officers of the court, and military for men of action. Within each of these two categories, there were nine degrees of official rank, the first being the highest. The garment for each rank was delineated both by the color of the robe and by the subject in the square of embroidery on the front and back of the garment. Birds, symbols of elevated intellect, were used to distinguish the civil ranks, and animals, indicative of physical strength, were employed for the military ranks. It is not known how the creatures were selected to represent their specific ranks, other than those connections that may be found in Chinese mythology.[35] The birds and animals were placed in a landscape facing towards the sun, an homage representing the emperor. The sun was located in different corners for civil and military officials: the birds faced the wearer's right, and animals faced the wearer's left.[36] The square patch was outlined with a frame to set it off (Fig. 5.8). In the court, the display of the proper rank on one's garments was quite important, but for traditional Jingju usage, precise rank no longer carries significance. Generally, only civil officers wear the *guanyi* onstage, so the badges are primarily embroidered with birds, although some *guanyi* have badges with a sun in the center for a more generic emblem. The *bufu* is the Qing-dynasty version of the garment with a rank badge, and it is used onstage for officials of foreign courts (Fig. 6.53).[37]

The *kao* developed for use as theatrical armor and the composition of the designs on the surface is unique, creating one of the most highly ornamented garments in the wardrobe. With elaborate embroidery on both the male and female versions, the animal and bird imagery projects the power of the wearer. Dragons are depicted on *kao* of the emperor's warriors. Symmetrical paired dragons can be featured on the padded front belt piece *(kaodu)*, or a single dragon may face sideways or appear with its head in the center of the band (Fig. 4.11). Dragons can also be used to embellish the hanging panels and the lower sleeves. In addition, the torso pieces, the upper sleeves, and the some of the panels below the waist are often decorated with a scale pattern that evolved from the use of segmented plates to facilitate movement in historical armor. A geometric design may be used in this area as well. Tigers are frequently used as motifs on the armor of characters who are uninhibited and straightforward. Large dimensional tiger heads can fill the space on the padded belt, and some forms of *kao* have dimensional tiger heads on the shoulders as well. A pair of fish tails finishes the lowest point on the apron panel over the legs in the front of the costume. The two tails evolved from the yin/yang symbol of two fish swimming in a circle. The fish emblem also means that the character thinks of clever strategies. An embroidered border emphasizes the shapes of all the panels. The border may contain ancient-style smooth dragons, geometric patterns of water, or a meander resembling the Greek key, called cloud-and-thunder by the Chinese (Fig 5.5).[38]

For female versions of armor, the phoenix, rather than the dragon, is the primary creature used, as women's armor is decorated with flying creatures, rather than the earthbound animals used for men's. The phoenix appears in the same locations as the dragon on the male armor, as well as on the larger cloud collar. Flowers, often peonies, ornament the additional narrow streamers and the borders on the edges of the shaped pieces. The embroidered designs on the rest of women's armor are similar to those on men's, with scales in the central parts of the panels and borders defining the edges (Figs. 1.11 and 6.10). Women's armor generally has a greater variety of colors in the embroidery than does the men's, which often is dominated by metallic couching to make it look impermeable.

The *kai chang* is worn by military and official men in their private quarters. The *kai chang* for *jing* features large, bold animal figures often stretching the length of the garment. Animals pictured include lions, leopards, tigers, elephants, and the *qilin* (Fig. 1.19). The *qilin* is a composite creature, often called a dragon horse or the Chinese unicorn, as it is sometimes depicted with a single horn emerging from its forehead, though some representations have two horns. The animal parts that comprise the *qilin* include the body of a deer, the tail of an ox, and the hooves of a horse. The body has scales with a ridge down the back, and the head has a flowing mane and two trailing antennae. The early *qilin* was an aggressive beast with the capacity to discern good and evil. Although the *qilin* later became more benevolent and not harmful to living creatures, it represented the first grade of military officers in the Qing court. In traditional Jingju, military men rarely wear their rank badges, but *qilin* imagery appears on their *kai chang*.[39]

Imperial Imagery. The imperial format of embroidered patterns, a terrestrial composition with waves, clouds, mountains, and dragons described above, appears in traditional Jingju costumes on the *mang*, the most important garment at court for both male and female characters. As the precise duplication of the emperor's robe was prohibited onstage, the decorations were modified. Water is a dominant feature of the *mang* design, covering as much as the bottom third of the garment. The embroidery of the waves is particularly impressive as these large areas are solidly filled with stitches. The standing waves can be rendered in rows of satin stitch using three or more gradations of color. The concentric semicircles above have similar gradations in color to define the shapes. An even grander effect comes from couching the entire water area in gold threads, separated by a contrasting color thread (Fig 4.3). The simplest version has curved standing water made with wavy diagonal lines in a single chevron in the center front and back of the robe, topped with a series of con-

centric semicircles to indicate still water. More complex patterns employ more chevrons or a greater proportion of semicircles. On some *mang,* dragons play in the waves (Fig. 4.5). The mountains are satin stitched in straight lines, using gradations of colors of thread, or solidly couched. The rest of the surface of the *mang* around the dragons may be left plain or have decorative clouds incorporated into the composition. Clouds take on several shapes, either round and fluffy or long and narrow.

In addition to the terrestrial design, the dragon comprises a major component of the composition on the *mang*, as the dragon has long been an important symbol in Chinese culture. Probably inspired by an alligator, the dragon is associated with water and rain, and therefore with ancient emperors, who through performing rituals properly, were responsible for ensuring enough water and rain to guarantee crops to feed their subjects. The first reliable reference to dragons as the principal design on these robes dates from the Tang dynasty.[40] Dragon designs come in many shapes and sizes, the dominant arrangement of the dragon's body being a serpentine twist to form a roundel, repeated several times over the surface of the garment. On garments with these round dragons, there are usually ten roundels dispersed over the surface of the *mang*, one at the center of the chest and back, two above the wave patterns on the front and back and two on each sleeve. This placement pattern comes from Han design, rather than the Qing, which used only nine dragons. The central dragons at the chest and back are generally arranged with the head facing forward at the top of the circle; the dragons near the knees are in profile facing each other (Figs. 4.1 and 6.1). Gentle, intelligent, and courageous male characters and young generals who are handsome and elegant wear the *mang* with rounded dragons.[41]

In his *China's Dragon Robes*, Schuyler Cammann delineates several other categories of dragon placement on court robes. In addition to the formal arrangement of dragon roundels, he describes examples of garments with larger dragons twisting around the neck or writhing down the front and sleeves of the robe. These additional dragon shapes have been incorporated into traditional Jingju costumes, being particularly effective for their larger scale. The bolder military *jing* roles wear them (Figs. 6.2 and 7.8). Dragons are often depicted playing with a round object variously described as a flaming orb, ball, or pearl (Figs. 4.11 and 5.9). The pearl, or pearl of wisdom, comes from the Buddhist symbol of enlightenment and represents the emperor's search for the wisdom of heaven needed to benefit his kingdom.[42]

The Chinese dragon reflects a composite creature created in the imagination of the Han people. Ancient dragons were smoother and simpler in design, and they often appear in secondary areas of embroidery around the neckline or on the extensions of the *mang*. The style of dragon used in the main embellishments of traditional Jingju costumes comes from the Ming and Qing dynasty version. Descriptions vary, but dragons are generally made up from parts of other animals including "the head of a camel (now thought to be a horse), the horns of a deer, the eyes of a rabbit, ears of a cow, neck of a snake, belly of a frog, scales of a carp, claws of a hawk and the palm of a tiger."[43] In most representations, jagged whiskers surround the mouth, which is filled with fangs. Under the nostrils is a "mustache" and above, two long trailing antennae. Behind the head grow a mane of twisted tendrils and two forked horns. Scales cover the serpentine body, which has a peaked ridge down the spine. The tail ends in a flame-shaped piece. The toes are always spread and have claws on the ends. Several colors of thread are used to distinguish each part of the dragon. The head usually matches the body, with contrasting colors used for the mouth, horns, mane, and antennae. The scales are depicted by three gradations of thread, with the darkest color on the inside, much the same way that the petals of a flower are defined. The direction of

the scales and the twisting of the back ridge describe the undulation of the dragon's body. Couching further outlines and defines the details. Cammann points out that theatrical dragons differ from imperial portrayals, as they are drawn more boldly for increased visibility. In addition to gold couching and bright colors, the features of the dragon are enlarged, with protruding eyes and a bulbous nose (Figs. 5.9 and 5.11).[44]

The number of dragon claws is now all but ignored in theatrical dress. Perhaps this can be explained by looking at late Qing dynasty usage. Existing robes show examples of robes with the dragon claws added later, indicating that more of the higher officials were gaining the right to wear the five-toed version, making the five-toed dragons less exclusive.[45] Furthermore, with the end of the dynastic era, there was no longer any pressure to subscribe to imperial regulations of dress. Now most dragons on traditional Jingju costumes have the full complement of five claws per foot.

A third component of imperial design composition was the twelve emblems of the sovereign (sun, moon, constellation of three stars, mountains, dragon, pheasant, pair of bronze cups, waterweed, grain, fire, ax, and *fu* [a symbol of power]). Every emperor since the Han dynasty wore these twelve symbols. Though early Manchu emperors appear to have avoided using them, perhaps because they were regarded as Han Chinese, the Qianlong emperor restored the symbols in the eighteenth century.[46] These symbols could be worn only by the true emperor, so on traditional Jingju garments, the twelve symbols have been replaced by either the eight symbols of Buddhism or Daoism or the eight precious objects of Confucianism, discussed below in the section on emblematic imagery. In traditional Jingju, significantly, both the emperor and empress have symbols on their garments, whereas at the historical court, the empress's garments would not regularly include this detail.

Women of the onstage court, the empress and high-ranking princesses and concubines, wear the *nümang*.

The embroidered images on *nümang* are similar to those of the men's, employing the composition of terrestrial elements, and scattered emblems, but with phoenixes instead of dragons. Because the women's version of this garment is shorter, the scale of the waves is reduced. Legend portrays the dragon and the phoenix as lovers in ancient times, so these two mythological creatures have come to symbolize the emperor and empress. The phoenix, like its counterpart, the dragon, is also an imaginary creature made up from parts of existing beasts: it resembles a wild swan in front and a unicorn behind, with "the throat of a swallow, the bill of a fowl, the neck of a snake, the tail of a fish (with twelve feathers), the forehead of a crane, the crown of a mandarin drake, the stripes of a dragon and the back of a tortoise."[47] The phoenix generally appears in a roundel shape, with the feathers of the tail curled gracefully around the body. As the phoenix has many colors, a variety of hues are applied, such as aqua, lavender, yellow, and cerise. The textures of the feathers are portrayed with careful detail, using a long-and-short stitch on the tail and couching on the body and wing feathers (Fig. 5.7).

Emblematic Imagery. Emblematic imagery includes the groups of objects that are associated with religious contexts in Buddhism, Daoism, and Confucianism, and the rebus, or punning devices. The nature of the Chinese language, composed as it is of a limited number of homophones that are written in distinct forms, creates many words that sound the same but have different meanings.[48] Some of these written characters have come to represent abstract concepts merely because they have the same sound.

The number eight has special significance in Chinese culture as an even, feminine, or yin number. Combinations of eight objects *(babao)* carry social significance. By the mid-eighteenth century, the "eight objects" had come to refer to several sets of symbols: the eight precious objects, sometimes associated with Confucianism, the eight symbols of Buddhism, and the eight symbols

of the Immortals of Daoism.[49] Because, as mentioned earlier, the twelve objects of the emperor could not appear onstage, one or more of these eights might be embroidered onto the stage emperor's gown in their place.

The eight precious objects of Confucianism, also known as the emblems of the scholar, are drawn from items that the scholar might use in the study. The list includes the pearl, the lozenge with interlocking diamond shapes, the stone chime, a pair of rhinoceros horns, coins, a mirror, books, and a leaf.[50] The eight symbols of Buddhism, said to be on the sole of Buddha's foot, are derived from traditions in Indian royal ceremonies: the wheel, the canopy, the umbrella, the lotus, the vase, the goldfish, and the knot.[51] The third group of symbolic objects is ascribed to Daoism. The eight Immortals of Daoism are represented by their attributes, or items that are associated with their legends: the fan, the bamboo tube, the sword, castanets, the gourd and crutch, the flute, the basket of flowers, and the lotus pod.[52] The objects are depicted entwined with ribbons to indicate that they are immortal, or lucky, charms.

Of these groups of objects, the objects of Buddhism seem to be the most commonly employed on the *mang* (Fig. 5.11). Variations in their application occur; on some robes, not all eight of the objects are used, and in other cases, the items are mixed or all three sets appear. An imperial precedent exists for mixing these symbols, as Cammann mentions that on some court robes, articles from one of the other symbol groups, such as a golden wheel or a vase from the eight Buddhist symbols were included with symbols of another set.[53] While the Buddhist symbols originally had a sacred meaning, and the Daoist set was associated with the semidivine persons whose attributes they represented, by the middle of the Qing dynasty, both had become disassociated from any religious connotations and were merely sets of lucky symbols.[54] As a result, later court robes displayed many auspicious symbols as incidental decorations with no ritual importance. Without their original meanings, the symbols were no longer written into the sumptuary laws, and "such trifles were left up to the designers of the robes or the artisans who made them."[55] That the symbols lost their significance in court functions may explain their mostly decorative usage in traditional Jingju dress.

In addition to objects representing religious and cultural meanings, the Chinese also incorporate written characters and language puns into their designs. In some cases the word means what it says, and in others, the character or image can be a form of a riddle or rebus. Because the language uses specific tones as well as pronunciation to express words, many words with vastly different meanings sound the same except for their tone. As a result, the Chinese take joy in the creation of word-play puns translated into visual representations. The image becomes a word that can be read like any character. For example, in Chinese morphology, the bat reigns supreme as a symbol of good luck and happiness, and in the Chinese language, the word for bat (*fu*) is the same as the word for happiness. The auditory representation, when translated into a visual design, makes the bat become an icon for happiness.[56] Five is considered a most auspicious number, so five bats together in a circle represent the five blessings of a long life, riches, health, love of virtue, and a natural death.[57] Bats are also scattered in the clouds of terrestrial compositions. Chinese written characters expressing good wishes are incorporated into surface design. The character for longevity (*shou*) appears frequently on costumes and is embroidered on the chest of the armor, protecting the heart (Figs. 2.11 and 5.14).

While stage dress may be rampant with anachronisms, a significant portion of the embellishment relates to authentic usages in the past. The principles of symbolism used in imperial garments illuminate the roles, while continuing to reflect the cultural context.

FIGURE 5.14. Five bats, representing the five blessings, encircle the written character for longevity. *Gailiang kao* from the collection of the ATCO, Beijing, China.

As traditional costume has been rapidly disappearing in China, the wardrobe of traditional Jingju has remained a repository of imperial clothing styles and has preserved the spirit, if not always the letter, of the laws of dress in former times.[58] The garments in traditional Jingju are costumes, and, as such, the significance of the imagery may be diluted from its original purpose. The overall characteristics of placement and meaning are heeded, however, with the addition of theatricality. Because the costumes are viewed from a distance, the theatrical need for scale may overtake cultural heritage. Embroidery supports the visual image by telegraphing personality, while contributing to the overall beauty of the production. Traditional Jingju is still a living art form, and generations of new artists will add their own contribution to the continuation of the tradition. In addition, as time has moved away from the era of the imperial courts, much of the significance of the imagery has passed from importance in daily life. As the guardians of the heritage disappear, so does the strength of the tradition. Since the range of embroidered imagery is not as great on traditional Jingju costumes as it was in imperial dress, the historical vocabulary has become more limited. At the same time, other embroidery designs have been added, which expand the imagery but may muddle the meanings. Although the origins and specific meanings of many of the symbols may not be common knowledge, those images still convey the general meanings from the past, and the patterns heighten the exquisite beauty of the costumes of traditional Jingju performances.

The Costume Compendium

The compendium catalogs a significant sample of the costumes worn in traditional Jingju. The costumes are classified by form and then organized by status or occupation. Four principal costumes comprise the majority of those worn by traditional Jingju characters. The *mang* (court robe) is considered the highest-ranking garment, and is worn by officials for court appearances. After the *mang*, the *pi* (formal robe) comes next in status, and it is worn by the some of the same characters for scenes outside of court. The *kao* (armor), worn by generals either at court or in battles, falls third in ranking, followed by the *xuezi* (informal robe), the lowest because all characters may wear it. All other costumes are consolidated into a single group simply called clothing *(yi)*. The range of clothing generally divides into four categories: long, falling from the shoulder to the floor; short, combining two pieces to cover the body, as in jacket and skirt or trousers combinations; special costumes for specific characters who require unique costumes, including some of the designs by the famous twentieth-century actor Mei Lanfang, and pieces that are added to the other garments, such as capes, vests, belts, shoes, and inner garments. The sections in which the costumes are listed reflect the trunk system and the method in which the costumes were stored for easy retrieval (see Chapter Eight). The basis for applying this system and developing this chapter was inspired by Tan Yuanjie's invaluable *Zhongguo Jingju fuzhuang tupu (An illustrated guide to costume in Jingju)*. While employing Tan's sys-

tem, the precise sequence has been modified to arrange like garments in proximity. This chapter also applies the theoretical analysis found in Chapters Three through Five to explicate the use of form, color, and embroidery for each garment.

Each garment is named in pinyin, a system for the romanization of Chinese words, with an explanatory translation. The Description and History sections explain the garment and detail its source, identifying whether it resembles a historical garment, was modified from a historical garment for stage, or created for stage usage without a historical precedent. The Usage sections define the conventions of wear, describe how the garment fits into the overall system of dress, and give some examples of when it is worn and which roles regularly wear it. The Color and Roles sections describe the colors of the garment and how they distinguish which roles and characters will wear it. In the Ornamentation and Roles portions, the range of embroidery designs is delineated and related to specific roles, while the Accessories and Headdresses sections describe some of the typical accessories, hair, and headdresses that are worn with the particular garment to give an impression of the entire image.

In some cases costumes have been modified to create another form of usage. These changed garments have the word *gailiang* (reformed) added before their name. Such improvements often came about through the inspiration of a performer desiring to express something new for a specific role. The *gailiang* versions follow the originals in the listing. When garments are worn by both male and female roles, there may be distinctions in cut, color, or ornamentation to indicate gender. In some of these cases, the women's garments are distinguished by the addition of the word *nü* (woman) before the base name of the piece.

Most of the costumes fit into one of the standardized forms as they are described in this chapter. Not every costume has been detailed, as there are many varieties within each category, but each of the major classifications has been included.

The Major Costumes

Mang (Court robe)

Description and History. Different forms of dragon robes *(longpao)* span almost one thousand years in Chinese history from the first recorded imagery of dragons on garments in the Tang dynasty (618–907) to the end of the Qing era (1644–1911). In the Ming era (1368–1644), robes with dragon decorations were considered one of the most prestigious articles of clothing, and they were conferred as gifts on those worthy of the honor. The robes became so popular that many officials arranged to have them made illegally, ignoring the 1459 law forbidding such practice.[1] During the Qing dynasty, the dragon robe became an official garment for court, earned through achieving an appointment from the emperor.

The cut of the male *mang* costume closely resembles the Ming dynasty's version of dragon robes. The historical robes had a rounded neckline and a curved crossover closing tied on the right. The front and back pieces were continuous, without a shoulder seam. The armscye was straight and occurred at the width of the fabric. Full length, trapezoidal shaped, and voluminous, the garment had side seams left open, and the fronts were widened with extensions *(bai)* that were several inches wide. These flaps lapped over the back of the robe and were tied to the center back of the neckline, while flaring at the hem. The sleeves of the historical garments could be very wide; however, the *mang* costume sleeves are tubular, longer than wrist length, and have water sleeves *(shuixiu)* attached at the hems. The historical robe was worn with a hoop-shaped jade belt *(yudai)*, and the stage version follows that fashion. The name *mang,* meaning python, refers to the four-clawed creature embroidered on the court robes in the Ming and Qing dynasty. The *mang* ranked below the five-clawed dragon *(long)* (see Chapter Five).

When the Manchu rulers came to power in the Qing dynasty, they further developed the dragon robe and renamed it *jifu* (lit. "auspicious attire or coat"). The cut of the *jifu* was based on Manchu tastes; it had the front and back slit to permit horseback riding and narrow sleeves ending in horseshoe-shaped cuffs. The surface design was refined to elaborate on the composition of dragons in a terrestrial environment of waves, mountains, and clouds. During the Qing era, the *jifu* was worn for all but the most formal events. The *jifu* was often concealed under the *bufu* (court surcoat) when worn to court.

As traditional Jingju costumes are not intended to replicate history, the *mang* court robe costume is a hybrid of its Ming and Qing predecessors, using the cut of the Ming robe and the surface design of the Qing *jifu*. The *mang* is the most respected of garments, indicated by the dragons on the surfaces representing the emperor. As the most prestigious costume, the *mang* has rich embroidery, with complicated, symbolic designs in solid gold or beautiful colors. Elegant enough for the imperial court, the stage image could easily be mistaken for reality, despite the obvious distinctions (Fig. 6.1 and Appendix 1.1).

Usage. Emperors and the highest-ranking members of the court wear the *mang* primarily for court or official scenes. *Sheng* (standard male) and *jing* (painted face) wear the *mang*, and it is only infrequently donned by the *chou* (clown), when he plays a shady official or a eunuch.

Color and Roles. The use of color in the *mang* exemplifies the system of upper *(shang wuse)* and lower colors *(xia wuse)* and their communication of character onstage. (The color system is discussed in Chapter Five.) The more pure upper colors, red, green, yellow, white, and black, appear more frequently and are used on the higher-ranking characters. A red *mang* with round dragons is considered among the highest combinations of color and design. Worn by *sheng* and *jing* roles, it designates important and good characters of noble rank, important relatives to the emperor, court officials, and army commanders (Fig. 6.1). A red *mang* with large dragons indicates a strong, dominating character when worn by *jing*, such as Cao Cao, the antagonist in the Three Kingdoms saga *Lü Bu and Diaochan (Lü Bu yu Diaochan)* (BJC, Beijing, China. July 15, 2000) (Fig. 1.12). Men with high-ranking or military functions wear a green *mang* (Fig. 4.2) The emperor is exclusively entitled to wear yellow, regardless of his virtues or role type (Fig. 4.3). Both *xiaosheng* and *laosheng* may wear a white *mang,* which represents loyalty (Fig. 1.2 and Table 6.22.N). Black *mang* usually appear on *jing* with a black facial design. The black robe projects both their rough and honest characteristics as well as the fact that they enforce laws and punishments (Fig. 4.5). The lower colors, maroon, pink, blue, lake blue, and olive green, are mixed, except for blue, and therefore less emphatic onstage. Maroon *mang* are worn by civil servants, as well as usurpers and barbarians, who are generally played by *jing* (Fig. 7.28). Pink *mang* are worn only by *xiaosheng* roles, as pink implies handsome youths (Fig. 2.2 and Table 6.22.B). A *mang* in blue indicates high status or military function (Fig. 4.8). The *mang* does not come in lake blue. An olive-green or neutral-color *mang* indicates an elderly *laosheng* character (Fig. 4.10 and Table 6.2.N).

The color of the embroidery can be either predominantly metallic couching or a limited range of color threads. Green, black, maroon, and blue dragon robes are most likely to have gold couching as the predominant color on the surface. Blue is the most common single color used to embroider a *mang*, appearing on the yellow, white, pink, and olive-green *mang* court robes. Red *mang* can have either blue or gold surface ornamentation. The *sheng*-style *mang* tend to be embroidered with colored threads, while the *jing*-style *mang* more often use metallic threads.

Ornamentation and Roles. The overall design of the *mang* costume reflects the diagram of the universe designed for the Qing *jifu*. The hem has a deep band of waves in straight or wavy diagonal lines. At the crest of the water, four mountains emerge, designating the earth and the four point of the compass, at the centers of the front and back, and the side seams. Clouds representing the sky complete the terrestrial composition (see Chapter Five). Dragons are placed within this environment, emblematic of imperial authority over all. The dragons are focused on a pearl that symbolizes the emperor's search for the wisdom needed to rule wisely.

The pose of the dragon on stage costumes represents a key to the character's nature or position. Because round designs are considered the most perfect, representative of the heavens, round dragons were designated for the emperor's informal wear in the early Ming dynasty.[2] On the stage *mang*, ten round dragons are distributed on the surface, one at chest level center front and back, two at the knees front and back and two on each sleeve, one above the other. In one favored arrangement, the chest dragon faces front, while the knee-level dragons face each other. Round dragon *mang* are worn by *laosheng* and *xiaosheng* (Fig. 6.1).

In the Ming and early Qing dynasties, larger dragons were designed covering more expanse of the surface of the robes. Traditional Jingju dragons have continued in this vein, with several examples depicting creatures

FIGURE 6.1 The *mang* for a *xiao-sheng,* seen here, or a *laosheng,* has a round dragon pattern and water sleeves, and it is usually worn with a hooped jade belt and *zhongsha* headdress. *A Sorrow that Transcends Life and Death (Sheng si hen).* Character: Cheng Pengju, actor: Ji Zhibin. BJC, Beijing, China. July 30, 2000.

in increasingly larger sizes and more dramatic poses. A design of six dragons will have two on the front and back opposing each other, loosely forming a circle, and two more decorating the sleeves. Four dragons may be distributed with one large dragon on the front and back and smaller ones on each sleeve. On robes with two large dragons, one of them covers the front and one sleeve, while the second stretches over the back and the other sleeve. *Jing* characters wear *mang* with larger dragons, because they represent intelligence, capability, high position, and power (Fig. 6.2 and 7.11).

A single walking dragon appears above the waves on one style of black *mang* worn by Judge Bao, who is known for his stern but fair judgments (Fig. 4.5). Additional dragons are depicted cavorting in the waves on this *mang* used for Judge Bao and other *jing* who wear

FIGURE 6.2. A *jing* wears a *mang* with large dragons and a jade belt. His makeup is *sankuaiwa lian* (three-tiled face) with the forehead, nose, and cheeks in the same color. *Reconciliation of the Prime Minister and the General (Jiang xiang he).* Character: Fu Bao, actor: Han Juming. PRSCJ, Beijing, China. April 24, 1996.

mang made from black fabric. The Qiu school of *jing* performers wears a distinctive style of *mang* embroidered with a yoke of waves and dragons surrounded by the ancient version of dragons rendered smoothly without scales, and rings of roundels containing the characters for happiness, long life, and smaller dragons (Figs. 4.5 and 5.9). This distinctive design was developed by Qiu Shengrong, a famous *jing* player in the twentieth

century, to be embroidered on a *mang* he would wear instead of the *mang* with the larger dragons.

The different styles of water on the hem are lesser forms of character identification, after the dragons and the color of the garment. There are three areas of water depicted: standing water *(lishui)*, depicted with long straight or wavy diagonal lines at the base; resting water *(woshui,* also called *pingshui)*, on the surface in the semicircles; and frothy bubbles *(jiangya)* at the top. A wave design with a single chevron pointing up in the center occurs often and can be worn by *sheng* or *jing* characters (Figs. 1.1 and 4.1). More complicated wave designs, with multiple chevrons in odd numbers, three and five, are worn by some *jing* characters. The standing, lying, three-rivers water design *(sanjiang shui)* and standing, lying, five-rivers water *(wujiang shui)* designs are for powerful officials just below the emperor. In some cases the diagonal waves are replaced entirely with semicircles of water couched in gold. This version was originally designed for Guan Yu, a character who must present a bold and impressive image. All three of these water configurations appear on high-ranking officers, fathers-in-law of princesses or princes, and wicked characters of high rank. When the *mang* has solid gold couching, the sections of water are delineated by black lines that define the wave design (Fig. 6.2). If the waves are embroidered in color, three shades of blue *(sanlan)* are likely to be used (Figs. 1.1 and 4.13).

As with historical garments, the traditional Jingju *mang* have four mountains rising above the waters. They are located at the center front and back and on the side front of the hems. The mountains are depicted as layers of trapezoids (Fig. 4.13). Loosely scattered over the surface are clouds and lucky symbols. Since the traditional twelve symbols of the emperor could not appear on stage, they are replaced by some of the eight lucky symbols *(babao)* drawn from Buddhism, Daoism, or Confucianism. Today, those replacement emblems have strayed from their original symbolism, and the motifs may appear in less than a full complement, or mixed with icons from another group (Fig. 5.11).

Accessories. A matching collar *(shanjian)* surrounds the neck of military characters wearing the *mang*. The collar has the same shape as the collar worn with other military garments, including the *kao* and the *jianyi* (archer's robe), and is viewed as a protective piece for the shoulder area. Generally the *mang* is worn with a hoop-shaped jade belt that encircles the body. The belt passes through loops under the arms and is balanced to hang lower in the front. If a eunuch wears a *mang*, he wears the small cord *(xiao taozi)* instead, representing lower rank than the jade belt. The *mang* is usually worn with padding *(pang'ao)*, a white collar *(huling)*, red trousers, and high-soled, high-topped boots *(houdi xue)*.

Headdresses. As several head coverings can be worn with the *mang* robe, depending on the character and the situation, only a few of the prominent ones will be mentioned. The *mang* is generally worn with either a version of the *shamao* (lit. gauze hat, official's headdress) or one of a number of *kui* (helmets). The *zhongsha* (loyal hat), a style *of shamao* in black velvet with the double crown and wings *(chi)*, is often worn by the *sheng* roles who wear *mang* (Fig. 6.1). This combination reflects a Ming precedent, when the *shamao* was worn with official garments. The *xiangsha* (prime minister's hat) is an angular version of the *shamao* that is worn by prime ministers (Fig. 7.4). The *fenyang mao* (also a prime minister's headdress) is a golden filigree headdress resembling the same double crown as the first two headdresses, but it has wavy wings (Fig. 7.31). A filigree helmet that can be worn with the *mang* is the *fuzi kui* (four-pronged helmet), which has four upright pompoms flanked by wired circles of pearls (Fig. 6.55, worn with a *kao*).

Nümang (Female court robe)

Description and History. The *nümang* has two cuts, one with straight edges and a traditional shape, and another with an additional border that has a wavy edge. The straight-edged *nümang* is said to have developed from the male *mang* for traditional Jingju purposes. As with many of the women's costume robes, it reflects the men's form, only in a shorter length (Fig. 6.3). Onstage, the *nümang* is knee length, the side front extensions have been eliminated, and the side seams are open only to the hip. The newer design has an attached bor-

FIGURE 6.3. A straight-edged *nümang* may be worn by a *laodan,* here the example is the prime minister's wife. She has a cord tied at the waist and the gray *zongfa* hairstyle for older women, with a *leizi* ornamentation centered on her forehead. *The Red-Maned Fiery Steed (Hongzong liema).* Character: Madam Wang, actor: Zhai Mo. BJC, Beijing, China. October 6, 2001.

der of contrasting fabric with wavy edges around the hems and side seams, and a wide cuff on the hem of the sleeves (Fig. 6.4 and Appendix 1.15). An embroidered contrasting border, such as the one used to create the undulations on this robe, signifies higher social status. The wavy edges are usually blue and embroidered with images of cranes. Both versions of the *nümang* have sleeves longer than the wrists and long water sleeves.

Usage. The two styles of *nümang* have different uses. The straight-edged version is worn by mature women of the court of both higher and lower rank and by dowagers, standard wives, princesses, and concubines. These characters are played by *laodan* (mature women) and *qingyi* (young to middle-aged women). The wavy-edged *nümang* appears on younger women of higher rank who are connected with the emperor as wives, princesses, or

FIGURE 6.4. A high-ranking *qingyi* may wear a wavy-edged *nümang* with a jade belt and a phoenix headdress in scenes of the court. *The Red-Maned Fiery Steed (Hongzong liema)*. Character: Wang Baochuan, actor: Deng Min. BJC, Beijing, China. October 6, 2001.

concubines; they are played by *qingyi*. In the past, noble women might have worn a *guanyi* (official's robe), but those robes have been replaced by the *nümang*.

Color and Roles. There are fewer color options for the fabric of women's *nümang* than for the men's *mang*. The straight-edged style *nümang* comes in yellow for the empress, and red for high-ranking imperial concubines and ladies with titles. Olive-green, orange, bronze, yellow-green, and apricot straight-edged *nümang* are used for *laodan* roles to indicate the older important women, such as the dowager empress. The wavy-edged *nümang* comes in yellow for the empress and red for the queen consort, princesses, and concubines. A pink *nümang* can also be used for concubines who are skilled at dancing and singing.

The colors of embroidery on men's *mang* tend towards monochromatic, and the same holds true for the women's straight-edged *nümang*. Shades and tints of blue threads are used for the yellow, red, olive-green and orange straight-edged *nümang*. In contrast, the embroidery on wavy-edged *nümang* uses a wider spectrum of pretty colors. The difference can be explained by the surface images; the straight-edged robe is designed with dragons on the surface, while the wavy-edged *nümang* has phoenix designs. The phoenix, a very colorful bird, requires a multitude of colors (Fig. 5.7). Pastels, including pink, lavender, turquoise, green, and yellow, are generally used to portray the variegated feathers of the phoenix, although some versions are rendered in silver and gold exclusively. The colors of the feathers are repeated in the waves at the hem. The cranes in the blue border, however, are less brightly rendered and usually appear in metallic, black, white, and gray threads.

Ornamentation and Roles. The distribution of the design on the surface of the straight-edged *nümang* shares the scheme of the universe that appears on the men's *mang* with roundels. The men's robes have ten dragon roundels, but the women's wavy-edged *nümang* have only eight, for the ones on the lower sleeve have

been replaced with flowers, wave designs, and the contrasting cuff. Both styles of *nümang* have waves and mountains at the hem, although the band of water is not as wide on the *mang*. The straight-edged *nümang* robe also is embroidered with clouds and lucky symbols. While historically the actual empress would not have had the twelve symbols of sovereignty on her robe, the traditional Jingju *nümang* are decorated with the same kinds of lucky symbols used on male court costumes. The dowager empress wears a straight-edged robe with dragons on it to represent her position as the mother of the emperor. Wives of officials who serve the emperor are also entitled to wear dragon imagery. The phoenix appears on the surface of the wavy-edged *nümang* robe worn by the empress and imperial concubines. In legend, the dragon and the phoenix were lovers, so the phoenix, as the queen of birds, represents the empress. Although historically the phoenix was not used regularly on clothing for royal women, it was connected with feminine imagery and has now emerged as a standard design in traditional Jingju dress. Peonies, an emblem of feminine beauty, often adorn the rest of the surface of the wavy-edged *nümang*.

Accessories. The straight-edged *nümang* is worn with or without the cloud collar *(yunjian)* by the *laodan* and with the cloud collar by *qingyi*. When the *nümang* is worn with the cloud collar, a jade belt is also worn to indicate higher rank. If the character does not wear a cloud collar, a white collar fills in the neckline and a Buddhist rosary *(chaozhu)* encircles the neck. A cord is tied around the waist with this combination to indicate a lower rank. A cloud collar with deep-knotted and tasseled fringe and the jade belt are worn together with the wavy-edged *nümang*. *Laodan* roles wear a green or blue skirt *(chenqun)*, olive-green trousers, and *fuzi lü* (lit. "good fortune" shoes) in olive green with black trim and a raised sole to complete the set. *Qingyi* wear a pleated white skirt *(baizhe qun)*, pink trousers, and embroidered flat slippers *(caixie)*.

Hair and Headdresses. The *qingyi* wear the phoenix headdress *(fengguan)* with both styles of *nümang*. The phoenix headdress is a wide silver-filigree headdress with the look of kingfisher feathers inlaid in the phoenix ornaments, and it is scattered with pearls mounted on springs. Long tassels frame the face and short tassels cover the nape of the neck. It is worn over the *datou* (complete hair), which has flat curls on the forehead and long silk cords representing hair in the back (Fig. 7.27). When dowagers wear the higher-ranking version of the *nümang* robe with the jade belt, they wear another style of phoenix headdress. Smaller than the one worn by younger women, this version is gold filigree with pearls and no tassels. In the lower-ranking configuration with the cord belt, the *laodan* does not wear a crown. Instead she wears the *zongfa* (lit. "palm fiber" hair, a bun), surrounded by a scarf with a single pearl on the *leizi* (lit. "to tighten," black velvet piece) at the center of the forehead (Fig. 6.3).

Qimang (Manchu court robe)

Description and History. The cut and ornamentation of the *qimang* resembles the dragon robe worn by Manchu noblewomen late in the Qing dynasty at about the time when the *qimang* was incorporated into traditional Jingju costumes.[3] As with the historical version, the Jingju *qimang* is a full-length gown with a round neck, an S-curved closing that crosses over to the right, tubular sleeves, and a trapezoidal-shaped body. The side seams are slit to the hip. The historical dragon robe had wide, horseshoe-shaped cuffs popular during the regency period of Dowager Empress Cixi.[4] The sleeves of the *qimang* are finished with a broad horseshoe-shaped cuff that is stitched in place where the historical cuffs would have been folded up. The *qimang* does not have water sleeves. The cuff, the band that goes around the neckline, and the closing to the underarm are often made from a contrasting fabric. The schematic ornamentation on the surface of the *qimang* reflects the terrestrial designs on Qing dynasty *jifu,* though simplified for the stage (Fig. 6.5 and Appendix 1.13).

Usage. The *qimang* is worn by high-ranking *qingyi* in stories involving characters from ethnic groups other than Han Chinese. One of the plays performed most frequently that uses the *qimang* is *Silang Visits His Mother (Silang tan mu)* (BJC, Beijing, China. October 7, 2001). Silang is a Han general captured by northern barbarians who eventually marries the daughter of the empress of the foreign tribe. The dowager empress, Xiao Taihou, and Silang's wife, Princess Iron Mirror (Tiejing Gongzhu), both wear *qimang* in the court scenes of this play. The women characters who wear the *qimang* at court change into the *qipao* (Manchu gown) for more casual scenes (Fig. 6.52).

Color and Roles. The colors for *qimang* are different from those used in clothing representing Han people. An ethnic empress will wear a blue *qimang,* as the highest robe for foreigner royalty. A red *qimang* will be used for younger foreign princesses. The embroidery tends to use multicolored threads, but they are not as brilliantly colored as the threads in the phoenix designs on the *nümang* court robes.

Ornamentation and Roles. The surface of the *qimang* is embroidered with the same scheme of designs as the men's *mang* and uses waves, mountains, clouds, and lucky symbols. *Qimang* have only eight dragons, rather than ten, as the sleeves are shorter and cuffed. The contrasting borders are embroidered with a different design from the rest of the garment.

Accessories. As was true of the historical Qing dynasty women's dragon robe, the stage *qimang* are worn with a separate blue collar *(lingyi)* under the gown. It has a stiff standing band with a short falling collar that is rounded in the front. The collar attaches to a bib that reaches to the waist. A Buddhist rosary also encircles the neck. Since the *qimang* does not have water sleeves, the *qingyi* may carry a handkerchief to accentuate their

FIGURE 6.5. The Qing dynasty style *qimang* is worn with the *qitou* hairstyle and *huapen di* pedestal shoes by characters of non-Han origin. *The Red-Maned Fiery Steed (Hongzong liema).* Character: Daizhan Gongzhu, actor: unidentified. BJC, Beijing, China. October 6, 2001.

hand gestures. The *huapen di* (flowerpot sole shoes) worn with this robe have a tall pedestal in the middle of the arch (Fig. 6.66). The stage shoe reflects the genuine shoe Manchu women wore to give the impression of bound feet without actually reshaping the toes. Movement is affected by these supports, and women wearing these shoes walk with a swaying gait, swinging their arms. In the historical dress, the robe was long enough to conceal the feet so the illusion was complete, but on-stage, the robe has a shorter hem so that the pedestal is exposed. Straight-leg trousers are worn under this gown, as all women in China wore trousers regardless of their heritage.

Hair and Headdress. To complete the Manchu look of this ensemble, actresses wear the *qitou* (Manchu hair) with the *liangba tou* (lit. "two pieces of hair"), an "archway" or "big wings" shape made of satin black fabric mounted on the head. Large flowers, jewels, and tassels decorate the upper piece. Flat waves or curls are placed around the forehead, along with gemstones and small flowers (Figs. 6.5 and 6.52).

Gailiang mang (Reformed court robe)

Description and History. The introduction of the *gailiang mang* is attributed to Ma Lianliang (1901–1966), who was interested in a simpler look from ancient times. The cut of the *gailiang mang* is narrower than the standard *mang*, and the surface ornamentation has been reduced as well (Figs. 6.6 and 7.41).

Usage. The *gailiang mang* can be worn in informal scenes by *sheng* in the role of officials, current and retired.

Color and Ornamentation. The *gailiang mang* comes in maroon, black, olive green, beige, and other colors in the subdued range. The nature of the surface decoration indicates the level of importance. High officials may have a single large dragon embroidered on the chest and back or have an additional pair of walking dragons placed above the waves on the front and back. The simpler smooth dragons from archaic Chinese designs can be used for lower or retired officials. Clouds and other emblems are not depicted; instead, there are bands of embroidery around the neckline and sleeve hems. The waves may be standard size or reduced.

Accessories. Either a jade belt or a fitted cloth belt of matching fabric can be worn with the *gailiang mang*. High-topped, tall-soled boots are worn as well.

Headdress. The *gailiang mang* may be worn with a *zhongsha,* or one of the gold filigree hats appropriate for court, such as the *xiangdiao* (prime minister's hat) (Fig. 7.32).

Pi (Formal robe)

Description and History. The *pi* evolved from the *beizi* (symmetrical robe), which gained popularity during the Song dynasty (960–1279). The *beizi* was worn for nonofficial and informal events. It opened down the center front, had a narrow neckband that continued to the hem, and had wide sleeves. By the Ming dynasty, the neckband had shortened to mid-chest and grown wider, while the sleeves were narrower. The traditional Jingju *pi* resembles the Ming form of this garment; it has the same front closing, with a wide band going around the neck and then stopping at mid-chest, and tubular sleeves. The base of the neckband in the theatrical garments is straight across for *sheng* and *laodan*, but it is finished with a fungus-shaped arabesque *(ruyi tou)* for *qingyi*. A single frog or fabric tie at the bottom of the neckband closes the front. Cut without a shoulder seam, the body of the garment is slightly trapezoidal, side-vented, and the straight sleeves are longer than the wrists with water-sleeve extensions. The water sleeves of the *pi* for women are longer than those for the men. The men's *pi* is full length, but the women's is only knee length, as was true for historical clothing. The *pi* worn by young men and women is made of crepe, while ma-

FIGURE 6.6. The *gailiang mang* has a simplified version of the *mang* surface pattern. Here it is worn with a *zhongsha* headdress. *Lü Bu and Diaochan (Lü Bu yu Diaochan)*. Character: Wang Yun, actor: Li Jian. BJC, Beijing, China. July 15, 2000.

ture men and women may wear a *pi* made of satin (Fig. 6.7 and Appendix 1.2).

Usage. The *pi* is a formal garment that falls between the *mang* and the *xuezi*. It is considered more formal than the *xuezi* because symmetry is a higher form than asymmetry, but less important than the *mang*, which has more significant surface decoration. The *pi* robe is commonly worn for daytime wear at noncourt functions. When *laosheng* officials of high to middle rank

or gentry are off duty, they wear a *pi*. Young male roles wear a *pi* less often; one may don a yellow *pi* if he plays an emperor or a red *pi* if he is getting married or has achieved number-one-scholar ranking. *Jing* and *chou* rarely appear in the *pi*.

Color and Roles. The color range for *pi* follows the standard convention for color and character meanings. In addition to yellow being designated for the emperor and red for grooms (Fig. 1.20 and Table 6.23.B and 6.23.N), mature men of wealth and influence wear blue, maroon, olive green, or other neutral colors (Fig. 7.35 and Table 6.1.B and 6.1.N). Married couples usually appear in matching colors and surface ornamentation.

Ornamentation and Roles. As roundels are considered the highest form of design, the ten round designs found on the *mang* are also used on the *pi*, signifying status, dignity, and formality, qualities related to maturity as well. For the emperor, the *pi* will have ten dragon roundels. For *laosheng* roles, the roundels could be formed from geometric designs, flowers, or a *shou* (Chinese character for long life). A *shou* surrounded by five bats conveys a desire for the five happinesses as well: long life, wealth, tranquility, love of virtue, and achieving one's destiny before dying (Fig. 5.14).[5] The *xiaosheng* wedding *pi* has circular designs made from flowers, sometimes combined with geometric designs (Fig. 1.20 and Table 6.23.B and 6.23.N). Pairs of wedding robes are usually made at the same time at the factory so that the color and design both match.

Accessories. Because the *pi* closes with a single tie in the center front, a *xuezi* is worn underneath to fill the gap beneath the opening. *Xiaosheng* wear light-colored *xuezi* and red trousers, while *laosheng* wear darker colors. A white collar is put between the *xuezi* and the *pi*, so the neckline has a white inner layer. Both young and mature roles wear body padding and high-soled, high-topped boots.

Headdresses. The emperor wears a *huangmao* (yellow crown) made of filigree and decorated with pearls

FIGURE 6.7. A husband and wife often wear matching *pi/nüpi* in maroon, with roundel embroidery. His headdress is the *xiangjin. The Goddess of the Green Ripples (Bibo xianzi).* Character, female: Lady Jin, actor: unidentified. Character, male: Squire Jin, actor: unidentified. AMSCO, Beijing, China. April 28, 1996.

with his *pi.* For official functions, the *laosheng* and *xiaosheng* wear the *zhongsha* (seen in Figs. 6.1 and 6.23 with other garments). The *xiaosheng* will also wear the *zhongsha* for his wedding, or a *yawei jin* (ducktail hat) with a crescent of short fur from side to side over the crown (Fig. 1.3, worn with a *xuezi*). When not on duty, the *laosheng* puts on a *yuanwai jin* (soft square hat), which is worn with one of the creases at the center of

the forehead (Table 6.1.B , 6.1.N a and b), or one of the other soft hats such as the *xiangjin* (informal prime minister hat) (Fig. 6.7).

Nüpi (Female formal robe)

Description. The *nüpi* shares the history and characteristics of the *pi,* with a trapezoidal-shaped torso cut without a shoulder seam and reaching to the knee, and long straight sleeves. The water sleeves are generally longer on the *nüpi* than the *pi* (Appendix 1.3).

Usage. The *nüpi* is an important garment for the *qingyi* and the *laodan*, as they wear it for most scenes except the most formal court appearances. The *nüpi* is not worn by the *huadan* (lively young women), although it may be worn by *daoma dan* (lit. "sword and horse" women) in private quarters.

Color and Roles. *Qingyi* wear pastel and brighter-colored *nüpi* in the pink, blue, aqua, and green ranges, as well as pale yellow and white, to name a few (Fig. 6.8). They wear red for their weddings and then switch to darker colors once they are married (Fig. 1.20, Table 6.14.B and 6.14.N, and Fig. 1.8). When playing the empress in private quarters, they will wear a yellow *nüpi*. The *laodan* most often wear *nüpi* in maroon and olive green, and the color will correspond to the *pi* worn by their husband (Fig. 6.7).

Ornamentation and Roles. Young ladies wear crepe *nüpi* and mature women wear a *nüpi* of satin. The two styles are usually distinguished by different shapes in the collar bands, a straight ending for *laodan* and the fungus-shaped arabesque for *qingyi* (Fig. 5.4, Table 6.29.N b, and Appendix 1.3). The embroidery on the *pi* of a young *qingyi* tends to have more color, while that of the *laodan* has more gold or silver metallic couching. *Laodan* and married *qingyi* may wear *nüpi* with ten roundels on it. The empress's *nüpi* has ten rounded phoenix designs on it, the symbol for high-ranking imperial women. The dowager empress's *nüpi* has ten roundels as well, but hers include both the dragon and the phoenix in each circle, as she is both a queen and the mother of the emperor. Her collar also has the fungus-shaped arabesque at the bottom, though she is usually played by a *laodan*. A bride wears a red *nüpi* that has floral roundels and either a red or white skirt (Table 6.14.B and 6.14.N). After the marriage, the couple wears the matching ten-roundel robes almost exclusively when the *pi/nüpi* are the garments to be worn. The roundels can be embroidered in flowers or geometric designs. Widows wear a low-level *nüpi* in black, with round flowers, after the period of official mourning is over.

Young, unmarried women wear a *pi* with freely arranged floral fragments that represent their beauty and gentle ways. Scattered flowers in a balanced design are used for free-willed, outgoing characters, while symmetrical sprays indicate a more restrained young lady. The commonly used flowers are chrysanthemums, peonies, plum blossoms, orchids, and roses.

Accessories. A *xuezi* with the center-front closing is worn under the *nüpi* to fill the gap at the neck. A rhinestone pin is worn at the base of the *nüxuezi* collar. Young women generally wear a white skirt, while older women wear a green or blue skirt. Both also wear trousers underneath their skirts. The *laodan* wear *fuzi lü* with a lift, but flat shoes are worn by the *qingyi*.

Hair and Headdress. The empress wears a phoenix headdress with tiny ornate phoenixes and pearls, and long tassels in front of the ears. Her hair will be dressed in the *datou* style, with flat curls and jewels on the forehead. The headdresses of the dowager empress and other older women consists of a scarf and the *leizi*, which is worn exclusively by older women. The hair of the dowager empress will be gray or white and dressed in the round bun for older women. Young ladies and young married women have highly ornamented hairstyles, either the *datou* or *guzhuang tou* ("ancient-style" hair), each covered with elaborate bejeweled ornaments and flowers (Figs. 1.8 and 6.8).

Kao (Armor)

Description and History. Decorative armor with images of fierce beasts and complex layers and pieces has bedecked Chinese generals for years. Ming dynasty armor included multiple protective pieces and large animal representations at the shoulders and waist, while in

FIGURE 6.8. The *nüpi* for young, unmarried *qingyi* often has symmetrical flower embroidery. She wears a one-hundred-pleats skirt, and her hair is dressed in the *guzhuang tou* (lit. "ancient style"). Her costume is framed by white edges created by the collar, water sleeves, and skirt. *Hongniang (Hongniang)*. Character: Cui Yingying, actor: Tang Hexiang. NJC, Beijing, China. October 5, 2001.

the Qing dynasty, armor was made of padded fabric that was covered with metal studs. Both of these periods appear to have contributed influences to the current stage version of armor, although the traditional Jingju design has also clearly incorporated theatrical invention (Figs. 3.4–5, 6.9 and Appendix 1.16). The *kao* is constructed of thirty-one embroidered pieces. A tabard, with front and back sections left open on the sides, except for small tabs under the arms, comprises the main part of the garment. The tabard closes on one shoulder and at the wrists with frogs. The front of the *kao* has a wide padded section at the waist *(kaodu)* that adds to the overall scale of the character and helps to balance the shape, which is enlarged by the width of four pennants spreading behind the shoulders and head. The waist piece in the back is soft, conforming to the contour of the body; it is tied around the hips and connects to the front piece with tapes. Below the front and back waist are two layers of rounded aprons, the upper one reaching to the knees and the lower one to the ankles. This tabard unit also has sleeve pieces attached, with larger flaps that cover the shoulders and upper arm and a fitted inner sleeve that protects the lower arm sewn together as a single unit. The sleeves are set into the upper half of the armscye along with the shoulder flaps, but they are left open under the arm and only tacked together below the elbow. Beneath this main piece, leg flaps *(kaotui)* resembling chaps are worn. A matching collar piece encircles the neck, the same style worn by military characters in other garments. The four armor flags *(kaoqi)* are mounted on a stand with four poles and lashed to the actor's back. The ropes are concealed with a piece of red silk. Several theories exist on the inspiration for the flags. Flags are thought to have come from history, when generals would give a pennant to their messengers as a token of authority to verify messages. Some examples from historical images portray generals with small flags attached to their headdresses.[6] Another theory is that they represent the army behind the general, which

involves numbers far too great to appear onstage. The many moving parts of the *kao* increase the excitement in battle, for the flags and their streamers wave, and the skirt and leg flaps swirl to create a blur of color and movement.

Usage. High-ranking generals and military officers wear the *kao*, including *jing, laosheng, wuxiaosheng* (military young men) or *wusheng* (military men). The characters wearing the *kao* engage in battle with movements based on dance and the martial arts. They twirl and fight with poles and halberds, actions that permit them to fight upright primarily, although some scenes require the actor to perform a back flip despite the flags on the back.

There are two ways to wear a *kao*. When the flags are strapped onto the back, the garment becomes the *yingkao* (hard or complete armor) or *dakao* (big armor). The *yingkao* is worn by military officers of various ranks. When the flags are not worn, the armor is called *ruankao* (soft armor) and indicates either that the figure is not fully ready for battle or else is half-defeated.

In some scenes a *mang* can be worn over the *kao* (Fig. 1.2). One arm goes through its sleeve, but the other sleeve is folded to the inside. This allows the garment to reach around the additional bulk of the *kao* so it can be closed in the front. This combination of *mang* and *kao* signifies a ceremonial event prior to battle, such as selecting the soldiers who will fight in the front lines. While the wearing of *kao* with flags is an impressive image, the addition of the *mang* creates the most spectacular combination of costumes worn in traditional Jingju. In contrast, when a general loses a battle, he removes the flags and one sleeve of the *kao*. When completely defeated, the general removes his helmet and may take off all the pieces of his armor except for the leg flaps, which are worn over the *jianyi* and trousers (Fig. 8.2). A *magua* (riding jacket) may be added to this combination. This stripped-down costume is the image of despair.

Color and Roles. The *kao* comes in most of the

FIGURE 6.9. The *yingkao* has four flags strapped on the back, indicating a high official in battle dress. His headdress is a *zhajin ezi. Turning Aside the Iron Carts (Tiao huache).* Character: Gao Chong, actor: Wang Feng. ACTO, Beijing, China. June 2, 2002.

upper and lower colors, though yellow *kao* are rare, and light-blue and olive-green ones are not likely to be made for men. The color of the *kao* reveals information about the male wearer, and *jing* are assigned *kao* colors according to the colors of their painted face, as well as their personalities. Red *kao* are for the straightforward characters with a high rank in the military, including commander-in-chief. Green *kao* are worn by military *sheng* and more particularly by red-faced *jing* roles because of the Chinese preference for red and green together. Loyal generals wear white. A character in mourning wears a white *kao* with silver embroidery. The black *kao* is reserved for *jing* with aggressive or rude personalities indicated either by red or black face makeup. Young generals who are handsome and romantic sport a pink *kao*. Extraordinarily brave men wear a blue *kao*. Maroon *kao* are for *jing* with maroon painted faces and are usually high-ranking generals. The color of the *kao* carries more significance than the surface design in determining what a character will wear.

Ornamentation and Roles. The centers of the front and back pieces on the chest and the aprons are embroidered with either the fish-scale design from historical armor or an interlocking three-pronged geometric shape, also seen on historical armor (Fig 3.5). The edges of these pieces can be embroidered with a border of waves or the ancient style of smooth dragons depicted without scales. A long-life character is often embroidered on the chest over the heart for protection (Figs. 2.11, 5.14, and 8.7). The padded waist piece showcases dragons or tigers (Fig. 4.11). The animals can be in pairs facing each other, or there can be a single large, forward-facing image that fills the space. The center point of the knee-length apron flap has an animal emblem: a lion's head on a fish body, dragons, or two fishes (Fig. 5.5). The leg flaps are embroidered on the inside as well as the outside because all surfaces are exposed in the heat of battle (Fig. 2.11). Guan Yu has a special *kao* created specifically for his character, made in green fabric, with red and gold peacock embroidery. The edges of the segmented pieces are sometimes fringed *(Zhuge Liang Leaves His Thatched Roof Study for the First Time) (Chuchu maolu)* (NJC, Beijing, China. October 4, 2001) (Fig. 6.55). Xiang Yu, the king who faces certain defeat in *The Hegemon King Says Farewell to His Concubine (Bawang bie ji)*, has a black *kao* with a row of thick, knotted fringe sewn below the front of the padded waistband (BIBOAP, Beijing, China, July 10, 2000).

Accessories. The *kao* is worn with the padded vest underneath to increase the scale and presence of the figure. Generally, men wear red trousers under their *kao*. Because the *kao* has no sides, the garments worn underneath may be visible to the audience when the character spins in a battle scene. Male characters sometimes wear a *jianyi* underneath, if they must change quickly.

Otherwise they may put on a dark-colored water jacket *(Shui yizi)*, to create a dark shadow under the *kao,* as well as absorb perspiration. The white collar fills in the round neck. All men in *kao* wear high-soled, high-topped boots.

Headdress. Filigree helmets, such as the *zhajin ezi* (lit. "tied cloth" helmet with *ezi,* lit. "forehead," here implying a diadem), with rows of pompoms and pearls encircling the face (Fig. 6.9), and the *fuzi kui*, with pompoms mounted on four upright wires behind, are worn with the *kao* (Fig. 6.55). The headdress is usually flat in back so that it does not get entangled with the flags, and the front is decorated with pompoms and pearls mounted on springs to enhance movement. Some headdresses also have tassels hanging in front of the ears. The color of the pompoms and tassels coordinates with the color of the *kao*. Many helmets also have six-foot-long pheasant feathers *(lingzi)* attached on either side of the face.

Nükao (Female armor)

Description. The *nükao* resembles the men's version of armor, although it has a narrower padded belt, two additional layers of multicolored pastel streamers in the skirt area, and sometimes matching multicolored bands on the lower sleeves. It is worn with a more elaborate, larger cloud collar, which has deep, knotted fringe around the lower edge. All of the edges of the *nükao* and the lower edges of the streamers are fringed (Fig. 6.10 and Appendix 1.17).

Usage. *Daoma dan*, the highest-ranking women warriors, wear the *nükao* for important battles. The *daoma dan* engage in energetic combat involving complicated martial arts with weapons and swirling movements. The *nükao* is generally worn with the flags on the back, and the ropes that tie them on are covered with decorative silk rosettes. For ceremonial occasions, women generals also wear the *nümang* over the *nükao*.

FIGURE 6.10. The *nükao* has additional tabs to form a skirt for *daoma dan*. The headdress is a *qixing ezi*. The red tasseled stick in her right hand indicates her mount. *Mu Ke Stockade (Mu Ke zhai)*. Character: Mu Guiying, actor: Li Guangfu. ACTO, Beijing, China. June 1, 2002.

Color and Roles. *Nükao* are most commonly constructed in red and pink. In *Women Generals of the Yang Family (Yang men nü jiang)* (NJC, Beijing, China. October 3, 2001), when the widowed women in the household volunteer to fight, a wide range of beautiful pastel *nükao* fill the stage. An olive-green *kao* is used for the rare elderly woman warrior.

Ornamentation and Roles. Rather than the animals and geometric designs used for the men's *kao*, multicolored phoenixes and peonies are embroidered on the padded belt section of the female generals' armor, and beautiful flowers are used for the borders and streamers. The central chest and apron sections usually have a fish-scale pattern (Fig. 3.9).

Accessories. Women generals wear padded vests, pink trousers, white skirts, and flat-soled, ankle-high boots *(baodi xue)* or embroidered slippers.

Hair and Headdresses. The *qixing ezi* (lit. seven-star forehead helmet) is often worn with the *nükao*. It is a filigree diadem decorated with pearls and pompoms, with long, multiple tassels on either side of the face, usually augmented with long pheasant feathers. Women generals wear the *datou* hairstyle, with rows of flat curls and gems on the forehead (Fig. 6.10).

Gailiang kao (Reformed armor) and Gailiang nükao (Reformed female armor)

Description and History. The *gailiang kao* was designed by the actor Zhou Xinfang in the twentieth century.[7] Originally it was created to enable actors to wear battle gear under a robe. Designed for theatre but with history in mind, it resembles the segmented, layered armor of the dynastic styles, as well as the *kao* design. The shapes of the layered pieces are similar to those of the *kao*, retaining the look of defense, while slimming and streamlining the form to facilitate movement in martial arts scenes (Figs. 6.11, 7.12, and Appendix 1.18). The rounded collar for the male version, the cloud collar for the female garment, and the shoulder flaps and sleeves are quite close to the design of the *kao*. The key distinctions are the absence of the four flags on the back and the padded belt at the front waist. The *gailiang kao* also has much greater variation than the *kao* in the shapes of the layered pieces. The jacket has either a center-front opening or a crossover flap to the right side and shares the shoulder, armscye, and sleeve construction of the *kao*. The peplum, cut without a waist seam, can either be a part of the decorative layering or plain and covered by the leg flaps. The greatest deviations in shape occur below the waist where the panels may take on various profiles. The lower sections generally include two or three full-length, trapezoidal leg flaps

on the sides and back, and shorter rounded layers in the front and back. These pieces are mounted on two waistbands that tie around the waist. The shaped segments of the torso and apron panels are all edged with fringe. A shaped belt completes the ensemble. The female version has essentially the same overall look, but with different colors and embroidery designs.

Usage. The *gailiang kao* can be worn by male and female generals or members of the entourage. When acrobatic movements require more mobility, the *gailiang kao* may be worn to facilitate action. The roles most likely to wear the *gailiang kao* are the *laosheng, wusheng, jing,* and *wudan* in supporting roles. Characters about to die may remove one sleeve of the *gailiang kao* jacket to indicate that they have been wounded.

Color and Roles. The male garments are usually made from the upper colors of red, green, white, and black, as well as blue, and are likely to be decorated with gold couching to simulate the effect of armor. The *gailiang nükao* comes in pastel colors, with a similar range of colors for the embroidery.

Ornamentation and Roles. The *gailiang kao* can be heavily embroidered in designs similar to those of the *kao*, with scales in the central sections and water designs on the borders. Other examples have lucky symbols and geometric borders. Dimensional tiger heads found in historical precedents often decorate the shoulders and waistband. The arabesques on the edges of the layers vary and may include fish-tail shapes at the lower peak in the front. The *gailiang nükao* usually has floral rather than animal motifs but may also utilize geometric patterns and scales. The leg flaps of both versions have embroidery inside on the linings for additional visual interest when the character is in motion.

Accessories. The *gailiang kao* is worn with matching-color trousers and high-soled, high-topped boots for men or flat-soled, ankle-high boots for women. The female warriors usually have an additional silk rosette decoration on the center front of the cloud collar. A

FIGURE 6.11. The *gailiang nükao*, worn by women warriors, is smaller than the *nükao* to facilitate movement, and it is decorated with flowers. Male warriors may wear a similar *gailiang kao*, with animal imagery. Her headdress is a butterfly helmet *(hudie kui)*. *At the Mouth of the River at Jiujiang (Jiu jiang kou)*. Character: low-ranking general, actor: unidentified. PRSCJ, Beijing, China. April 23, 1996.

curved, round, shiny disk, called a heart-protecting mirror *(huxin baojin)*, is sometimes worn at chest height with the *gailiang kao* (Fig. 6.27 worn with a *hua jianyi)*.

Headdress. Both male and female characters wear a helmet with a crest of furry balls and pearls framing the face, tassels or streamers on either side of the face, and pheasant feathers. The female warriors may wear a butterfly helmet *(hudie kui)*, which has a large butterfly on the crown (Fig. 6.11). The tassels and furry balls on the headdress complement the color of the garments. A flap of material embroidered to match the garment covers the back of the neck.

Xuezi (Informal robe)

Description and History. The *xuezi* is a simple, geometrically cut robe that can be traced at least to a Song dynasty garment, the *jiaoling pao* (long robe). The *jiaoling pao* was worn for daily wear, and the *xuezi* is worn for the same purpose onstage. The front and back are cut in a single, floor-length, flared piece, with a fold on the shoulder. The wide sleeves are straight, longer than the wrists, and have water sleeves at the hem. The *xuezi* ties closed under the right arm, and the side seams are vented to the waist. The distinctive feature of the *xuezi* robe comes from the straight crossover closing to the right, which is finished with a wide straight band. In addition, the right side of the neckband of the *xuezi*, unlike the left, drops straight down from the neck, so the fronts are not symmetrical (Fig. 6.12 and Appendix 1.4).

Usage. The *xuezi* is the most widely used garment because in its many forms it can be worn by almost all the characters in traditional Jingju, male, female, rich, and poor, and for almost any event outside of the formal court and battle scenes. Both a young, well-to-do scholar and a peasant will wear a *xuezi* for everyday use. It is the variations in color, fabric, cut, and surface embellishment that determine the different forms that the

xuezi can take. The *xuezi* can also be worn in different ways for further versatility, belted or unbelted, sleeves on the arms or off, and the front open or closed. Additional costume pieces can be added to the *xuezi* for other looks, including vests or an overskirt. The *su xuezi* (plain *xuezi*) is also a universal inner garment worn under the other robes, including the *mang* and the *pi*.

Color, Ornamentation, and Roles. The *xuezi* for each of the role types and circumstances is distinguished by its color and ornamentation, which conform to the conventions of traditional Jingju dress. Five types of *xuezi* are described to indicate a representative sample.

Xiaosheng hua xuezi (xiaosheng flowered xuezi). *Xiaosheng* wear a *hua xuezi* most of the time when they are at home or at large in a nonofficial capacity (Figs. 1.3 and 6.12). The *xiaosheng hua xuezi* are made of silk crepe and come in a range of pastel colors, lake blue, green, lavender, and pink, with pink being reserved for those who are handsome and romantically inclined. The other colors are not assigned specific meaning or circumstances and can be used by this role type for a wide range of scenes. The *xiaosheng hua xuezi* is embroidered with a garden of pretty flowers, with chrysanthemums, peonies, plum blossoms, and roses most commonly used. A geometric pattern entwined with flowers often decorates the neckband. Additional floral designs occur outside around the neckband and on the left side near the hem front and back. Men rarely wore garments with floral designs in actual Chinese dress, so this development for the traditional Jingju male characters seems to be based on a theatrical choice to beautify their clothing.

If the characters are impoverished, then the embroidery only occurs in the area on and around the neckband, called a double collar pattern. The flowers on such a *xuezi* are usually plum blossoms, to imply nobility. In even more impoverished circumstances, the *xuezi* will have embroidery only on the collar band or will be completely plain (Table 6.19.B and 6.19.N).

FIGURE 6.12. The *xiaosheng hua xuezi* has floral embroidery around the neck and on the opposite hem. He is also wearing a *qiaoliang jin* headdress. *Hongniang (Hongniang)*. Character: Zhang Junrui, actor: Song Xiaochuan. NJC, Beijing, China. October 5, 2001.

Headdresses and Accessories for *Xiaosheng hua xuezi*. The headdresses worn with the *xiaosheng hua xuezi* are soft folding hats of either matching fabric and embroidery or of a solid color. The matching hat can be a *xiaosheng jin (xiaosheng* hat), with a crest ridge from ear to ear with fungus-shaped arabesques on the end (similar to Figs. 6.13 and 7.34 without the tassels and flame at the crest), or a broad gable from front to back, the *qiaoliang jin* (bridge hat) (Fig. 7.36). The *yawei jin* has a semicircular crest of black fur from ear to ear (Fig. 1.3). Some of these headdresses may have a small piece of white jade *(maozheng)* over the center of the forehead when worn by a *xiaosheng*. The *xiaosheng* wear light padding, a white collar, high-soled, high-topped boots, and light trousers, often pink or blue.

Wuxiaosheng hua xuezi (wuxiaosheng* flowered *xuezi). Young men in martial roles wear *wuxiaosheng hua xuezi* made of satin, with surface designs that often contain more metallic threads than the *xiaosheng hua xuezi*. The *wuxiaosheng hua xuezi* is usually in either strong colors or white. In contrast to the asymmetrical embroidery on the civil *hua xuezi*, the martial version for *wuxiaosheng*, worn by high-ranking young generals, has borders of flowers around the vents and across the front and back hems, as well as around the neckline and at the base of the sleeves. Another *wuxiaosheng hua xuezi* for high-status characters has ten flower roundels in the typical locations, one at the chest and two at the knees front and back, and two on each sleeve and an embroidered border (Fig. 6.13). *Jing* may also wear a satin martial *hua xuezi* in bold upper colors, with couched roundels and border design.

Headdresses and Accessories for *Wuxiaosheng hua xuezi*. The *wuxiaosheng* wear a version of the *xiaosheng jin*-style headdress worn by young scholars called a *wusheng jin* (military male hat). The outline of the hat is the same, but with the addition of tassels hanging from the arabesques on either side and a decorative flame-shaped ribbon at the crest of the crescent. A hel-

FIGURE 6.13. The *wuxiaosheng hua xuezi* may be embroidered with ten flower roundels and a floral border. The headdress is a *wusheng jin*. *The Gathering of Heroes (Qunying hui)*. Character: Zhou Yu, actor: Li Hongtu. BJC, Beijing, China. July 23, 2000.

met combining filigree and fabric, called the *jiangjin*, may also be worn with the *wuxiaosheng hua xuezi* with roundels (Fig 6.21, worn with a *kai chang*).

Hualian hua xuezi (hualian* flowered *xuezi). Bold, uninhibited martial *jing* can wear a *hualian hua xuezi* (*hualian* being another word for *jing*) opened like a coat over another garment or thrown over the shoulders. For these characters, the *hualian hua xuezi* is often black and decorated with a scattered pattern of birds or butterflies, indicating the wearer's agility and strength, or a dispersed arrangement pattern of clouds (Fig. 6.14). In addition, these robes may be embroidered on the inside so that another design shows when it falls open.

Headdress and Accessories for *Hualian hua xuezi*. A helmet style of headdress can be worn with these *xuezi*, or a *zongmao* (lit. "mane hat"), a tall truncated cone of sheer black mesh. With the *hualian hua xuezi* worn open, the characters wear a robe such as the *jianyi*, a padded vest, and high-soled, high-topped boots.

Wenchou hua xuezi (wenchou* flowered *xuezi). *Wenchou* wear their *hua xuezi* when they are portraying petty officials, disreputable sons of higher-ranking officials, or other characters of rank who lack scruples. The *wenchou hua xuezi* come in harsh colors, including fuchsia and a green that is different from the pure green, and they are decorated with scattered ornaments, flowers, lucky symbols, or other motifs. The *wenchou* may wear *hua xuezi* that are shorter than those worn by other characters to draw attention to their lesser stature (Figs. 6.15 and 7.38).

Headdress and Accessories for *Wenchou hua xuezi*. *Wenchou* may wear a cord belt over the *hua xuezi* to cinch the waist. A soft hat, often the *heye jin* (lotus-leaf hat) covers the head (Fig. 6.15). It is a small cube shape, with a larger square of fabric placed on the top so that it hangs over on all four edges. Another soft hat worn by *chou* is the *bangchui jin* (lit. "wooden club" hat) with a pinched crown and leaf-shaped wings in the back (Fig. 7.38). These characters wear boots with shorter sole heights *(chaofang)* and a white collar. *Chou* do not wear padding.

***Su xuezi* (plain *xuezi*).** The *xuezi* also has many lives in an unembroidered version called a *su xuezi*. Some of these *su xuezi* may also be shorter in length or be lacking water sleeves as other indicators of the wearer's poverty. The different colors of plain gowns have particular functions.

***Su xuezi* Color, Headdresses, Accessories, and Roles.** The *su xuezi* may be worn by both older and

FIGURE 6.14. The *hualian hua xuezi* is worn open in this example, with a scattered pattern of butterflies. The headdress is a *zongmao*. *Li Kui Visits His Mother (Li Kui tan mu)*. Character: Li Kui, actor: Chen Zhenzhi. NJC, Beijing, China. April 27, 1996.

younger men. For lower-status *laosheng*, the *su xuezi* robe can be "rice color," maroon, dark blue, olive green, gray, blue, or brown, for example (Fig. 6.16). The trousers will be in a related color range and worn with low-soled shoes, similar to those for *laodan*. A black *su xuezi* with a white collar band represents poverty for ordinary people, such as a failed Confucian scholar. Such characters may also wear it with a cord tied at the waist. A black *su xuezi* with a black velvet collar *(haiqing xuezi)* can be worn by an assortment of household servants. A wide, firm, orange-colored sash *(luandai)*, about three

FIGURE 6.15. The *hua xuezi* for *wenchou* usually has a scattered pattern. This *chou* wears his contained by a tasseled waist cord. The hat is a *heye jin*, and his boots are unembroidered *chaofang*. The beard is a hanging, dangling beard *(diao da)*. *The Gathering of Heroes (Qunying hui)*. Character: Jiang Gan, actor: Ma Zengshou. BJC, Beijing, China. July 23, 2000.

yards in length with long tasseled ends, often accompanies this style, along with a *ying luomao* (upright hexagonal black fabric hat) (Table 6.3.B). The *laodou yi* style of *su xuezi* is worn by destitute elderly men and women, *laodou* being a scornful name for old people on the lower edge of society.[8] Ivory-colored, the *laodou yi* hue is described as "rice color." It may be worn with a string belt or sash (Fig. 6.17). The hem of the *laodou yi* style of

xuezi is folded up when the waist cinch is applied so that the reduced length creates a disheveled look that reinforces the perception of poor circumstances. The trousers may be tucked into white sock-like gaiters *(baibu dawa)*, worn with flat or low-soled shoes *(daxie)*. The foot coverings may also be straw sandals *(caoxie)*. A soft white felt hat *(zhanmao)* with a pompom or a straw hat brim *(caomao quan)* may be worn for the headdress.

Nüxuezi (Female informal robe)

Description and History. A *nüxuezi* with the same asymmetrical cut as the men's robe is worn by elderly and poor women (Fig. 6.16). As with other women's garments, the *nüxuezi* is knee length and worn with a skirt. Younger and slightly higher-ranking women wear a second form of *nüxuezi*. As it would be unseemly for dignified women to appear in a garment with even a slightly lowered neckline that does not button tightly, this type of *nüxuezi* has a standing band collar and a center-front closing secured with frogs (Fig. 6.18 and Appendix 1.5). A similarly shaped knee-length robe with tubular sleeves and a standing band collar was worn by women in the Ming dynasty. This garment was introduced into the traditional Jingju wardrobe in the first half of the twentieth century. Other than the neck and opening, the two stage versions of the *nüxuezi* are essentially the same, with a slightly flared body and long straight sleeves with water sleeves attached. As with other robes, the women's water sleeves are longer than the men's.

Usage. These two garments actually look quite dissimilar and are worn by different characters, but they are both worn for informal daily life and can indicate poverty. The crossover *nüxuezi* appears on older women who are not well off. Young ladies of common families or who have lost their husbands and income may wear the center-front opening *nüxuezi*. It may also be worn in casual circumstances or as an alternative to the *nüpi*.

Color, Ornamentation, and Roles. The center-front opening *nüxuezi* has different embroidery and borders for a variety of uses. When this cut of *nüxuezi* has a symmetrical floral fragment on the front, back, and sleeves, it may be worn by higher-ranking women as an outer garment (Fig. 2.3, left, and Table 6.13.B and 6.13.N). This style of *nüxuezi* also comes in a wider range of pretty colors so it can be used as a foundation under higher-status women's *nüpi*. The hem is slightly shorter than the other robes so that it does not hang below the outer garment. A jeweled pin is worn at the neck when that area shows. Generally, the inner-garment version of the *nüxuezi* has borders of flowers embroidered around all the edges, necklines, collar, and hems. This same cut can be worn by lower-ranking women as an outer garment, in which case the simple design projects the wearer's lower social status. The lower five colors are used for this style, particularly blues. A low-ranking woman in the palace will wear this style of *nüxuezi* with a cloud collar to dress it up. A woman in mourning wears a white version of this style, with only white lotus flower embroidery. Although mourning dress was not allowed to have adornment in real life, the theatrical version has modified this regulation.

An even lower form of dress is the plain black *nüxuezi* with blue borders and white piping. Called *qingyi* (black clothing), this garment gave *qingyi* their name because several characters in this role type are assigned this garment. Women who are dignified, although they come from poor families or have fallen into reduced circumstances may wear this type of *nüxuezi*. A variation on the borders comes with the introduction of a fungus-shaped arabesque at the front waist and top of the side vents. The colors may also vary on this *nüxuezi* now as well, with gray, blue, and dull green versions being made to express more distinctions among the characters who wear this garment. The plain-bordered *nüxuezi* is worn with a plain white skirt with matching contrasting borders, trousers, and flat shoes. This *nüxuezi* may also be worn with a sash *(yao jinzi)* at the waist, a further sign of poverty (Fig. 6.18).

Young women may wear the *nü su xuezi* to indicate lower status. The *laodan su xuezi* follows the crossover cut of the male *su xuezi*, but with a shorter hem. It is usually constructed in maroon, olive green, and other typical colors for older women (Fig. 6.16). The rice-colored *nü laodou yi* is used for the very poor (Fig. 6.19). The *laodan su xuezi* and *nü laodou yi* are worn with a

FIGURE 6.16. The unembroidered *su xuezi/laodan su xuezi* is used for both male and female poor characters. *Tears in the Wild Mountains (Huangshan lei)*. Characters: Gao Mu and Gao Fu, actors: unknown. PRSCJ, Beijing, China. April 24, 1996.

plain green or dark blue skirt and may be cinched with a cord belt or a scarf sash. A more destitute character may wear her skirt on the outside, with a scarf tied at the waist. Elderly women wear only one layer of these robes, so the white collar is worn underneath to fill in the neckline area. Their trousers are usually olive green, and they wear *fuzi lü* with raised soles.

Hair and Headdress. Regardless of how low a young woman's circumstances drop, she retains her beauty in her hair ornaments. The scale and number of decorations is reduced, but they are still lovely. With some of these *nüxuezi*, a woman may wear a scarf that partially conceals the jewels, and with the *qingyi nüxuezi*, a woman may have no rhinestones or flowers at all, but wear only silver hairpins (Fig. 6.18). *Laodan* wear white or gray hair covered with a scarf. Their sole ornamentation is a single pearl on the *leizi*, worn at the center of the forehead (Fig. 6.19).

Fugui yi (Garment of wealth and nobility)

Description and History. The *fugui yi* is ironically called the garment of wealth and nobility. Although it is covered in patches and worn by those in impoverished circumstances, it nevertheless projects the audience's wish that the character will come to better times. The men's form of the garment is the same as the *xuezi,* with the trapezoidal body, elongated rectangular sleeves, and crossover diagonal closing, with a band at the neck that can be white or black with white piping around the edge. The body of the garment is black silk crepe and, as with other lower-status garments, it does not feature embroidery. Instead, the *fugui yi* is distinguished by multicolored three- and four-sided silk scraps, a stylized version of the patched clothing of the poor. The female garment adds the patches to the *qingyi xuezi*, which closes in the center front with a small standing collar that has a narrow blue border applied around the edges. Mei Lanfang introduced this garment for the character of Han Yuniang in *A Sorrow that Transcends Life and Death (Sheng si hen)* (BJC, Beijing, China. July 30, 2000) (Fig, 6.20). The women's patched garment does not share the aspiration for a better future signified with the men's *fugui yi*.[9]

Usage. Usually the characters wearing this garment are only temporarily in a penniless state and are viewed sympathetically by the audience. They are often *xiaosheng* whose fortunes have taken a turn for the worse, or *qingyi* wives whose husbands have been absent for a long time. Although the audience (and the characters) hope that the character's circumstances will improve by the end of the story, in some plays the reverse occurs, and a character starts with higher status that is lost by the conclusion of the play. Because this garment is con-

FIGURE 6.17 The *laodou yi* represents destitute elderly characters. The elderly *chou* role wears it with a blue pleated skirt, straw sandals, and a straw hat brim. *Zhuge Liang Leaves His Thatched Roof Study for the First Time (Chuchu maolu)*. Character: Lao Nong (old peasant), actor: Jin Lishui. NJC, Beijing, China. October 4, 2001.

sidered lucky, tradition says that it is to be stored on top of the other costumes in the trunks, but a practical reason for this arrangement is that the *fugui yi* is placed on top to protect the more valuable costumes with metallic threads.[10]

Color. The *fugui yi* was originally made in black, but

FIGURE 6.18. The black clothing *nüxuezi* gives the *qingyi* role type their name. This example wears it with a scarf tied outside, indicating her meager circumstances. Her hair is simply adorned with silver ornaments. *The Red-Maned Fiery Steed (Hongzong liema)*. Character: Wang Baochuan, actor: Deng Min. BJC, Beijing, China. October 6, 2001.

FIGURE 6.19. *(Left)* The *nü laodou yi* is worn by destitute elderly women. *A Sorrow that Transcends Life and Death (Sheng si hen)*. Character: Li Yu, actor: Ye Ping. BJC, Beijing, China. July 30, 2000.

FIGURE 6.20. *(Right)* The poorest characters are dressed in the patched *fugui yi*. *A Sorrow that Transcends Life and Death (Sheng si hen)*. Character: Han Yuniang, Actor: Li Huifang. BJC, Beijing, China. July 30, 2000.

can now appear in several colors, including blue, maroon, and off-white.

Ornamentation. It would not be appropriate for a beggar to appear truly ragged or dirty onstage. In keeping with the basic desire for everything in traditional Jingju to be beautiful, this costume is made of silk and carefully embellished with colorful silk patches. In real life, patches are used to cover stains or rends, and so one usually makes an attempt to have the color of the patches blend with the color of the original garment. In the costume version, however, a bolder choice stylizes that reality and exaggerates for stage purposes. In earlier times, each patch stood for an amount of money, so the more patches on the garment, the more money the wearer would be able to accumulate later.

Accessories. The women wear flat-soled shoes and may tie a scarf around their waist. Men wear shoes with only a slightly raised sole.

Hair and Headdress: The male character wearing the *fugui yi* wears a soft, black hat. The *qingyi* wear a simpler version of the *datou* hairstyle, with fewer ornaments than usual, and a scarf tied around the crown. The decorations may be silver or pearl instead of rhinestones to reduce the glitter, but the concept of beauty keeps the women from being entirely unadorned.

The Long Costumes

Following the four major costumes, the remaining garments are generally referred to simply as clothing, and are divided into four categories, long, short, specialty, and accessories. The long costumes reach from the shoulder to the knee for women's clothing or to the ankle for men's garments. The women's robes for the most part are worn with skirts, though the robes and skirts are not always made as a set. For this reason, skirts are considered separately, in the section on accessories.

Kai chang (Open robe)

Description and History. The *kai chang* is a traditional Jingju-developed garment that blends the cut of the *mang* and the *xuezi*. The hybrid form is a logical combination as the *kai chang* falls between ceremonial and leisure wear in usage.[11] As with the other long robes, the *kai chang* has a trapezoidal-shaped body and long rectangular sleeves with water sleeves (Fig. 6.21 and Appendix 1.20). The front neckline resembles the *xuezi*, with a straight crossover closing to the right finished with a wide straight collar band. The sides and back are taken from the *mang* cut; the fronts lap over the back at the side seams with extensions tied to the center back of the neck. The *kai chang* is distinctive because of an undulating edge on the front and back hems. The *kai chang* receives its name from the habit, sometimes employed by coarser characters, of wearing it open and thus allowing for easy removal in combat.

Usage. The *kai chang* is worn for informal or private occasions by *wusheng* and *jing* as high-ranking officials, such as chancellors, advisors, military strategists, and generals. With different ornamentation, it may also be worn by civilian *laosheng*.

Color and Roles. The *kai chang* is made in the upper colors, as well as maroon and blue. Civilian and military officials wear white; red is for *laosheng*; and black is worn by uncivilized characters such as Zhang Fei from the Three Kingdoms saga *Zhuge Liang Leaves his Thatched Roof Study for the First Time (Chuchu maolu)* (NJC, Beijing, China. October 4, 2001). In some versions of the *kai chang*, a contrasting color fabric border with an undulating edge surrounds the hem and continues into the opening on the right front and up around the neckband, as well as the extensions. This border has different embroidered designs from the rest of the robe, often geometric or symbolic. The presence of a contrasting border indicates a higher social status, because two pieces of embroidered fabric are more valued than having all the embroidery on a single piece.[12]

Ornamentation and Roles. For military generals played by *jing*, the *kai chang* will have large powerful animals on the surface, including lions, tigers, leopards, elephants, and the *qilin* (Chinese unicorn), as well as incense burners, calligraphic characters, and geometric designs. The gold couched embroidery can be quite bold, with one large rampant animal stretching the length of the garment, or two smaller creatures arranged opposing each other (Fig. 1.19). The *kai chang* of important *wusheng* may have smaller lions in ten roundels spaced symmetrically on the surface. Ten circular motifs with flowers, usually chrysanthemums or orchids, or geometric designs are used on the *kai chang* of high-ranking civilian officials. The *wusheng* and civilian *kai chang* are embroidered primarily in colors with metallic accents (Fig. 6.21).

Accessories. The *kai chang* is worn with high-soled, high-topped boots and the padded vest, along with the white inner collar. The trousers are usually red.

Headdress. The *kai chang* can be worn with either a soft matching fabric hat, such as the informal prime minister's hat *(xiangjin)* (Fig. 6.7, worn with a *pi*), or a filigree helmet with pompoms or a helmet, such as the *jiangjin* (general's cap) (Fig. 6.21).

FIGURE 6.21. The *kai chang* for *sheng* roles has embroidered borders and roundels, in this case, lions. This headdress is a *jiangjin*, and the beard is a *sanliu ran* (three-part beard). *Zhuge Liang Leaves His Thatched Roof Study for the First Time (Chuchu maolu)*. Character: Liu Bei, actor: Huang Bingqiang. NJC, Beijing, China. October 4, 2001.

Guanyi (Official robe)

Description and History. The *guanyi* comes from the official robe worn by officers of the court in the Ming dynasty. The Ming version was made from a brocade, but in traditional Jingju, the *guanyi* fabric is satin. The cut reflects the original robe, as well as the *mang* costume, for it has a round neckline and curved crossover closing to the right (Figs. 1.13, 6.22, and Appendix 1.1). The front and back are made in one piece, without a shoulder seam. The armscye seams are straight lines placed at the width of the fabric. The square-cut loose sleeves are longer than the wrist and have water sleeves attached at the hem. The body of the *guanyi* is trapezoidal, with side seams open almost to the underarm. The fronts are finished at the side seams with extensions made from a contrasting color. These flaps are stiffened at the top, worn overlapping the back piece, and secured at the center back at the neck with a tie and loop. The *buzi* (rank badge), used in the Ming and Qing dynasties, appears at the front and back of the *guanyi* at chest height. The size, shape, and ornamentation of the stage *buzi* resemble the Qing rank badges (Fig. 5.8).

Usage. When the emperor and the uppermost men of rank at court wear *mang,* the middle-ranked civil and military officers appear in *guanyi,* though military *guanyi* are rarely seen. Occasionally, the *guanyi* can indicate a character who has recently passed the imperial examinations for civil service.[13] Infrequently, a *laodan* may wear an olive-green *guanyi.*

Color and Roles. Color was an important factor historically in expressing the nine ranks of the officers of the court. Onstage, the ranks are designated with red and maroon indicating the upper ranks, and blue for the lower-ranking officers. The use of red and blue reflects the system used by Ming dynasty, except for the Ming inclusion of green robes for the lowest ranks.[14] A black *guanyi*, also called *qing guanyi* (dark *guanyi*) or *qingsu* (plain black), is worn by those in service positions outside the ranking system and can therefore ap-

FIGURE 6.22. This red *guanyi* has an animal on the *buzi*, indicating the *laosheng* wearer's military status, and is worn with a black jade belt and the typical *zhongsha* headdress. *The Gathering of Heroes (Qunying hui).* Character: Gan Ze, actor: unidentified. BJC, Beijing, China. July 23, 2000.

pear without the *buzi*. The *qingsu* may also be worn by officials recently removed from their offices, defeated generals, or removed officials waiting for interrogation. In traditional Jingju, selection of the color for a character's *guanyi* seems to take precedence over the image on the rank badge.

Ornamentation and Roles. In history, military officers wore beasts on their rank badges as an indication of their brute strength, and civil officials wore birds, symbolic of their soaring intellects. These badges were embroidered on a black or blue background; each badge had a frame, waves at the bottom, a sun and clouds, and the creature of rank in the center (Fig. 5.8). The format of these badges has transferred to the costumes. If a character's rank is known, a *guanyi* with the correct symbol may be used, but the badges used in traditional Jingju do not necessarily follow the historical ranks. In some cases, generic symbols such as a sun have been substituted for the creatures, thus avoiding the rank issue altogether. The stage *guanyi* is generally worn by civilian officers, played by *laosheng,* and *xiaosheng* or *chou* portraying corrupt, funny or clever officials (Fig. 1.13).

Accessories. Like the *mang,* the *guanyi* is always worn with a stiffened hoop-shaped jade belt suspended from fabric loops under the arms and worn dipping down in the front. The belt has imitation jade ornaments that would have indicated rank in the imperial court. The *guanyi* is worn with the padded vest, white collar, and high-soled, high-topped boots of the *sheng* roles. The *chou* wear medium-soled boots *(chaofang),* and a white inner collar, but not the padded vest. Both roles wear trousers.

Headdress. A *zhongsha,* a headdress for court, is most commonly worn with the *guanyi* robe (Fig. 6.22).

Gailiang guanyi (Reformed official robe)

Description and History. The *gailiang guanyi* has the same cut as the conventional *guanyi,* but instead of

FIGURE 6.23. The embroidery on this *gailiang guanyi* includes a round motif at the chest and a border near the hem. *The City of Baidi (Baidi cheng).* Character: Lu Xun, actor: Chang Jianzhong. PRSCJ, Beijing, China. April 22, 1996.

having a square of embroidered fabric stitched on to indicate the rank, the *gailiang guanyi* has a round motif embroidered onto the chest of the robe. One or two additional bands are embroidered parallel to the hem at the height of the knee, and the neckline is encircled with embroidery (Fig. 6.23).

Usage. The *gailiang guanyi* is worn at court by *laosheng* or *chou,* depending on the nature of the character.

Color and Ornamentation. The *gailiang guanyi* comes in the colors of the standard *guanyi*: red, blue, and black. The embroidery usually includes an early form of the dragon with a smooth body in a round design.

Accessories and Headdress. A hoop-shaped jade belt and high-soled, high-topped boots are worn with this garment, along with the inner collar, trousers, and the padded vest used only for the *sheng* roles. The *gailiang guanyi* is worn with the *zhongsha*, the same headdress worn with the standard *guanyi*.

Eunuch Robe *(Taijian yi)*

Description and History. Historically, eunuchs were the personal attendants to the emperor and protectors of the concubines. In this position they also guarded the legitimacy of heirs sired on these women. The eunuch robe has two different styles of closing, a round neckline with a curved crossover closing to the right *(yuanling taijian yi)* and a *xuezi*-style straight-neckband style that laps to the right *(xieling taijian yi)* (Fig. 6.24 and Appendix 1.22). The eunuch robes have a unique cut, distinguished by a stitched-on broad waistband of contrasting color that has a deep tasseled fringe hanging below. A border of the same color surrounds the round neck and is also used for a collar band of the *xuezi* style. The contrasting border continues down the side openings and goes across the hems with either straight or wavy edges. Eight matching circles of this second color are sewn on the eunuch robe, one each at center front chest and back, two at the knees front and back, and one on each shoulder. While historically eunuchs wore garments similar to those of other men in the various dynasties, in traditional Jingju performance, unique robes were expressly developed for eunuchs.

Usage. The straight-collared style eunuch robe is for younger or lower-ranking eunuchs, while older or higher-ranking eunuchs wear the round-neck version.

FIGURE 6.24. The red eunuch robe has a curved crossover closing, and the yellow one is cut with the straight neckband. The front figure is wearing a eunuch helmet *(taijian kui)* and carrying a horsetail brush. A small cord belt with tasseled ends is tied around the waist of the other character. *The Cosmic Blade (Yuzhou feng)*. Characters: eunuchs, actors: unidentified. NJC, Beijing, China.

Eunuchs are usually played by *chou*, although any male role can play a eunuch. The head eunuchs generally wear the curved-closing eunuch robe, but other eunuchs may dress according to the event, which may include wearing the *jianyi* and *magua* combination or the *mang*.

Color and Roles. The eunuch robe with the straight

neckband comes in yellow when the wearer attends the emperor or in red either for lower-ranking eunuchs or when the wearer is not in the presence of the emperor. On the yellow robes, the contrasting borders are black or blue. The round-neck eunuch robe comes in red, maroon, blue, and green. The green robes have yellow trim and are worn by the chief eunuch, usually played by a *chou,* while the red robes, for lesser eunuchs attending the emperor, have blue trim.[15]

Ornamentation and Roles. The embroidery on the eunuch robe appears on the contrasting color areas. The straight-collared version generally has gold couched geometric designs, while the round-collared version usually uses a combination of couching and multicolored embroidery.

Accessories. The eunuch robe is usually worn with red trousers and a white collar. In addition, a small cord is wrapped and knotted at the waist with a bow in front. Eunuchs generally wear the medium-soled boots and carry a horsetail brush *(fuchen).*

Headdress. The eunuch helmet *(taijian kui)* has a spray of pearls framing the face and a central ornament topped with a single pompom. There are tassels on either side of the face, and the back of the headdress has a crescent-shaped tall crown piece, open at the top. The headdress resembles the style of headdress worn by eunuchs in paintings from the Ming dynasty.[16]

Xueshi yi (Scholar's robe)

Description and History. Though a *xueshi yi* was worn in the early years of the Republic, the stage version does not resemble this garment.[17] The rounded neckline and curved crossover closing of the stage *xueshi yi* reflect Ming traditions, while the hem that curves up on the side vents has a theatrical basis. The *xueshi yi* is usually worn with a tight belt of matching fabric, with two tabs hanging down at the center front. The sleeves are tubular with water sleeves. The robe is softer, like the *xuezi,*

FIGURE 6.25. The *xueshi yi,* a robe for scholars is usually worn with the *xueshi jin,* seen here. *Zhuge Liang Leaves His Thatched Roof Study for the First Time (Chuchu maolu).* Character: Zhuge Liang, actor: Yu Wanzeng. NJC, Beijing, China. October 4, 2001.

rather than resembling the stiffer robes of court officers (Fig. 6.25).

Usage. The *xueshi yi* is worn by well-read and well-educated young men of no special status or rank.

Color and Ornamentation. The *xueshi yi* comes in black, blue, and white. Black reflects the lowest rank of the scholar officials. The ornamentation on the *xueshi yi* includes borders around the edges and a medallion at the chest. The border at the intersection between the hem and side vent curves to follow the contour of the outer edge.

Accessories and Headdress. The tight belt of matching fabric indicates a lower rank than the jade belt. Rather than wearing the *zhongsha* of higher court officials, scholars in the *xueshi yi* may wear a *xueshi jin* (scholar's hat), a soft hat that comes together into a flange on the crown, with matching fabric wings at the back. The standard array of inner garments is worn under the *xueshi yi*: the padded vest, white collar, trousers, and high-soled boots.

Jianyi (Archer's robe)

Description and History. The *jianyi* is one of the Manchu-influenced garments that transferred virtually unchanged into the general wardrobe for traditional Jingju roles. In the second half of the nineteenth century Cheng Changgeng (1812–c.1880), the leader of the Sanqing Troupe, began to introduce Qing-styled garments to the wardrobe.[18] One of those garments, the *jianyi*, directly correlates with the Qing dynasty garment, the *jifu*, commonly known as the dragon robe. The cut of the *jianyi* is virtually identical to its Manchu counterpart, developed to suit the Manchu nomadic life. The overall shape includes a trapezoidal body, tapering sleeves, rounded neckline, and rounded crossover front flap closed on the right with toggles and loops. Unlike Han clothing, which was worn loose and flowing, the *jifu* was belted for ease of movement. The narrow sleeves ending in horseshoe-shaped cuffs were designed to protect the wearer's hands when riding, and the center front and back slits allowed the garment to spread over the horse for mounted travel. Because of the narrow cuffs, the *jianyi* does not have water sleeves. There may or may not be a center front and back seam to accommodate the slit in the *jianyi* skirt. Cut without a shoulder seam, the *jianyi* has a small gusset under the arms to aid in fitting the narrow sleeves and accommodating arm movement. A separate matching collar is worn around the neck of the higher-status characters. The *jianyi* comes in satin for the higher ranks and cotton for workers (Figs. 3.3, 6.26, and 6.28, and Appendix 1.9).

Usage. During the Qing dynasty, the *jifu* was worn under the *bufu* for semiformal appearances at court. In traditional Jingju, the *jianyi* is a quite versatile garment worn for a range of events by a number of characters. When worn with the *bufu* onstage, the combination indicates officials of foreign courts. Less formal than the *kao* or *gailiang kao*, the *jianyi* is worn under the *magua* by traveling Han court officials and supernumeraries or by the military in times when armor is not required.[19] The *magua* collar is worn when the two garments are worn together. The *magua* is usually removed for battle scenes. When the *jianyi* is worn alone, a collar matching the *jianyi* is used. In more important battles, the roles wearing the *long jianyi* (dragon archer's robe) decorated with dragons will change into the *kao*.[20]

The horseshoe cuff on the sleeves of the *jianyi* is usually worn turned back, revealing a contrasting color lining. Upon arrival at court, a character may turn the cuff over the hand and kneel, placing both hands on the floor in front of his superior in an act of obeisance. The *jianyi* skirt can also be worn in two different ways to indicate the situation. In a nonmilitary situation, the skirt flaps are worn down. In a battle scene, the front gap is pulled slightly open and the outer right flap is lifted and tucked into the sash, a dashing look that also allows greater leg freedom for the performance of martial arts movements.

Color and Roles. The *jianyi* comes in a full range of colors, with their standard meanings. An embroidered white *jianyi* is worn by promising young warriors, and pink is used for those young warriors who are also handsome and romantic (Fig. 4.7). Red represents loyal characters (Fig. 6.30), and intense upper colors are worn by the *jing* figures.

Ornamentation and Roles. A range of roles from high-ranking generals to household staff may all wear the *jianyi*. The *long jianyi*, decorated with dragons in colors for standard males or couched in gold thread for *jing*, is worn by emperors and other high officials

FIGURE 6.26. The *long jianyi* for male warriors is generally worn with the wide, firm belt, and the *zijin guan* headdress may have feathers attached. *Lü Bu Shoots an Arrow (Yuanmen she ji)*. Character: Lü Bu, actor: Jiang Qihu. NJC, Beijing, China. April 29, 1996.

FIGURE 6.27. The *hua jianyi* may be worn by women disguised as men, as with this *wudan*. A heart-protecting mirror covers her heart. Her headdress is the *qixing ezi*, and she wears decorated high-topped, high-soled boots on her feet. The tasseled stick in her right hand indicates her mount. *Blocking the Horse (Dangma)*. Character: Eighth-Sister Yang, actor: Huang Hua. BJC, Beijing, China. September 9. 2001.

connected with the court. It is made of satin and embroidered in a fashion similar to the *jifu*, with the diagram of the universe using waves, mountains, clouds, and eight round dragons. Two of the dragons have been eliminated because of the narrower sleeves of the *jianyi*. The chest dragons face front, and the skirt dragons are in profile. The rounded dragons are the only design that appears on the *jianyi* because it is bisected by a sash, and larger dragons would be obscured (Fig. 3.3).

The *hua jianyi* (flowered *jianyi*) has flower roundels and a border around the edges or simply a flower border. Worn by ordinary fighters, this represents one of the few cases when a warrior will wear a garment embellished with a floral design. Eighth-Sister Yang, a woman disguised as a foreign general to go to a barbarian country in *Blocking the Horse (Dangma)*, also wears a *hua jianyi* (BJC, Beijing, China. September 9, 2001) (Fig. 6.27).

The *su jianyi* (plain *jianyi*) is made of satin and comes

FIGURE 6.28. The *bu jianyi* is made of cotton fabric, often blue, indicating those among lowest status, usually played by *chou* roles. The under wrap is visible on his right at the hem. The *chou* facial hair can be cut short, in a humorous fashion, as with this moustache. He is wearing a felt hat *(zhanmao)* and his trousers are tucked into wide white fabric socks. *The Beating of the Dragon Robe (Da longpao)*. Character: a community policeman (Di Bao), actor: unidentified. NJC, Beijing, China. October 9, 2001.

The *bu jianyi* (plain cloth *jianyi*) is made of cotton fabrics, indicating an even lower status of the wearer. This version may or may not have the contrasting borders around the edges. The solid-color blue cloth *jianyi* signifies the lowest rank and is worn without the matching collar or the white inner collar (Fig. 6.28).

Accessories. The stage version of the *jianyi* is worn close to the body, just as it was during the Qing dynasty. It is cinched with a wide firm sash. For some *wusheng* roles, long silken cords *(si taozi)* are knotted across the chest. The cords are a theatrical addition, designed to make the wearer look strong, as well as to help hold the costume in place (Figs. 4.7 and 8.6 with the *kuaiyi*). Because the *jianyi* has an open rounded neckline, the white inner collar appears at the neck of the higher-ranking characters. *Jing* and *sheng* wear a padded vest under the *jianyi*. In some cases, a matching *xuezi* may be worn over the *jianyi*, often open like a coat, and it is removed to fight. Trousers are worn under the *jianyi*, usually red for *laosheng* and *jing* and white or pink for *wusheng*. The high-soled, high-topped boots are worn on the feet.

Headdress. The higher-ranking characters wear metal filigree helmets with pearls, pompoms, and long pheasant feathers, such as the *zijin guan* (purple gold headdress) (Fig. 6.26), while the plainer *jianyi* used by lower-ranking characters is worn with one of the many soft-cap styles. In the *long jianyi* and *magua* ensemble, the headdress is usually a *da banjin* (flat-board headdress) with a neck flap and streamers draped in front of the shoulder, worn with a metal filigree *ezi* (diadem) (Fig. 7.39).

Longtao yi (Attendant robe)

Description and History. The *longtao yi* is a flared garment with a straight center-front closing that uses either ties or frogs. The neckline has a standing band collar or a plain round neck. The tubular sleeves have short water

in black, white, gray, blue, and maroon. Contrasting borders highlight the edges of the robe, blue, for example, on the black garments. Messengers and lower assistants wear this version (Table 6.32.B and 6.32.N).

sleeves at the hem. Borders of a contrasting fabric may be sewn around the neck, sleeve hems, garment hem, the center-front opening to the waist, and sometimes the side seam and center back slits. The shape of the border around the neckline resembles a Peter Pan collar. The fungus-shaped arabesque finishes the top edge of the center front and side slits. The borders are edged with a bias binding in a third color. Another style is made from a single fabric, but has more elaborate embroidery (Table 6.33.B and 6.33.N). *Longtao yi* is also a general category of attendant robes that includes the *dakai* (big armor), a style of attendant garment that resembles the *kao* (see below).

Usage. As scenery is kept to a minimum, an entourage is what creates the court environment. Those characters, wearing the *longtao yi*, are also called *longtao* (nonspeaking male attendants), and they usually come in groups of four. They process onstage carrying banners at the beginning of the scene and stand symmetrically on either side of the central table and chair. The costume sets for these attendants are stored together in the wardrobe cabinets as they are always used as a group.

Color and Roles. The *longtao* costumes are made in red, green, white, and blue. The color is selected to match or harmonize with the principal role they serve.

Ornamentation and Roles. The attendants wearing the *longtao yi* in the service of the emperor or high court official have eight dragons embroidered on the garments. Round dragons are placed on the shoulders, front and back chest, and two each at the knees in the front and back. The surface is additionally decorated with cloud designs and sometimes waves at the hem. The borders are couched with gold geometric designs. Lower-ranking entourage members will wear a *longtao yi* with a less formal arrangement of flowers on the body of the garment and contrasting fabric borders embroidered with a geometric design.

Accessories and Headdress. The *longtao yi* is worn

with coordinating trousers and flat-soled ankle boots. The *da banjin* headdress in a color and pattern that matches the *longtao* is worn on the head. Streamers from the crown projection piece are worn over the front of the shoulders (Table 6.33.B and 6.33.N).

Dakai (Big armor)

Description and History. The *dakai* is a subset of the *longtao* category of garments worn by attendants and guards. The *dakai* is a variation of the *kao*, with similar shoulder flaps and padded front waistband. The distinction in design happens below the waistband. Both have a short curved flap at the center hanging from the waist, but the *dakai* lacks the decorative fish at the deepest point of this curve. Beneath this piece, the *dakai* has squared flaps, either a knee-length one and two ankle-length ones or just two longer ones. With the additional width of the panels in the front and back, the *dakai* does not have the inner side leg panels of the *kao*. The separate collar of the *dakai* may have a squared edge rather than the curved edge worn with the *kao*. Another distinction is that the *dakai* does not have flags (Table 6.34.N).

Usage. The *dakai* is worn by the guards of the imperial palace and high-ranking nobles. They can also be less important generals than those dressed in the *kao*. The extras who play these parts are *liuhang* (lit. "flowing role type," that is, nonspeaking attendants).

Color and Ornamentation. The *dakai* is most often red, orange, or apricot yellow. It usually has an array of geometric motifs couched in gold on the main pieces and paired animals on the padded front waistband. The embroidery is less flamboyant than that on the *kao* in both the color and design. Because the performers wearing this style are not leading characters, the design details are not fixed.

Accessories, Hair, and Headdress. Red trousers are worn with the *dakai*, along with a white collar and thin-soled short boots. These characters usually carry a weapon and wear a matching *guanzi kui* (lit. "bucket-shaped helmet"). It has a diadem front and peaked crown with a tuft of fur on the end of a stalk that comes from the point. A flap of cloth falls over the neck (Table 6.34.N).

Gongzhuang (Palace garment)

Description and History. One of the more complicated garments in traditional Jingju, the *gongzhuang* is a stunning and colorful image onstage. The *gongzhuang* is quite unlike many of the other garments worn by women because it is full length, and that length is composed of layers of streamers. The rectangular shape of the bodice and wide sleeves are typical of the cut for the Han people. The round-necked bodice fits loosely on the body and is slightly high-waisted. The tubular sleeves are longer than the arms, wider than the sleeves of other costumes, and decorated with seven colorful bands with wavy edges separated by contrasting bias binding. The water sleeves may be plain white or have three layers in white, pink, and blue. The multiple colors of the sleeve bands are repeated in the streamers of the skirt area, which are also finished with contrasting bias trim (Figs. 3.6, 6.29, and Appendix 1.23). The *gongzhuang* was reformed by Mei Lanfang, and those who follow his school have three layers of streamers. In addition to the streamers, the front and back have layered apron panels, and there are leaf-shaped tabs inserted under the waistband. Underneath the streamers, a pleated skirt of lightweight silk is also attached to the waistline. The *gongzhuang* closes at the center front with frogs and Velcro at the waist. The cloud collar has a standing band collar and a shoulder cape, with a shaped edge finished in tasseled fringe. A shorter fringe is attached to the lower edge of all the streamers and apron panels.

Tracing the derivation of this garment reveals a number of possible connections between historical and theatrical dress. The floating narrow panels and multiple colors were inspired by the phoenix, for the phoenix image represents the females in the palace, from dowager empress to princesses, and is a symbol for their beauty.[21] The streamers are also believed to have developed for dancing at court, which would have been one of the activities for concubines and princesses. In addition, the streamers may relate to bridal dress. Other elements of the *gongzhuang* can be connected to the dress of daily life. The stripes on the sleeves may be an extension of the Qing practice of adding borders to garments. The cloud collar is similar to ones that were worn for ceremonial events. The combination of all of these elements creates a unique garment that reflects and expands on the historical aesthetic.

Usage. The *gongzhuang* is worn by princesses and concubines, played by *qingyi* or *huadan,* for leisure, dancing, and other activities in the inner palace. The garment's rank is lower than the *nümang,* so it would not appear for important ceremonial occasions or on higher-level wives.[22] One of the most famous characters to wear this garment is Yang Guifei in *The Drunken Beauty (Guifei Zuijiu),* a concubine of Emperor Minghuang.[23] She becomes intoxicated while pining for her emperor, as he has chosen to turn his attentions to another. She dances her lament for herself, gradually getting more inebriated and performing more elaborate movements, as the costume enhances the gestures of her dance.

Color. The colors of the *gongzhuang* include much of the color vocabulary in traditional Jingju costumes. The bodice is generally red, although yellow may be used as well. The pleated underskirt is a pale blue. The streamers and sleeve bands use a range of pastel colors, including green, pink, pale blue, yellow, and teal.

Ornamentation. The *gongzhuang* is richly embroidered in a wide range of beautiful colors. The floral imagery on the streamers, aprons, and sleeve bands often

FIGURE 6.29. Princesses and concubines may wear the *gongzhuang*, an elaborately embroidered garment for dancing or leisure in the palace. This example has three colors for the water sleeves. The phoenix headdress is usually worn with the *gongzhuang*. *The First Scholar as Matchmaker (Zhuangyuan mei)*. Character: Princess Chai, actor: Zhao Xiujun. PRSCJ, Beijing, China. April 24, 1996.

includes peonies, as they are emblematic of feminine virtue and beauty. The phoenix, with its associations with imperial women, appears on the bodice and the front aprons, embroidered with a wide range of pretty colors to depict the flamboyance of this mythological bird. Some garments have a diaper pattern couched in gold on the bodice (Fig. 5.7). The intricate embroidery adds to the visual delight of the overall image.

Accessories. Although the *gongzhuang* has a built-in underskirt, it opens in the front, so a second skirt is worn beneath it for modesty, as well as trousers. Flat-soled shoes are also worn.

Headdress. The *gongzhuang* is worn with a silver-and-blue phoenix headdress with a round silhouette comprised of pearls and filigree phoenix ornaments mounted on springs covering the crown. Long tassels hang on either side of the face and shorter ones fall over the nape of the neck (Fig. 6.29).

The Short Costumes

The short costumes extend from the shoulder to the hip and are generally worn by lower-ranking characters and for less formal scenes. In some cases, the short garments are made to match other garments to create a set that covers the body.

Magua (Riding jacket)

Description and History. The *magua* is a short surcoat drawn directly from the Qing dynasty garment with the same name. During the Qing era, the ordinary *magua* was worn for informal dress and travel, and a *huang magua* (yellow *magua)* was reserved for the highest-ranking ministers and the imperial bodyguard.[24] It was also considered a gift of the highest honor from the emperor, worthy of display in the ancestral hall.[25] After the 1911 revolution, the *magua* became a component of formal wear worn with a long robe. The *magua* has a simple rectangular cut in the Han tradition, with a plain round neckline, straight sleeves, and hip-length slightly flared body. Historically, the front closed in the center, crossed over to the right, or had a *pipa* (shape resembling this musical instrument) line that curved to the right and cut back to the center in a straight line at the waist. The center-front closing is most common onstage, secured with frogs. The neckline is plain and the sleeves are tubular, reaching between mid-forearm and wrist. It has a matching separate collar in the same shape as those used with the *jianyi* and the *kao* (Fig. 6.30 and Appendix 1.10)

Usage. The *magua* combines with the *jianyi* to indicate informal or convenient dress for traveling onstage,

just as it served for travel in real life. The *magua* may also be worn to disguise a character's identity and for close or informal fighting scenes. The horseshoe cuffs of the *jianyi* fold back over the straight sleeves of the *magua*.

Color and Roles. In the Qing dynasty, the color of the *magua* was normally blue, but a different-colored *magua* could also reflect the colors of the wearer's regiment when attending the emperor. The stage *magua* is most often black satin, but is also made in colors, including red, green, white, maroon, yellow, and orange. The *huang magua* has lost some of its prestige onstage and is now used for the military entourage of a high-ranking official or by court attendants in the presence of the emperor.

Ornamentation and Roles. The Qing dynasty *magua* was made of a jacquard or plain fabric, while the stage version is made of satin and either embroidered or plain. A lesser version of the *mang* terrestrial design appears on the *long magua* (dragon *magua*), but uses only four dragon roundels, one on each shoulder and one center front and back at the chest, and the *long magua* may or may not have the wave pattern embroidered at the hem. Higher-ranking characters, including princes and generals, wear the *long magua* (Fig. 6.30).

The *tuanhua magua* (flower-roundel *magua*) is usually black, with four roundels of flowers on the shoulders and the center front and back. Having this less-prestigious design, it is worn by those who are lower in rank than those who wear the *long magua*, such as a governor or inspector.

Accessories. The *magua* is most often worn with the *jianyi* underneath. Both costumes come with separate collars, and the *magua* collar is worn on the outside. The standard garments underneath the *jianyi* include the padded vest, a white collar, complementary-colored trousers, and high-soled, high-topped boots.

Headdress. The *long magua* is usually worn with a

FIGURE 6.30. The *long magua* combined with the *jianyi,* both absorbed from Qing-style clothing, indicates travel for court characters. The two garments may be worn with the *damao* (Mongolian hat) of barbarian kings. (This character is Han, but he is married to a barbarian princess.) His beard is the *san liuran. The Red-Maned Fiery Steed (Hongzong liema).* Character: Xue Pinggui, actor: Yan Shiqi. BJC, Beijing, China. October 6, 2001.

filigree helmet with pearls and woollen balls or a fabric *da banjin* with a neck flap worn with a metal filigree *ezi* (Fig. 7.39 worn with a vest and *jianyi*).

Baoyi (Lit. "leopard" or "embracing" clothes)

Description and History. The precise meaning of *bao* in *baoyi* is unclear, as it could refer to "leopard/panther" or "embracing," as the costume is held tight to the body by silken cords. And because heroes wear the *baoyi*, the garments are also referred to as hero clothes *(yingxiong yi)*. Worn for martial arts, the *baoyi* is also called *dayi* (fighting clothes). The *baoyi* is a two-piece set of martial arts garments consisting of a jacket and trousers. A traditional Jingju invention with historical connections, the front of the jacket has a straight, diagonally lapped closing with a wide collar band that fastens under the right arm. The sleeves are wrist length and fitted with toggle closings. The *baoyi* is distinguished from other martial arts costumes by two layers of pleated light-weight silk skirts called moving water *(zoushui)* that are fastened to the hem of the jacket. The moving-water layers have been added to enhance the martial arts action. The trousers are the typical form, with an unfitted muslin waistband and straight legs. The waistband is folded to fit and tied with a string. Cotton is used for the waistband to prevent slippage. The trousers are often made of a lighter-weight silk than the jacket so that they are more practical in the fight scenes (Fig. 6.31 and Appendixes 1.6 and 1.7).

Usage. The *baoyi* is worn in particularly demanding fight scenes because it is less cumbersome than other military wear. The *duanda wusheng* ("quick fighting" soldiers) are among the role types who would wear the *baoyi*, as well as the *jing, laosheng,* and *wuhang* (soldiers). The men wearing the *baoyi* are gallant and chivalrous and must often fight alone rather than in an army formation, along the lines of Robin Hood. Ren Tanghui wears a white *baoyi* in one famous scene of a lone combatant in *Fight at Crossroads Inn (Sancha kou)* during a fight that takes place in the dark for the characters, but occurs on a fully illuminated stage (ACTO, Beijing, China. June 2, 2002) (Fig. 1.6).

Color and Roles. The jacket and trousers are of matching colors, and the moving water layers have one or two contrasting colors. White or pink *baoyi* represent brave youths, *jing* often wear black or green *baoyi*, and a *laosheng* will likely wear olive green. The *baoyi* also comes in red and blue.

Ornamentation and Roles. There are two versions of the *baoyi* hero's jacket and trouser set, one embellished and the other more plain. The *hua baoyi* (flowered *baoyi*) has borders on the collar band, the sleeve cuffs, and around the hem and side slits of the jacket. The borders may have abstract geometric or floral designs, and this is one of the few examples where flowers may appear on a male warrior. In addition, the fungus-shaped arabesque appears on the hem at center front and on top of the side seam slits. The surface of the jacket has roundels of embroidery or free-form flowers in a scattered pattern that repeats on the trousers. The roundels can include the long-life symbol, as well as floral or geometric designs. The *jing* version may have eight lucky symbols on it. The moving-water layers may have matching designs or lucky symbols embroidered on them. The *su baoyi* (plain *baoyi*) in olive green is decorated only with a black fungus-shaped arabesque around the collar band. Older warriors who solve problems through strategy rather than fighting may wear this version. Both the fungus shape and the collar band are now made out of stiff black velveteen, with white piping trim.

Accessories. The jacket is pulled close to the body with a large box pleat in the back and held in place by a long firm sash knotted in the front, and by long silk cords elaborately lashed around the torso in a honeycomb pattern. If the sash has hanging tasseled ends, then the two pieces are tied together so that the hero

FIGURE 6.31. *Duanda wusheng* may wear the *baoyi* with a *ruan luomao* (soft beret) for vigorous fight scenes. His foot coverings are *kuai xue* (lit. "fast boots"). *Fight at Crossroads Inn (Sancha kou)*. Character: Ren Tanghui, actor: Yin Dongjun. ACTO, Beijing, China. June 2, 2002.

can kick them out of the way over his shoulders in the flurry of combat. Sometimes, a vest is worn in combination with the *baoyi*. The front of the vest is worn open and secured at the waist with the sash. When dressing, the lower right front edge of the *baoyi* is lifted to permit kicks. Inside the jacket, the actor wears a small padded vest, not only to enhance his silhouette, but also to lift the cap of the sleeves away from the arm for easier movement.[26] The white collar band is worn over the padded vest to fill in the neckline. If traveling or going to court, the character may wear a matching *xuezi* over the *baoyi*. If the *xuezi* is worn for fighting, then it is worn asymmetrically and tied in a knot at the right hip. Because of movement demands, flat-soled, ankle-high boots or *kuai xue* (lit. "fast boots") are worn with this combination. The trousers are tied at the ankle and tucked into the boot tops. The olive-green *baoyi* may be worn with black gaiters *(bangtui)*. These lower leg pieces are solid, firm, curved shapes, with Velcro closings on the back of the leg (Fig. 6.35 worn with the *bingyi*).

Headdress. The style of hat worn with the *baoyi* depends on the character and the situation. A matching soft beret-style hat *(ruan luomao)* completes the image for a *duanda wusheng* in battle (Fig. 6.31), and when he goes to court on a civilian mission, he will wear one of the firm helmets decorated with pearls and woolly balls. A *jing* may also wear the helmet, while the *laosheng* may wear a broad straw hat brim, with no crown, covered in blue satin.

Kuaiyi (Lit. "fast" clothes) and *Bingyi* (Soldier's clothes)

Description and History. *Kuaiyi* translates variously as fast, tight, or simple clothing. This set of garments, used for martial arts, consists of a jacket and trousers, which reflects the informal clothing of the Qing dynasty. The jacket has a round neck with a convex crossover curved closing that is fastened to the right with frogs. The front

FIGURE 6.32. The black *kuaiyi* is for stealthy fighters, and the velvet version of the jacket is specific for this character, Wu Song. He wears the *su luomao* (plain beret) on his head. *Wu Song Causes a Ruckus in the Inn (Wu Song da dian)*. Character: Wu Song, actor: Huang Jingping. BJC, Beijing, China. July 2, 2000.

and back are cut together without a shoulder seam, with a slightly flared torso. An additional piece for the wrap is added in the center front. The attached sleeve pieces are tapered and fastened at the wrist with frogs. The trousers are unfitted, with ties used for the waist and cuffs (Fig. 6.32 and Appendix 1.11).

Usage. Characters who wear the *kuaiyi* are adept at the martial arts, but they are nonofficial warriors who are not as well situated as those who wear the *baoyi*. Positive roles in the Robin Hood mold or negative roles such as outlaws, both played by the *duanda wusheng*, may wear the *kuaiyi*. Those who wear this set have a strong sense of justice.[27]

Color, Ornamentation, and Roles. The most common *kuaiyi* set is black. As the black color of the garments aids in their disguise in the dark, they are sometimes called clothes for the night. The functional closings are concealed, and decorative frogs in contrasting colors go down the center front, the side seams, and from shoulder to wrist outside the sleeves. *Kuaiyi* with white decorative frogs, known as heroes' buttons, are worn by warriors and those with gold frogs are worn by *jing*. A black velvet *kuaiyi* jacket worn with silk trousers and a white or yellow sash is specific to Wu Song, a principal character in the Water Margin stories (Fig. 6.32).

The *hua kuaiyi* comes in many colors and has designs of birds or butterflies embroidered on it to represent the wearer's agility and strength. This style is usually worn by chivalrous characters and *wuchou* (martial clowns), such as Liu Lihua in *Fight at Crossroads Inn*, in the famous night-fight scene (Fig. 6.33).

The *bingyi* (soldier's clothes) version of the *kuaiyi* costume is worn by soldiers in the armies of the principal generals. The design on these garments can be a simple circular medallion on the chest and borders on the hem, cuffs, and neck, or a more elaborate scattered composition of animals, mythological creatures, or lucky symbols. The color of the *bingyi* relates to the color of the leader. Two opposing armies generally wear different colors of the same style *bingyi*. Both groups will have either the simpler medallion decoration (Fig. 6.34) or the version with more detailed embroidery (Figs. 1.15, 2.12. and 6.35). Immortal soldiers may have lucky charms embroidered on their costumes.

Accessories. All styles of the *kuaiyi* are worn with a white collar inside the neckline. One of several belts is used to constrict and secure the waist: a stiffened fabric belt matching the jacket, a sash, or a firm belt with tasseled ends. The excess fabric of the jacket body is pulled into a box pleat in the back to create a smooth line in

FIGURE 6.33. *Wuchou* may dress in the *hua kuaiyi* with butterfly embroidery. This character wears a scarf tied around his waist and "fast boots" on his feet. *Fight at Crossroads Inn (Sancha kou).* Character: Liu Lihua, actor: Liu Yao. ACTO, Beijing, China. June 2, 2002.

FIGURE 6.34. *(Left)* Armies wear matching *bingyi* with jacket, trousers, and belt of the same fabric, here simply embroidered with a circular medallion and borders. This headdress is a small tasseled helmet *(xiao daoying kui)* with a stiff diadem and soft neck flap. *Attacking Pei Yuanqing with Fire (Huo shao Pei Yuanqing).* Character: soldier, actor: unidentified. ACTO, Beijing, China. May 31, 2002.

FIGURE 6.35. *(Below)* A more decorated version of the matching *bingyi* has animal and cloud patterns embroidered on the surface, with trousers, jacket, belt, and gaiters of the same fabrics. Their headdresses are *ying mao* (tasseled hat). *Yandang Mountain (Yandang shan).* Characters: soldiers of He Tianlong, actors: unidentified. BJC, Beijing, China. September 9. 2001.

the front. Individual characters may wear padding, but the *wuchou* and ranks of soldiers do not. Some soldiers wear triangular kerchiefs knotted around their necks. A vest can be added to this set. The feet are covered with ankle-high fight boots or soft, thin-soled slippers *(daxie)* that either match the costume or are black. Some roles may call for the addition of gaiters or leg bindings to constrict the ends of the trousers and facilitate movement.

Headdress. The plain black *kuaiyi* is worn with a plain soft beret *(su luomao)* pulled down over the right ear (Fig. 6.32). The *wuchou* wear a fitted soft cap with springs and pearls around the rim (Fig. 6.33). The characters wearing the *bingyi* usually have a matching flap on the back of the head that protects the neck and a filigree *ezi* with woolly balls on top. If the fabric piece and *ezi* are combined into one piece, it is called a *daoying kui* (tasseled helmet). This version has a pointed crown with a red tail mounted at the peak. Another style of headdress has a headscarf *(toubu)* knotted around the head under the *ezi* (Fig. 1.15). Immortal soldiers have streamers of silk on either side of the face that are tied into rosettes at chest height and additional adornments (Fig. 2.12). The ends of the silk are caught in the belt to control them during fight sequences.

Chayi (Lit. "tea" clothes)

Description and History. *Chayi* are so named because of their color. Tea is a necessity of life and therefore has come to symbolize the ordinary.[28] In the Song dynasty, there was an edict that ordinary people could only wear a beige color, therefore light brown has been associated with the working class for hundreds of years.[29] *Chayi*, clothes for workers, are made of cotton rather than silk. The jacket opens in the center front and has a black collar band piped in white that ends in the fungus-shaped arabesque usually reserved for women's garments. The incongruity is considered a visual joke, as the characters who wear these garments are often comic. The sleeves of the jacket are three-quarter length and cuffed as though they have been rolled up for duty. The trousers are similarly shortened and cuffed. The cuffs on both the jacket and the trousers are white. The style of garment comes from lower-status wear that was modified for stage usage (Fig. 6.36).

Usage. *Chayi* indicate poor men, often boatmen, woodsmen, or fishermen.

Color and Ornamentation. In addition to browns and beiges, *chayi* may also come in blue, such as the big-sleeved servant robe *(daxiu)* (see below). They are not embroidered.

Accessories. A white double-layered pleated apron *(shuiqun,* lit. "water skirt"*)* encircles the waist. The name theoretically comes from the association of this costume with boatmen. The two pleated pieces are stitched to a white cotton waistband that is wrapped around the waist and tied in place. As they have nothing else to indicate that they are on the water, the ripples of the skirt

FIGURE 6.36. *Chayi* represent lower-status workers, such as this boatman, who is also wearing a double-layered pleated apron. His headdress is a straw hat brim, and his white hair bun shows above it. His beard is a white *chousan* (three-part clown beard). *Autumn River (Qiu jiang).* Character: Shao Weng (old boatman), actor: unidentified. BJC, Beijing, China. May, 1996.

can project the movement of the waves as the boatman rows his boat.[30] This set is worn with practical flat straw sandals tied at the ankle and short black wraparound ankle guards. If the character is a boatman, he will have an oar for a prop.

Headdress. The boatmen wear a wide straw crownless hat brim. It is worn twisted on the head so that the back edge is turned to the inside of the hole where the crown would have been.

Big-sleeved Robe (Daxiu)

Description and History. The big-sleeved robe is distinguished by its sleeves, which are wider and longer than usual and are finished with water sleeves. The neckline crosses over to the right in a diagonal line and is finished with a wide collar band, similar to the *xuezi* (Fig. 6.37).

Usage: The big-sleeved robe is worn by waiters, innkeepers, and other commoners. Although large sleeves and water sleeves may seem to indicate elegance, the large sleeves of the big-sleeved robe can be used more humbly, to wipe off tables.[31]

Color and Ornamentation. The jacket and trousers are blue or black, and the collar band may be white. Although there are other colors, these are considered part of the tea-garment group worn by servants. The blue is likely to have come from indigo, an inexpensive source for dyeing garments. There is no ornamentation on this costume.

Accessories. A white collar band is worn inside the jacket neckline. The jacket comes to mid-thigh, but the bottom half is covered by a white double-layered pleated apron. This set is worn with flat black shoes and white socks of heavy cotton tied at the ankle. The trousers are tucked into the top of the socks.

Headdress. A soft black tall felt hat with a pompom on the end is often worn with this set.

Prisoner's Clothes (Zuiyi)

Description and History. Male and female prisoners are dressed in the prisoner's jacket and trousers *(zuiyi)*. The men's jacket has a standing collar and a curved crossover closing to the right. The women's version has a standing band collar with a center-front closing and blue banded trim with white piping around the collar, front hem, and cuffs. The women's trousers may have blue banding around the hem as well. The waist of the

FIGURE 6.37. Lower-status workers can wear a big-sleeved robe with a double-layered pleated apron. This character also has his trousers tucked into his fabric socks, which he wears with slippers. *The Magic Cistern (Ju dagang)*. Character: Xiao Lujiang, actor: Jiao Jingge. ACTO, Beijing, China. June 1, 2002.

women's pants may be cut like trousers, with a waistband and side zipper because the leg of the trouser is slimmer than the usual shape. The prisoner's clothing is a Jingju costume development (Fig. 6.38).

FIGURE 6.38. A female prisoner may wear prisoner's clothes, with a skirt wrapped around her legs. *Yutang Chun (Yutang Chun)*. Character: Yutang Chun, actor: Jiang Yang. Jiangsu Province Beijing Opera Company (Jiangsu sheng jingju yuan), Jiangsu, China. May 22, 1980. Photograph courtesy of Elizabeth Wichmann-Walczak.

Usage. The prisoner clothing is worn by male and female criminals and prisoners. Some higher-ranking prisoners may instead wear a red *xuezi*.

Color, Ornamentation, and Roles. In Chinese tradition, red has opposing connotations, both auspiciousness and bad luck. While red as a symbol for happiness is used for weddings and festive events, it is also

employed for negative occasions and has connections to blood. In the past, a criminal sentenced to the death wore red. Jingju adopted that tradition and expanded it to include most prisoners.[32] However, some prisoners are dressed in black, white, or blue for lesser sentences. Some of the women's jackets have a fungus-shaped arabesque pattern on the center-front closing, but both men's and women's versions are unembroidered.

Accessories. Both male and female prisoners can wear a white prisoner skirt *(zuiqun)* (Fig. 7.37), but male prisoners may appear without the outer skirt. The skirt has very small pleats and no embroidery. It is worn with the hem pulled up to the waist in the front so that the lower edge falls down the center front into a U-shaped curve around the back of the legs. Women wear a waist scarf, and men have a fringed sash tied over the skirt and under their jackets. Men wear white fabric socks on their lower legs and tuck their trousers into them. Both wear flat shoes.

Hair and Headdress. Some prisoners wear a distinctive hairstyle called a *shuaifa* (lit. "to toss the hair"), a long ponytail on a post mounted on a 3-inch leather circle. This hairpiece is placed on top of the head and held in place by tying it to the hair skullcap *(wangzi)*, which is further secured with a headscarf. When characters are particularly distressed, they kneel down and swing the ponytail in a circle (Fig. 2.10). Women can wear either a simplified version of their usual hairstyle with a scarf around the crown or the *shuaifa*.

Executioner's Clothes *(Guizishou yi)*

Description and History. Consisting of a red jacket, skirt panels, and trousers, the executioner's costume is recognizable by its distinctive black borders with white piping. The contrasting borders on the jacket usually include a hem decoration that also outlines the side seam slits, cuffs, and a detail at the neckline. Although the design of the black borders may change from set to set,

the aggressive look projects in each version. The jacket has a center-front closing with frogs and straight sleeves without water sleeves. There are usually four skirt panels, with the front and back panels shorter than those on the sides. They all have black borders. The typically shaped trousers are plain red (Fig. 6.39).

Usage. Executioners usually come in even numbered sets, from two for an informal execution, to six or more for important prisoners. They flank the prisoner to escort him or her onstage, or in more dramatic moments, they carry them off lying face up above their heads.

Color and Ornamentation. The red color on the executioner's costume stands for blood. In some versions, a black shape is appliquéd on the leg flaps in addition to the borders.

Accessories. Short black boots with flat soles are worn by executioners. These roles wear either an asymmetrical painted face, symbolizing that they are out of balance, or standard *sheng* makeup.

Headdresses. A matching red *da banjin* and metal filigree *ezi* is worn with this set. A single short pheasant feather is attached to one side of the headdress.

Jacket and Skirt *(Aoqun)* and Jacket and Trousers *(Aoku)*

Description and History. The jacket, skirt, and trousers combination comes from the dress of the Han women during the Qing period. The three costume pieces are made as a matching set and are stored together. The jacket collar closes in the center front, and from that point the bodice has a curved crossover closing to the right that is secured with frogs. The collar, front closing, hem, and cuffs are edged with contrasting piping. The torso is fitted with curved side seams and has a hip-length peplum slit on the side seams. The sleeves are narrow and do not have water sleeves. The skirt is made of two pieces mounted on a single waistband. The front and back are flat panels, and the sides are knife pleated.

These pleats are larger than those of the skirt worn with more formal garments. The trousers have the characteristic shape (Fig. 6.40).

Usage. The skirt is usually worn by *huadan* when they are at home and for interior scenes. The short length on the jacket of this set is considered less elegant than the longer *nüpi* worn by the *qingyi* characters, implying the women wearing these clothes have lower status. The slender line of the jacket accents the vivacious movements associated with those who wear this set. The three pieces are worn together by higher-ranking *huadan* characters. Tradition originally did not permit showing women in trousers, but in the last hundred years women's trousers have been seen onstage in several roles.[33] The jacket and trousers worn without the skirt indicates a lower social position of *huadan* (Fig.1.9).

Color, Ornamentation, and Roles. The colors are selected from the pastel range used for young ladies, pink, aqua, pale blue, yellow, and others. The jacket and skirt are embroidered with matching free-form flowers. A large sprig usually decorates the front and back of the jacket, with a similar arrangement on the front and back panels of the skirt. The sleeves and side sections of the skirt have smaller motifs. The trousers can have sprigs or a border embroidered at the hem. An assortment of flowers, including chrysanthemums, peonies, and pear blossoms can be used in a variety of floral colors. Generally the flower color is darker than the color of the garments.

Accessories. The jacket and skirt or trousers may also be worn with a hip- or knee-length vest having a similar collar and front closing. The addition of a vest lowers the rank of the wearer, who in this costume may act as a go-between or personal maid.[34] A long scarf worn around the waist over the vest is knotted on the right with streamers hanging to mid-calf (Table 6.24–25.B, and 6.24–25.N).

The jacket and trousers can be worn with a small apron *(xiao fandan)* tied at the waist and a separate panel hanging from the waist. The apron has a curved top that is attached to the upper bodice by a button and loop (Fig. 1.9). The lower part is tied around the waist. The panel that drops from the waist conceals the gap between the legs for a more modest look. The apron and panel are usually made of black silk, with brightly embroidered flowers that are not as refined as those for the higher-ranking characters.[35] Both sets are worn with flat shoes.

Hair and Headdress. The hairstyles worn with these garments include the *datou* and the *guzhuang tou*. Despite the lower rank of the women characters wearing these garments, they still have rhinestone hairpins and flowers in their hair, but perhaps with fewer ornaments than a woman with higher status.

Zhan'ao zhanqun (War jacket, skirt, and trousers)

Description and History. The *zhan'ao zhanqun* combines traditional clothing styles with theatrical innovations to create an image for vigorous young fighting women warriors. The jacket has a standing band collar, like Qing dynasty garments, and a center-front closing secured with frogs. It is fitted through the torso, and the sleeves are tapered to the wrist. The jacket is worn belted with a self-fabric band or a soft scarf or both. The self-fabric band may have two tabs on the front; if not, then a scarf might be worn under the jacket so that the ends hang down to conceal the gap between the legs. If worn alone, the scarf is tied on the outside. The peplum of the jacket is worn over the skirt panels and trousers. The skirt *(xiajia)* has two flat panels with a center-front opening and a vented overlap in the back to allow for martial movements. The fronts are curved at the bottom. The edges of all the pieces are sometimes finished with a contrasting color bias banding. The trousers are the conventional shape (Fig. 1.10 and Appendix 1.19).

Usage. *Wudan* (martial women) with expertise in

FIGURE 6.40. A matching set of jacket, skirt, and trousers is used for *huadan*. *The Magic Cistern (Ju dagang)*. Character: Wang Daniang, actor: Huang Hua. ACTO, Beijing, China. June 1, 2002.

fighting wear the *zhan'ao zhanqun*. The jacket and trousers are similar to those worn by male combatants, and the skirt was added to create a feminine grace without hindering movement. Where the *zhan'ao zhanqun* is worn by active fighters, the *nükao* is worn by military women who sing and engage in less rigorous combat.

Color and Roles. The *zhan'ao zhanqun* comes in red, blue, yellow, and pink, among other colors. A white set is used for Bai Suzhen, the White Snake, and a specific color of blue is also worn by her friend, Xiao Qing, Little Blue *(The Legend of White Snake [Bai she zhuan]).* Guest artists with NKKCO, Taipei, Taiwan. November 5, 1995).

Ornamentation. These sets are ornamented with an assortment of pretty flowers. The flowers often form a border around the edges of the jacket and skirt panels, and additional scattered flowers are worked across the surface. The trousers are embroidered to match.

Accessories. The *zhan'ao zhanqun* is worn with ankle-high boots called small "barbarian" boots *(xiao manxue),* and the trousers are folded, tied, and tucked into the top of the boots.

Hair and Headdress. Although they are fighting vigorously, the female fighters maintain their beauty in hairstyle, with rhinestone ornaments and flowers arranged similarly to their *qingyi* counterparts. Their long silk strands of hair are caught into a waist cinch to keep them from getting entangled in the heat of the battle. They may also wear filigree helmets, including the butterfly helmet and *qixing ezi*.

Caipo ao (Colorful jacket for old women)

Description and History. The *caipo ao* has a standing band collar, wide sleeves, and a full-cut trapezoidal torso, all characteristics that come from the casual dress of women in the Qing dynasty. The banded trim around the sleeves, curved front closing, and hem are typical of Chinese taste. To a contemporary audience, the shape

FIGURE 6.41. The *caipo ao* has an awkward cut to add to the humor of the role, usually a *caidan*. This character is holding a pipe in her left hand. *Picking Up the Jade Bracelet (Shi yuzhuo).* Character: Matchmaker Liu (Liu Meipo), actor: unidentified. Independent players, Beijing, China. September 8, 2001.

of this jacket looks cumbersome and awkward, giving a humorous appearance to the comic characters wearing it (Fig. 6.41).[36]

Usage. The *caipo ao* is worn by *caidan*, played by a male clown actor. "Because it is the ugliest shaped robe in the history of Chinese dresses, it is used by the ugliest women characters on the stage."[37]

Color and Ornamentation The jacket is usually made in drab colors, with bright or very dark trim. The borders, trim, and embroidered flowers on this garment are sometimes overdone for a woman of this age and position, another comic turn. Generally, the outer band is broader than the others. A fungus-shaped arabesque appears at the intersection between the front neck curve and the side opening and at the top of the side slits.

Accessories. The jacket is worn with trousers that are shorter than usual and can be drawn in at the cuff for additional comic effect. A vest can also be worn with this combination, and the character may carry a pipe.

Hair and Headdress. The hairstyle worn with the *caipo ao* is arranged as it would be for *laodan* roles, with the hair drawn up into a bun on the top of the head and wrapped in a scarf.

Duantiao (Lit. "short and convenient for playing" robe) and An'anyi (Children's clothing)

Description and History. Children's clothing is used to dress characters from small walking children through teenagers. Infants are depicted by dolls (Fig. 6.52). The ensembles for children, which resemble adult clothing in a simpler form, consist of trousers and a top, with a variety of closings. The top can close with a round collar and curved closing to the right, or a center-front closing with a tie at mid-chest. The *duantiao*, also called *xiao xuezi* (small *xuezi*) has a diagonal straight collar overlapping to the right, like its adult counterpart. It is calf length and may or may not have water sleeves (Fig. 6.42). The *an'anyi* is shorter, with a white crossover collar and contrasting cuffs without water sleeves.

Usage. The children's roles are often played by female actors, and the gender of the child is not always visually discernable. Younger children have shorter garments, while older children have robes that go past the knees.

Color and Ornamentation. Most often, children's clothes are made in the blue range, from lake blue to a deep turquoise. The embroidery on children's garments

FIGURE 6.42. Children are dressed in the *duantiao*, a small version of the *xuezi* belted with a cord. They may wear wigs with knots at the temples. *Hongniang (Hongniang).* Character: Lute boy, actor: Song Yi. NJC, Beijing, China. October 5, 2001.

is quite simple, focusing on the collar band and chest area. The straight-fronted garment may have black borders and a fungus-shaped arabesque at chest height. The trousers may have a band of trim near the hem.

Accessories. The longer garments are worn with a small cord belt on the outside of the waist. The shorter version is worn with a scarf tied around the waist of the trousers under the top. All tops are worn with the white collar underneath and simple flat-soled black shoes.

Hair. Children's roles are distinguished from others by their wig *(hai'er fa)*, which has bangs and long hair.

The Specific Costumes

Specific costumes have evolved for some Jingju characters because of their distinctive personalities or circumstances. Four broad categories encompass these dedicated costumes: religious dress for monks and priests; gods, devils, and spirits for mythological and spirit-based characters; ethnic minorities for all non-Han roles; and garments that are worn by only one character because they are unique in some way. This last group includes some of the costumes designed by Mei Lanfang.

Religious Costumes

BAGUA YI (EIGHT TRIGRAMS ROBE)

Description and History. The basic form of the *bagua yi* resembles the *kai chang*, with a wide, straight collar band on the diagonal overlap closing on the right. Where the *kai chang* has just an undulating hem, the *bagua yi* has a border of wavy edges on both the hem and the side slits, eliminating the extensions that finish the side seams of the *kai chang*. These borders are couched with a geometric floral design. The sleeves are slightly flared, and the length is extended with water sleeves attached to the lower edge. The form of the garment is further distinguished by a band of matching fabric applied at the waist and two streamers that fall from the center front. The *bagua yi* is made from satin. Both the shape and the ornamentation of this garment are a theatrical invention intended to express the Daoist knowledge of the wearer, since an actual Daoist would not need to convey his wisdom through his clothing (Fig. 6.43 and Appendix 1.21).[38]

Usage. The *bagua yi* costume evolved for characters possessing magical talents related to Daoism. Zhuge Liang, the prime minister of Shu-Han in the period

FIGURE 6.43. The eight-trigrams design distinguishes the *bagua yi* for characters possessing magical talents related to Daoism. The hat is a *bagua jin* and has the trigrams embroidered on the crown. *The Gathering of Heroes (Qunying hui)*. Character: Zhuge Liang, actor: Li Chongshan. BJC, Beijing, China. July 23, 2000.

of the Three Kingdoms, often appears in the *bagua yi* (*The Gathering of Heroes*) (*Qunying hui*) (BJC, Beijing, China. July 23, 2000). He wears this garment to demonstrate his noble-minded, brilliant qualities, although he is not a Daoist priest. Characters with the attributes that entitle them to wear this garment will not appear in anything other than this costume and its variations.

Color and Ornamentation. The *bagua yi* is usually maroon, dark blue, or the deep *qing* color. Any of these colors can be worn in a given scene. The distinctive feature of the *bagua yi* is the pattern of the eight trigrams arranged around the surface, along with the yin/yang symbol that appears on the front and back chest. The eight trigrams are thought to have come from the markings of a tortoise shell that were then developed by the legendary emperor Fuxi (2852 BC) into mystic symbols. The symbols are made from the eight possible patterns that can be derived by combining a continuous line, the yang principle, with a broken line of the yin principle, in sets of three.[39] Each symbol contains a different meaning, and they are typically arranged on the garment for maximum effect. The sky *(qian)* is on the left shoulder, and the earth *(kun)* is on the right. On the lower left front is the symbol of the wind *(zhuan)*, while opposite it on the lower right is thunder *(zhen)*. On the back, the mountains *(gen)* are located on the lower left, and lakes *(tui)* are on the lower right. The outside of the left sleeve is decorated with the sign for water *(kan)*, and fire *(li)* appears in the same location on the right. The overall meaning of the eight trigram emblems is "to shoulder the sky and earth, to have wind and thunder in the heart, to rely on the mountains and rivers on the back, and to store water and fire in the sleeves."[40] The trigrams are couched in gold or platinum, and in some versions of this costume they are surrounded by a circular floral design.

The yin/yang symbols on the chest and back represent the positive and negative forces in the universe. The dark yin symbolizes the earth, moon, darkness, and feminine aspects, while the light yang represents heaven, sun, light, and maleness. The combined symbol is usually couched in two colors of metallic thread. The combination of the trigrams and yin/yang represent the wearer's knowledge in astronomy and geomancy, religion, and military strategy.

Another version of the *bagua yi* robe is the crane robe *(hechang)*. With an identical cut and surface pattern distribution, the eight *bagua yi* symbols and two yin/yang circles are replaced with ten cranes in roundel designs. The crane means longevity and refinement and is also believed to carry people to heaven.[41] The color of this robe is a light blue gray. Zhuge Liang, for example, wears a crane robe in an episode in *The Battle at Red Cliffs (Chibi aozhan)*.[42]

Accessories. Zhuge Liang always carries a flat feather fan, a symbol of his wisdom, and wears a string of Buddhist rosary beads. The use of the beads started as the result of a performance at the Qing court. The actor Tan Xinpei (1847–1917) performed Zhuge Liang in *The Gathering of Heroes / Borrowing the East Wind (Qunying hui / Jie dongfeng)* and particularly pleased Dowager Empress Cixi with his interpretation. As a reward, she presented him with her own Buddhist rosary beads after the performance. From then on, it would have been an insult to Cixi for anyone portraying Zhuge Liang to appear without the Buddhist beads, even though the *bagua yi* is Daoist garb. The *bagua yi* is worn with black or olive-colored trousers and high-soled, high-topped boots.

Headdress. A matching hat *(bagua jin)* with similar decoration is generally worn with this robe.

FAYI (PRIEST'S CHASUBLE)

Description and History. Daoist priests wear the *fayi* (lit. "magic power clothing") for religious ceremonies. It is a large rectangle, with front and side openings. A contrasting border surrounds the *fayi* on all open edges. The stage garment resembles the actual chasuble in shape, although the decoration is quite different. The base of the stage garment is a solid color, and the border is embroidered with designs appropriate to the character wearing the cape, whereas the historical version has imagery over much of the surface. On the costume there are two tabs of a third color that hang on either side of the center front from about the waist level (Fig. 6.44).

FIGURE 6.44. This *fayi* has the eight trigrams symbols embroidered on the border. The hair is *pengtou* worn long in back, and the crown combines the *lianhua guan* specifically for this character, and the *erlong gu* (double dragon ring, not visible). *The Gathering of Heroes (Qunying hui)*. Character: Zhuge Liang, actor: Li Chongshan. BJC, Beijing, China. July 23, 2000.

Usage. The *fayi* is worn by both priests and immortals, including Zhuge Liang, the Daoist military strategist in the Three Kingdoms stories in *The Gathering of Heroes (Qunying hui)* (BJC, Beijing, China. July 23, 2000).

Color and Ornamentation. When worn by Zhuge Liang, the *fayi* is blue gray with dark blue borders. The *fayi* can be decorated with the eight Daoist attributes or the eight trigrams.

Accessories. Underneath the *fayi*, the actor will wear high-soled, high-topped boots, black trousers, and a black *xuezi* or *bagua yi* robe.

Hair and Headdress: The *fayi* can be worn with the *lianhua guan* (lotus crown) with religious symbols. Zhuge Liang has a hairpiece of long hair *(pengtou)* worn loose on the back of his head when he is wearing this headdress. Hair spread in the back *(pifa)* is a Daoist characteristic.

SENGYI (BUDDHIST ROBE)

Description and History. Monks appear regularly in traditional Jingju stories, and they are dressed in garments similar to those worn by their real-life counterparts. The long *sengyi* has a straight crossover closing to the right, with a wide collar band similar to the *xuezi* and the garment worn by actual Buddhist monks. The sleeves are wider than those of the *xuezi*, and there are no water sleeves (Fig. 6.45).

Usage. An abbot in a Buddhist monastery wears this style of robe.

Color. This robe comes in colors worn in Buddhist monasteries: gray and shades of light brown, beige, and yellow, with the yellow being worn by the head monk. The garment is unembellished as befits the lifestyle of a monk.

Accessories. Characters wearing this costume carry a small string of brown wooden prayer beads in their hand and wear flat-soled shoes on their feet.

Headdress. The *sengmao* (monk hat) is peaked in front and has upturned flaps above the ear area. The character for Buddha is embroidered above the forehead.

XIAO SENGYI (YOUNG MONK'S ROBE)

Description and History. Robes for young monks are calf length and have standard-width sleeves, al-

FIGURE 6.45. The abbot in a Buddhist monastery wears an unembroidered *sengyi* with the *sengmao* headdress. *Hongniang (Hongniang)*. Character: Dharma Source, actor: Song Feng. NJC, Beijing, China. October 5, 2001.

FIGURE 6.46. The *xiao sengyi* and shaved head indicates a younger monk. His trousers are tucked into wide fabric socks. *Hongniang (Hongniang)*. Character: Dharma Wit, actor: Chen Guosen. NJC, Beijing, China. October 5, 2001.

though some examples have the wider sleeve of the *sengyi*. These robes have no water sleeves. The collar band is wide and straight, closing diagonally to the right (Fig. 6.46).

Usage. This style of robe is worn by lower-ranking and younger monks, played by either *chou* or *xiaosheng*.

Color. The robe is usually gray and may have a black collar band.

Accessories. A long string of wooden beads is worn with this garment. Flat-soled shoes in gray or black and heavy white cotton socks cover the lower legs and feet. Black trousers are tucked into the tops of the socks.

FIGURE 6.47. The red cloak of the head monk is worn over a wide-sleeved yellow robe and with a *wufo guan* headdress. *Mulian Saves His Mother (Mulian jiumu).* Character: Mulian, actor: Zhang Miao. ACTO, Beijing, China. June 2, 2002.

Hair and Headdress. A shorter black *sengmao*, with a front peak and the character for Buddha embroidered at the center front, is worn with this lower-status version. The character's head may be shaved, and he may wear no headdress, one of the few examples of a bare head in traditional Jingju.

HEAD MONK CLOAK (*JIASHA*)

Description and History: The red cloak for the head monk is an essentially square wrap worn under the right arm, over the left shoulder, and secured at the chest. The head monk's cloak comes from a real-life monk's garment, the *qingjing zhuang* (lit. "clean garment"). The closing can be either simple ties or an auspiciously shaped S-hook and jade ring. The robe worn underneath is yellow, with a straight crossover closing finished with a wide straight collar strip that has black piping around the edges and wide sleeves without water sleeves (Fig. 6.47).

Usage. The actual monk's cloak is worn with the five-paneled hat described below for reading the rites in Buddhist ceremonies. The name of the garment implies the situation in which it is worn. In traditional Jingju, however, the garment has been transformed into status dress and represents who the monk is rather than the situation.[43]

Color and Ornamentation. The head monk cloak comes in red only, with a couched linear pattern resembling bricks to provide symbolic protection from demons and ghosts. In the past, there were ninety-nine bricks, with eighty-one lines between them, a numerical combination relating to the Chinese belief in nine as an auspicious number.[44]

Headdress. The *wufo guan* (five-Buddha headdress) is flared, has five Buddha figures on the front panels, and white streamers that hang over each ear.

SENG KANJIAN OR WUSENG YI (MILITARY MONK VEST)

Description and History. A military monk wears a black *kuaiyi* under a distinctive black *seng kanjian*, with two moving-water layers of pleated fabric in red-orange and yellow attached to the hem. The neckline of the vest falls straight from the shoulder and is decorated with a contrasting band that ends with the fungus-shaped

Color and Ornamentation. The vest is made only in black, with red-orange and yellow moving-water layers, and it has no embroidery.

Accessories. A white collar and padded vest are worn under the black jacket. The character wears the wide firm sash over the vest and may have the fighter's long silk cords. Trousers and ankle boots or fabric socks and slippers are worn with this combination.

Hair and Headdress. Characters who wear this vest practice Buddhism without getting their hair cut, so they wear a hairpiece made of human or yak hair that is about eighteen inches long. Their head may be encircled with a fillet *(jiegu)*, with or without a crescent shape over the forehead meaning the "ring to forget desires."

SANSE DAO BEIXIN
(THREE-COLOR DAOIST VEST)

Description and History. The three colors of patches on the *sanse dao beixin* come from actual Buddhist garments and are said to symbolize Buddha's ragged clothing.[45] The vests are also called paddy-field clothing *(shuitian yi)* because the patches resemble the squares of the rice fields.[46] The women's *sanse dao beixin* is knee length, with a center-front opening and collar band that ends in the fungus-shaped arabesque at mid-chest (Fig. 6.49). The men's patched vest has a straight lower edge on the collar band and is floor length.

Usage. Both male and female monks may wear the *sanse dao beixin*. Although the vest originated for Buddhists, as with the anachronisms in dress, traditional Jingju usage does not clearly distinguish the religions. The word *dao* in the name of the garment refers to Daoism, and it can be worn by Daoist characters as well. When male monks wear the three-color Daoist vest, it indicates that they possess outstanding martial arts skills.

Color and Ornamentation. The *sanse dao beixin* has a distinctive diamond pattern usually created from a patchwork of one or two tones of blue sewn together

FIGURE 6.48. Military monks dress in the *seng kanjian* over a black *kuaiyi*. This character also wears fabric socks and slippers. His headdress is a circular fillet and as a military monk, he wears the red version of the *sengdao lian* (Buddhist/Daoist monk face). *Hongniang (Hongniang)*. Character: Benevolent Perception, actor: Hou Lianying. NJC, Beijing, China. October 5, 2001.

arabesque at chest height. The front of the vest is worn open and contained with the sash, while the back hangs freely over the sash (Fig. 6.48).

Usage. Warrior Buddhist monks skilled in acrobatics wear the *seng kanjian*.

FIGURE 6.49. A young nun can wear the *sanse dao beixin,* made of pieced fabrics in different colors. *Autumn River (Qiu jiang).* Character: Chen Miaochang, actor: Xu Cui. NJC, Beijing, China. October 7, 2001.

cord hangs on the right for women. The men's *sanse dao beixin* is tied with the wide firm sash with a flat bow in front. The back of the vest is not caught in the sash, but left to hang freely, as in the style for monks' vests. It is worn over a *jianyi* and trousers.

Hair and Headdress. Young Buddhist nuns who retain their hair wear the women's Buddhist hat *(daogu jin).* It is distinguished by embroidered circular pieces in a panel hanging down the back. Martial monks wear filigree helmets with the *sanse dao beixin.*

DAOIST NUN VEST *(DAOGU KANJIAN)*

Description and History. A plain gray or neutral-color vest resembling a real nun's clothing can also be worn by older Daoist nuns onstage. Similar to the knee-length vest worn by other older women, it has the same style of neckband as the *laodan pi,* which ends at mid-chest with a flat edge on the bottom (Fig. 6.50).

Color and Ornamentation. The vest is usually neutral-colored and unembellished, as is appropriate for the character.

Accessories: The Daoist women's vest is worn un-belted over a short garment with a *xuezi*-like closing and without a skirt. Plain black shoes with a slight height in the sole are worn, along with wide white socks of woven fabric that reach to mid-calf. The trousers are tucked into the socks.

Hair and Headdress. An older nun wearing the plain vest has hair similar to that of the *laodan,* with a bun on the top of the crown. A wide flaring headband encircles the crown.

Mythological Creatures and Beings

Description and History. As Chinese tales often contain references to the spirit world and mythological creatures, these characters frequently appear in traditional Jingju stories as well. Since many of these figures are involved in battles, their costumes are based on martial

with white fabrics, although other colors may be incorporated. This is the only traditional Jingju garment that utilizes this form of pieced surface. Although the surface is quite lively with this pattern, the costume is considered plain because in some versions it has embroidery only on the neckband, while others have embroidery in the patches.

Accessories. The women's *sanse dao beixin* is worn with a *nüpi,* skirt, and trousers. A tasseled small cord is tied with a bow around the waist, and the two loops are flipped around behind the cord. Two end tassels hang down the center front, and the third tassel on a sliding

FIGURE 6.50. The Daoist nun vest is unadorned and worn with trousers tucked into wide cloth socks. This character is portrayed by a *caidan*. *A Sorrow that Transcends Life and Death (Sheng si hen).* Character: Old Nun (Lao Nigu), Actor: Li Yingjun. BJC, Beijing, China. July 30, 2000.

FIGURE 6.51. The Crane Boy has costume pieces embroidered to look like feathers to identify his character. *White Snake Steals the Immortal Herbs (Dao xiancao).* Character: The Crane Boy (Hetong), actor: unidentified. NJC, Beijing, China. October 4, 2001.

garments, the *kuaiyi* or *bingyi*, with additional pieces added on over the basic jacket and trousers. The extra collars, peplums, and specialty designs have individualized shapes that often make visual the unique characteristics of the creature, such as a shell for a turtle, fins for a fish, or feathers for a bird (Fig. 6.51).

Usage. Specific costumes are assigned to specific characters.

Color, Ornamentation, and Roles. Color most often indicates the nature of the spirit, with sea creatures dressed in the colors of water and forest animals in earth tones. All of the accessory pieces are embroidered with matching imagery to indicate the type of creature. Frog costumes have a repeated round textured pattern that emulates frog skin; a turtle has an embroidered shell pattern; birds have feather shapes; and fish have scales, and so on.

Accessories. The decorative pieces may include a segmented peplum with overlapping pieces, a wide shaped collar, a belt, and a matching hat. The collar pieces usually have long tabs that can be fixed firmly under the belt so that they stay in place during acrobatic movements. Ankle boots are worn with these sets.

Headdress. The headdresses often have a three-dimensional image of the creature being represented, in a style similar to that of the children's headdresses of the Qing dynasty, which had animal figures on the crown. There can also be a flap over the back of the neck and a diadem framing the forehead.

Ethnic Clothing

QIPAO (MANCHU GOWN)

Description and History. The *qipao* used for traditional Jingju costumes is a descendant of the *qipao* worn as everyday dress during the Qing dynasty by the Manchu women. The *qipao* represents a significant difference in silhouette from most garments worn by Han Chinese women onstage and off. Han women's clothing consisted of two parts, a short robe or jacket and a pleated skirt, while the *qipao* was a single full-length garment. The *qipao* is a narrow trapezoidal-shaped dress with tubular sleeves. It closes to the right with an S-shaped curve and frogs typical of Manchu styling. A standing band collar finishes the neckline. The side seams are open to the top of the thigh. A slimmer, more shapely form of the *qipao* continues to be worn today by Chinese women who have a taste for classical styles (Fig. 6.52 and Appendix 1.14).

The *qipao* entered the traditional Jingju costume vocabulary towards the end of the Qing dynasty, along with other Manchu-styled clothing used to identify women from ethnic minorities. The contrasting silhouette provides a readily identifiable clue of the origins of the character onstage. The onstage convention of wear reflects that of real life to some extent, with Han

women in traditional Jingju retaining the two-piece garments of Han women in history and women of all other groups dressed onstage in the one-piece garments of the Manchu women of the Qing dynasty.

Usage. The *qipao* is worn for everyday scenes onstage by ethnic minority women of higher status and their maids. *Silang Visits His Mother (Silang tan mu)* is one of the most regularly performed traditional Jingju plays where the women wear this style of clothing (BJC, Beijing, China, October 7, 2001). Silang's second wife, Tiejing Gongzhu or Princess Iron Mirror, comes from the Liao state that existed during the Northern Song dynasty (960–1127). Although the Liao clearly came long before the Qing dynasty, the character wears the *qipao* to designate that she is not Han.

Color, Ornamentation, and Roles. The *qipao* comes in many colors, and the designs on the surface distinguish the roles. For higher-status women, the *qipao* is embroidered with sprays of flowers and sometimes butterflies or birds. In addition, the sleeve cuffs, neckline, lap, side vent, and hem edges may have contrasting color borders. There are usually two borders in this version, with the wider border on the outer edge. The inner border may have embroidery on it or possibly a machine-woven pattern. The lower edge of the lapped closing and the upper point of the side vents may be further decorated with the fungus-shaped arabesque in a color matching the attached border fabrics. The serving maids will wear plainer versions of the *qipao*, generally in a pale blue. Sometimes, their robes have narrower bands of trim at the cuff and hem.

Accessories. The *qipao*, like other forms of Manchu dress onstage, is worn with the *huapen di*, footwear developed in the Qing dynasty to imitate the bound feet of the Han women. Hand movements in this robe are distinct, as the *qipao* do not have water sleeves, so these characters carry a handkerchief instead. Straight-legged trousers with bands at the cuffs are worn under

FIGURE 6.52. The Qing-style *qipao,* worn with the *qitou,* represents characters of non-Han ethnicity. Princess Iron Mirror carries a doll to represent her infant on her left arm, and the handkerchief used by non-Han ladies in the absence of water sleeves on their garments. *Silang Visits His Mother (Silang tan mu).* Character: Princess Iron Mirror (Tiejing Gongzhu), actor: Dong Yuanyuan. BJC, Beijing, China. October 7, 2001.

the *qipao*. The serving maid's *qipao* may be worn with a hip-length vest.

Hair and Headdress. The *qitou* hairstyle, with the *liangba tou* ("big wings") is worn with the *qipao*.

In addition to the ethnic clothing covered here, the female *qimang* described in the Major Garments section and the feathers and foxtails in the Accessories section in this Chapter may be used for ethnic characters.

BUFU (COAT WITH A BADGE)

Description and History. The *bufu* dates from the mid-seventeenth century as the Qing court's version of a robe with a rank badge. The Ming dynasty rank badge robe had been full length and broad, and it became the *guanyi* in traditional Jingju usage. The historical *bufu*, in contrast, was a knee-length surcoat with three-quarter length sleeves, reflecting the Manchu preference for more fitted garments. Another significant distinction is that the earlier *guanyi* style opened on the right side, while the *bufu* opened in the center front. The rank badges *(buzi)* were therefore divided in the front and whole on the back. The *bufu* had a rounded neckline, closed with five sets of frogs, and the side seams were vented. The original garment was made of lacquered gauze. In history, the *bufu* was worn over the beautifully enriched dragon robes known as *jifu* for semiformal, public, and informal occasions. The garment was a social equalizer of sorts, as all who were required to wear it were dressed in a similar simple garment, with only the rank badge to distinguish them. Many of these characteristics have been retained by the stage costume (Fig. 6.53). The stage *bufu* so resembles the historical garment that genuine *bufu* have been used as a costume.

Usage. Onstage, ruling-class bureaucrats from the minority nationalities wear the *bufu*. As was the case in real life, it is worn over the *jianyi*, a stage transformation of the historical dragon robe. The *bufu* is usually worn by *chou*.

FIGURE 6.53. The *bufu*, with a rank badge on the chest, is worn by non-Han characters with the *nuanmao*, both items adapted from Qing dress. *Silang Visits His Mother (Silang tan mu)*. Character: Imperial Brother-in-Law, actor: Lang Shilin. BJC, Beijing, China. October 7, 2001.

Color and Ornamentation. All *bufu* are the same black or almost black color and are generally made from a translucent gauze fabric in imitation of the original lacquered gauze. The significance of the images on the rank badge is no longer important.

Accessories. A string of Buddhist rosary beads is worn with the *bufu*, and flat-soled boots cover the feet. A separate collar is worn under the *bufu* robe, as it was historically. It has a blue satin standing collar band and fall collar and attaches to a bib that reaches to the waist in the front.

Headdress. The headdress most often worn with the *bufu* is also a direct copy of the Qing dynasty headdress *jiguan*, called a *nuanmao* (warm hat) for stage usage. Made from black velvet, it has an upturned brim and a rounded crown covered with long red fringe that emanates from the center. A round decoration sits on top of the center of the crown, and a feathered strip reaches from the base of the ornament to past the brim in back. In Qing times, the round ball and the feathers were an expressive of rank, but as with other rank indicators, these distinctions are not retained onstage.

Special Characters

YULIN JIA (FISH-SCALE ARMOR)

Description and History. The *yulin jia*, also named *Yuji jia* for the character Lady Yu, who wears it, was designed by Mei Lanfang. Lady Yu is a favorite concubine of King Xiang Yu in *The Hegemon King Says Farewell to His Concubine*. Lady Yu accompanies Xiang Yu to battle where they are led to believe that they are surrounded and facing imminent defeat. Lady Yu, to divert Xiang Yu from his troubles, performs a sword dance wearing this specially designed set of garments, before committing suicide.

There are two main parts to this set that create the look of armor, the shaped shoulder cover similar to the cloud collar and the paneled skirt cover *(kuazi)*. Both

have curved edges bordered with a band of trim or contrasting color fabric and edged with fringe. The two armor pieces are worn over the *guzhuang* ("ancient" costume), also designed by Mei, which consists of a short jacket with tubular sleeves without water sleeves and a two-piece pleated skirt with wider pleats than the standard skirt. Mei's designs for this character were developed in the second quarter of the twentieth century during his peak as a performer of female roles. With the introduction of Mei's design, the look of this character became conventionalized, and she has achieved the status of a unique image with a costume specific to her role (Fig. 6.54).

Usage. A concubine character usually wears the phoenix headdress and *nümang* or a *gongzhuang*, but this character has unique circumstances as a concubine at a war camp. She possesses skills in the martial arts and in one scene visits the battlefield. Therefore, she requires a distinctive garment to indicate the duality of her position. The fitted style of this garment and the absence of water sleeves also suits the sword dance movements more than the looser *gongzhuang* would.

Color and Ornamentation. The armor is red or blue, and the inner garment is yellow. She is entitled to wear the yellow because of the rank of her lover, the king. As this garment represents armor, it has the fish-scale pattern often used in other armor designs. The scales are couched in gold thread to indicate the high status of this character. In addition to the scale pattern, the front apron also takes the shape of a stylized fish. In some versions there are contrasting borders that are decorated with metal studs.

Accessories. A white collar may be worn at the neck depending on the cut of the cloud collar and the jacket. Flat slippers are worn on her feet. She carries two swords to perform her dance.

Hair and Headdresses. Lady Yu's unique headdress evolved from a Zhou dynasty (1100–221 BC) crown *(mianguan*, lit. "face crown*)* that was worn by officials

FIGURE 6.54. Lady Yu wears the *yulin jia* specifically designed for her by Mei Lanfang to combine women's dress with the look of armor. Her headdress is the *ruyi guan* and she holds the swords for her ill-fated dance. *The Hegemon King Says Farewell to His Concubine (Bawang bie ji)*. Character: Lady Yu, actor: Mumu Sanjinzi. BIBOAP, Beijing, China, July 10, 2000.

throughout Chinese history into the Ming dynasty. It consisted of a flat board that was worn front to back on the head with strings of pearls suspended from the ends of the board. The stage version, the *ruyi guan* (sacred

fungus headdress), was also designed by Mei Lanfang and is smaller than the original headdress. The graceful curve of the emperor's scepter is replicated in the stage headdress, which replaces the flat board of the earlier *mianguan*. The ends are shaped in the fungus-style arabesque, from which hang the strands of pearls. This headdress indicates Lady Yu's status as concubine to a king. The narrow shape also facilitates dancing with swords.

GUAN YU

Description and History. One of the three blood brothers of the Three Kingdoms epic story, Guan Yu appears in many plays adapted for the stage from the Three Kingdoms novel. He has long been greatly admired for his abilities as a brilliant and indomitable warrior, and as he has been deified, portrayals of him onstage are handled with great reverence. Guan Yu has unique movements, musical accompaniment, and some of his costumes are exclusive to his character. For example, he has a specific green *kao*, often worn without flags as they would dilute the impact of his specially designed headdress and beard. Guan Yu's role type is a *hongsheng* (*laosheng* with a red face) rather than a *jing* (Fig. 6.55).

Color and Accessories. All of Guan Yu's specially designed costumes are green, as that is considered the most complementary color for his red face. Guan Yu carries a special weapon, and his distinctive boots are green, with tiger heads on the toes.

Hair and Headdress. The *fuzi kui* was originally designed for Guan Yu, although other characters now wear it as well. It has four upright wires on the back of the crown and wired circles of pearls on either side. Based on descriptions in the novel, Guan Yu also wears a five-strand beard *(Guan Gong ran)*, which is made with extra length and fullness, sometimes of human hair, and is designed specifically for him.

Zhiduyi (Combat clothes for the Monkey King)

Description and History. The Monkey King, Sun Wukong, is a much-beloved character in traditional Jingju as well as Chinese lore. He has a delightful combination of magic, strength, wit, and mischief. His story is told in the epic tale *Journey to the West*, and several of his adventures have been transformed into stage plays. The Monkey King and his monkey soldiers are all dressed in similar styles of matching yellow color garments that have distinctive patterns of fur embroidery. The facial makeup design for the Monkey King and his followers is a pictogram of a monkey's face (Fig. 1.16).

The *zhiduyi* includes a robe and matching trousers. The cut of the *zhiduyi* robe varies slightly from the *jianyi*. The right front is cut straight across at the waist, eliminating the right outer flap, although the underwrap still covers the right leg. The center-front opening can therefore be arranged to have a wider opening, enabling the extreme leg movements that go along with this role. The neckline, right overlap, center-front and back openings, and cuffs have contrasting black borders, and roundels are embroidered on separate fabric and appliquéd onto the chest, back, and shoulders (Fig. 6.56).

Usage. The Monkey King can be played by either a *wusheng* or a *wuchou*, and because of the demands on the performer, more than one actor may portray the Monkey King in a single performance. This costume is worn for the vigorous fighting scenes.

Color and Ornamentation. The Monkey King's *zhiduyi* is solid yellow, with applied black borders and roundels that are surrounded with blue bias edging. The borders are embroidered with whorls and wavy line pattern associated with fur, and the roundels are filled with round dragon designs. The dragons on his garment symbolize that the Monkey King is a god, while the hair is a reminder that he is an animal.[47] The embroidery is done primarily in a range of blues, with gold couching.

FIGURE 6.55. Guan Yu wears green costumes, such as this *kao*, that are unique to his role, along with the *fuzi kui* headdress and a beard of human hair. His make up is *zhenglian* (whole face) with reclining silkworm-style eyebrows. He is played by a *hongsheng* (*sheng* role with a red face) rather than a *jing* performer. *Zhuge Liang Leaves His Thatched Roof Study for the First Time (Chuchu maolu)*. Character: Guan Yu, actor: Wang Zhongwei. NJC, Beijing, China. October 4, 2001.

drill through the sky" helmet), is a flared filigree head-dress with pearls and yellow furry balls. A yellow fur ball is tucked into the headdress in front of each ear. A black strip of fabric circles over the top of the head and ties under the chin, although it does not help to hold the headdress in place. He may also wear a *caowang kui* (self-proclaimed king's helmet) for illegitimate regional rulers, with yellow pompoms, indicating his unsuccessful claim to the throne of heaven (Fig. 7.28, worn on another character).

Monkey Clothes *(Houyi)*

Description and History. The monkey clothes are a variation on the *hua baoyi*. They have two pieces, the jacket, with a crossover closing to the right and two rows of pleated lighter-weight fabric attached to the hem, and matching trousers. The Monkey King's version has a rounded neck with a convex-curved closing rather than the straight diagonal closing of the standard *baoyi*. Contrasting black borders are sometimes stitched around the neckline, closing, hem, and cuffs (Fig. 6.57).

Usage. The Monkey King also wears this garment for combat scenes, such as when he is fighting the eighteen Luohans (*Eighteen Luohans Fight Wukong*) (*Shiba luohan dou Wukong*) (BJC, Beijing, China. May, 1996).

Color and Ornamentation. The garment is usually yellow with black trim. The two-part fur pattern of whorls and wavy lines is scattered on the surface of this set and on the pleated layers as well. The blue and black embroidery threads are couched in gold.

Accessories. A matching belt is worn tightly at the waist, and a kerchief ties around the neck. Thin-soled ankle boots are worn on the feet to help with the acrobatics.

Headdress. The monkey soft beret *(hou luomao)* is worn with the monkey clothes. It has the same surface design as the Monkey King garments.

FIGURE 6.56. The Monkey King wears the *zhiduyi* for scenes of acrobatic combat. This figure wears the simplified version of the *zuantian kui*, with yellow pompoms. The traditional version has three levels. *Causing an Uproar in the Heavenly Palace (Nao tiangong)*. Character: Sun Wu-kong, actor: Jia Yongquan. NJC, Beijing, China. October 7, 2001.

Accessories. The *zhiduyi* is worn with matching flat-soled, ankle-high boots. It is belted with the wide firm sash that has fringed ends. The white collar fills the rounded neckline. A padded vest is worn if needed.

Headdress. The Monkey King's *zuantian kui* (lit. "to

FIGURE 6.57. The monkey clothes resemble the *baoyi*, with fur embroidery. A monkey soft beret with a similar pattern is often worn with the monkey clothes. *Eighteen Luohans Fight Wukong (Shiba luohan dou Wukong)*. Character: Sun Wukong, actor: un-identified. BJC, Beijing, China. May, 1996.

FIGURE 6.58. The *houjia* represents armor for the Monkey King, and his companion wears little monkey clothes. *Causing an Uproar in the Heavenly Palace (Nao tiangong)*. Character, right: Sun Wukong, actor: Jia Yongquan; Character, left: small monkey, actor: not identified. NJC, Beijing, China. October 7, 2001.

Houjia (Monkey armor)

Description and History. The *houjia* has a torso section made of stiffened yellow satin, with elbow-length flared sleeves and rounded peplums. Inner sleeves in red silk crepe go from the shoulder to the wrist. Ornamented yellow gauntlets cover the wrists. The peplum is made in two pieces, with three rounded pieces on the front and sides and a single rounded piece to cover the back. The waist is covered with a wide matching flat belt. Orange tiger fur with black stripes edges the arm-scye seams, the belt, and the hems of the sleeves and peplums (Fig. 6.58).

Usage. The Monkey King wears the *houjia* for battles that are more serious than when the *houyi* is worn.

Color and Ornamentation. As with other monkey garments, the armor is made from yellow fabric. The embroidery is castellated black lines with red dots in between, which resembles armor rather than fur.

Accessories. The red inner sleeves are built into the bodice of the armor. Matching red trousers and kerchief are worn with this set.

Headdress. A *hou luomao*, with matching embroidery and tiger fur trim, sits squarely on the head. A yellow fur ball is tucked in front of one ear, and a black cloth strip goes over the head and ties under the chin in a bow.

Little Monkey Clothes *(Xiao houyi)*

Description and History. The costume for young monkeys is based on the *kuaiyi.* The set includes a jacket with a round neck and a curved crossover closing to the right, matching trousers, and auxiliary pieces. The neckpiece is shoulder width and may have long tabs in the front and back that are secured in the belt. The peplum is made of four sections that are split into two units, one with three pieces and one with one (Fig 6.58).

Usage. This costume is for little monkeys who are soldiers in the service of the Monkey King.

Color and Ornamentation Little monkey clothes are yellow, with the scattered pattern of the two stylized representations of fur, whorls in circles and three wavy lines. The patterns are embroidered in blue and black and surrounded with gold couching.

Accessories. The little monkey set is worn with a solid yellow or red kerchief and flat-soled yellow ankle boots with matching embroidery.

Headdress. A yellow *hou luomao*, with matching embroidery and round ball on top, is worn with this set. Yellow puffs are inserted in front of each ear.

MEI LANFANG DESIGNS

Mei Lanfang was the premier performer of female roles in the first half of the twentieth century. He was involved in the creation of a new category of role, the *huashan* (lit. "flower shirt"), that combined the qualities of *qingyi, huadan,* and martial *dan,* a movement led by his teacher, Wang Yaoqing (1881–1954). His newly created role type subsumed the former role types and allowed performers to exhibit more complex skills and to create more multifaceted characters. These new female characters needed reformed costumes, and Mei drew his ideas from ancient Chinese paintings, often those of mythological figures. His designs are called *guzhuang* ("ancient-style" or pre-Qing dynasty dress) because of their relationship with the past. He wanted to introduce a costume style to complement dance movement and emphasize a more feminine form. In an attempt to overcome the straight lines used in traditional Jingju female dress, Mei switched from having the skirt worn inside a flowing robe to having it more visible on the outside, with shaped hip panels over it. The loose robes were replaced by smaller jackets or blouses tucked into the waist and embellished with small capes or collars that were wide at the shoulder but tapered into the waist. All of the pieces were secured with a wide belt, creating an innovative X-shaped silhouette. The style not only introduced ancient Chinese dress, but it also overthrew the voluminous clothing worn by women at court for centuries, revolutionizing the traditional Jingju costumes into a more twentieth-century, western style of dress. The roles using the reformed styles were released from the confines of knee-length robes, and the fitted form enhanced the overall impression of grace.

Guzhuang ("Ancient-style" dress)

Description and History. The *guzhuang* has many manifestations, the most typical version of which is generally composed of several pieces, with an inner layer of jacket and skirt and an outer layer of variously shaped collar and peplum pieces. Most sets of garments with short peplum pieces worn over the skirt fall into this category of costume. The jacket is worn tucked into the skirt and has a lapped closing with a round neck or

FIGURE 6.59. The *guzhuang* style of dress is worn with the *guzhuang tou* form of hairdressing in ancient-style plays. This character also wears a floral embroidered cape to indicate she is traveling. *Xi Shi (Xi Shi)*. Character: Xi Shi, actor: Ma Shuai. ACTO, Beijing, China. June 2, 2002.

a center-front closing similar to that of the *nüpi*. The sleeves are tubular and may or may not include water sleeves at the hem. The skirt is unusual in that it is sewn shut rather than being made of two separate panels like the standard skirt. The pleats can be formed in more than one way, either with knife pleats all going in the same direction around the skirt, or a central panel in the front with knife pleats folded towards the back on either side. The jacket and skirt of the *guzhuang* can be made of silk chiffon that is lined with a regular-weight silk fabric in a matching color. The two layers of fabric are intended to complement the flirtatious movements of the *huadan* roles or dancing characters. Matching accessories are worn over the jacket and skirt and include a cloud collar or bib with tabs to the waist, a belt, and a peplum with an apron and streamers (Fig. 6.59). Other

FIGURE 6.60. This reformed version of the cloud-terrace costume eliminates the collar and peplum while retaining the wide belt. The hair is dressed in the *guzhuang tou* style. *The Heavenly Fairy Spreading Flowers (Tiannü sanhua)*. Character: Tiannü (Heavenly Fairy), actor: Li Jie. PRSCJ, Beijing, China. April 24, 1996.

schools followed Mei's designs, and this has created similar costumes for characters beyond Mei's repertoire.

Usage. The *guzhuang* is worn by some fairies, dancers, *huadan* roles such as Hongniang, and occasionally a *qingyi* character.

Color and Ornamentation. The *guzhuang* garments are made in pretty pastel colors, with flowered and geometric-patterned embroidery. The accessory pieces are either the same color as the foundation garments or a darker color. The pattern on the accessory pieces is often different from the main garments, but they are united

by similar color choices in the surface ornamentation. The jacket, skirt, and accessory pieces are constructed as a set to be worn together.

Accessories. The actor wears a white collar inside the round neckline, trousers, and flat shoes.

Hair and Headdress. The *guzhuang* costume is usually worn with the *guzhuang tou* ("ancient" hairstyle), also designed by Mei. Upright loops of soft hair emanate from the crown of the head and a long ponytail falls behind. Rhinestones pins and flowers decorate the hair.

Cloud-terrace Costume *(Yuntai zhuang)*

Description and History. The cloud-terrace costume originated as a style of *guzhuang* with decorative pieces worn over the short jacket and full-length skirt. The outer items included a combination collar and bib piece that wrapped around the neckline and a fitted peplum around the hips. The pieces were masked at the waist by a wide cinched belt. Other versions have since evolved, altering the outer pieces, while maintaining the fitted waistline (Fig. 6.60).

Usage. The cloud-terrace costume is worn for roles that involve dancing, either solo or in groups, and represents fairies who fly.

Color and Ornamentation. The cloud-terrace costume is made in pretty pastel colors with floral embroidery.

Accessories. The title character in *The Heavenly Fairy Spreading Flowers (Tiannü sanhua)* (PRSCJ, Beijing, China. April 24, 1996.) has a long streamer wrapped behind her neck that extends several yards beyond the ends of her hands. The length of fabric is used to express her tossing of flowers during the dance.

Hair and Headdress. The *guzhuang tou* is worn with this form of costume. It has the loops of soft hair springing from the crown, in the ancient style, and a long ponytail down the back; it is decorated with pins and other ornaments.

In addition to these costumes, Mei Lanfang also designed the *Yulin jia* armor for Lady Yu (Fig. 6.54) and a version of the *gongzhuang* palace garment with three layers of streamers instead of two and sometimes three layers of water sleeves in yellow, blue and pink (Fig. 6.29).

Accessory Pieces

This section includes basic pieces such as trousers, skirts, vests, belts, and inner garments that can be worn with a range of costumes. The skirts and trousers are either made as a set with the upper garments, as introduced above, or as separate units, discussed below. Footwear is also described. Although water sleeves are a part of the robes, they are included here to present a single description that applies to all garments with water sleeves.

Trousers *(Kuzi)* and Colored Trousers *(Caiku)*

Description and History. The style of unfitted trousers used for traditional Jingju is taken from the trousers that were worn in daily life, which had been absorbed from the steppe nomads into the Chinese wardrobe around the third or fourth century BC. The trousers are made of two tubular legs, with some additional shaping in the crotch, but the hip and waist circumferences are about the same. Both the men's and women's versions are made essentially one size fits all. The trousers for stage use are made of silk in most cases, with a straight wide waistband of muslin or similar cotton fabric sewn to the top of the joined legs, following earlier construction techniques (Fig. 6.61 and Appendix 1.7). Plain inner trousers are called colored trousers *(caiku),* while the embroidered trousers worn either inside or outside have many names, depending on the usage.

Usage. All traditional Jingju characters wear trousers of some kind, as did all Han people. The men of

FIGURE 6.61. The top of the trousers has a wide, open waistband that is folded to fit and secured with a string tie. Note the unpainted chin for this painted face, as the beard will conceal this part of the face. Actor: Christopher Doi. DTD, UHM, Manoa, Hawaiʻi.

privilege wear their trousers under all of their robes and armor (Fig. 4.7). The cuffs of the trousers are generally tied at the ankle and tucked into the tops of their boots. Lower-status males wear trousers, also tied and tucked into their boots or socks, or rolled and cuffed to indicate hard work (Figs. 6.36–37). Soldier's trousers are visible under their short jackets (Figs. 6.34–35). Women's trousers are either concealed by their skirts or long gowns, or are visible when worn with shorter jackets (Fig. 6.38). Their hems are left to hang straight.

Color, Ornamentation, and Roles. If the trousers

are not visible, such as those for *qingyi, laodan* and nonmilitary *laosheng,* and *xiaosheng,* they are generally plain. In recent usage, however, nonmilitary men have begun to wear the embroidered trousers more frequently. Well-to-do *laosheng* generally wear plain red trousers, and *xiaosheng* are dressed in solid color pink, blue, lavender, or other pastel-colored trousers, while *jing* roles generally wear black or maroon trousers. Elderly *laosheng* and *laodan* usually have plain olive-green trousers. Servants wear solid black trousers, and lower-status characters wear plain tea-colored pants. *Qingyi* generally have pink or white trousers, with some floral embroidery.

Trousers worn by *wusheng* and *jing* with military clothing such as the *kao* are often embroidered, as they may be revealed in movement. This is also true of trousers that are visible when paired with short garments. Soldiers have trousers to match their jackets, and both pieces are either plain or embroidered. Jacket, skirts, and trousers sets for women will have embroidered trousers, as they may be worn without the skirt (Fig. 1.9).

Skirts *(Qunzi)*

Description and History. The skirt worn in traditional Jingju resembles a women's style of skirt worn during the Qing dynasty, but this version of a pleated and flat-paneled combination skirt dates back as early as the Song dynasty (960–1279). The skirt is sometimes referred to as paired aprons because it is made of two separate pieces that are mounted on a single cotton waistband that is wrapped and tied around the waist. Each piece consists of a flat panel on each end and a section of knife pleating in the middle. The flat panels are worn in the center front and back overlapping each other, with the pleats on the sides of the body. To secure the folds, the pleats are basted together by hand on the inside in an alternating pattern that creates a honeycomb effect called fish-scale pleating.[48] Women

in the Ming dynasty preferred light-colored or white skirts, and this choice transferred to the stage.[49] There are varying widths and densities of the pleats for different characters. The tighter pleats, requiring more fabric, indicate a higher-status wearer; the one-hundred-pleats skirt *(baizhe qun),* for example, is often worn by *qingyi* roles (Fig. 6.8). Wider pleats are used in the combination of jacket and skirt *(aoqun)* (Fig. 6.40 and Appendix 1.8) often worn by the *huadan,* and in the skirts for the *laodan,* where they are called inside skirts *(chenqun)* (Figs. 1.7 and 6.3). Some skirts for the *huadan* roles are made without the center panels and may have a layer of pleated chiffon over the basic skirt. When the skirt is wrapped around the body, the hem is placed a little longer than the toe of the shoes so that the feet are covered. Because of the open-panel construction (rather than closed seams) as well as tradition, the skirt always has trousers underneath.

Usage. The skirt is a multipurpose item that is worn for formal and informal dress by many of the female roles. As most of their robes are knee length, the skirt is needed to cover the lower legs. The combination of skirt and robe is considered a set of clothes and is worn together, although they are not constructed or stored as a set. When a woman is ill, she wears a pleated white *yaobao* (bloated skirt), which ties above the bust. The ends of the front panels are attached to her fingers to exaggerate her gestures. When the White Snake is pregnant in *The Broken Bridge (Duan qiao)* scene from *The Legend of the White Snake (Bai she zhuan),* she wears this variation (BJC, Beijing, China. July 2, 2000) (Fig. 1.17). A man who is ill will also wear the *yaobao* over his usual garments, as the aging Liu Bei does in *The City of Baidi (Baidi Cheng)* (NJC, Beijing, China. September 30, 2001).

Both male and female prisoners wear the criminal's white skirt *(zuiqun).* The edges of the front panels are drawn up to the waist so that the hem falls from the center front of the waist to the back of the legs, creating a curved line and bringing out the fish-scale pattern basted into the pleats (Fig. 6.38). A skirt worn in this manner may also indicate a fisherman.

Color and Roles. The skirt for *qingyi* is made of white silk, a neutral color enabling it to be worn with many different colors of robes. The white color is an effective complement to the white water sleeves on the upper garments. The skirt for the bridal costume is usually red to match the *nüpi* worn with it (Fig. 1.20 and Table 6.14.B). *Laodan* wear a skirt in either dark blue or green (Figs. 1.7 and 6.3). These three color designations used in traditional Jingju come from the clothing practices of the Qing dynasty.[50] When the skirt is worn with a jacket by a *huadan*, the two pieces match in color (Fig. 6.40).

Ornamentation and Roles. The embroidery on the skirt is focused on the lower half because the top portion is usually covered by a robe. The center panels have sprigs of flowers reaching from the hem to just above the knee. The pleated sections have a border of flowers embroidered around the hem. A skirt worn by the very poorest of characters is solid white with a blue border (Fig. 6.18). An unadorned white skirt is used for the sick and for prisoners (Figs. 1.17 and 6.38).

Vests *(Kanjian)*: Male

Description and History. Men's vests onstage generally have the sloping shoulder and rounded armscye cut of hide-based garments. They are either hip length or to the toe. Men's vests generally close in the center front with either a deep collar band and a tie at mid-chest or a rounded neckline and frogs. Long vests may be worn with a small cord belt with tasseled ends.

Usage. Vests are worn by military characters, gentlemen, and peasants.

Color, Ornamentation, and Roles. Long vests *(da kanjian)* may be worn by a wide range of characters. Emperors and their officials may don a full-length vest

FIGURE 6.62. One example of a man's vest is this short one worn by a military boatman, as well as soldiers, guards, and gatekeepers. The headdress here is a small tasseled helmet *(xiao daoying kui)* with a red tassel. His oar presents his boat. *The Gathering of Heroes (Qunying hui)*. Character: The Boatman (Chuanfu), actor: unidentified. BJC, Beijing, China. July 23, 2000.

made of silk with embroidery, while a plain vest with banded edges will appear on commoners. Soldier's vests *(zu kan)* are also worn as livery for servants, guards, gatekeepers, boatmen, and so forth (Figs. 6.62, 7.39, and Appendix 1.12). They are hip length, red in color, and decorated with gold couching in borders and medallion patterns.

Vests: Female

Description and History. Sleeveless vests were often layered over women's robes with sleeves for decoration or additional warmth. Vests came in lengths from high hip to the floor. In the Ming dynasty, the vests tended to be full length and were worn by serving girls and women of common families.[51] A shorter version of the vest was introduced in the Qing era, and the court vest (*chaogua*), a highly ornamented knee-length vest, was a significant part of female quasi-official dress.

Usage. Women's vests are worn by servants, ladies' maids, and occasionally, middle-ranking women. Vests are combined with several garments, including the crossover and center-front-closing *nüxuezi* and jacket, trousers, and skirt sets. When worn by a *qingyi*, the vest is the longer knee-length version, while *huadan* and servants generally wear the short vest (*xiao kanjian*) (Table 6.24.B and 6.24–25.N).

Color, Ornamentation, and Roles. The color range and decoration of women's vests follows the patterns of color in their other garments. The color of the vest is usually the same value or darker than the rest of the costume. The vests are embroidered with floral imagery appropriate for the nature of the role.

Form and Roles. The shape of the front of the vest often, but not exclusively, reflects the form that is usually associated with each role type. *Qingyi* and *laodan* tend to wear vests with the same center-front closing and collar band shape as their *nüpi*, with a fungus-shaped arabesque on the base of the *qingyi* collar and the straight finish on the *laodan* collar. *Huadan* wear jackets and vests with S-curved lapped closings and standing band collars. This style indicates female roles of common character, including prostitutes and serving maids, and the latter may wear this vest style with pants.

Large Apron (*Da fandan*) and Small Apron (*Xiao fandan*)

Description and History: Women in Southern China used to wear a garment resembling the large apron to protect their clothing while cooking.[52] The top is peaked and secured at a single point at the neck. The rest of the apron is a flat panel that reaches to the knees and is tied at the waist. The small apron is the same shape, but reaches only to the upper thigh. A similar garment can still be seen worn by itself on Chinese infants and toddlers in the summertime.

Usage: The apron is used to indicate working women The large apron is worn over a *nüpi* or *nüxuezi* by the *qingyi* roles in lower circumstances or when at work, and the small apron is worn by the *huadan*, often with the jacket and trousers (Fig. 1.9).

Color, Ornamentation, and Roles: Both sizes of the apron usually have the fungus-shaped arabesque worked in embroidery at the top of the bib and an assortment of pretty flowers on the rest of the surface. The apron fabric is usually dark, in blue or black. With the shorter version, a narrow scarf or panel is tied around the waist to modestly conceal the gap between the legs. Although the shape of the garment is taken from real life, the fabric and embroidery have been made prettier for stage purposes.

Capes (*Doupeng*)

Description and History. Capes (*doupeng*) can be full- or knee-length wraps worn by both male and female characters. The cape is essentially rectangular, with a flare at the front edges and slight curve for the hem. The top edge is pleated into a fitted neckband and is closed at the neck with ties. There are versions of the cape for male and female characters, with different images embroidered on each. A cape with a very similar form was worn during the Qing dynasty and is the likely source of the stage version (Fig. 6.59).

Usage. Capes are used onstage to indicate being outside or traveling because they imply protection from the cold and dirt of the roads. They are not used to represent the cold that comes from changes in the climate or seasons. Capes may also be worn for ceremonial needs, such as newly appointed officials or people traveling on special missions for the emperor.

Color and Roles. The selection and assignment of colors on capes corresponds with that of other garments. Red is often used for warriors and high-ranking officials, and women have pretty colors that match or coordinate with their costumes.

Ornamentation and Roles. Dragons embellish the capes worn by emperors, princes, and high-ranking roles. Men's capes may also be decorated with flowers or left plain. Women's capes have phoenix or floral imagery or may be plain with banded edges. Embroidered capes often have a border that may or may not be of a different fabric color.

Variations. Characters of lesser status or rank may wear a shorter cape. In addition, stage peasants can wear a fringed cape *(suoyi)* designed to imitate the straw or palm bark cape worn as a raincoat by the people in China south of the Yangzi (Fig. 6.63).

Belts

Chinese clothing in history has favored an abundant form, with a volume of fabric, but belts have also appeared throughout the centuries as an accessory. They were particularly useful as a place to hang personal items, as the clothing was constructed without pockets. Belts at court took on assorted profiles, from small cords to wider sashes to the oversized hoop-shaped jade belt worn with official garments. While many traditional Jingju costumes are worn unbelted to give the figure volume and allow for an unbroken view of the embroidery design, several forms of belts are worn with another range of the garments.

Scarf (Yao jinzi). A rectangular embroidered scarf with fringed ends can be used to tie around the waist of both men's and women's costumes. The scarf wraps around the waist twice, and ties in a bow, with the

FIGURE 6.63. A straw cape is imitated with fringe onstage. *Lian Jinfeng Stabs the Giant Clam (Lian Jinfeng)*. Character: Lian Jinfeng, actor: Guo Lingling. ACTO, Beijing, China. June 1, 2002.

streamers of the scarf hanging down the center front or to the left side. Liu Lihua, the *wuchou* in *Fight at Crossroads Inn*, wears a short sash around his waist over his *hua kuaiyi* (ACTO, Beijing, China. June 2, 2002.) (Fig. 6.33). When women wear a scarf at the waist, it generally indicates that they have the lower status of maidservants or else have meager means. Serving maids often wear waist scarves with their jacket, trouser, and apron set or over the jacket and skirt set (Table 6.24–25.B and 6.24–25.N). Poor *qingyi* characters may wear a scarf outside the waist with the *nüxuezi* with a center-front closing, thus indicating their reduced circumstances (Fig. 6.18).

**Wide Firm Sash *(Luandai* or *Dadai). Luandai* and *dadai* are both names for the same sash. The name implies that the belt resembles a phoenix's tail. The firm sash is four inches wide, woven in solid colors or lengthwise stripes, with deep tassels on the ends. The wide firm sash is about three yards long and is wrapped around the waist from front to back and around to the front again, where it is knotted and tied into a bow. A second version of this sash comes in two pieces to facilitate the tying of the knot at the center front. The wide sash looks heroic and is generally worn by warriors wearing the *jianyi* and the *baoyi*, among others (Figs. 4.7 and 6.26). To signal readiness for combat, a performer may kick the ends of the sash over one shoulder. An orange wide firm sash is worn with a black *xuexi* by some household stewards (Table 6.3.B).

**Small Cord *(Xiao taozi).* The small cord has tassels on the ends and a third tassel on a cord looped around the main cord. The spare tassel is worn on the right for women and on the left for men. The small cord is about one-half-inch thick, and with the length of the tassels, it is long enough to go around the waist twice, make a bow, and hang to mid-calf in front. The loops of the bow are generally tucked under the tie forming a "W" at the front of the waist. The small cord comes in a variety of colors, from dark to light, and a complementary one is chosen for each costume. The small cord is quite versatile and is worn with a cross section of garments from the empress dowager to nuns and servants. When worn with the *nümang*, the cord indicates a lower rank than a jade belt (Fig. 6.3). The eunuch's court robe is worn with a cord belt at the waist over the stitched band on the middle of the costume (Fig. 6.24). *Chou* and household attendants can wear a cord belt with the *xuexi* (Fig. 6.15).

**Silk Cord *(Si taozi).* The silk cord is a longer set of cording that is tied around the chest of some of the fighters who wear the *jianyi* or the *baoyi*. The silk cords come in a variety of colors and have long tassels on either end. The silk cord is tied in ornate knots resembling either a modified spoke or honeycomb pattern. The tassels are tucked into the cords at the shoulders and hang down the back (Figs. 4.7 and 8.6).

Fabric Belts. Some of the costumes are made with matching fabric belts about three inches wide that may have decorative streamers in the front. The fabric belts fasten in the back with Velcro. A matching-fabric belt may be worn with the *gailiang mang*. The *jianyi* occasionally has a matching girdle, but more often the waist is pulled in with the wide firm sash. Other men's garments with matching-fabric belts include the *gailiang kao* (Fig. 7.12) and many of the *bingyi* (Figs. 6.34–35). Women's garments with matching-fabric belts include the *gailiang nükao* (Fig. 6.11) and the female counterpart to the *bingyi*, the *zhan'ao zhanqun* (Fig. 1.10). In the case of these fighting roles, the belt has obvious benefits for keeping the costumes in place and facilitating acrobatic movements. The women's *guzhuang* in the "ancient" style introduced by Mei Lanfang also come with matching-fabric belts, as one of his goals was to create a more figure-revealing line for the female roles (Fig. 6.59).

**Jade Belt *(Yudai).* The style of jade belt used in traditional Jingju dress was worn in the Ming dynasty with the dragon robe and the robe with the rank badge. When these two garments morphed into the *mang* and the *guanyi* onstage, the jade belts transferred as well (Figs. 6.1–2, and 6.22–23). A rigid hoop made of leather or bamboo, the circumference of the belt extends significantly beyond the silhouette of the wearer. The jade belt is covered with silk and decorated with plaques made from horn, gold, silver, or jade. Now they are formed of plastic. The jade belt is passed through and clipped to two fabric loops high on the side seams of the *mang* or *guanyi* and closed in the front by a long tongue that fits into a channel on the other side of the belt opening. The jade belt hangs balanced at an angle that slopes down in the front. The jade belt worn with the *mang* is a complementary color, while the *guanyi* version is always black. A woman's wavy-edged *nümang* is worn with a jade belt (Fig. 6.4), and the conventional *nümang* can be worn with either a jade belt or a small cord (Fig. 6.3).

Footwear

Traditional Jingju footwear can be loosely divided into three categories: tall boots, short boots, and slippers. In the case of tall boots and slippers, the footwear seems closely derived from the historical precedents of the Ming and Qing dynasties in both shape and color. Ankle boots appear to be a theatrical development for acrobatics. Jingju footwear does not generally distinguish left and right.

High-soled, High-topped Boots (Houdi xue). Footwear for male official characters in traditional Jingju is closely related to the style of boots worn in the Ming and Qing courts. Numerous portraits of emperors and officials in these dynasties show them wearing boots that are made of black satin and have white soles one-half-inch thick.[53] The historical boots, *maxue* (lit. "horse boots"), indicated that the wearer never left home on foot.[54] Although the top of the boot cannot be seen in the portraits, extant examples in the Palace Museum and other locations indicate that they were knee high and tubular, with either straight or curved tops.[55] While the boots for officials were plain black, those for the emperor were made of black and yellow satin, with embroidered ornamentation. Also, a variety of dimensional toe ornaments could be designed on the boots at court, including cloud- and tiger-shaped toes. This pattern of usage transferred to the stage, where officials continue to wear unadorned black satin boots, but special characters have more distinctively colored and ornamented boots.

In history, the depth of the rigid sole varied from the half inch shown in the sedentary portraits to a three-inch-thick version used for horseback riding. The Manchus ruling in the Qing dynasty developed a thicker sole to permit them to stand up in the stirrups while riding. The sole was made from a combination of paper, cotton, and leather felted together and painted white. It has also been said that the soles were made from the Bibles distributed by missionaries.[56] In both court and stage usage, the bottom of the thick-soled boot is tapered in at the front to make it easier to walk (Figs. 4.7, 6.27, and 7.13). In performance, the characters who wear these boots walk with a slow gait, extending their legs unbent in front of them and then rocking forward to change feet. *Laosheng*, *xiaosheng*, and *jing* may wear this style of boot. The thickness of the sole varies from two to three-and-a-half inches to indicate rank and status, with the lower-soled boots worn by lower-ranking or elderly characters. The cake of white makeup used for drawing the *jing*-painted faces and *chou doufu* makeup patch is also used to maintain the white soles of the boots.

***Chaofang* (Medium-soled boots).** The *chaofang* style of boot has the same tall top as the *houdi xue* style of boot, but the sole is only one-half-inch thick. This kind of boot is worn by some eunuchs and *chou* officials and emphasizes their smaller stature and spirit; it is also worn by older men, household servants, and secondary characters (Fig. 6.15).

Martial Boots (Baodi xue). The male and female combat roles wear ankle-high boots with a soft, flat sole to permit the performance of acrobatic feats. *Baodi xue* is the overall category for short boots, and within this category are the "fast boots" (*kuai xue*) (Fig. 6.33), referring to those boots that have pointed, curled toes and may be embroidered, and the small "barbarian" boots (*xiao manxue*), which are specifically embroidered boots with pointed, curled toes worn by women warriors. Martial boots come in black as well as a range of colors to match the costumes. Combatants in the *kuaiyi* and *baoyi* wear this style of boots, as do *longtao* (attendants) and other servants and *chou* (Fig. 5.1). Female roles may wear them with the *nükao, gailiang nükao,* and the *zhan'ao zhanqun.*

Slippers *(Daxie* or *Zaoxie).* The lowest-ranking men wore shoes rather than boots in the Qing dynasty, and this tradition continues onstage. Boatmen, waiters, prisoners, and the comic *caidan* all can wear a style of slipper. In some cases the slippers are worn with white sock-like pieces made from heavy woven fabric. These reach to the mid-calf, where the bottom of the trousers is tucked into them. The shoes are tied on at the ankle over these socks (Figs. 6.37 and 6.48).

Embroidered Slippers *(Caixie).* Women's shoes onstage diverged from historical fashion, for the Han women had been binding their feet since around the beginning of the Song dynasty. Until recently, some *dan* performers imitated the look of the bound foot with *caiqiao* (stilts) supporting the foot in a tip-toe position, allowing the performer to walk on their toes. *Qingyi* and *huadan* now wear flat slippers in a variety of colors to match or blend with the costumes. The shoes are embroidered and have a large silk tassel on the toes (Fig. 6.64).

***Fuzi Lü* ("Good fortune" shoes).** Shoes for older *laodan* and other roles, the *fuzi lü* have a slipper-style upper similar to those worn by younger women. The sole is thicker and referred to as the "bottom of the vessel" shape because it is tapered in the front like a boat. The shoes are usually olive green, with a black velvet appliqué that includes bats in the design (Fig. 6.65).

***Huapen di* (Flowerpot sole shoes).** Another style of shoe worn onstage resembles the platform soles that were worn by Manchu women at the Qing court, the *huapen di,* also called *qixie* (Manchu shoes). Although they did not wish to bind their feet, the Manchu women still desired the look of a small foot. Binding feet distorts them to about three inches long and four inches high. By wearing a pedestal shoe with a curved

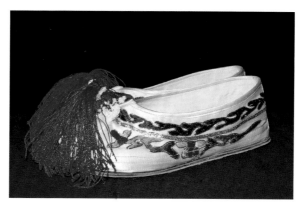

FIGURE 6.64. Young women's slippers have embroidery and tassels on the toes. From the collection of DTD,UHM, Manoa, Hawai'i.

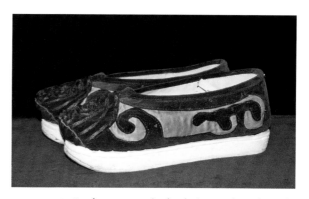

FIGURE 6.65. *Laodan* can wear the *fuzi lü* shoes with an elevated sole and black velvet appliqué. From the collection of DTD,UHM, Manoa, Hawai'i.

block of wood under the arch, similar to a shape of a flower pot, the sole gave them the additional height and small profile achieved with foot binding. The gait is altered by the elevation of these shoes, and a jaunty, swaying step, with arms swinging, is used, rather than the demure, restrained glide of the standard female roles. The *huapen di* are worn exclusively with other items of Manchu dress, including the *qipao* and *qimang* (Figs. 6.5 and 6.66).

Straw Sandals *(Caoxie).* Some lower-status male characters, including boatmen, wear straw sandals. The

FIGURE 6.66. The *huapen di* imitate Manchu women's shoes with the pedestal lift. From the collection of DTD, UHM, Manoa, Hawai'i.

sole is woven straw, and the sides are partially open. They are secured with ties (Fig. 6.17).

Socks *(Baibu dawa)* and Gaiters *(Bangtui).* Socks and gaiters provide a different silhouette at the bottom of the leg. Some roles, including waiters and monks, wear a pair of socks made from a heavy white fabric. The socks are wide at the top, and the bottoms of the trousers legs are tucked into them (Figs. 6.28, 6.37 and 6.48). The gaiters can be worn with the *bingyi* or *kuaiyi* and usually match the costume in color and ornamentation. They are curved and trapezoidal to fit snugly around the lower leg; they reach to mid-calf and fasten in back with Velcro (Fig. 6.35).

Inner Garments

Actors are dressed in layers of clothing to complete the look of the garments as well as to protect the costumes from perspiration and makeup. In addition, many performers will wear their own simple trousers and T-shirts under the inner garments provided by the troupes. During the Ming dynasty, undergarments for men included a short jacket, loose trousers, and an inner robe of lightweight silk.[57] It appears that the layering of garments for traditional Jingju has evolved from this pattern of wear, for beneath the robes for court and leisure wear, all characters, male and female, wear similar layers of clothing. In addition, outer garments may be worn on the inside, depending on the needs of the play. In addition to the garments listed, the *jianyi, baoyi,* and sometimes the *mang* or *kao* may be worn underneath other garments.

Water Jacket *(Shui yizi).* In the Qing dynasty, people wore an inner garment made from the tiniest branches of a bamboo tree to protect their clothing from perspiration. The tubular branches, about the size of bugle beads, were strung together in a diamond-shape pattern to create either a sleeved or sleeveless garment opening in the front. In earlier periods, actors may also have worn this garment to protect their costumes, but now the bamboo garments have been replaced by the water jacket, a simple crossover-cut absorbent top with long sleeves, made from light blue, dark blue, or white cotton woven fabric. It ties closed in the front. All actors wear the water jacket onstage, and the color is usually coordinated with the garments and the roles. The dark blue is worn with the *kao* to create a dark shadow as the *kao* is open on the sides and underarms. Male and female characters wear the light blue or white water shirt (Figs. 6.61 and 6.67).

***Xuezi* (Informal robe).** Male roles wear a solid color, unembroidered *xuezi* underneath the *mang* or *pi.* If the outer garment will be removed onstage, the inner *xuezi* may be embroidered. This inner *xuexi* has the same cut and water sleeves as the outer *xuezi,* and as a consequence each actor wearing a *xuezi* as an inner garment has two water sleeves on each arm. In the Ming era, women wore a center-front closing jacket with a high-standing collar as an inner garment.[58] Female roles now wear the center-front closing version of the *xuezi* under their *nüpi,* filling the gap at the base of the neck. A brooch is worn at the join between the standing collar

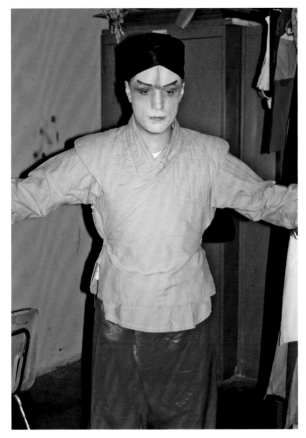

FIGURE 6.67. A water jacket, an absorbent cotton garment, is worn under most costumes to protect them from perspiration. The smaller padded vest is worn over it for *sheng* roles. Actor: Andy Utech. DTD, UHM, Manoa, Hawai'i.

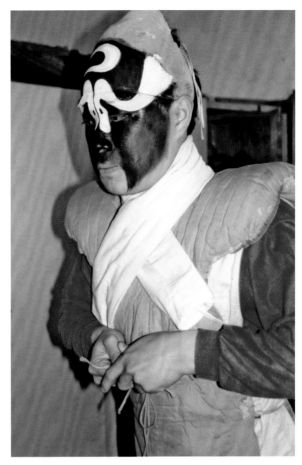

FIGURE 6.68. Under many of the costumes, a *jing* actor wears a heavily padded vest and white collar. This performer is wearing his own shirt rather than the water jacket. AMSTCO, Beijing, China.

band and the neckline on the inner *xuezi* as a decorative detail (Fig 1.8).

Inner Collar *(Huling).* The inner collar is a rectangle of white cloth that is wrapped around the neck, crossed in front left over right, and tied around the waist. The inner collar has an additional string on the center back of the neck that hangs to the waist. where it is caught by the waist ties. During the Ming dynasty, the emperor Hongwu (1368–1398) ordered all ladies-in-waiting to wear a paper collar guard. As it was inexpen-

sive and convenient, the inner collar became popular for everyone and transferred to stage use.[59] Now virtually all male and female roles wearing robes and armor wear an inner collar made of fabric. The male version comes in different thicknesses designated for different role types and garments. The inner collar is worn directly under the outer garment, creating an attractive white edge at the neck (Fig. 6.68).

Padded Vest *(Pang'ao,* lit. "fat jacket"). To shape the torso, *jing* and *sheng* actors wear a padded vest. The padded vest is a theatrical convention, and it balances the increased height that comes from the platform shoes and the elaborate headdresses. The amount of padding on the chest and shoulders varies with the nature of the role; *jing* wear the largest and the broadest shoulders and *xiaosheng* use the smallest. The vest is open on the sides and closes with a crossover flap in the front, with ties at the waist (Figs. 6.67–68).

Water Sleeves *(Shuixiu)*

Water sleeves are the lengths of white silk attached to the sleeve hems of court robes and upper-status dress. Water sleeves never appeared in historical daily dress; they originated from period dance costumes. The combination of long sleeves and beautiful dancing was an admired theme in classical Chinese poetry and literature.[60] Originally the sleeves of the garments were extended to lengthen the line of the arm and enhance the arm movements, but when they proved to be too heavy, the garment sleeves were shortened and augmented with a lighter-weight length of silk.[61] A female dancer shown in a painting from the Qin and Han period (221 BC–220 AD) has long, lightweight extensions of fabric on her sleeves.[62] Images from the later Tang dynasty Dunhuang frescoes show additional examples of this fabric technique used for enhancing the movement of the dancers.

Although theatre performance added words to the dance form, the telling of the story relied on an integration of choreography that continues to play a significant part in the convention of style. As a result, the costumes have evolved in a way that gave movement prime importance, and so stage garments retained the graceful lines that come with the gestures of water sleeves.[63] In courtly attire, the sleeves were often enlarged, but they were more likely to extend in width than in length. The patterns of etiquette that developed to avoid dragging these sleeves through dinner were probably additional contributors to the many movements now related to sleeve usage onstage. Both the dance and historical gestures with water sleeves are an essential aspect of choreography in traditional Jingju.

Water sleeves are found on most traditional Jingju garments, except for those used for combat, the garments of Manchu extraction, and some lower-status roles. The length of the water sleeve is correlated to the character. Attendants and servants, if they have water sleeves on their garments, have the shortest versions. Higher-ranking men have longer water sleeves, and the longest water sleeves, about two feet in length, are reserved for the *dan*. The sleeves of the garments extend about six inches beyond the hand as well, adding to the abundance of fabric in the silhouette. Rather than continuing the tubular line of the sleeve, water sleeves are left open on the underarm seam (Figs. 2.8, 6.1, and throughout).

Makeup, Hair, and Headdresses

Between the rich colors and textures of the costumes, and the bedazzling, animated headdresses, the faces of the performers would be lost without the benefit of makeup. The enhanced visage has long been a tradition in both daily life and performance in China, and consequently, makeup designs have evolved into elaborate expressions of the countenance, from the epitome of beauty to the amplification of character through vibrant color and intricate patterns. The makeup, more than any other aspect of the stage image, converts the actors from mere mortals into the theatrical ideal. With their stylized movement and altered voices, these breathtaking beings transcend the worldly image of humans, becoming icons on the stage.

The concept of painted faces developed from the facial disguises created through mask and makeup in ritual, legend, literature, and theatrical invention. As early as 4,000 years ago, in the kingdom of Shu, shamans used masks while performing ritual activities. Over 2,400 years ago, during the Warring States period, warriors used colors to dye their faces and skin and to blacken their teeth.[1] The famous legend of Prince Lanling, who lived during the northern dynasty of Qi (550–577), tells of another use of masks that is often related when recounting the early use of facial makeup in Chinese theatre. The prince was a valiant warrior with unusually attractive features. In order to appear more ferocious to his enemies, he wore a mask with a vicious visage in battle, and by this device he proved himself to be a powerful warrior. His people celebrated his success with a song-and-dance performance that featured actors wearing masks. By the Tang (618–907) and Song (960–1279) dynasties, records show that actors wore masks or makeup, indicating that the transfer of facial modification to performance had occurred by this time.

The process of applying makeup in the Tang and Song eras was called *tumian* (to smear the face), and two versions were applied in theatrical presentations. The *jiemian* (smart face) used makeup to beautify the features for the male and female roles. The *huamian* ("flower" face) was used on the faces of the *jing* (painted face) and the *chou* (clown) roles.[2] The design of the *huamian* was relatively simple in this era, for only white, black, and red were used, and in uncomplicated patterns. A patch of white paint was often put in the center of the face for the comic roles, an apparent precursor to the current facial design used for *chou*. The use of the word *hua* to describe the patterns in the face makeup continues to the present day, and the current *jing* roles are sometimes referred to as *hualian*, another way of saying "flower face," which also has connotations of being patterned, complicated, and painted. The *jiemian* and *huamian* designations established a tradition of two opposites in face painting that continues to be practiced in traditional Jingju.

In the Yuan dynasty (1271–1368), black, white, and color were used in theatrical makeup, as can be seen in a mural painted in 1324 in the Guangsheng Temple in Shanxi province depicting Yuan variety drama.[3] The practice of distinguishing the roles with face painting had continued according to this image, with the *chou* identified by white patches and the *jing* face blackened in the eye and nose areas. It was not until well into the Ming dynasty (1368–1644) that the use of additional colors and decorative patterns began to emerge. During this era, face paint blossomed from the original minimal designs to more complex patterns and colors that were codified for the individual roles. It is believed that painted faces were used more in the Ming years because military dramas had become very popular. While the costumes projected the social status of the characters, the makeup was used to suggest their moral qualities and disposition.[4] The term *lianpu* (lit. "face chart"), used to describe the designs of face paint, emerged in the Ming dynasty and continues in use today. By the Qing dynasty (1644–1911), the highly ornamented facial patterns were well established in both color and detail. Coincidentally, the fashion in men's hair during the Qing dynasty assisted the application of the painted face patterns. The front of the hair was shaved back to a line that went from ear to ear over the top of the head, leaving the back hair long and worn in a queue. The heightened forehead gave the actors a larger canvas on which to paint designs, and the proportion of the pattern was now equal above and below the eyes.[5] While some actors today still shave their heads for performances, an alternative is to place a piece of fabric around the forehead and apply the face design over it. The ornate patterns usually obscure the line of the fabric across the brow.

While masks still play a limited role in traditional Jingju, makeup has become dominant, probably because it preserves audibility and facial expression. Where the mask obliterates the actors' appearance, the makeup heightens the features and thus intensifies the actor's facial expressions. Paint, while not the same kind of barrier as a mask, still alters the face enough to significantly affect the normal expectation of recognition and human interaction, and so can successfully separate the *jing* and *chou* from the natural world.

Today, styles of makeup for traditional Jingju characters remain clearly divided into two categories. The *jiemian* of the Song dynasty has evolved into the *mocai* (ink coloring), the style of makeup seen on the *sheng* (standard male) and *dan* (female) roles; it employs white or natural face color, with rouge accents and blackened details around the eyes and brows, thus enhancing and idealizing the natural appearance of the face (Figs. 7.3 and 7.34). The Song dynasty *huamian* continues in *goulian* (lit. 'to outline the face") procedures, which are used for the *chou* and *jing* roles.[6] The *chou* facial pattern still features a small patch of white makeup on the center of the face (Fig. 7.29), while the *jing* or painted face designs enlarge and overstate the original facial contours with intricate patterns and artificial colors (Figs. 7.4–13). In each case, the natural face is obscured, and the identity of the character is visualized in the external appearance of the face.

Women's Makeup

Since ancient times Chinese women have used makeup to enhance their appearance. The Tang dynasty was a highpoint in feminine beauty, with lovely layered gowns in sheer silk fabrics and layering in the colors of makeup as well. Because the Chinese admired pale skin, white powder was used to cover the face. A red powder was put on the cheeks, while the eyebrows and mouth were enhanced with black makeup. Sometimes women also painted flowers between their brows and used additional glazes of blue or yellow powder.[7] In the Qing dynasty, women continued to favor a white face and drew in eyebrows that were long and thin. The lips were very small and round, with just a bit of color applied in the middle of the mouth, or only on the lower lip.

The attraction to white faces in court fashion possibly contributed to the use of white makeup for female characters in traditional Jingju. As early as the beginning of the twentieth century, the makeup design for the female roles used white powder and black around the eyes and brows, while adding a spot of red on the lips. Gradually the amount of red was increased from the cheeks up past the eyes and above the brow, creating a peony blush, as seen today. The famous *dan* actor Mei Lanfang is credited with adding this technique of coloring to the *dan* makeup design.[8]

Using black makeup, the natural eyebrow line is replaced by an uplifted arch, called the silkworm shape, and the eyes are gracefully outlined with an extension painted beyond the outer edge. The upward angle of the eyes and the brow is further amplified when the skin at the temples is drawn up by the tapes of the headdress. A rim of bejeweled flat shiny black hair coils arranged across the forehead and two sweeping sideburns complete the egg-shaped face desired for the feminine ideal. This stunning contrast of white, black, and red creates the facial appearance now used by female performers for the *qingyi* (young to middle-aged women), *huadan* (lively young women) and *wudan* (martial *dan*) roles (Fig. 1.8). The color and design of their stylized makeup augments the facial features, making them strong enough to balance the complex beauty of the headdress and the costume. The elderly *laodan* (mature women), in a simpler costume and without the blush of youth, have a more natural skin tone, a bit of rouge, and a few age lines (Fig. 1.7).

Two types of makeup are used for the *dan* and *sheng* characters, *junban* (lit. "handsome/beautiful makeup"), using red or pink pigments, and *shuaiban* (old makeup), which has less color. The distinction is determined by age, health, and status. The young and fit characters, such as the *qingyi* and *xiaosheng*, use the *junban* makeup. The *laodan* and *laosheng* can wear either the *junban* or the *shuaiban*, with the elderly, weak, and poor characters typically wearing the *shuaiban* version. Before the 1980s, all *laodan* wore the pale facial color of *shuaiban*, but since then the style has been reformed by Wang Shufang (1947–), and most *laodan* are seen in the more colorful *junban*. *Laosheng* with black beards wear the *junban* style, regardless of their status. When *laosheng* use the *shuaiban*, they always wear a white beard with it.

The Makeup Process: *Qingyi*, *huadan*, and *wudan*. While a honey-and-water mixture was originally used to prepare the face, a petroleum jelly may now be applied liberally to cover the skin before beginning the makeup process. A pale pink foundation of grease paint is patted over the entire face area, using the outside of the palm of the hand to spread the color (Fig. 7.1). The light pink makeup reads as white onstage. The rouge (*dahong*) is a bright crimson or pinkish-red grease-based makeup. It is applied using the middle finger, starting at the center of the eye sockets where the color is the most intense. Then the rouge is fanned out towards the temples and down past the cheekbone, blending into the pale pink. The inner edge creates a straight line down the nose from the inside edge of the brow to below the nostril. The location of this line can help to shape the nose, making it broader or narrower as desired. Then the face is powdered with a pale powder to set the colors. The red may be reinforced with a red-orange powdered rouge, particularly to bring out the area above the eye (Fig. 7.2).

The black for the eyes and the brows is a powder mixed with water to make it darker and applied with a brush to paint a softened edge. The line is darker at the base of the lid and grayer towards the top of the stroke. The form of the darkened area is an S-shape, without the extra curl on the outer corner of the eye. A second line drawn under the eye starts at the inner corner, without meeting the upper stroke, and encircles the eye at the outer edge. The brow line starts at the natural brow at the bridge of the nose and sweeps up-

FIGURE 7.1. *(Left)* The makeup for *qingyi* starts with a smooth application of pale pink foundation. Li Yanyan, ATCO, Beijing, China.

FIGURE 7.2. *(Right)* Red rouge is added around the eyes and upper cheeks. Li Yanyan, ATCO, Beijing, China.

ward towards the temple. The lips are painted with a brush in the same color as the cheeks. The shape is natural and full (Fig. 7.3). For the completed image of this performer, see Fig. 8.1.

The Makeup Process: *Laodan*. The makeup for the *laodan* uses a more natural color for the base. The rouge is applied very subtly, just round the eyes, without moving down over the cheeks. The eyes are barely outlined in black, as are the brows, which are drawn in a less exaggerated shape than the younger ladies. *Laodan* also have three lines at the outer corner of the eye to indicate crow's feet wrinkles (Fig. 1.7).

Men's Makeup

The Makeup Process: *Xiaosheng*. The makeup for *xiaosheng* (young men) uses the same pale base and rouge color as the young ladies, along with the black liner around the eyes and accenting the brows. The process of application and resulting visual effect is similar to the women's, with the addition of an area of red rouge between the inner corners of the eyebrows. The area

FIGURE 7.3. Black lines accent the eyes and brows, and the lips are brushed with red lipstick. Her hair is applied in Figs. 7.21–23, and the completed character can be seen in Fig. 8.1. Li Yanyan, ATCO, Beijing, China.

is arched for *wenxiaosheng* (civil *xiaosheng*) (Fig. 7.36) and pointed for *wuxiaosheng* (martial *xiaosheng*) (Figs. 7.34–35). In some plays a character shifts between these two role types, but rather than changing makeup, the actor will apply one or the other form of face design and use it throughout the performance.

The Makeup Process: *Laosheng*. *Laosheng* wear a more natural facial color, similar to the *laodan*. Their rouge color is scarlet or orange red *(zhuhong)* and is applied around the eyes and in a wedge or arc shape on the forehead. The eyes and brows are accented with black (Figs. 4.1–2 and 7.32).

The Makeup Process: *Wusheng*. The *wusheng* (martial male) base color varies with the character and his age. Some can have a color that is closer to the *xiaosheng*, while others may be more like the color of the *laosheng*. The *wusheng* also have a wedge shape of rouge between their brows, with the point facing upwards. Black lines reinforce their eyes and eyebrows (Figs. 1.6 and 7.24).

Lianpu (Lit. "face chart") Makeup

Lianpu designs are used with all *jing* and *chou* roles. Both role types developed from the clown roles in Song dynasty performances, and both acquired at that time the use of face paint. The *jing* roles gradually became larger than life, men of power, with the patterns of face paint that came to reinforce the essence of their characters; they have makeup that reaches beyond the natural area of the face. The *chou* roles, on the other hand, became comics and were considered smaller than life. The white patch that appears in the center of the *chou* face appears coincidentally to shrink face size.

Each character has a standardized design for his face that has been developed by successive generations of performers based on the temperament and personality traits of that character, so there are as many face designs as there are *chou* and *jing* characters. In addition, each school that trains performers has a distinctive approach to the application of the makeup for each character. The design features of *lianpu* are also modified to complement the bone structure and musculature of each actor. Though the specific interpretations of a character's designs can vary, each version works within an established pattern for that character, so the audience can still identify and recognize the significant designs expressing the personality.

Jing **Makeup.** The design of the *jing* face is not a portrait, but rather is closely linked to the disposition, moral nature, and age of the character represented. The color and overall pattern reveal internal personality traits that are further denoted by the shapes of the features. Some of the design compositions came from the study of facial anatomy, the shapes of the bones and

muscles, along with the folds and wrinkles that come with age. While at first makeup merely enhanced facial features, many of the designs have evolved into highly artistic, exaggerated, and purely theatrical forms that go far beyond human facial characteristics. In most cases, the distinct areas of the face are still identifiable within the elaboration, for the patterns heighten the eyes, brows, and nose with intense shapes that increase the three-dimensionality of the face, but for other designs, the underlying face is virtually obscured.

Jing **Color.** The colors were imbued with meaning during the Ming dynasty, with a red face designated for loyal generals, a blue face for arrogant rascals, and yellow for devious and shrewd characters. These meanings have remained essentially the same to the present day. A limited number of additional colors are also used as the basic hue for the faces. When the pattern is simple, the color of the face is apparent, but when the design is complex, the dominant color, or the color of the forehead, or the color in the center of the forehead determines the designation of a facial color. While the colors applied to the face are sometimes the same as colors used in the costumes, the meanings of the colors are not related, nor are facial colors ranked as the costume colors are. In most cases the color of the face contrasts with the hue of the costume so that the face is not lost in a sea of color and pattern. One exception is the black-painted face roles, who generally wear black costumes.

The choice of color in face painting sometimes derives from the written literature about the historical characters who appear in traditional Jingju plays. Guan Yu, from the Three Kingdoms story, was referred to as having a "red ochre complexion," and his stage makeup is a plain red face. Bao Zheng, the famous judge from the Northern Song dynasty (960–1127), was called "iron face" because he was impervious to bribery and influence, but he was also so ugly that his parents did not want to raise him. His stage counterpart, Judge Bao, is now depicted with black and brown face paint.

The color characteristics described below depict a representative sample of meanings.

***Jing* Color Characteristics.** Red faces are for straightforward men who are loyal and courageous. In Chinese culture, such characters are considered "men with the nature of blood," hence the choice of red for their makeup. The red signifies that the character is an intrinsically good man who can be trusted to be steadfast in his bravery. Guan Yu has red makeup, but he is actually played by a *hongsheng* (red-faced *sheng*) rather than a *jing* actor (Fig. 6.55).

Purple, which reads as maroon or brownish red, when covering the lower part of the face, is for well-respected characters who have reached an age of maturity (Fig. 7.5). They are also strong willed. A full maroon face indicates a barbarian.

A full pink face is used for high officials who are stubborn and arrogant (Fig. 7.6). When pink is used on the lower part of the face, in the 60 percent face, the color indicates age.

Gray faces convey several meanings. Bandits may wear gray faces as an alternative to blue or green, for the color resembles the shell of a shrimp or other sea creatures long ago associated with pirates. Gray also relates to silver and may appear on mythological characters. Gray may also represent elderly characters.

Black or very dark faces may be used for upright characters with absolute integrity, but they are also temperamental or choleric. The black denotes their unfaltering adherence to the laws of the state. Other characters with black makeup can be brave, but they are rough and less educated or polished in social behaviors (Fig. 4.5).

A white visage is the most treacherous and is reserved for characters of the deepest infamy. Two forms of white makeup carry different meanings. A white powder makeup prepared with a layer of white cake makeup creates a dry shell. This matte surface *(fenbai)* appears to conceal the blood color or humanity of the character

(Fig. 7.4). Such matte-white-faced characters are intolerant and unsympathetic. A second category of white face is the shiny white *(youbai)* created with oil-based makeup; this is used with somber, arrogant, and overbearing characters (Fig. 4.8).

Blue-faced characters are often Robin Hood hero types who are upright. Blue can also indicate fierce generals with bold courage, who are capable of intense loyalty, although they can be obstinate and calculating.

The color yellow indicates characters who are ferocious, cunning, clever, and crafty, with a reserve of hidden strength and a bit of mystery about them (Fig. 7.30).

Green-faced characters are formidable bandits, heroes, and generals, who are excitable, impulsive, and violent, tending towards being evil and wicked. This color is also used for characters from the spirit world.

Gold is used for gods and immortals because gold is associated with Buddhist images of gods in the temples (Fig. 7.12). Lesser immortals are indicated by silver face paint.

***Jing* Patterns.** The facial design is another important tool for projecting the character of the painted-face roles. The simpler designs indicate individuals with stable characters and serious natures. The more complicated patterns reflect more tempestuous natures, with less control over their emotions, and this is expressed by the face makeup. One color generally dominates, with the possibility of minor colors being used along with white for the boundaries and black lines for details. As opinions vary as to the number of classifications of face patterns, as well as the subsets within them, the goal here is simply to identify the essential features of the generally agreed upon forms of designs. In addition to the basic pattern of each category, some of the main forms have a variation with *hua* (flower) added before the name, meaning it has been embellished with multiple colors and layers of patterns. This feature has also contributed to the name *hualian* that is sometimes used

FIGURE 7.4. The *zhenglian* is a solid-color face with linear accents. A flat white makeup represents the most treacherous of characters. His beard is a *man rankou* and the hat is a *xiangsha* for prime ministers. *The Gathering of Heroes (Qunying hui).* Character: Cao Cao, actor: Luo Changde. BJC, Beijing, China. July 23, 2000.

for this role category. Most of the painted-face characters wear beards that conceal their mouths, so that area is not featured in those designs.[9]

***Zhenglian* (Whole face).** The *zhenglian* is the oldest and simplest design, where the entire face is painted in one color. The features, which resemble the human face, are painted with small brushes using black or white paint. Characters with solid face patterns have integrity and are models of virtue. Judge Bao has a black full face with a crescent moon on his forehead, a symbol of his ability to go from the upper to the netherworld (Fig. 4.5). At the other end of the spectrum, Cao Cao, the ruthless warlord in the Three Kingdoms stories, has the white face painted with cake makeup to conceal his deceitful nature. The purity of the white symbolically hides his evil intentions (Fig. 7.4).

***Liufen lian* (60 percent face).** The *liufen lian* has two large blocks of color that divide the face horizontally above the eyebrow area. The lower part of the face comprises about 60 percent of the face and has a darker color, while the upper part of the face is white, with a narrow wedge of color in the center of the forehead that matches the base and determines the color by which the face is known. This style evolved from the full face. The *liufen lian* is usually used for an old general or government minister, and the principal colors are red or purple (reddish brown), which represent faithfulness and maturity (Fig. 7.5).

***Sankuaiwa lian* (Three-tiled face).** The *sankuaiwa lian* has the forehead, nose, and both cheeks in a single color, with the eyes, eyebrows, and mouth separating those forms into three areas. This pattern and its variations are the most widely used of the designs, and most of the other faces evolved from this concept (Figs. 6.2 and 7.6). The *hua sankuaiwa lian* also has three divisions on the face, but the pattern is richer, with more colors

FIGURE 7.5. The *liufen lian* has a white forehead and the lower portion of the face is in color, here purple, which appears brownish red. This character's headdress is removed, revealing his looped hair, though he is only pretending to be in a desperate situation to confound his enemies. *The Gathering of Heroes (Qunying hui)*. Character: Huang Gai, actor: Wang Wenzhi. BJC, Beijing, China. July 23, 2000.

FIGURE 7.6. The *sankuaiwa lian* is divided into three areas, with the forehead and two cheeks in the same color, as with the pink in this example. He wears an orange *yingkao*. *The City of Baidi (Baidi cheng)*. Character: Ding Feng, actor: unidentified. NJC, Beijing, China. September 30, 2001.

added to it. This facial pattern indicates a more complicated character, but the blocks of color still indicate the inner nature. The fractured *sankuaiwa lian* pattern divides the areas with patterns and lines even further so that the three tiles become virtually obscured and no longer resemble the original pattern. Low-ranking generals and displaced fighters use this extreme design. With the variegated *sankuaiwa lian* pattern, the forehead and cheeks no longer are painted in the same color.

Shizimen lian (**Ten face**). In written Chinese, the number ten is a cross shape. When there is a vertical line that goes from the forehead to the nose bisected by a horizontal line going across the bridge to the eyes, the resulting pattern is called a *shizimen lian*. The cross face evolved from the three-tiled face. The color that symbolizes the character is the narrow strip down the center of the forehead (Fig. 7.7). Characters with this face have a cruel nature and may die a violent death.

Yuanbao lian (**Ingot face**). The *yuanbao lian* has a shape on the forehead that is similar to traditional Chinese gold or silver ingot, and originally this makeup indicated the character's interest in wealth. Now it seems

FIGURE 7.7. The *shizimen lian* face makeup has a cross, the Chinese character for the number ten, centered at the nose. The character is also wearing the *bamian wei* style of helmet. *Reconciliation of the Prime Minister and the General (Jiang xiang he)*. Character: Lian Po, actor: Wang Wenzhi. BJC, Beijing, China. July 2, 2000.

more related to stupid or humorous roles. One color appears in the area above the brows and another on the cheeks. Characters with *yuanbao lian* makeup have some evil qualities, but they are not without redeeming features (Fig. 7.8).[10] The *hua yuanbao lian* has the same kind of color division, with additional lines and details when a more complicated design is desired.

Wailian (**Asymmetrical face**). The *wailian* has mismatched sides. This asymmetrical design reflects either an ugly visage or a flawed character who is devious and dishonest and may die miserably. This pattern is often used for executioners (Fig. 7.9).

Suihua lian (**Scattered-pattern face**). The *suihua lian* is complicated by many details and colors that roam over the parts of the face, obscuring rather than distinguishing them. One common pattern in this category is two dark-red kidney-shaped areas over the nostrils (Fig. 7.10). The *suihua lian* face appears on very complex characters with contradictory natures, who are often rough and uncouth.[11]

Sengdao lian (**Buddhist/Daoist monk face**). Buddhist and Daoist characters wear the *sengdao lian* de-

FIGURE 7.8. A *yuanbao lian* has the shape of old Chinese money on the forehead, in this case because the character is stupid and has a fondness for money. His hat is a *jiangsha* with diamond-shaped wings. *The Red-Maned Fiery Steed (Hongzong liema)*. Character: Wei Hu, actor: Gu Qian. BJC, Beijing, China. October 6, 2001.

sign, which is used exclusively for their characters. The design is distinguished by a red dot in the center of the forehead, representing a pearl. The facial color is typically light pink and white for venerable monks, with an addition of silver or gold for high-ranking monks. Monks with martial arts skills, contravening the rules of Buddhist teaching, may have makeup that is redder in the face and thicker, fiercer eyebrows (Fig. 6.48).

Taijian lian (**Eunuch face**). The *taijian lian* is similar to the monks' face, with a dot on the forehead, but

FIGURE 7.9. *(Above)* The asymmetrical *wailian* makeup is worn by negative, flawed, or ugly characters. This character wears a felt hat and blue cotton *jianyi*. *Reconciliation of the Prime Minister and the General (Jiang xiang he)*. Character: Parasitic Guest (Men Ke), actor: unidentified. BJC, Beijing, China. July 2, 2000.

FIGURE 7.10. *(Right)* The complicated *suihua lian* features intricate patterns and colors on the face. The headdress is a *bamian wei*. He is dressed in a *kao* for battle. *Attacking Pei Yuanqing with Fire (Huo shao Pei Yuanqing)*. Character: Xin Wenli, actor: Liu Kuikui. ACTO, Beijing, China. May 31, 2002.

here it represents a mock claim to be a disciple of Buddha, cleansed of sensual desires.[12] Eunuch faces are distinguished by heavy black eyebrows and tiny mouths that turn down at the corners. The entire face is visible, because they do not wear beards (Fig. 7.11).

Xiangxing lian (**Pictographic face**). *Xiangxing lian* have a pictogram of the animal character painted on the actor's face (Fig. 7.12).[13] The Monkey King is an exam-

ple of this category, although he is played by a *wusheng* or *wuchou* (martial *chou*) rather than a *jing* actor. He sometimes has a pearl on his forehead, indicating that he is a disciple of Buddhism (Fig. 1.16).

Shenguai lian (**God-spirit face**). If the spirit is a human deity, then the facial characteristics of the *shenguai lian* designs are related to the magic or special features of the spirit (Fig. 7.13). For example, the fire god

FIGURE 7.11. Eunuchs have the *taijian lian* makeup, with a dot in the forehead. The two strips of hair on either side of his face signify his hair from childhood, when he was castrated. Without a beard, the large dragons on his *mang* are revealed. *Li Yaxian (Li Yaxian)*. Character: Zhou Gonggong, actor: Liu Qingxian. BJC, Beijing, China. May 26, 2002.

FIGURE 7.12. *(Right)* This character is a golden-eyed panther. He wears the *xiangxing lian* style of makeup that pictures the creature, with the fierce lines around the mouth representing the panther's teeth. The red streamers coming from the headdress indicate he is also a god. His costume is a *gailiang kao*. *The Magic Cistern (Ju dagang)*. Character: Jinyan Bao (Golden-eyed Panther), actor: Liu Kuikui. ACTO, Beijing, China. June 1, 2002.

will have flames. On the other hand, animal spirits will have a pictogram of the animal designed on the face.[14]

In addition to the overall pattern of the face, the individual features, including the shapes of the eyebrows, eyes, and forehead decorations, are also classified and assigned significance. A sampling of the eye and eyebrow patterns are mentioned here.[15] The shape of the eye area suggests the nature of the character, a large open eye area indicates strong characters, while slender eyes are used on the faces of the more reserved characters. The narrowest eyes are used on the faces of villains. The shape of the brows ranges from a basic style that merely accents the natural brow to elaborate ornamentations that overtake the forehead. The triangular brow has a point at the inner edge of the brow and spreads out over the temples, which makes a sinister-looking face for villains. The elderly brow droops down on the outer edge of the face. The saw-toothed eyebrow used for thugs has rounded upturned spikes on the forehead. Judge Bao has ladle eyebrows that make his brow look knitted because his mind is troubled (Fig. 4.5). Guan Yu has reclining silkworm eyebrows that are used exclusively for his character (Fig. 6.55). Zhang Fei, the coarsest of the three sworn brothers in the Three Kingdoms saga, has butterfly eyebrows that symbolize his roughness along with his sense of humor (Fig. 7.25). Xiang Yu, in *The Hegemon King Says Farewell to His Concubine (Bawang bie ji)* has eyebrows drawn as the character *shou* (longevity), an irony because he dies young (BIBOAP [excerpt], Beijing, China. July 10, 2000). Xiang Yu's eye shapes give the impression of being full with tears, of knowing that he will not survive the ensuing battle or see his love again.[16]

Although the forehead is not an area normally featured in expression, because of the added space obtained by shaving the head, the painted-face designs use it to highlight evocative patterns. The future of a character may appear on his forehead, such as the Chinese word for long life. Jiang Wei, a student of Zhuge Liang in the Three Kingdoms saga, has the yin/yang symbol in the center of his forehead to show that he possesses knowledge of Daoist magic.[17] Cao Cao, the sinister leader during the Three Kingdoms saga, has a flying bat between his brows that coincides with nerve lines on the face (Fig. 7.4).[18] In addition, special features may be added to indicate a ruined face, such as a wound resulting in the loss of an eye.[19]

The Makeup Process: *Jing.* The art of face painting can be compared to calligraphy, where the graceful and confident stroke of the brush is essential for success. The actors paint the principal shapes on their faces in

FIGURE 7.13. The *shenguai lian* makeup represents gods and spirits. In this example of Juling Shen, the god of the giant spirit, he has two faces, the upper one is a laughing baby and the lower, an old man. *Causing an Uproar in the Heavenly Palace (Nao tiangong).* Character: Juling Shen, actor: unidentified. NJC, Beijing, China. October 7, 2001.

continuous sweeping lines, then sketch out the key patterns, fill in the areas of color, and apply the finishing details. Originally the face paint was in powder form and mixed with oil to create a glossy shine. Now the actors use a grease paint for all of the colors except the matte white, which comes in a compacted ball and is mixed with water for application. Depending on the arrangement of the colors, the process will be different, but the basic sequence of steps for a three-tiled face describes the common practice.[20]

FIGURE 7.14. *(Left)* The white cake makeup is applied first to the *jing* face, to establish the shapes and prevent the colors from running together. He has shaved his head to make his face area larger. Liu Kuikui, ATCO, Beijing, China.

FIGURE 7.15. *(Right)* The areas for color are outlined in gray in a technique similar to sketching with pencil; then the black areas of the pattern are painted on the face. Liu Kuikui, ATCO, Beijing, China.

FIGURE 7.16. The colors of the *jing* makeup are applied last. The completed face is pictured in Fig. 7.25. Liu Kuikui, ATCO, Beijing, China.

The foundation is prepared with a layer of petroleum jelly. Then a light layer of white makeup is dotted on and smoothed over the entire face with the hand to seal the surface. Most of the face patterns consist of white, gray, black, and a color, with some faces having additional details worked in another color. The makeup is applied in that sequence. The cake of white powder makeup, mixed with water and honey, is first brushed on the face to define the white areas of the design. Most of the designs use white borders between the colors as well as a color in its own right. The visual advantage of the white borders is that they clarify the areas of the design. On a practical level, the white powder, unlike grease paint, dries solid and creates a protective coating that prevents the other colors from running together (Fig. 7.14).

A light gray paint is mixed from a loose black powder and the white cake to outline the color areas. The gray acts like a pencil line to define the areas to be filled in with color. If the primary color of the face is red, then a pink outline may be used. The planes of the face are often obscured by the pattern, so the gray edge returns some dimensionality to the visage by creating a shadow around the new contours, though not all actors employ this step (Fig. 7.15).

Most facial designs have black around the eyes and mouth. The eye socket area is first covered with dry black powder before the black grease paint is applied; this prevents the black grease paint from leaking into the eyes. The black powder is also applied on the upper lip to create a matte surface on which to rest the beard. After this preparation, the black design is brushed on with grease paint that is mixed with water or oil for a more fluid consistency and to enhance the shine (Fig. 7.16).

The primary facial color is added next, if other than black or white, first brushed on in smoothly curved outlines to define the borders, and then the areas within are filled with a solid surface of paint. This completes the basic canvas, and any additional lines or details are then added to finish the design. A final version of this face can be seen in Fig. 7.25.

Chou **Makeup.** The diminutive figures of the *chou* are expressed in their face-painting design, in which the dominant feature is a small white patch of makeup around the nose, eyes, and cheek area. Called a *doufu* (tofu) face, this awkward visage contributes to the comic effect of *chou* roles. The shape of the patch can be rectangular, triangular, round, or diamond-shaped, and there are also special shapes for distinct roles. A *wuchou* will have a narrow white zone down his nose, while a *wenchou* (civil *chou*) has a wider area of white that covers the area around the eyes. The amount of the white reflects the degree of wickedness or cleverness, for white on the *chou* clown face means craftiness and disloyalty just as it does for the *jing* roles. One particularly rascally fellow, Lou Ashu (Lou the Rat), has a tofu patch in the shape of a rat running across his nose. He is a crafty thief in the play *Fifteen Strings of Cash (Shiwu guan)* (NKKCOC, Taipei, Taiwan. November 3, 1995). Elderly *chou* have white wrinkles painted around their eyes (Fig. 7.33). The *chou* facial features, painted in black and red, are also minimized, with small brows, noses, and mouths, and there is no attempt to accent the eyes. Like the *jing*, each *chou* character has a distinct design, but the motifs are not as widely divergent as the patterns for the *jing*.

The Makeup Process: *Chou.* To start the *chou* face, a makeup color is mixed to match the skin tone. This matching tone is dotted on the face in a circle around the outer edge of the face outside the region where the tofu spot will be placed and smoothed outwards, blending into the natural skin at the hair and chin lines. A skin-tone powder is brushed on to set this color. Then the scarlet red used by the standard males is brushed around the perimeter of the place where the white patch will be painted. It is applied more heavily at the inner edge and blended out about an inch into the natural tone (Fig. 7.17).

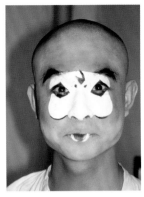

FIGURE 7.17. *(Left)* After the face is covered with a natural tone, the *chou* applies red around the outside of where the white patch will be around the nose and eyes. Jiao Jingge, ATCO, Beijing, China.

FIGURE 7.18. *(Right)* The white patch and character lines complete the *chou* makeup. Fig. 1.13 shows the final version of this character. Jiao Jingge, ATCO, Beijing, China.

The white makeup used for the patch is the same solid cake applied on the *jing* faces. A mixture is made fluid enough to paint on the face smoothly with a small brush, and the area for the white patch is filled in inside the rouged border. The area around the eyes is blackened with powder mixed in water, as with the *jing* makeup. Then a small brush with grease paint is used to define the brows, create lines or shapes around the eyes, and draw other marks that determine the design for each character. A small amount of red usually describes the mouth, along with white and black accents (Fig. 7.18). The completed version of this makeup is in Fig. 1.13.

Hairdressing and Accessories

Chinese women have had a protracted fascination with elaborate hairdressing and long hair. Throughout imperial China, women devoted time and effort to arranging their hair in the current fashion using wires, frameworks, and supplemental hairpieces, as well as glittering combs and jeweled pins for ornamentation. The stage

FIGURE 7.19. The components for building hairstyles, left to right: *dawan,* above, *leitoudai,* below, *xiaowan. xian lianzi,* bun, above, *wangzi,* below, *dafa,* and *shuisha.* DTD UHM, Manoa, Hawai'i.

hairstyle is not a wig; it is, rather, constructed and created out of several pieces that are applied to the actresses' heads prior to each performance. The concept of making hair from several pieces seems a logical extension of the historical approach to styling that supplemented the natural hair with additional pieces. This system of hair design was developed for the stage in the eighteenth century and continues to be used today. While all performers apply their own makeup, there are specialists who help dress the hair. The hairpieces are made of several materials, and some of the items are interchangeable among the different styles of hair dressing.

For all of the young women's hairstyles, the hairpieces around the face are sculpted and glued to the forehead and cheeks using a gel made from boiled wood shavings *(baohua).* The wood comes already cut into paper-thin strips that are crumbled into a pan of boiling water. The shavings are left to soak until a gel forms from the resin, and they are then strained out of the gel. The hair wefts are immersed in the gel, which is worked through the hair and then the excess is squeezed out. The gel-soaked wefts are carefully combed on a wooden board until they are straight and smooth, with the gel evenly dis-

tributed. Once prepared, the wefts can be formed into any of the shapes needed for the hairstyles. Depending on the complexity of the hairstyle, the application can take from a few minutes to about a half an hour. Men's hair is considerably less complicated, although it still is created on the head out of many of the same pieces. The hairpieces are listed in the order that they are often applied, considering the similar sequences used for creating the base for the different styles, along with the additional items that are used to create the different silhouettes (Fig. 7.19).

Leitoudai (**Lit. "tighten hair ribbon"**). A small square of fabric with long twill tape ties, the *leitoudai* is used to protect the actors' own hair and to provide a foundation for the other pieces. When the tapes are wound around the head, they are used to lift the outer edge of the eyebrows. The women's *leitoudai* is made of muslin, with white tapes, and the men's is black, with a fabric square almost large enough to encircle the head.

Xiaowan (**Small curls**). Wefts of human hair in black, the *xiaowan* are about ¾ inches wide and 14 inches long; they are used to create flat loops across the forehead.

Dawan (**Big curls**). The *dawan* are larger wefts of

human hair in black, about 2 inches wide and 18 inches long, used to shape the sideburns that frame the face.

Pianzi (**Small pieces**). The *dawan* and *xiaowan* together are called *pianzi*.

Shaved Plant Gel *(Baohua)*. Tree shavings create a gel when soaked in boiling water. The gel is used for styling the *xiaowan* and *dawan* and for affixing them to the face.

Xian lianzi (**Drape of hair**). The *xian lianzi* is a strip of long black silk cords tied to the back of the head to simulate long tresses that fall to the knees (also called *xian weizi* or tail of hair).

Wangzi (**Skullcap**). A skullcap or circlet made of horsehair, the *wangzi* is about 4 inches wide and 20 inches around. The bottom is woven together with cotton cord and finished with a black twill tape for tying it to the head. The top is finished with loops and a drawstring is used to shape the *wangzi* to the head.

Hairpin *(Dazan)*. A hairpin is used to secure the back of the *wangzi*. Pieces of hair and cording are wrapped round it to fasten the *wangzi* in place. The hairpin comes from historical usage.

Bun *(Fadian)*. The bun is a ball of human hair covered with a hair net and used as the base of the bun on the back of the head.

Dafa (**Hair switch**). A hank of human hair, the *dafa*, is used to cover and fill out the bun on the back of the hairstyle.

Zhuaji (**Hair coil**). The *zhuaji* is another name for the bun worn on the back of the head in a variation of the *datou* style.

Shuisha (**Water gauze**). A piece of black silk gauze 4 feet long and 16 inches wide, called the *shuisha*, is dampened and wrapped around the head at the base of the hair style to create a smooth finished edge.

Hair Coil *(Fajiu)*. The *fajiu*, also called *faji*, is a coil of hair used to form a small looped bun, on the top of some hairstyles. A gray or white coil is employed in older character's hairstyles, and a black coil appears on younger men who remove their headdresses. The hair coils are also used to form the larger and more elaborate top loops or buns for the "ancient" style of hair. The loops are also called *yunhuan* (cloud loops).

Swallowtail *(Yanwei)*. The swallowtail piece, worn on the back of the head for the Manchu-style hairstyle, is shaped like a fiddle. It has a ridge of hair down the center, and then the remaining hair is dressed horizontally over the rest of the surface.

Liangba tou (**Lit. "two pieces of hair"**). The bridge-shaped piece that forms the top of the Manchu-style hairstyle is a *liangba tou*. It has a circular wire base and an upright framework structure that is covered with black fabric.

Guzhuang tou (**"Ancient" wig**). The "ancient" wig is a fall of hair for the back of the "ancient" hairstyle.

Shuaifa (**Lit. "to toss the hair"**). A long black ponytail on a 3-inch stick, the *shuaifa* has a round leather base that is tied to the top of the headdress.

Children's Wig *(Hai'er fa)*. Children's wigs are made of human hair, with short bangs in front and longer hair behind.

Pengtou (**Loose hair**). The *pengtou* is a full wig made of human or yak hair; it is worn longer for Daoists and shorter and in bright colors for spirit characters.

Pifa (**Spread hair**). A subset of *pengtou,* the *pifa* is a black or white, full, long wig made of human or yak hair. It is worn spread across the back of the neck for Daoist priests and gods.

Women's Hairstyles. Women's hair onstage can be loosely divided into four categories: the *guzhuang tou* (lit. "ancient-style" hair), which has soft loops of hair on the crown and a ponytail in back and is often used for *qingyi* and *huadan*, as well as dancers and fairy maidens; the *qitou* (Manchu hair), which adorns the female characters from non-Han families and has the "big wings"-style construction; the *datou* (complete hair), used for young women's roles, with curls rimming the face and long tresses down the back; and the *zongfa* (lit.

"palm-fiber" hair, now horsehair) a simple bun style that identifies older women.

Guzhuang tou. Mei Lanfang introduced the *guzhuang tou* in the twentieth century, based on his interpretation of early historical models. In the Qin and Han periods (221 BC–220 AD), women arranged their hair in coils, often with an additional section of long hair left to fall straight down the back. The overall silhouette was rounded, with the hair softly raised around the face. The loops, braids, or buns took on many different fashionable shapes over the centuries, from firm standing coils over one foot high to softer versions that rested on the head or fell to the sides. A larger number and greater height of loops projected wealth. By the Ming dynasty, pre-formed switches arranged on a bun and supported with iron wire were available in jewelry stores.[21] Qing dynasty women sometimes wore short thin bangs, with curved sections of hair framing the face. The *guzhuang tou* onstage includes the characteristic loops of hair on top, bangs in front, and a ponytail drawn together at the base of the head and reaching down near the waist, while the front can be styled in several ways. This hairstyle appears on dancers, fairy maidens, and mythological characters, as well as some *qingyi* and *huadan* roles (Figs. 2.6, 6.8, 6.59, and 6.60).

Guzhuang tou **Hairdressing Process.** The *leitoudai* foundation is centered on the forehead around the hairline. The twill tape ties are dampened and wrapped around the back and brought around to the forehead. As an uplifted line on the outer eye is admired, the tape is then used to lift the ends of the eyebrows at the temples. The tapes are brought around to the back again and tied (Fig. 7.21).

Two *dawan*, already treated with the gel mixture, are combed flat on the board. One version of the front design will start by placing a *dawan* slightly off center on each side of the face. Then each *dawan* is curved around the temple, shaped down the side of the face, and curled towards the chin in an S-shaped curve.

A small fringe of hair is placed in the gap between the two *dawan* pieces to form bangs. Then the *shuisha* is wrapped around the head to create a neat hairline. Over this is placed a fall of human hair that has a fairly complete wig cap foundation inside. The fall is tied at the nape of the neck to form a ponytail that reaches about to the waist.

Over this base, the loops, buns, or braids can be styled on top of the head using the additional hairpieces. The loops stand above the head about 4 or 5 inches. Jewels for this kind of headdress include a row of round jewels surrounded by rhinestones mounted on a black band encircling the face, and a single large rhinestone spray almost the height of the hair loops. A symmetrical front-facing phoenix can be used for *qingyi* roles (Fig. 6.8), and an asymmetrical side-facing phoenix can be worn by a *huadan* when she has a major role in the play (Fig. 2.6). While her position in society does not reward her with such beautiful jewelry, her position in the play does.

Qitou (**Manchu hairstyle**). The *qitou*, which is based on Qing dynasty fashion, was introduced into the traditional Jingju vocabulary around the late nineteenth or early twentieth century, along with Qing clothing styles. The Qing dynasty saw a dramatic shift in the way that women's hair was dressed; the rounded line of loops and buns was replaced by the *liangba tou*, an angular shape that was a large, flat upright structure resembling "big wings."[22] The hair itself was worn parted in the middle and slicked closely to the back of the head, where the excess was used to create a swallowtail piece (*yanwei*) that was shaped over a form. This design was dressed once or twice a week, using the same gel now employed for creating the stage hairstyles. A framework of wire or rattan covered with black gauze was pinned to the top of the head. From the front, it is quite wide and imposing, but from the side it has virtually no dimension. This supplemental piece was also decorated with flowers, sequins, and jeweled ornaments. The Manchu style of hair is used for the ethnic minority roles and is less common than the other two hairstyles for young women (Figs. 2.4, 6.5 and 6.52).

Qitou Hairdressing. The *leitoudai* foundation is placed at the forehead and the tape ends are wrapped round the head, lifting the eyebrows at the temples. The front of the hair can be arranged in several styles, and the following description details one version. The hairpieces used to create the front of the design are first treated in the styling gel. A single piece of *xiaowan* hair is placed on the left side of the forehead above the middle of the left eye; it curves out over the brow and then back at eye level to create a single, wider loop. A second piece starts at the same point and curves to the right looping down across the forehead, up at the middle of the right eye and back off the face at the same level as the left side. The two pieces together create an off-center part. The tip of the second piece is used to make tiny spit curls in the gap of the part. Two *dawan* pieces are then used to make symmetrical loops from the temple to the chin line and back beneath the earlobe. The pieces blend together in a graceful S-shaped curve on either side of the face.

A *wangzi* is then wrapped around the head and secured. A bun is mounted on top of the head to serve as the base for the bridge piece. The swallowtail-shaped piece is placed on the back of the head, tied on with string around the head and another around the bun (Fig. 7.20). The *liangba tou* with its wire base is then placed over the bun and pinned firmly. The *shuisha* is wrapped around the head to create a neat edge. It wraps around the middle of the swallowtail and then the ends are opened up to cover the top half of it. They are then tied around the base of the *liangba tou* to conceal the wire frame.

With the hairstyle completed, ornamentation can be attached. The wire base can be covered with a sequined band, and then flowers arranged over the vertical front surface of the *liangba tou*, one on each side and an enor-

FIGURE 7.20. The swallowtail is mounted on the back of the *qitou* style of hairdressing, with the *liangba tou* on the crown. The *dawan* pieces loop under the ears. Katrin Zimmerman, ATCO, Beijing, China.

mous one in the middle that conceals much of the surface. The stage version of this design adds a gold filigree bar across the top of the arch, with long tassels hanging off the ends. In addition, jewels and flowers are placed asymmetrically around the face.

Datou (Complete hair). The *datou* strays from the historical precedents more than the other traditional Jingju hairstyles. Developed in the eighteenth century by the accomplished actor Wei Changsheng (1744–1802), who introduced a number of lasting innovations, the feature that distinguishes this hairstyle from real life is the arc of seven curls framing the forehead, which diverges from the emphasis on long sweeps of hair in the imperial courts. Sideburn-like hairpieces were introduced to the *datou* by one of the great *dan* players of the twentieth century, Xun Huisheng (1900–1968), to help shape the face. Both of these attributes were developed when men were playing women's roles as a way to reshape their faces into a more feminine form.

The jewels and floral decorations reflect the historical models more closely than the hairstyle does. As early as the Qin and Han period, metal artisans had developed a high level of skill to create delicate hair ornaments. The pins were designed to flutter with the head movements, increasing the sparkle and interest of the pieces.[23] During the Tang dynasty, the placement of the pins became quite dense, and when worn in combination, they could cover the head more like a headdress than individual pieces.[24] A Ming dynasty portrait from the Palace Museum shows a concubine of the Zhengtong emperor wearing a black headband with nine jewels of graded size stretched across her forehead.[25] While no definitive connection can be made between the historical and stage fashions, it is conceivable that the style worn in the historical image may have inspired the row of jewels now commonly placed in the center of each curl. Worn by *qingyi*, *huadan*, and *wudan*, the *datou* has the most widespread usage in traditional Jingju performances (Figs. 1.8 and 1.9).

***Datou* Hairdressing Process.** The *leitoudai* is placed around the front hairline, and the twill ties are crossed around the back to the front, lifting the eyebrows at the temples (Fig. 7.21). The stylist shapes the gelled *xiaowan* pieces into the different-sized flat loops on the combing board before placing them on the face. The largest curl is placed in the center, slightly above the others. The remaining six curls arch to the temples. The placement of the *xiaowan* around the forehead is important to help shape the face into the desired egg shape. After the curls have been arranged, the *dawan* are set from the

temple to the chin line in a graceful curve, also sculpting the desired shape for the face. All of the extra ends of these pieces are held in place by another wrapping of the twill tape (Fig. 7.22). Each hairstylist learns the proper proportions for the curls and sideburns and how to make them complement each performer, making the face wider or narrower as needed. Some actresses have become proficient in this step of the process and place their own curls and sideburns.

The *xian lianzi* is tied on next. It curves under the back of the head and the cords reach to below the knees (Fig. 7.42). The main body of the hair dressing is then created by the *wangzi* as it is tied around the head from the forehead to the base of the skull at the neck. The tapes are brought to the front, then crossed and wrapped around the head at the base of the *wangzi*. As the *wangzi* is not large enough to encircle the head completely, the back is secured with a hairpin and tied with extra twill tape and a few lengths of the silk cord. The bun is placed over the gap in the back of the *wangzi*, over the hairpin. A *dafa* is tied on above the bun, with pieces of the silk cord spread over to cover it. The *shuisha* is dampened, folded on the bias, and wrapped around the base of the *wangzi* to tidy up the edges. It can also be wrapped around the bun and then tied at the top (Fig. 7.23). See Fig. 8.1 for the completed hair for this character.

Some women characters wear a complex set of ornaments that emulate the kingfisher feathers of the imperial court (Fig. 1.8), while other roles wear colored jewels encircled with rhinestones around the face. Rhinestone pins, with articulated pieces mounted on spring wires, and beaded fringes provide fluttering movement as well as sparkle (Fig. 1.9). The pins are in the shapes of animals such as bats and butterflies, meaning happiness and youth, and phoenixes for princesses and concubines to indicate their imperial status. The pins are placed on the top of the head and side fronts, and the fringes hang on either side, as well as on the back under the bun.

FIGURE 7.21. The *leitoudai* forms the foundation of the hairstyles, and the tape ties are used to raise the eyebrows. Li Yanyan, ATCO, Beijing, China.

FIGURE 7.22. The *xiaowan* across the forehead and *dawan* sideburns contour the face into the admired egg shape, and are secured with the tape ties. Li Yanyan, ATCO, Beijing, China.

FIGURE 7.23. The *dafa* and *xian lianzi* comprise the back of the *datou* hairstyle. The *wangzi* encircles the head. Li Yanyan, ATCO, Beijing, China.

Dangling earrings can be worn as well. While most of the style is symmetrical, the front is often arranged with unmatched pins and flower sprays. Adhering to the concept of beauty, the accessories of the *huadan* are often as elaborate as those of their higher-ranking mistresses. The *wudan* may have fewer ornaments in order to facilitate their movement, but they will still be well appointed. The poorest women will have plain silver embellishments in a symmetrical placement and a rhinestone pin in the center of the forehead (Fig. 6.18).

Zongfa (**Bun**). The extremely simple design of hair wrapped in a scarf worn by *laodan* is likely to have been based on working-class hair rather than fashion. A sweatband originally worn for protection later evolved into a pretty band worn for decoration, much like the colored scarves used in traditional Jingju.[26] Those who could not afford precious decorations might also use a turban to cover their hair. As many *laodan* are of mod-

est means, the wrapped headdress is commonly used for their characters. The hair for elderly women consists merely of white or gray hair with a *zongfa* on the top of the head (Figs. 1.7, 2.3, and 6.3).

Zongfa **Hairdressing Process.** The *laodan*'s hair is generally assembled by the wardrobe person in charge of headdresses rather than by the hairstylist. The *leitoudai* foundation is tied in place, lifting the eyebrows only a little for older women's roles. A gray or white *wangzi* surrounds the head. A hair coil is formed into a bun on the top of the head and then a hank of hair *(binfa)* is separated from the coil on either side and drawn down in front of the ears. These pieces are either left to hang straight or looped up behind the ears. The order of applying these two pieces may be reversed depending on the finished design. Next, the *leizi* (for poor women this is a black velvet strip with a single pearl) is centered on the forehead. Then a scarf *(choutiao)* in a color for elderly characters is wrapped front to back and back to front around the head, tied in a square knot centered over the forehead, and the ends are tucked in either side. A higher-status arrangement of the bun hair is called *laodan guan (laodan* headdress); this has a larger bun, a wider scarf wrapping pattern, and a jade ornament on the *leizi*.

Children's Wig *(Hai'er fa)*. Children's wigs have a fringe of bangs and a center part. Two topknots of hair are looped and tied in place just above the temples. Two strands of hair on either side of the face are separated from the rest and secured with colored bands to hang in front of the shoulders. The children's wigs are made in one piece and of human hair (Fig. 6.42).

Men's Hair

The history of men's hair in China is not as complex as that for women, because men tended to wear head-dresses that covered their hair. Examples of hairstyles from the early Qin era can be seen in the terra-cotta figures of Emperor Qin Shihuang's army, found in his tomb in Xi'an. The individualized sculptures of the soldiers reveal a variety of loops of hair tied on top of the head in bands of fabric. Men also used jade pins to fix their hair in this era.[27] In the Jin (220–420) and in the last dynasty, the Qing, men wore their hair long and braided. Generally, though, men's hair has been pulled to the top of the head, knotted, and then concealed by a headdress, turban, kerchief, or soft hat as it was worn in the Ming dynasty (1368–1644). During that era, the hair was first secured in place "by a black net cap made of knitted horsehair" that was worn alone or with another headdress over it.[28] The *wangzi* used for creating traditional Jingju hairstyles is also constructed from twisted and tied horsehair, although a definitive connection cannot be established between the two articles. The men's hairstyles onstage follow the tradition of being covered by a headdress. In most cases the hair

is barely visible unless the hat is removed, which indicates a character in trouble, who has been captured or imprisoned.

The Hairdressing Process: Men. One simple style of hair can be worn by all of the men's role categories with only slight variations. This common dressing for men's hair uses simply the *leitoudai* and the *shuisha*. The *leitoudai* is placed around the head, with the opening in the back, and the eyebrows are lifted with the tapes a little, for the *sheng* roles only. The *jing* actors do not have their eyebrows lifted as the painted design defines the shape of the brow area and can be placed where needed. The *chou* characters are of lower dignity, and therefore their eyebrows are not lifted.

The base of the *leitoudai* is then concealed when the dampened *shuisha* wraps around the head in a narrow band. For the *sheng* roles, the gauze is carefully shaped into a half moon around the face, with a smooth curve over the forehead that dips down at the temples. The *jing* and *chou* roles have a rounded shape without the additional shaping at the temples. The damp silk creates a shiny black edge that appears to be a neat hairline when the headdress is placed over it on the head (Fig. 7.24). In addition to this main style, variations occur for given circumstances, including the *shuaifa* for characters in distress, a hair-coil style of hair with loops on top, and hair designs for older men.

***Shuaifa* Process of Hairdressing.** Characters who have been defeated in battle, are prisoners, or otherwise in a state of distress, will have their headdress removed, revealing their hair. The loss of the headdress or helmet indicates humiliation and loss of status, and any male role type can be faced with this situation. These characters require a more complete hairstyle that features a ponytail at the peak of the crown. The black *leitoudai*, the *wangzi,* and *the shuisha* are used as a foundation. Then the *shuaifa* is tied to the top of the head, where the drawstring of the *wangzi* is closed around the leather base of the *shuaifa*. The long hair of the *shuaifa* is then

FIGURE 7.24. The men's hair is created simply by wrapping the *shuisha* around the forehead to form a hairline. The makeup is for a *wusheng*. Unidentified actor, ATCO, Beijing, China.

Elderly male characters wear a gray or white *wangzi*. A matching switch is secured on top of the head, with strings that are tied to the tape ties of the *wangzi*. Two hanks of hair are divided from the switch to hang in front of the ears, while the rest of the hair is looped on top of the head. The wet silk gauze *shuisha* is then wrapped round the head. A black piece of gauze is used even though the hair is gray or white (Fig. 7.5).[29]

Beards

Written and pictorial records indicate that false beards were used onstage as early as the Yuan dynasty. Extant Ming copies of Yuan-era plays list "vital items of attire" including beards.[30] The fourteenth-century wall painting in the Guangsheng Temple in Hongdong county, Shanxi province, referenced earlier illustrates two bearded characters from Yuan dynasty drama. One quite clearly has an imitation beard suspended from his ears. Both beards are dark and short, no more than six inches long. From this simple beginning, the beards have increased in size and complexity to include a vast variety of styles and colors that may be worn by many of the male roles in contemporary performances. Beards are now stored with the props and are under the supervision of the wardrobe person who takes care of the male headdresses.

Rankou (whiskers) were originally made from horsehair, but they are now created from yak hair, plastic, or occasionally human hair. The beard hair is knotted over a flexible wire frame that hooks over the ears and rests on the upper lip. The beards come in many styles, with each representing character qualities of the wearer. Court officials tend to wear beards because the beard adds majesty and authority to their appearance. The longest, thickest beards are worn by the *jing*, as men of great power. These *man rankou* (long, full beards) can be as much as 30 inches long and cover the lower part of the face as well as much of the embroidery on the fronts of their costumes (Figs. 4.5 and 7.5–7.6). A thin-

coiled into a knot around the post, in a way similar to the way men's hair was worn in history. Once the hat is removed, the hair comes unfurled, and these characters often get down on one knee to swing their hair in a circle to express their anguish (Fig. 2.10).

Hair-Coil Process of Hairdressing. Other male characters may remove their hats in slightly less dire circumstances, which requires a different design of the hair. Using the same black *leitoudai*, *wangzi*, and *shuisha* as a foundation, variations in styles can be created by the different hair coils used to create a loop, twist, or bun of the hair on top of the head, all of them resembling men's styles from history.

FIGURE 7.25. The *zharan* beard with an open mouth is worn by coarse characters and is often paired with *er maozi*, upright tufts in front of each ear. The makeup pattern is *shizimen lian*, with butterfly eyebrows, shown in process in Figs. 7.14–16. *The Battle at Reed Marshes (Luhua dang).* Character: Zhang Fei, actor: Liu Kuikui. ACTO, Beijing, China. June 2, 2002.

ner, shorter beard, the *sanliu ran* (three-part beard), is divided into three sections; it is worn by scholars and officials in the *laosheng* roles (Figs. 6.21 and 6.30). This design, with the center section broader than the two outside pieces, represents dignity and integrity. The beards cover the mouth when the actor is singing, for the open mouth is considered ungraceful, while a covered mouth is more decorous. When this beard is gray,

it is called *cansan* (Fig. 1.2). With another type of beard, the *zharan* (beard "with a fierce outlook"), the center of the beard around the lips is suspended from the main wire, just barely revealing the mouth area. This style is worn by *jing* roles for rough characters whose courage surpasses their intelligence, like Zhang Fei, the coarse sworn brother in Three Kingdoms (Fig. 7.25). *Er maozi* (two upright tufts of hair) are often worn in front of the ears with the *zharan*.

Chou, if they wear beards, have an assortment of humorous and bizarre shapes including dangling goatees and upswept moustaches (Fig. 6.28). Drooping facial hair is for the uncouth, while upturned facial hair exemplifies a roguish nature. The *chousan* (clown three-part beard) is the comic version of the *sanliu ran* worn by officials of the court. When *chou* actors portray corrupt officials, their *chousan* is shorter and thinner than its more dignified counterpart (Fig. 1.13). A thicker version of the *chousan* may appear on elderly, lower-status *chou* characters (Figs. 6.17 and 6.36). *Chou* playing old men of the working class may also wear a short, wispy, white five-part beard *(bai wuzui)* or a moustache and goatee combination, with additional strands in front of the ears. Another goatee style is the hanging, dangling beard *(diao da)*, a comic addition to the *chou* visage (Fig. 6.15). Their beards are shorter than those of the *laosheng* and *jing*, as they would have been in real life for practical reasons. Men who perform manual labor for a living could not afford to cultivate a luxurious beard. A few of the *chou* and *jing* roles wear a *qiuran* (curly beard) in black or colors to indicate their coarseness.

The beards range in natural colors of black, gray, and white, and a less natural version of red. A purple that is closer to maroon is another possibility, although rare (Fig. 7.28). The first colors indicate the age of the characters, with black being used for those in the thirty-to-forty-year range, gray for those between forty and sixty, and white for those who have passed their milestone sixtieth birthday. Beards are not a universal sign of age though; not all mature men wear them and occasionally younger characters have beards. The various cuts and colors also represent character qualities that transcend the concept of age.[31] Red beards are reserved for bandits, thieves, foreigners, and fierce-tempered characters, including Dou Erdun, a hero in *Stealing the Imperial Horse (Dao yu ma)*.[32] A rare number of beards are more than one color, and they are designated for specific characters. Liu Tang, or Red-Haired Devil, in *Black Dragon Residence (Wulong yuan)* wears a black beard with red streaks on either side of his mouth, along with red *er maozi*.[33] The beard itself is the most important aspect for the *laosheng* and some *jing* characters, while the frame is more significant for *chou* and other *jing* roles.

Some male role types do not wear beards. *Xiaosheng* roles are beardless, as they have not reached the stage of maturity and position that a beard symbolizes. Soldiers who perform acrobatics are not bearded, because a beard would encumber their movement. Palace attendants, eunuchs, and most monks are also clean-shaven.

Headdresses

Headdresses and hats complete the visual image, and only characters in great distress or lowly monks appear without a headdress of some kind. The headdresses are specifically assigned to a character by dignity, rank, and position, and they are generally linked to particular garments. In some cases only certain headdresses can be worn with given garments, while in others, any item within a category of headdresses may be worn with the garment. As with the costumes, some of the headdresses may be traced to historical examples, while others were designed for their theatrical impact. Also following the precedent with the costumes, a larger portion of the headdresses are related to headgear from the Ming and previous dynasties, while only a few Qing

hats have been worked into the conventionalized styles. Female characters wear either the hair ornaments described above, or an item from the range of women's headdresses detailed here.

The general pattern of usage for real-life headdresses is reflected in the choices of headgear for characters onstage. Official men of court and generals wear sculpted and firm headdresses, while scholars and lesser soldiers wear soft fabric headdresses. The fabric headdresses are often made using the same fabric and embroidery designs as the garments they are worn with, while the golden filigree helmets can be worn with a variety of garments, although an effort is made to coordinate the color of the pompoms (*rongqiu*) and the tassels with the hue of the garment.

The headdresses can be grouped in many ways, but four loosely defined categories will be used here: ceremonial headdresses and crowns (*guan*), helmets (*kui*), hats (*mao*), and fabric caps (*bu*, also called *jin*). The connection between historical headgear and traditional Jingju designs is apparent in the some of the ceremonial headdresses, hat, and soft caps, but the helmets are an area of dress where theatricality has overtaken historical references. While court headdresses had their share of fanciful designs, the range of creativity is much more extensive in the stage helmets, with dazzling gold filigree bases topped by animated pearls and woollen balls mounted on springs. Some of the helmets are augmented with 6-foot-long pheasant feathers that gracefully arch back from the sides of the head. The helmets add a dimensional texture that is otherwise lacking in the image, for garments provide primarily a flat visual texture through embroidery. The headdresses, with their expressive feathers and articulated decorations, also present opportunities to exploit movement. There are numerous headdresses, and the ones described below are merely a representative sample of those most frequently used.

The ceremonial headdresses include the court headdresses of the emperor, princes, and the emperor's mother, wives, concubines, and princesses. The headdress of the head monk is also classified in this group.

King's Crown *(Wangmao/huangmao)*. The king's crown resembles the gold mesh crown with dragon ornaments now in the museum of the Ming Tombs of Dingling (Ultimate Peace Imperial Tomb) outside of Beijing. This crown has the characteristic double-crown shape of the historical *futou* (official's hat). The gold relic is decorated with metallic filigree dragons chasing a pearl. In typical fashion, the stage version has been further embellished to heighten the visual impact. The stage emperor's crown, the *wangmao,* has a hard inner framework covered with colored fabric, and an outer layer of gold filigree decorated with more dragons and pearls overlaid on top and long tassels on either side. When the fabric is yellow, it is called a *huangmao* (Fig. 7.26).

Phoenix Headdress *(Fengguan)*. The phoenix headdress worn by empresses, princesses, and concubines closely resembles its historical counterpart that emerged in the Song dynasty and continued into the Ming dynasty. An extant phoenix headdress from the Ming dynasty was also discovered in the Ming Tombs of Dingling. The crown is rounded, and three wings project on each side, curling outwards above the shoulders. The surface is composed of delicate filigree ornaments made of gold inlaid with a mosaic of pieces of the iridescent blue feathers from the kingfisher bird. The kingfisher bird was hunted almost to extinction because of the Chinese love of their beautiful, brilliant feathers. Several images of the phoenix, the bird that symbolizes the empress and other royal women, adorn the surface, along with gems surrounding the filigree and strings of hanging pearls. The stage silhouette has been modified to a fuller, rounded shape, small and gold for mature women, large and silver for the younger ladies of the court. The sur-

FIGURE 7.26. The gold filigree king's crown is the headdress for a king. *Reconciliation of the Prime Minister and the General (Jiang xiang he).* Character: King of the Zhao State (Zhao Wang), actor: Yao Yucheng. BJC, Beijing, China. July 2, 2000.

faces of both theatrical headdresses are highly ornamental, using similar filigree images of flowers and phoenixes crafted in metallic colored pastes, with the blue "kingfisher feathers" now made of a mosaic of little pieces of blue satin fabric. Many of the figures are separate pieces intermixed with gems and pearls that are mounted on springs or dangling from picks to add movement. The dainty pearled strings with figured ornaments that are suspended over the temples in the original have been

FIGURE 7.27. *(Above)* The phoenix headdress imitates kingfisher-blue feather hair ornaments with pieces of blue fabric and is further decorated with pearls and tassels. *The Red-Maned Fiery Steed (Hongzong liema).* Character: Wang Baochuan, actor: Deng Min. BJC, Beijing, China. October 6, 2001.

FIGURE 7.28. *(Right)* The *caowang kui* (self-proclaimed or illegitimate king's helmet) is worn by regional kings without legitimate claims to the throne. This character also wears a purple beard, as described in the novel *The Romance of the Three Kingdoms*; the purple resembles maroon in western color terms. *The City of Baidi (Baidi cheng).* Character: Sun Quan, actor: Wei Jijun. NJC, Beijing, China. September 30, 2001.

recreated on a larger scale in the stage version, and long pearl tassels hang down in front of the shoulders. A row of shorter tassels covers the back of the headdress onstage. The phoenix headdress is masterfully crafted to create a stunning effect suitable for royalty onstage; it is worn with the *nümang* (woman's court robe) (Figs. 6.4 and 7.27) or *gongzhuang* (palace garment) (Fig. 6.29).

***Caowang kui* (Self-proclaimed or Illegitimate king's helmet).** The *caowan kui* is second in importance only to the *wangmao.* Used for regional kings with illegitimate claims to the crown, the *caowang kui* has a long-life symbol over the forehead, two pompoms on the crown, and is covered with pearls and blue and metallic filigree decorations (Fig. 7.28).

Zijin guan (**Purple gold headdress**). Lower in rank than yellow gold, the purple gold in the name refers to a color of gold worn by princes and young noblemen. Gold and silver filigree versions are now constructed with a diadem of pearls, pompoms, and a distinctive filigree ball on the top of the crown. Feathers may be attached to this style. The *zijin guan* is worn with the *mang, jianyi* (archer's robe), and *kao* (armor), signifying it can cross from court to battle (Figs. 1.4, 2.2, 4.7, and 6.26).

Ruyi guan (**Sacred-fungus headdress**). The *ruyi tou*, a symbol derived from a sacred fungus, appears frequently in ornamentation on clothing, costumes, and the emperor's scepter. The crest of the *ruyi guan* is shaped in a graceful S-curve similar to the emperor's scepter, with fungus-shaped arabesques on the ends, from which it takes its name. The *ruyi guan* also has dangling pearl strings off the front and back of the crest, similar to the imperial crown, the *mianguan* (lit. "face crown," a flat board with strings of pearls over the face and neck). Though the *ruyi guan* resembles the *mianguan*, its use and meaning are dissimilar, and the two headdresses are not considered related. Mei Lanfang designed the *ruyi guan* for Lady Yu, the concubine in *The Hegemon King Says Farewell to His Concubine (Bawang bie ji)*, to wear when she performs her famous sword dance prior to committing suicide.[34] The narrow profile of the headdress facilitates the refined sword movement essential to successful execution of the dance (Fig. 6.54).

Eunuch Helmet *(Taijian kui)*. Eunuchs have a distinct design for their court headdress that follows the style the eunuchs are wearing in a painting from the Ming dynasty in the National Palace Museum collection.[35] The front of the hat fits the shape of the head, while the back has a piece that wraps around the back

of the head and stands above the crown, curving into a cone shape. The Ming dynasty version is plain black, but the surface of the stage headdress is gold filigree, decorated with pearls and woolly balls (Fig. 6.24 and Table 6.26.B and 6.26.N).

Wufo guan (**Five Buddha headdress**). The *wufo guan*, worn by head monks, is in a category by itself. It is flared and petal-shaped at the top edge, with five Sakyamuni figures on panels in the front and white streamers hanging over each ear (Fig. 6.47).

Xiao ezi (**Small diadem**). The White Snake, Bai Suzhen, wears a distinctive headdress with snake-like loops, sometimes made from pearls, that frame her face and with a central red pompom on top (Fig. 1.17).

HELMETS

The shapes and decorations of military helmets throughout history reveal no source that can readily be matched with the helmets now used in traditional Jingju. The gold mesh headdress from the Ming Tombs indicates a precedent for decorative golden headdresses for men, but the shape is related to the historical double-crowned *futou* rather than the rounded forms of stage helmets. The level of complexity and the vocabulary of ornament on the historical phoenix headdresses seems a possible inspiration for both the ceremonial headdresses and the helmets onstage. While pearls were plentiful in historical ornamentation, pompoms appear to be the traditional Jingju addition, beginning as early as the nineteenth century.

The type of helmet is generally predetermined for the character who wears it. From the stock of helmets of that type, the dresser will select one with pompoms that complement the garment. The tassels and the fur-decorated shafts *(lingzi tao)* for connecting the pheasant feathers to the helmets are selected with the same goal in mind. The same basic materials, buckram, paste filigree, and blue pseudo-feathers, are used in constructing the stage versions of ceremonial headdresses and helmets. The helmets are often built in two pieces that can slide together to fit the head.

***Zhajin ezi/Zhajin kui* (Lit. "tied cloth" helmet with diadem).** The distinctive shape of the *zhajin ezi* originated with a tied head scarf, along the same lines as the *futou*, hence the name of "tied cloth." Like the *futou*, the *zhajin ezi* was constructed out of firmer materials as it evolved. Onstage, the *zhajin ezi* is a filigree helmet and diadem combination creating a grand headdress to be worn with the *yingkao* (hard *kao*) by both *sheng* and *jing* generals. It can also be worn with the *mang* for court appearances. The full and richly decorated *zhajin ezi* has rows of pearls and pompoms framing the face. Behind the crescent of decoration are four upright supports, with pompoms on top. In the center of the forehead is a long-life character *(shou)*. The *zhajin ezi* may or may not have pheasant feathers attached, depending on the character (Fig. 6.9). Without the *ezi*, as a *zhajin kui,* this headdress can be worn with the *kao, jianyi,* or *kai chang* (Fig. 8.7).

***Fuzi kui* (General's helmet).** The *fuzi kui* is a gold mesh and filigree helmet with four upright pompoms on curved wires rising from the back of the crown. The pompoms are flanked by wired circles of pearls. A diadem of pearls and pompoms frames the forehead, and tassels hang on either side of the face. This headdress may also have pheasant feathers attached. Guan Yu, from the Three Kingdoms epic, wears the *fuzi kui. Fuzi* is a term of respect applied independently to Guan Yu and Kong Fuzi (Confucius), hence the name *fuzi kui* for this headdress. It was developed by the actor Wang Hongshou (c. 1850–1925), who was well known for performing the role of Guan Yu towards the end of the Qing dynasty (Fig. 6.55). Years later another actor, Yang Xiaolou (1878–1938), designed a *fuzi kui* in black for Xiang Yu to wear in *The Hegemon King Says Farewell to His Concubine* and a white *fuzi kui* for Zhao Yun in *The Long Slope (Changban po).* Now the *fuzi kui* appears on many generals.

***Bamian wei* (Eight-sided helmet).** The *bamian wei* has an eight-sided brim of gold mesh, and the peak of each section has a tassel suspended from it. The front has a crescent of pearls and pompoms rimming the face. The *bamian wei* is worn with the *kao* by powerful *jing* (Figs. 7.7 and 7.10).

Tasseled Helmets/Small Tasseled Helmets (*Daoying kui/Xiao daoying kui).* Fighting acrobats wear simple hats knotted tightly on their heads so they do not interfere with their movement. There are one-piece and two-piece versions, with both large and small dimensions. The one-piece small tasseled helmet is a combination of a stiff diadem with soft flap hanging behind the head. When worn by a soldier, the small tasseled helmets usually match the *bingyi* (soldiers' clothes) in fabric color and embroidery (Figs. 6.34), or they contrast when worn by a servant (Fig. 6.62).

***Guanzi kui* (Lit. "bucket-shaped helmet," attendant helmet).** A *guanzi kui* is worn with the *dakai* (attendant armor) and is made of matching fabric. It has a diadem in front and a peaked stiff crown with a tuft of fur on the end of a stalk coming from the point. A flap of cloth falls over the back of the neck (Table 6.34.N).

***Qixing ezi* (Seven-star diadem).** A crescent-shaped helmet, the *qixing ezi* is the helmet for *daoma dan* (lit. "sword and horse" woman warriors) wearing the *nükao* (women's armor) and *wudan* (military women) dressed in the *zhan'ao zhanqun* (martial jacket, trousers and skirt). The *qixing ezi* is worn with the row of seven flat curls and gemstones on the forehead. Rows of pearls frame the face and are topped with rows of pompoms as well. Pheasant feathers are generally attached to this helmet for additional beauty (Figs. 1.10, 1.11, 4.4, 6.10, and 6.27).

Butterfly Helmet *(Hudie kui).* Women warriors dressed in the *gailiang nükao* (reformed women's armor) or *zhan'ao zhanqun* may wear a butterfly helmet with a large decorative butterfly image on the peak of the crown (Fig. 6.11). It is further embellished with pompoms and feathers, and foxtails are added for a nongovernmental female general.

HATS

Shamao (Lit. "gauze hat," officials' hats). For much of the history of China prior to the Qing dynasty, men wore their hair long and drawn up on top of the head into a bun. To protect their hair, they wrapped turbans around their heads, which repeated the silhouette of the hair, fitting close to the head in the front and having a higher rounded section in the back. During the Tang dynasty there were dozens of variations on the turban wrap, which also had streamers created from the ends of the wrapped fabric tied behind the head. Some of the head wraps gradually changed to a solid material, taking on a firm, double-crowned form. The streamers were also stiffened, causing them to stand away from the back of the hat.

By the end of the Tang dynasty and the beginning of the Song, the turban evolved into a full-fledged *futou* of lacquered gauze over a rattan frame. The *futou* was worn extensively by court officials during the Song era and beyond. The ties on the back of the turban were stiffened and transformed into two wings *(chi)* that projected side to side in back of the crown. The wings came in different shapes indicative of rank. One style of Song wings became quite long and narrow, projecting as much as two feet from either side of the wearer's head. According to legend, one of the Song emperors decreed that this shape must be worn to prevent his officials from plotting treason, for they could not whisper in each other's ears while wearing their official headgear at court.[36] The *futou* made of stiffened gauze continued to be worn through the Ming dynasty, when it was paired with the official's robe with the rank badge. This later version of the *futou* had the rounded trapezoidal wing shapes regularly seen on traditional Jingju characters. Both items are now costume pieces that frequently appear together on stage officials, the *futou*

being renamed *shamao* and the official's robe *guanyi* (official's robe).

Shamao **Description.** The *shamao* is a general category of hats that have the same basic double-crowned shape with wings. They vary in the materials used, the amount of decoration, and the shape of the wings. The lower front and the raised back crowns are built as separate pieces, to allow for multiple head sizes. Worn by many officials of the traditional Jingju court, a version of the *shamao* is often paired with the *mang*, the *guanyi,* and the *pi* (formal robe). One version of the *shamao* is the *zhongsha* (loyal hat), which is widely used for *laosheng* and *xiaosheng* characters (Figs. 4.2, 4.6, 6.6, and 6.22). A small square of white jade *(maozheng)* on the front of the hat indicates a *xiaosheng* (Fig. 6.1). The hats worn by both *laosheng* and *xiaosheng* are made with black velvet fabric stretched over a firm foundation. The wings on the *zhongsha* are flat, upright, and made from golden filigree with wired edges. While the rank of the wearer could be determined by the wings in the past, onstage the wing shape reflects personality characteristics of the wearer. Upright, wide-rounded trapezoidal wings are reserved for intelligent and loyal court officials. Diamond or peach-shaped wings on the *jiansha* (lit. "sharp or pointed" *shamao*) indicate dubious characters, including traitors and corrupt officials in *jing* and *chou* roles (Figs. 4.8 and 7.8). *Yuansha* are *shamao* with rounded wings; these are worn by foolish, dishonest, and funny officials who may take bribes. They are played by *chou* actors (Fig. 7.29). The *shamao* may be worn at home as well as for official events.

Xiangsha (Prime minister's hat). The *xiangsha* is a trapezoidal version of the *shamao* (*xiangsha* being shortened from the term *xiangshamao*) that is worn by high-ranking characters such as a prime minister or Judge Bao. The surface and structure are the same as the *shamao*, with squared rather than rounded tops on the crowns. The wings are long, narrow, and parallel to the floor. The ends of the wings are slightly upturned,

FIGURE 7.29. *(Above)* The round wings on the back of this *yuansha* headdress indicate a foolish official. *Mu Guiying Takes Command (Mu Guiying gua shuai)*. Character: Menguan (doorkeeper), actor: unidentified. BJC, Beijing, China. July 16, 2000.

FIGURE 7.30. *(Right)* The *taiding,* a variation on the *houmao,* has two side flaps and a horn-shaped ornament atop the squared crown. *Xie Yaohuan (Xie Yaohuan).* Character: Wu Sansi, actor: Zhang Feng. ACTO, Beijing, China. May 31, 2002.

and they are solid black rather than the golden filigree seen on rounded versions of the *shamao* (Fig. 7.4). The squared version of this headdress was also worn in real life during the Song through Ming dynasties.

Houmao and ***taiding*** (**Marquis's hats**). The *houmao* is square, and the two sides of the square slope down into wide ear flaps edged in fringe. A single pompom is perched on top of the crown and a long life symbol is placed over the forehead. This headdress is nicknamed

"unable to hear" *(er buwen)* because the broad stiff flaps covering the ears give the impression that the wearer does not want to listen to intrigue. The style derives from a story of a real general, Guo Ziyi, a famous leader who refused to listen to the advice of suspected traitors and covered his ears with his hands.[37] When a horn-shaped decoration is added to the top of the headdress, the combination is called a *taiding.* The horn, because it is shaped like a weapon, indicates the wearer's military

FIGURE 7.31. The *fenyang mao* is a gold filigree version of the prime minister's hat. *The Carefree Ford (Xiaoyao jin)*. Character: Cao Cao, actor: Wang Zhongwei. NJC, Beijing, China. October 4, 2001.

status and therefore it is usually worn by a noble who has a military position (Fig. 7.30 and Table 6.27.B).

Fenyang mao (Prime minister's hat). The *fenyang mao* (also called a *wenyang mao*) is a golden filigree headdress with the double crown worn by prime ministers and other very high civil or military officials, or the father of the emperor's wife, son-in-law, or daughter-in-law. The surface is highly ornamented with pearls and pompoms, and the *fenyang mao* has shaped wings, called cloud wings *(yunchi)*, that are upright and decorated as well (Fig. 7.31).[38] The *fenyang mao* is usually worn with a *mang* that has the *liwo sanjiang shui* (standing, lying, three-rivers water) design on the hem.

Xiangdiao (Decorated prime minister's hat). The *xiangdiao* version of the prime minister's hat is made of gold filigree and a blue fabric mosaic, and is trimmed with three-dimensional decorations. The base has the

FIGURE 7.32. The prime minister's *xiangdiao* is decorated with filigree and may have dimensional dragons on the wings. *Women Generals of the Yang Family (Yangmen nüjiang)*. Character: Kou Zhun, actor: Li Yuanzhen. NJC, Beijing, China. October 3, 2001.

squared double-crown shape. The wings are parallel to the floor rather than upright and may have dimensional dragons walking on the upper surface (Figs. 4.1 and 7.32).

Luomao (**Beret**). The *luomao* is a six-sided fabric hat mounted on a tall circular band that fits around the crown of the head. This hexagonal beret-like bag is either stiff and worn upright, *ying luomao* (Table 6.3.B and 6.3.N), or soft and worn collapsed to one side, *ruan luomao* (Fig.1.6). It has a padded ball at the apex of the six pieces. This hat can be either plain or embroidered, and the use changes depending on the version. A solid-color hat is called *su luomao* (plain *luomao*). Head servants or attendants wear a black *su luomao* with the top standing up, and a black *su luomao* is worn tilted to the right by unattached soldiers wearing the black *kuaiyi* (martial clothing) (Fig. 6.32). When worn with the embroidered *baoyi* (hero jacket and trousers), the *luomao* is made with matching fabric and embroidery patterns (Fig. 6.31).

Straw Hat Brim *(Caomao quan).* Many woodcutters, fishermen, and water sellers wear a straw hat brim without a crown. They often twist it so that the back of the hat is flipped to the inside of the brim and pressed up against the rear of the head (Figs. 6.17 and 6.36).

Felt Hat *(Zhanmao).* The felt hat has a round crown and upturned brim. It comes in white and colors and is used for servants (Figs. 6.28 and 7.9). The boatman's version is called *shaozi mao*.

Qinjiao mao (**Pepper-shaped hat**). The *qinjiao mao* is cuffed at the base and has a long soft crown that sometimes has a pompom on the end. It is worn collapsed on top of the head. It comes in white, red, blue, and black and is worn by lower-status characters to indicate they are silly (Fig. 7.33).

SOFT CAPS

An array of soft caps is used in traditional Jingju, and images from the actual headgear of the Ming and

FIGURE 7.33. The *qinjiao mao* is a soft felt hat for lower-status characters. *A Visit to the Family Grave (Xiao shangfen)*. Character: servant of the county magistrate (Ya Yi), actor: unidentified. ACTO, Beijing, China. May 31, 2002.

earlier dynasties can be matched to many of the stage styles. Onstage the soft hats are worn by civilians and scholars for scenes in private quarters. Made from fabric, with stiffened interfacing and lining, most of these caps fold flat for storage. The folding is similar to that of a paper bag, with the sides pleated in. The crown is often based on a squared shape that rounds out when placed on the head. Soft hats are often constructed from the same fabric as the garments and embroidered with similar colors and designs to create a unified look.

Jiangjin (**General's cap**). The *jiangjin* combines filigree and fabric into a war helmet worn by *wusheng* (martial men) dressed in the martial *xuezi* (informal robe), the *kai chang* (lit. "open robe"), or the *gailiang kao* (reformed armor). The front has a filigree diadem, while the crown is a hard shape covered by fabric. A soft fabric flap falls over the back of the neck (Fig. 6.21).

Yuanwai jin (**Gentry hat**). A square hat, the *yuanwai jin* relates to the shape of an informal hat worn from the Song to the Ming dynasties. The historical version had a short upright divided brim, but this does not carry over to the stage form.[39] The tip of the hat is square, and the side has four creases to create the square shape. The *yuanwai jin* is about 4 to 5 inches tall and usually matches the costume in fabric and embroidery. On either side of the center-back crease, there are two short streamers dropping from the tip. The hat is positioned on the head with the crease opposite the streamers in the center front. Worn by retired or rich men, it often has the long-life character embroidered on the surface (Table 6.1.B and 6.1.N a and b).

Xiangjin (**Informal prime minister hat**). The *xiangjin* resembles the *yuanwai jin* in shape, but it is worn by prime ministers for informal events, with a flat side facing forward. The rows of embroidery on the *xiangjin* are similar to the ridges on historical imperial crowns (Fig. 6.7).

Xiaosheng jin (***Xiaosheng* hat**). *Xiaosheng* characters wear the *xiaosheng jin*, which has a two-dimensional crescent reaching across the crown to the ears. The crescent ends on either side with a fungus-shaped arabesque. The hat has two streamers hanging down the back, and it is made in fabric with embroidery that matches the robe worn with it (similar to Fig. 7.34, see below).

Wusheng jin (**Military crescent hat**). A variation on the *xiaosheng jin*, the *wusheng jin* is worn by military

FIGURE 7.34. The *wenxiaosheng jin* and *wusheng jin* share the same crescent shape. The *wusheng jin,* seen here, is distinguished by a flame-shaped ribbon rosette at the crest and tassels over the ears. The robe is a martial *hua xuezi. The Gathering of Heroes (Qunying hui).* Character: Zhou Yu, actor: Li Hongtu. BJC, Beijing, China. July 23, 2000.

FIGURE 7.35. This character is wearing the *xueshi jin*, a fabric cap with fabric-covered wings on the back. This role of a husband may be played by either a *xiaosheng* or *laosheng* actor; here it is depicted as a *xiaosheng* dressed in a blue *pi*. *Mu Guiying Takes Command (Mu Guiying gua shuai)*. Character: Yang Zongbao, actor: Yu Wanzeng. BJC, Beijing, China. July 16, 2000.

men. The shape is the same, with the addition of tassels suspended from the fungus shapes over the ears and a ruffled ribbon rosette shaped like a flame mounted at the peak of the crescent. The *wusheng jin* is made of fabric and embroidery to match the garment worn with it (Fig. 7.34).

Xueshi jin (**Scholar's hat**). The crown of the *xueshi jin* is shaped by bringing together the long flat edges of the front and back of the hat to create a flat panel on top of the head. The *xueshi jin* is distinguished by curved wings on the back. Unlike the wings for court, these are fabric covered and embroidered to match the rest of the hat and the gown worn with it. The wings slope downward and have fungus shapes on the ends. The *xueshi jin* is worn by virtuous *xiaosheng* and *laosheng* (Figs. 6.25 and 7.35).

Qiaoliang jin (**Bridge hat**). The *qiaoliang jin* resembles a historical soft hat from the Ming dynasty.[40] The "bridge" comes from a distinctive piece of peaked fabric mounted on the headdress from front to back, with the highest point lining up from ear to ear. The *qiaoliang jin* is embroidered and has a pair of streamers in the back. It is worn by *xiaosheng* (Figs. 6.12 and 7.36).

Gao fangjin/di fangjin (**High/low square hat**). The top edges of the *fangjin* hats are stitched together forming a peaked, flat section from side to side, like the roof of a house. They are made of fabric and embroidered, but they do not always match the garments worn with them. The *gao fangjin* tends to be worn by educated characters who do not have an official position or wealth (Fig. 7.37). The *di fangjin* is shorter and can be worn by *chou*.

Yawei jin (**Ducktail hat**). The *yawei jin* is a soft hat made in black or colors. It is distinguished by a crescent of fur that reaches from ear to ear over the top of the head. Often worn by young scholars, including for their wedding, the *yawei jin* may also be assigned to older men and some *chou* (similar to Fig. 1.3, see below).

Xu Xian jin (**Small ducktail hat**). Xu Xian, the

FIGURE 7.36. The *qiaoliang jin* has a triangular crown and is worn by *xiaosheng* roles with a *hua zuezi*. *Calling to the Portrait (Jiao hua)*. Character: Liu Mengmei, actor: Zhang Miao. ACTO, Beijing, China. June 1, 2002.

FIGURE 7.37. The *gao fangjin* is tall with a peaked crown. The white scarf and skirt worn by this character indicate he is a prisoner waiting to be executed. *Exchanging Sons at the Execution Ground (Fa chang huan zi)*. Character: Xue Meng, actor: Cao Jin. ACTO, Beijing, China. May 31, 2002.

husband of the White Snake, wears a smaller version of the *yawei jin* ducktail hat designed specifically for him (Fig. 1.3).

Bangchui jin (**Wooden club hat**). The basic shape of the *bangchui jin* resembles the *di fangjin* hat. The peak of the hat is folded in to form a flat joined piece on the top that is wider than the head, and it is this characteristic that has produced its unusual name. Behind the flat piece are two small wings shaped like leaves; these point up and out to the left and right. Fops and spoiled sons of high officials wear this hat style. The term *bangchui*

has an alternate meaning, a person who knows nothing, which here indicates the wearer's ignorance (Fig. 7.38).

Heye jin (**Lotus leaf hat**). Another square hat worn with the flat side to the front, the *heye jin* is differentiated by the addition of another piece of cloth over the top of the crown. The cloth is larger than the square of the crown, so the edges fall down the sides, the way a tablecloth would. A similar headpiece was worn in the Ming dynasty.[41] This style is worn by educated officials played by *chou* (Fig. 6.15).

Bagua jin (**Eight trigrams hat**). The *bagua jin* is the

FIGURE 7.38. The *bangchui jin* is flattened on top of the crown and has two upright leaf-shaped wings behind. *A Sorrow that Transcends Life and Death (Sheng si hen)*. Character: Young Master Hu (Hu Gongzi), actor: Huang Dehua. BJC, Beijing, China. July 30, 2000.

headdress worn with the *bagua yi* costume. It is decorated with the eight trigrams and worn by those who have magical powers related to Daoism. It comes in the same colors as the garment, maroon, dark blue, or *qing* (dark blue-green black), and is embroidered with similar designs. The shape is a variation on *qiaoliang jin* style, although the bridge piece is more square (Fig. 6.43).

Da banjin and *ezi* (**Big board soft hat and diadem**). The peak of the crown of the *da banjin* has a flat trapezoidal-shaped board, with the narrow end of the trapezoid at the top of the hat. A protective flap falls from the trapezoid piece to the shoulders to cover the back of the neck. Similar neck flaps can be seen on the helmets of Qing dynasty armor. Streamers from either side of the crest piece fall in front of the shoulders. A crescent-shaped *ezi* made of filigree and trimmed with pompoms and pearls may be worn with the *da banjin*; this frames the face and makes a combination of helmet and soft cap styles. A round long-life character is usually centered over the forehead. Higher-ranking soldiers may wear a soft *da banjin* headdress with a *magua* (riding jacket) and *jianyi* (Fig. 7.39).

A variation of the *da banjin* and *ezi* combination is also used for executioners. For these characters, the fabric crest and flap are red, with black borders, similar to the costume executioners wear. White streamers from the top of the hat fall in front of the shoulders, and a black silk streamer draped over the head drops on either side of the face to the hip. The executioner's hat has a single pheasant feather, one meaning orphan or widow, which indicates that the wearer deprives people of their lives and breaks up families; it also signifies that the executioner's job of killing people is not a noble profession (Fig. 6.39)

Toubu and *ezi* (**Scarf and diadem**). The *toubu* can be worn alone or with the *ezi*. A triangular *toubu* is placed straight across the forehead covering the hair and tied outside on the back of the head, with the remaining fabric thus covering the back of the neck. An *ezi* is placed over the *toubu*, which is again tied with strings in the back (Fig. 1.15). This combination headdress, worn by acrobat soldiers, has a silhouette similar to the *daoying kui* described earlier, the one-piece version of this style with a tassel on top (Fig. 6.34).

SUPPLEMENTARY STYLES

Nuanmao (**Warm hat**) and *Liangmao* (**Cool hat**). As with the costumes, the Qing dynasty headdresses are less common onstage than the styles of other periods. One notable example is the *jiguan* (lit. "auspicious hat"), which has been reproduced virtually unchanged as the *nuanmao*. The *jiguan* was a Qing dynasty winter court headdress that had a round crown and a black velvet or fur upturned brim. Red floss fringe radiated from the center of the crown, which was topped by a gold ball. A tube on the right side was used for inserting a peacock feather. In history, the color and material used for the knob was a sign of rank, and the peacock feather was an award for meritorious service, but the items do not have this significance onstage (Figs. 5.1 and 6.53). The *nuanmao* is generally worn with the *bufu* (court surcoat) by non-Han characters. The *liangmao* is the stage version of the summer hat worn at court, a conical headdress made of split bamboo or woven rattan and decorated with the same red fringe seen on the winter hats.

ACCESSORIES

Feathers. A pair of majestic 6-foot pheasant tail feathers embellishes the helmets of many martial traditional Jingju characters. A single feather of the Northern Pheasant *(Phasianus reevesis)*[42] mounted on either side of the face creates a visual spectacle and presents the opportunity for an impressive variety of head and feather movements. The inspiration for headdress feathers may have developed from a number of sources, for feathers have been incorporated into ceremonies or prayer activities throughout the history of China. The use of feathers in dance and ritual has been traced back as far as the Zhou period, and feathers have long been used by the dancers in the annual celebration in honor of Confucius's birthday. Some drawings of military figures from the Qing dynasty indicate feathers on either

FIGURE 7.39. The *da banjin*, with a flat board across the crown and a flap over the back of the neck, is worn for traveling and by servants. This character's garments consist of a vest worn over plain *jianyi* with a wide firm belt. *Attacking Pei Yuanqing with Fire (Huo shao Pei Yuanqing)*. Character: Old Soldier, actor: unidentified. ACTO, Beijing, China. May 31, 2002.

FIGURE 7.40. Feathers may be worn by Han and non-Han characters. Foxtails represent non-Han characters, or in this case, a Han warrior who has married into a foreign court. *Silang Visits His Mother (Silang tan mu)*. Character: Yang Silang, actor: Du Peng. NJC, Beijing, China. October 7, 2001.

FIGURE 7.41. Gold flowers added to the *zhongsha* indicate that the character is the number one scholar in the recent examinations. This performer is wearing a *gailiang mang*. *Li Yaxian (Li Yaxian)*. Character: Zheng Yuanhe, actor: Liu Yuechun. BJC, Beijing, China. May 26, 2002.

side of the headdresses, arranged in much the same way as they are onstage.[43]

Originally feathers and fur were used onstage to indicate characters from non-Han roots, generally barbarians from China's northwest borders. As these historic tribes were hunters living in a cold climate, they made their protective clothing from the skins of their prey and used bird plumage for decoration. Over the years the ethnic distinction has blurred in performance, and while non-Han characters still wear the plumage, the use of feathers no longer distinguishes minority characters. Feathers have, however, taken on a new meaning in that they are thought to imbue the fighter with the power of the bird's spirit. The feathers now indicate the bravery and nobility of Han characters and they are proudly worn on the helmets of many warriors and generals. The feathers are attached to a short fur-trimmed shaft that fits into sockets on the sides of the helmets (Figs. 1.1, 1.4, 6.26, 6.27, and 7.40).

Foxtails *(Huliwei).* Long white foxtails are worn in concert with pheasant feathers to indicate non-Han characters. They are attached to the back of the headdress; for female warriors they are wrapped around to frame the face under the chin (Fig. 1.10), for male warriors they fall knotted down the back (Fig. 7.40). They are made from both real and artificial fur. The Monkey King, Sun Wukong, also appears in the feather and fur combination when he is in full regalia, because he truly is an animal.

Fuma taozi **(Hat ornament for the imperial son-in-law).** The *fuma taozi,* also referred to as *taochi* (wing cover), is a circular crown with tassels over the ears. When this piece is affixed to the *zhongsha,* the combination represents the son-in-law of the emperor. Silang in *Silang Visits His Mother* wears this version of the headdress. Because Silang is a member of the court of foreign barbarians, he also has foxtails added to his hat (Fig. 1.1).

FIGURE 7.42. The *hunpa* gauze over a headdress conveys that the character is a spirit. This back view of the *datou* hairstyle shows the long *xian lianzi. A Sorrow that Transcends Life and Death (Sheng si hen).* Character, right: Han Yuniang, actor: Li Huifang. Character, left: Cheng Pengju, actor: Ji Zhibin. BJC, Beijing, China. July 30, 2000.

Gold Flowers *(Jinhua).* The *zhongsha* can be further transformed by the addition of two upright wings on either side of the higher crown, indicating that the wearer is the number one scholar from the current examinations. The pieces are golden flowers in a peach shape (Fig. 7.41). The *jinhua* is part of a larger category of *dinghua,* lit. "top flower," which includes a variety of decorations for the *zhongsha.*

Hunpa (Black gauze). A shroud of black mesh over the headdress indicates the character is a spirit. Cheng Pengju wears this addition when he appears in a dream to his long-lost wife, Han Yuniang, in *A Sorrow that Transcends Life and Death (Sheng si hen)* (Fig. 7.42).

Gui suizi (Ghost fringe). Ghosts are indicated by a few narrow strips of white paper attached to their headdresses at the temple and hanging on either side of the face.

In the absence of a costume designer, the dressers are responsible for preparing the visual image and maintaining the integrity of the costume conventions. Rather than create newly designed costumes for every production, each Jingju troupe or academy collects a range of conventionalized costumes. The costumes can either be hand-embroidered and made to order from a factory or purchased from specialty shops. A troupe's costume stock normally contains an assortment of garments that can be used for each of the roles as well as the supernumeraries. An old saying, *"shi mang, shi kao"* (ten court robes, ten armor), refers to the standard costumes a troupe needs to present performances. The emphasis is on obtaining the expensive, highly embroidered costumes, one in each of the ten major colors and preferably duplicates in black and white. Then troupes either continue to expand their stock with an assortment of *pi* (formal robes), *xuezi* (informal robes), and other garments, or they borrow these costumes from others. When preparing the costumes for a traditional Jingju presentation, the dressers make selections for each character from the range of items available in their stockroom, or from other companies and the actors themselves, who sometimes have their own costumes prepared especially for them.

Training

The training for dressers usually begins around age fifteen, with preparation occurring in five fundamental

areas: the names of the garments and their patterns of wear, costume plots, which consist of lists of costumes worn in each play, dressing techniques, storage rules, and an overall understanding of traditional Jingju performance and Chinese culture.

Students begin by learning the names of all of the garments. The next step involves memorizing and understanding which garments are worn by each role type and when. This includes the necessary items of clothing and the colors needed to represent that specific image and the occasion. Since many role types wear garments with the same name and form, students learn to choose the color and ornamentation that make the ensemble specific to a given role type or a named character. In addition, only certain accessories are worn with each garment, and only the appropriate headdresses and shoes can be combined with each set of clothing.

The second aspect of learning the dressing skills is to commit to memory the costume plot for hundreds of plays. A costume plot represents an inventory of all the components of dress for every character and their scene-by-scene changes for each play. These plots are based on established dressing traditions, and the teacher will train the student dressers play-by-play and role-by-role. Students are also required to attend numerous performances and memorize the costumes in use. In the past, wardrobe workers were illiterate and could not record their art, so information passed orally from master to student. More recently, efforts have been made to record the costume plots for plays, and there are at least two books of costume plots published in Chinese.[1] Some of the playscripts also contain costume lists, but not all of them.

Student dressers also learn how to assemble the garments on the actors. Many of the images require layering, and the dresser not only learns the components but also the sequence of items for preparing each image. Every costume is worn in a specific manner, with some entailing complicated knots and lashing. Many of the garments are adjusted to fit the actor only in the process of dressing, and the dresser needs to know the folding and fitting techniques as well as how to secure the garments with belts and ties. Learning how to store the costumes so that they can be retrieved for subsequent performances is equally significant, for the system of costume storage is as closely regulated as the wearing of costumes. Each type of garment must be folded by a particular method so they can be stored flat in stacks on shelves in the wardrobe cabinets. Because the garments are folded inside out to protect the embroidery, each stack is arranged by color and frequency of use so that they can be easily located.

To assure an accurate representation of each character, dressers learn all aspects of the visual image, including makeup and headdresses. Dressers also need to comprehend the overall aesthetic that defines the style so they can make choices that are both accurate and pleasing from among the available garments. Their education may also include courses in Chinese culture and history to give them contextual knowledge of the garments appropriate for selection. The training lasts for two to four years.[2]

Patterns of Selection

When preparing costumes for a performance, the dressers make their choices of garments according to traditional patterns for the role types and specific characters that have been refined for generations, as well their own artistic sensitivities and the individual acting style of the performers in the production. In some companies, principal players may be involved in selecting their costumes or may even provide their own garments. The fundamentals of garment choice are organized by scale, as detailed in Chapters Three, Four, and Five, from the "outer," the form of the garment, to the "inner," the color and surface pattern. These three components combine to project the six identifiers of character: male/female, youth/age, upper/lower status, wealth/poverty, civilian/military, and Han/ethnic minority, explained in Chapter Two. The dresser needs to have command of these details for each character in order to attire them effectively. Each character wears a predetermined form of garment that cannot be altered, but tradition may or may not specify the color or range of colors. The embroidery designs were determined at the time the costumes were made, so dressers have little concern for this aspect at this point in the process. Each garment is guaranteed to have suitable designs on its surface. When dressers encounter an unfamiliar play, they first learn the roles and identities of the characters. Then they select particular garments based on their overall knowledge of the costume patterns. They may also consult with the actors or the director for additional insights. Using the conventions as a guideline, dressers still apply their own artistic and technical training to make specific choices from the available wardrobe.[3] If, for example, a dresser needs to find a *nüpi* (women's formal robe) for a *qingyi* (young to middle-aged woman) role, the dresser will examine the troupe's stock of *nüpi* in the appropriate colors and ornamentation. The ultimate choice involves an aesthetic eye as to which particular robe will create balance and beauty across the stage within traditional Jingju conventions.

When books from China discuss the costumes of traditional Jingju, the pieces are generally divided by garment. All versions of each item of clothing are grouped together by form; for example, *mang, gailiang mang* (reformed court robe), *nümang* (women's court robe) and *qimang* (Manchu court robe) will be covered as a category. Within this broad category, the next division delineates the distinctive color and embroidery of that garment for each role type. In this structure, which is the format used for Chapter Six, the focus is on the garments and their variations. However, in order to clarify the components of the wardrobe for each role type, this chapter reorients the information in Chapter Six to establish the patterns of costume by role type and to describe the contents of each role type's "closet," though this is merely a conceptual construct. The tables and descriptions offer an overview of the major role subtypes, with the main garments they most commonly wear. Characters within the role types are generally dressed according to these patterns, but certain characters have specific clothing images that may take precedence. The conventions described are meant to serve merely as guidelines. For further information on garments worn less often, refer to Chapter Six.

Sheng **(Standard male) Costume Conventions.** The *sheng* are divided into three major subsets: the *laosheng* (mature men), the *xiaosheng* (young men) and the *wusheng* (martial men). Each has a different wardrobe, with some overlapping pieces. The *laosheng* and *xiaosheng*, as statesmen and scholars, generally wear long robes. When at court, rules regulate their clothing, and depending on their status, they both will appear in one of two robes. Those of the highest status will wear a *mang* with round dragons and waves embroidery (Figs 1.1 and 6.1). If they are elderly *laosheng*, the *mang* will be beige or olive green (Table 6.2.N), while the middle-aged *laosheng* and the *xiaosheng* wear the *mang* in other colors, often red, if they are particularly important to the court and the plot. A *xiaosheng* will wear a white *mang* to show his loyalty or a pink one if he is handsome and romantically inclined (Table 6.22.B and 6.22.N). When either role type plays the emperor, the *mang* will be yellow (Fig. 4.3). In roles as a foreigner, the *laosheng* wear

the same *mang* as they would at a Han court, except feathers and foxtails are added to their headdress (Fig. 7.40). Civilian *laosheng* and *xiaosheng* officials of the court who have not earned the right to wear the *mang* wear the *guanyi* (official's robe) with the rank badge. The *guanyi* comes most often in red, maroon, or blue (Fig. 4.6). When *laosheng* are high-ranking civilian officials, such as a prime minister, they may then, in informal scenes away from court, wear a *kai chang* (official's informal robe) with crossover closing and embroidered roundels and borders (Fig. 6.21). While traveling, they sometimes wear the *jianyi* (archer's robe) with the *magua* (riding jacket) (Fig. 6.30).

In scenes away from court, *laosheng* and *xiaosheng* have greater differences in their wardrobes. If a *laosheng* appears at home, he will, as a mature male, wear a *pi* with roundel patterns in the embroidery (Table 6.1.B and 6.1.N a and b). The *pi*, which is daily wear for rich men, middle-ranking officials, and gentlemen, can be maroon or olive green for an elderly *laosheng*, and for the middle-aged, it can be dark blue and other sedate colors (Fig. 7.35). If playing an emperor in private chambers, both the *xiaosheng* and *laosheng* will wear a yellow *pi* with round dragon embroidery. When a *laosheng* does not have wealth or position, he wears a *su* (plain) *xuezi* with a crossover front closing (Fig. 6.16). A range of dull colors depicts the stages of poverty. Olive green, brown, and blue are some of the colors of *su xuezi* that indicate lower-status *laosheng*, and those wearing the off-white *laodou yi* (poor old man clothing) are at the very bottom of society (Fig. 6.17). When imprisoned, *laosheng* and *xiaosheng* could wear red *zuiyi* (prisoner's clothes) with a white pleated skirt draped around the back of the legs.

The *xiaosheng* are most often seen wearing *xiaosheng hua* (embroidered) *xuezi* in domestic scenes, rather than a *pi* (Figs. 1.3, 4.9, 6.12; also Table 6.20.N and 6.21.B). These pastel-colored *hua xuezi* have pretty flowers embroidered on and around the collar band and on the left side of the hem when they are worn by young scholars. When their fortunes are not promising, they may wear a *xuezi* in black or pastel colors, with simpler embroidery only on the collar (Table 6.19.B and 6.19.N). For their weddings, they wear a red *pi* with roundel embroidery (Table 6.23.B and 6.23.N). After getting married and having children, they may wear the *pi* as a sign of maturity, or they may become *laosheng* and change to the *laosheng* wardrobe of costumes (Fig. 7.35).

If they are failed Confucian scholars, both *xiaosheng* and *laosheng* wear a plain black *xuezi* with a white collar. Both also can wear the black garment with the patches, *fugui yi* (garment of wealth and nobility), used for characters who are penniless, but whose prospects imply better fortune in the future. The plain *xuezi* worn by other kinds of poor *xiaosheng* roles sometimes have brighter colors than those for the *laosheng* roles in the same position. When *laosheng* play servant roles, they often wear a black *xuezi* with a black velvet collar and a wide fabric sash in orange (Table 6.3.B and 6.3.N).

The *wulaosheng* are mature generals, and *wuxiaosheng* are young ones. When they are prepared for battle, they are dressed in the *yingkao* (hard *kao*) with four flags (Fig. 1.4). Their *kao* are embroidered with dragons or fierce animals and geometric patterns. Generally, *wulaosheng* wear white, red, or green *kao*, and the youthful *wuxiaosheng* are frequently dressed in white *kao* with blue borders, but this pattern is not exclusive. For casual dress, the military *sheng* roles may wear a martial *xuezi* made of satin with embroidered roundels and/or borders (Table 6.21.N).

The *wusheng* roles are divided into *changkao* (long armor) roles and *duanda* (short clothing) roles. The *changkao wusheng* generally wear a white *kao* as the *wuxiaosheng* do, but their flesh-toned makeup distinguishes them from the *wuxiaosheng*, whose makeup is pink and white (Figs. 1.4–5). When freedom of movement is required, they may wear the *gailiang kao* (reformed armor), which fits closer to the body and lacks

flags; it is generally in the upper colors (Fig. 7.12, *gailiang kao* on another role type). When *wusheng* are in informal scenes, such as in their private quarters, they are dressed in a *kai chang* with roundel animal decorations or a satin *xuezi* with roundels, usually in white or upper colors (Fig. 6.21). The *duanda wusheng* of rank wear the *baoyi* (hero's clothes) with moving water pleated silk on the hem of the jacket and matching trousers. Their *baoyi* will come in upper colors, with geometric or floral embroidery (Figs. 1.6 and 6.31). For traveling, they may add a matching *xuezi* worn as a coat over the basic *baoyi*. Lesser *duanda wusheng*, as acrobatic warriors, wear the black *kuaiyi* (martial clothing) (Fig. 6.32). For a graphic representation, see Table 1: Character and Representative Costumes: Men, and Table 3: Costumes by Rank, Role, and Event: Men.

***Dan* Costume Conventions.** The *qingyi,* when they are young ladies of high position, wear the knee-length *nüpi* or *nüxuezi* in pastel colors with floral embroidery over a white one-hundred-pleats skirt *(baizhe qun)* with flat panels in the front and back (Table 6.10–12.B). The base of the collar of their *nüpi* has a fungus-shaped arabesque at mid-chest. If they are demure unmarried ladies, the flowers on the *nüpi* are likely to be symmetrical sprigs on either side of the front and a single sprig in the center of the back, though they may also wear a *nüpi* with a scattered floral design. When the *qingyi* marries, she wears a red *nüpi*, generally with floral roundels (Table 6.14.B and 6.14.N). The skirt worn with a wedding *pi* can be either white or red, though red is preferred. A married *qingyi* usually wears a *nüpi* with flowered roundels in more sedate colors than she wore in her youth (Fig. 1.8). In less formal scenes, a *qingyi* can wear the center-front closing version of the female *nüxuezi*. This *nüxuezi* comes in pastel colors similar to the *nüpi* and has either flowered borders or symmetrical sprigs (Table 6.13.B and 6.13.N). A white version of this *nüxuezi* with lotus-flower decoration represents mourning. When her situation becomes dire, the *qingyi* may wear the garment for which the role type was named, the "black clothing" *nüxuezi* with blue borders (Fig. 6.18). The center-front closing *nüxuezi* can be worn with or without a sash. Rather than a flowered skirt, the black *nüxuezi* pairs with a plain white skirt with blue straight borders. Like the *sheng*, the *qingyi* also may wear a *fugui yi* when they are destitute, though theirs does not carry the same meaning for an improved future (Fig. 6.20). When *qingyi* are arrested and imprisoned, they are likewise dressed in the red *zuiyi* with a white pleated skirt draped behind the legs (Fig. 6.38). In a *guzhuang* (lit. "ancient-dress")-style play, a *qingyi* may appear in the *guzhuang*-style garments and hairstyle first designed by Mei Lanfang (Fig. 6.59).

When a *qingyi* plays an empress, princess, or concubine in informal scenes, her *nüpi* will be yellow with phoenix roundels. A more elaborate garment worn by these women to court or for dancing is the *gongzhuang* (palace garment), a full-length gown with two or three layers of streamers and striped sleeve bands on the extended length (Figs. 3.6 and 6.29). At court for the most formal events, a *qingyi* character will wear either a red or yellow *nümang*, with either the wavy-edged border or the straight-edged design and a hooped jade belt. Both versions are worn with a cloud collar (Fig. 6.4).

Qingyi may also play foreign princesses, for which they wear the Qing dynasty style costumes. In informal scenes, they are dressed in the *qipao* (Manchu gown), in white or pastel colors with sprays of flowers (Fig. 6.52). When at court, these princesses wear a full-length *qimang* (Manchu court robe), with roundel dragons and waves (Fig. 6.5). As these garments are full length, they are not worn with skirts. Trousers are worn underneath, as the sides of the robes are slit to the thigh. Distinctive shoes, *huapen di* (flowerpot sole shoes) with a pedestal in the arch, and the *qitou* (Manchu hair) complete this look.

The *laodan* (mature women) dress more discretely and appropriately for their age. Their skirts *(chenqun,* lit. "inside skirt") are usually forest green or teal blue, with larger pleats than the one-hundred-pleats skirt worn by *qingyi*. The embroidery is also less dense and is executed in gold. When well off, they usually wear a maroon, blue, or olive-green colored *nüpi*, with roundel embroidery and a collar with a straight base (Fig. 1.7, Table 6.29.B, and 6.29.N b). If they appear onstage with their husband, the couple are often dressed in matching robes (Fig. 6.7). When *laodan* are widowed or their fortunes fail, then their dress changes to reflect that situation. They wear plain crossover-style *laodan su xuezi* in olive green and other drab colors like their male counterparts in similar circumstances (Fig. 6.16). An off-white *nü laodou yi* (poor old women clothes) signifies the poorest of the poor (Fig. 6.18). These robes are generally belted with a small cord *(xiao taozi)* or scarf sash. When the skirt wraps outside of the *nü laodou yi*, it indicates the *laodan*'s destitution. A *laodan* does not wear the center-front-opening *nüxuezi*.

Dowager empresses and other noblewomen are usually assigned to the *laodan* role type. In court scenes, they wear an olive-green or orange straight-edged *nümang*. The olive green indicates age, while the orange color relates to the yellow hues reserved for the emperor and his family. Their *nümang* are embroidered either with dragons or a combination of dragons and phoenixes and worn with either a hooped jade belt and cloud collar or a small cord belt without the collar (Figs. 6.3 and 8.4). For informal scenes, they wear a yellow phoenix-and-dragon *nüpi* that is further distinguished by a fungus-shaped arabesque at the base of the collar.

Huadan (lively young women) are often maids or companions for the *qingyi* roles. In some cases, the *huadan* wear robes, but they also can wear a short jacket with either a skirt or trousers; the skirt has higher status than the trousers. Their skirt has fewer pleats than the *qingyi* skirts, indicating their lower position, and it may or may not have the center panels. These three-piece sets come in pretty pastel colors and are embroidered with sprigs of flowers (Fig. 6.40). They can be varied by the addition of an assortment of vests, in hip or knee lengths. The *guzhuang* style, with fitted waist, cloud collar, or long bib with matching peplum or long tabs, may also be worn by a *huadan*. (Fig. 2.6). The collar and tabs set are usually made in colors that are darker than the jacket and skirt set. The trouser sets can be enhanced with aprons and leg panels (Fig. 1.9).

The *daoma dan* ("sword and horse" women) wear the *nükao* (female armor) decorated with flower and phoenix embroidery and two layers of streamers in the skirt. The *nükao* most often comes in red or pink, but can be made in a variety of pastel colors (Figs. 1.11 and 6.10). Women warriors may also dress in a pastel *gailiang nükao* (reformed female armor), which fits more closely to the body; it has no flags and is worn when the need for freedom of movement calls for a less bulky costume (Fig. 6.11). The *wudan* are similar to the *duanda* and are more acrobatic in their movements than the *daoma dan*. To allow for their extreme motions, they wear the *zhan'ao zhanqun* (martial jacket and trousers), which is made in several colors, such as red, pink, white, and blue (Fig. 1.10). (See Table 2: Character and Representative Costumes: Women).

Jing **Costume Conventions.** The *jing*, as men of power, tend to be generals, prime ministers, and judges. When they are at court, they often have the highest status, which permits them to wear the *mang* (Figs. 1.12, 4.5, and 6.2). Their *mang* tend to be red, black, maroon, and blue, and are distinguished by large rampant dragons, unlike the more sedate rounded dragons worn by the *sheng*. In informal scenes outside of court, the men of rank dress in the *kai chang*; these are often red, green, black, or maroon (Fig. 1.19). As with their *mang*, their *kai chang* have large rampant animals embroidered on them, including lions, tigers, and *qilin* (Chinese unicorn). For battle, they don the *yingkao*, commonly in red, black, green, blue, or maroon; this garment is embroidered with dragons and geometric patterns (Figs.

7.6 and 7.10). In some battles, secondary *jing* wear either the *gailiang kao* or the *jianyi* in similar colors. Like the *sheng* roles, when traveling, *jing* are sometimes dressed in the *jianyi* and *magua*. A matching *xuezi* may be used for a coat instead of the *magua* if they are not in formation. For lower-ranking military characters, the *jing* can wear the *kuaiyi* in battle and a plain or scattered embroidered *xuezi* in dark or neutral colors for daily life (Fig. 6.14). The *jing* roles otherwise rarely dress in this robe. (See Table 1: Character and Representative Costumes: Men, and Table 3: Costumes by Rank, Role, and Event: Men).

Chou **Costume Conventions.** The *chou* cross the lines of rank and status, playing characters from emperors to servants. The civilian *chou* are called *wenchou*, or just *chou*; the military roles are played by *wuchou*; and when *chou* play female roles, they are called *caidan*. A court official *wenchou* rarely wears a *mang*; instead they usually appear in a *guanyi* (Fig. 1.13) or a eunuch robe *(taijian yi)*, for eunuchs are most often played by *chou* (Fig. 6.24, eunuch robe on another role type). In scenes outside of court, *wenchou* with status most often wear a *xuezi* in bright colors with scattered embroidery (Fig. 6.15). If they wear a *pi*, it would conform to the conventions of age and position of other role types.

Wuchou are comic fighters and are often dressed in the *hua kuaiyi*, sometimes embroidered with butterflies to indicate that they are quick and light on their feet (Figs. 1.6 and 6.33). They may also wear a matching butterfly-embroidered *xuezi* as a coat. *Wuchou* fighters can also wear the plainer solid-color version of the *kuaiyi*. For scenes off the battlefield, *wuchou* may don a *kai chang* with embroidery similar to their *hua kuaiyi*.

Chou actors also play a wide variety of servant and attendant roles. When traveling, they may wear the *jianyi* and *magua* combination. As waiters, they wear the dark blue or black big-sleeved robe with a double-layered white pleated apron (Fig. 6.37). *Chou* servants can also wear a blue cotton *jianyi*, plain black *xuezi*, and variations on those garments (Fig. 6.28). Their robes are often drawn up to the knees to give the impression of hard work. Boatmen may wear *chayi* (lit. "tea" clothing) (Fig. 6.36). *Chou* are also used as attendants in foreign courts, where they dress in Qing dynasty based garments, the *jianyi* with the *bufu* (court surcoat) (Fig. 6.53).

Caidan are the unattractive and comic female roles played by *chou* actors. For younger roles, they dress in a slightly comic version of the standard *qingyi* dress, a *nüpi* with odd color combinations or embroidery less pretty than their more favored peers. Their makeup can be slightly askew (Figs. 1.14 and Table 6.15–18.B). As older, nagging women or matchmakers, the *caidan* are dressed in garments very similar to those worn by older women in the late Qing dynasty, a *caipo ao* (colorful old-woman jacket), a loose-fitting, large-sleeved jacket with banded borders and short trousers with straight legs (Fig.6.41). (See Table 1: Character and Representative Costumes: Men, and Table 3: Costumes by Rank, Role, and Event: Men).

Ensemble Costume Patterns. As the settings are usually minimal, ensemble members are often used to dress the stage. At court, the *longtao* (male attendants) wear the *longtao yi* (attendant robe) if they are carrying banners (Table 6.33.B and 6.33.N). The attendants of the emperor and high officials wear the *dakai* (big armor) (Table 6.34.N). The colors of these garments often match that of their leader. If they are traveling, then attendants may be dressed in the *magua* and *jianyi*. *Gongnü* (female attendants) at court often wear the center-front-opening *nüxuezi*, with borders of flowered embroidery and a cloud collar around the shoulders. An alternative design for scenes with dancing is a *guzhuang*-styled costume. The *wuhang* (acrobatic fighters) are dressed in matching *bingyi* (soldier's clothing) that comes in a wide variety of colors and ornamentation (Figs. 1.15 and 6.34–35). Each army dresses identically and in contrast with the opposing army.

Layering Patterns

No garment is worn by itself; rather, each image has a sequence of layered garments to complete the effect. All of the images start with the fitted water jacket *(shui yizi)* as the innermost, hidden layer to protect the costumes from perspiration (Fig. 6.67). In the absence of this long-sleeved absorbent cotton inner garment, some actors wear a T-shirt to protect the costumes. Some male characters wear the padded vest *(pang'ao)* over the water jacket to enlarge their silhouette and give a straighter line to the shoulders (Fig. 6.68). The white inner collar *(huling)* is put on next, wrapping to the right for both men and women, for all garments close in the center or to the right, regardless of the gender of the wearer (Fig. 6.68). Male and female characters all wear trousers, but women usually add a skirt over the trousers. Some robes are worn with a plain solid-color *xuezi* underneath the principal garment to help cover gaps in the center front at the neck and the legs. When dressed in the *kao*, some of the male characters wear a *jianyi*, while females in *nükao* armor wear an additional skirt underneath. Many of the costumes themselves are made up of more than one piece or are complemented with accessories. The overall image of the character is completed with shoes and headdresses, as is detailed in representative samples in Table 4: Dressing Layers: Men, and Table 5: Dressing Layers: Women.

The basic patterns of dress illustrated in Tables 1–5 exemplify the concept of the conventionalized costume plot. The process of memorizing each plot for hundreds of plays is much less daunting than may appear, for the same patterns are applied to the preparation for each performance. Some flexibility for interpretation exists, depending on any number of factors, from the training of the dresser to the available stock to the image required by the specifics of a character, and the creation of the overall canvas, but the essence of standardized costumes creates prototypes for recurring usage.

Deviations from Dressing Patterns

Each article of dress conforms to a specific way of being worn and conveys a set message about the character to the audience. When characters wear clothes in another manner, the visual message is altered, indicating different circumstances. Sometimes the changes are subtle, while other shifts are more dramatic. This dressing technique adds versatility to the vocabulary of the limited number of costumes.

The skirt is an example of a garment that carries different meanings when worn in altered ways. Both male and female prisoners wear a plain white *zuiqun* (prisoner skirt) over their red *zuiyi*. The skirt draws up in the front, creating a U-shaped curve from the front of the waist to the back of the legs (Fig. 6.38). This arrangement of the skirt can also be worn over the *kuaiyi* by traveling warriors. The feeble condition of an ill male character is shown by his wearing an unembroidered white *yaobao* (lit. "bloated" skirt) worn around the waist over his long robe. Female characters in times of ill health or pregnancy will wear the *yaobao* above the bustline. The front edges of the woman's *yaobao* have small loops to put over the fingers so that it can be spread in graceful arcs on either side of her body (Fig. 1.17). When a *laodan* wears her skirt over her *xuezi*, it signals that she is impoverished.

Additions to the standard garments also vary the message of the original garment. When a general, male or female, adds the *mang* over the *kao*, this signifies that they are reviewing their troops and handing out official assignments (Fig.1.2). The *zhongsha* (loyal hat) can be altered with several accessories. Upright metallic wing-like flowers *(jinhua)* on either side of the higher crown indicate the wearer is the number-one scholar in the recent round of examinations (Fig. 7.41). The *zhongsha* indicates the wearer is the emperor's son-in-law with the addition of a *fuma taozi* (hat ornament for the imperial son-in-law) made of gold filigree with pearls, pom-

poms, and tassels (Fig. 1.1). Non-Han characters may add pheasant feathers and foxtails to their headdresses (Fig. 7.40). A strip of white silk fabric draped across the upper crown of the *zhongsha* means that the wearer is in mourning for his parents. A female in mourning may don a white silk rosette *(baise caiqiu)*, sometimes worn on the crown of her head, with long streamers on either side of her face (Fig. 8.1) or on the front of the *nükao* (Fig. 4.4). Subtractions can be equally telling. A *mang* worn without the jade belt, but with a small waist cord instead, indicates for male characters that the wearer is a eunuch. On the other hand, for *laodan,* the waist cord indicates lower rank than the jade belt. When a general has been defeated in battle, he appears only in his *kaotui* (leg flaps) and *jianyi,* signifying by the loss of his armor the loss of the battle. Removal of the headdress denotes total defeat (Fig. 8.2).

Asymmetry communicates changes in the character's position as well. Called *xiepi* (to wear placed on crookedly), this asymmetry is achieved by not putting one arm through its corresponding sleeve so that the excess garment folds to the inside under that arm. A *dan* role wearing an asymmetrical *nüpi* reveals extreme mental distress to the point of madness (Fig. 8.3). Disarrayed hair accompanies this usage, but not so much as to override the rules of beauty. A *xuezi* worn asymmetrically by a male character indicates that he is traveling. When a warrior removes one of the sleeves of his *kao,* the visual message shows his defeat.

Costume Plots

The costume plots, even when recorded, are merely a framework for selecting the costumes for a performance. The standard format features a brief synopsis of the production, a listing of the characters by name and role type, and descriptions of their costume and headgear. The descriptions include the name of the garment and sometimes the color, but generally no directions are

FIGURE 8.1. *(Above)* A white rosette on the head indicates a mourning headdress for female characters. For the process of applying this actor's makeup, see Figs. 7.1–3, and for the hair process, refer to Figs. 7.21–23. *A Visit to the Family Grave (Xiao shangfen).* Character: Xiao Suzhen, actor: Li Yanyan. ACTO, Beijing, China. May 31, 2002.

FIGURE 8.2. *(Right)* The stripped-down version of armor, with only *kaotui* and *jianyi*, represents characters who have been defeated. The figure portrayed here has volunteered to be beaten as a strategic ruse, so he is only pretending to be divested of his title and rank. *The Gathering of Heroes (Qunying hui).* Character: Huang Gai, actor: Wang Wenzhi. BJC, Beijing, China. July 23, 2000.

FIGURE 8.3. A *nüpi* worn asymmetrically with one sleeve removed indicates severe anguish, as for this *qingyi*, who feigns madness to avoid being forced to become a concubine for the emperor. *The Cosmic Blade (Yuzhou feng)*. Character: Zhao Yanrong, actor: Zhang Chunqiu. NJC, Beijing, China. October 9, 2001.

given for embroidered designs. The overall look of each character's attire and the particular production need to conform to the dressing patterns elaborated in the costume plots. The range of choices within the convention can be understood by imagining the daunting process of assembling truly identical costume stocks in traditional Jingju troupes across the vast regions of China. Instead, the dresser's goal is to work within the guidelines of their training to utilize the available stock, while drawing on their own sense of the aesthetic language.

When faced with pulling garments for a performance, the dresser still needs to decide which pink *nüpi* or undesignated color *xuezi* they will select for the roles. At this point, other factors may have an impact on their choices, including dramatic interpretation or theatre lore. While there are rules that are seldom broken, different dressers or actors may have distinct readings of a given character, creating a range of solutions within the rules. For example, when the circumstances of young women of dignity change for the worse, through loss of money or family, they can be dressed in the black *nüxuezi* with blue trim (Fig. 6.18). Now that garment also comes in a range of muted colors, from gray to sage green or dusty blue. The unadorned surface with simple blue borders remains the same, but the different colors of the body of the garment allow for projection of different moods for these characters.

Another factor is theatre lore. In a popular scene from *Yutang Chun Unjustly Accused (Yutang Chun)*, three judges are interrogating the female prisoner and prostitute, Su San (NFDA APOT, Taipei, Taiwan. December 2, 1995). She dresses in the red traditional for prisoners, and two of the judges also wear red, while the third is in blue. Originally the official in blue was designed to stand out because of his lurid interrogation process, but Mei Lanfang changed both the judge's words and his costume to shift the focus of the scene from the judge to the female prisoner. Mei Lanfang dressed all three judges in red to equalize their image. Now when this scene is performed, some dressers retain the traditional style, with two red and one blue costume, for the judges, while others choose the more modern version, now called *All in Red (Mantang hong)*.[4]

The actor has some discretion in the selection process as well. During preparations backstage at the Academy of Traditional Chinese Opera, one performer was observed bringing three different colors of the same costume into the dressing room to ask the others present which color they preferred. A principal performer for

Turning Aside the Iron Carts (Tiao huache) was attired in a green *kao* for the dress rehearsal (Fig. 6.9), but appeared in a blue *kao* for performance because he preferred the blue *kao* (Fig. 2.11). The general opposite him had been in the blue *kao* armor for the dress rehearsal, and he was switched to the green in performance so that they would not both be onstage at the same time in the same color. In this same performance, two actors were playing the principal role because of the extreme vigor of the acrobatics, yet the second performer of the role retained the green *kao* armor in his scenes. The opposing general did not appear in this part of the play.

Despite these variances, the patterns of dress also create repeated similarities among productions. Records of multiple performances in Beijing over several years reveal the following examples of recurring usages. The same actress appeared wearing the identical costume when playing the same character and role type in two plays produced by the same company in two different theatres over two year-long seasons (Fig. 8.4). The same costume appeared on a different actor playing another character of the same role type in the same week as one of the aforementioned performances (Figs. 2.4 and 6.3). In another example, two actors of the same role type played different characters in different plays wearing the same olive-green *mang* (Fig. 4.10 and Table 6.2.N). The repetitions are expected, rather than exceptions, given the system employed.

A Costume Plot and Two Performances

A Galaxy of Character Images in Traditional Jingju (Chuantong Jingju renwu zaoxing huicui). edited by Zhang Yijuan et al. and published in 2001, is one of the more current and complete records of costume plots for traditional Jingju plays. The written plots found in this book list the characters, their makeup, hair, headdress, costume pieces, accessories, and changes. By comparing the written version of a costume plot with two perfor-

FIGURE 8.4. The same costume ensemble was worn by this actor to play the same character in two plays and by another performer to play in the same role type in a third performance (see Fig. 6.3). *Mu Guiying Takes Command (Mu Guiying gua shuai).* Character: She Taijiun, actor: Wang Shufang. BJC, Beijing, China. July 16, 2000, pictured, and *Silang Visits His Mother (Silang tan mu)*, Character: She Taijiun, actor: Wang Shufang. BJC, Beijing, China. October 7, 2001.

mances, it is possible to envision both the patterns and the variations in dressing for traditional Jingju. Productions of *The Phoenix Returns to Its Nest* were presented in Beijing by the Beijing Jingju Company on July 9, 2000, and by the National Jingju Company on October 3, 2001. The recorded images of the costumes illustrate how a dresser follows the conventions for each role and character in the selection of the garments, while illuminating the feasible differences.

The Phoenix Returns to Its Nest was first brought to the Jingju stage by Mei Lanfang in the 1920s, and it is now a part of the traditional Jingju repertoire. Elizabeth Wichmann's synopsis of the plot introduces the characters.

> During the Ming Dynasty, Cheng Pu, a retired Vice Minister of War, met at a picnic the intelligent, but impoverished young scholar, Mu Juyi. Mu was the son of an old friend who had been framed by a highly placed eunuch, and then executed for the crime he did not commit.
>
> Cheng had two daughters; Cheng Xue'e, the younger one by his concubine, was clever and beautiful. Upon meeting Mu Juyi, he wanted his younger daughter to marry the poor young scholar.
>
> When he returned home and discussed the matter with his wife, however, problems rapidly arose. Madam Cheng had given birth to Cheng Xueyan, Cheng's eldest daughter (who was rather ugly), and wanted her own daughter to wed the promising young scholar instead of Cheng Xue'e. The old couple's discussion of the matter thus degenerated into a quarrel.
>
> Determined, Cheng Pu invited Mu Juyi to attend the celebration of his birthday and instructed his beautiful daughter to take a secret look at the young man. Prince Zhu, a friend of Cheng, was also invited and was taken by the beauty of the younger Miss Cheng. Cheng Pu, however, related to Mu his intention of giving to him, in marriage, his beautiful young daughter. Mu readily accepted this promise and remained to live in Cheng's study in the outer courtyard.
>
> Quite aware of Mu's presence, the elder Miss Cheng stole her way into his study to flirt with him. Startled by Cheng Xueyan's homely countenance, Mu Juyi angrily thought she was the promised maiden and that Cheng Pu was tricking him into marrying an otherwise undesirable daughter. Thereupon, he stalked out of Cheng Pu's mansion.
>
> At this time a rebellion occurred and Cheng Pu was appointed to a high post in Marshall Hong's army. Taking advantage of Cheng's absence from his home, and falsely claiming to be Mu Juyi, Prince Zhu sent a wedding sedan for the delicate Cheng Xue'e.
>
> Madam Cheng again seized what she thought was an opportunity to fob off to Mu Juyi her ugly-duckling daughter, Cheng Xueyan. Still, when the sedan chair arrived at its real destination and the expectant bride's face was unveiled by the scheming groom, both felt foiled.
>
> Meanwhile, following his departure from Cheng Pu's, Mu Juyi was also assigned to Marshal Hong's staff where he again met Cheng Pu, and distinguished himself in performing his duties. Upon the quelling of the rebellion, Mu Juyi was promoted to the rank of general. At that time, Marshal Hong and the eunuch Army Supervisor Zhou arranged for him to marry Cheng Xue'e. Smarting from the distasteful encounter with the first Miss Cheng, Mu Juyi was not willing to consummate a ceremony with one who he still mistakenly thought to be so unsightly. It was only when Cheng Xue'e's radiant face was unveiled that Mu Juyi saw that she was, in reality, an exquisite young lady. He kowtowed

profusely in apology to his bride, new father-in-law, Marshal Hong and Eunuch Zhou.

The curtain falls in an atmosphere of great happiness.[5]

An additional detail of the plot is that Zhu Huanran and his family are overcome by bandits and their fortunes are stolen, leaving them penniless until they meet Cheng Pu again.

The characters are described and arranged in the accompanying chart in the order listed in *A Galaxy of Character Images in Traditional Jingju* (see Table 6: *The Phoenix Returns to Its Nest: Comparative Costume Plots*). In most cases, when a costume piece such as an inner garment is not visible in the photograph, it can be assumed the actor is wearing the item as described or something near to the description, for less variation occurs with the inner garments and shoes. When an accessory is marked as not evident, it means it is not included in the photograph, but may have been used at another moment. For the characters indicated as not recorded, either they were not onstage long enough to capture in a photograph, or they did not appear. The makeup described for each character reflects their role types, and in the case of the *sheng* and *dan* roles, it is listed as *junban* (lit. "handsome/beautiful makeup") for well-to-do and healthy individuals.

Cheng Pu, as a father and a court official is a *laosheng* (mature male). In the costume plot, he is described as wearing a purple *pi* and *yuanwai jin* (gentry hat), purple resembling maroon in the western color sense. In the Beijing Jingju Company performance, he wore a *pi* in olive green, a color used in the same way as maroon to indicate age (Table 6.1.B), while in the National Jingju Company production, he initially appeared in the maroon *pi* as listed in the plot (Table 6.1.N a), and later changed to an olive *pi* (Table 6.1.N b). All of the *pi* worn by Cheng Pu had roundel embroidery suitable for a dignified character. In both productions, he wore a matching-color *yuanwai jin* as described in the written plots, and carried a folding fan *(zheshan)*. When Cheng Pu returns to official service, the costume plot has him change to a green *mang*. In the Beijing Jingju Company production, he wore a green *mang* (Table 6.2.B), while in the National Jingju Company's version he was dressed in an olive-green *mang* (Table 6.2.N). The green color represents his military function as the associate minister of the Ministry of Defense, while the olive green identifies elderly characters, so both choices are within the range for him. The embroidery on both included round dragons and *lishui* (standing water) at the hem, in the style designated for dignified men. The costume plot indicates he should wear a *zhongsha* (loyal hat), as he did in both performances. Both Cheng Pu actors wore the *cansan* (gray three-part beard) listed in the plot.

The House Manager is the gatekeeper in the courtyard of Cheng Pu's home. He is described as wearing a black *ruan luomao* (soft beret hat) and black *xuezi*, though both *luomao* were hard instead. The plot lists a white beard and yellow silk headscarf *(choutiao)* for him, but he wore a black beard without the headscarf in the Beijing Jingju Company version (Table 6.3.B) and a white beard with the headscarf in the National Jingju Company production (Table 6.3.N). This shows a distinction in age, for the headscarf would not be worn by a younger character. The orange sash worn by the Beijing Jingju Company actor is more common for characters of this type than the yellow worn in the other production.

Zhu Huanran, because he is foolish and tries to trick the Cheng family, is played by a *chou* actor. As a princeling in the imperial clan, he is entitled to wear yellow, although the color of yellow for someone of lesser rank is not the same hue as that worn by the emperor. In both productions, Zhu Huanran first appeared in a yellow *pi*, although in the Beijing Jingju Company version, it was his main garment (Table 6.4.B) and in the National Jingju Company performance, he wore it like an open coat over a red *xuezi* (Table 6.4.N). Wearing the robe in this incorrect fashion communicates that he is not an upright character.[6] Both yellow *pi* had dragon roundels embroidered in blue, another indication of Zhu's imperial rank. The visible inner *xuezi* was embellished with a scattered pattern typical of *chou* characters of status. He wore the *bangchui jin* ("wooden club" hat) listed in the plot in both productions, although one was orange and the other was yellow. In scene 4, Zhu changes clothes several times, saying, "I must remove these traveling clothes and change into some felicitation clothes, in order to properly give the Vice Minister birthday greetings."[7] Both of the actors in this role dressed and redressed in a series of brightly colored embroidered *xuezi*, more specifically the *wenchou hua xuezi* with scattered floral patterns on them, reciting the lines, "Aren't these the same clothes I wore when I came in? . . . Didn't you bring any others? . . . It's not as though I have no other clothes!"[8] The colors were green, red, and true purple, and just a bit brighter than what noncomic roles would wear (Table 6.5–6.B and 6.5–6.N). Zhu's change for the wedding was inexplicably omitted from the written costume plot. In both productions, when Zhu appeared for his wedding, he was dressed in the traditional red *pi* with roundels of embroidery, a combination reserved for grooms (Table 6.7.B and 6.7.N). In the Beijing Jingju Company performance, he wore a red *xueshi jin* (scholar's hat) to match his *pi*, but in the National Jingju Company version, he retained the yellow hat that he had worn from the beginning of the story. After the wedding, Zhu's fortunes slide when bandits raid his home, and he now is dressed in lower-class clothing. In both versions, he wore a white pleated skirt over a plain black *xuezi* as listed in the plot, the first with a black velvet collar band used for household servants (Table 6.8.B) and the second with a contrasting white band for ordinary people (Table 6.8.N). In

the plot and the Beijing Jingju Company production, his headdress was a black *gao fangjin* (high peaked hat), but in the National Jingju Company version, he wore a *di fangjin*, a shorter version of the same hat. For the Beijing Jingju Company production, he wore tall black boots with low soles and had his trousers tucked into the tops.

Two *chou yuanzi* (courtyard keepers) are described and appeared in black *ruan luomao* (soft beret), black *xuezi*, and cloth sash. In both performances, orange sashes were selected. In the Beijing Jingju Company, these characters were played by *chou* actors as indicated in the plot (Table 6.9.B), but in the National Jingju Company performance, they were depicted by *laosheng* (Table 6.9.N). Such servants can be played by either role type. The *qing pao* supporting roles were not recorded in performance.

Cheng Xue'e, the attractive younger daughter, is a *qingyi*. In the plot, she is listed as having a total of three changes: a *nüpi*, a *nüxuezi*, and a wedding outfit, but in both productions, she had several additional costumes. In the Beijing Jingju Company version, she wore three different *nüpi*, green, red, and lake blue, each with embroidered floral sprays (Table 6.10–12.B). She then changed into a blue *nüxuezi* that also had floral-spray embroidery (Table 6.13.B). In the National Jingju Company version, Xue'e wore three *nüpi* in green, yellow, and pink, then changed into a lavender *nüxuezi*, before returning to the first *nüpi* in blue (Table 6.10–13.N). In both cases, the *nüpi* and *nüxuezi* worn were among the many colors and floral patterns suitable for a *qingyi*, and she changed to a *nüxuezi* as described. The colors for these garments are not delineated in the plot, allowing for the variations in selection. Her skirt is designated as white in the plot and she appeared in a white skirt in both versions because white is standard for young women of her status. In both productions and the plot, Xue'e was dressed in a red *nüpi* and wedding veil (*gaitou*) for the wedding scene, the color and garments being constant as required by the event. In the Beijing Jingju Company production, both her wedding *nüpi* and skirt were red (Table 6.14.B), but in the National Jingju Company, although her *nüpi* was red, her skirt was white with red embroidered flowers (Table 6.14.N). The *nüpi* in the Beijing Jingju Company production had large golden-flower sprig embroidery, while in the National Jingju Company version, she was dressed in the more traditional surface design of multicolored roundels. Wedding garments for the bride and groom are usually embroidered as a set, but Xue'e matched her husband's garment only in the National Jingju Company version. Xue'e's hair, *datou* (complete hair), *xian lianzi* (drape of long hair), and ornaments were executed as described in the plot in both productions, with diamonds (rhinestones) and kingfisher feather decorations.

Cheng Xueyan, the unattractive daughter, is played by a *caidan*, or comic *chou* actor. Given the overriding desire for beauty in performance, it would not be suitable for a *qingyi* actress to play the role of the ugly elder sister. The Beijing Jingju Company actor applied a distorted version of the *qingyi* cherry-blossom makeup, and both wore the typical *qingyi*-style headdress and ornaments listed in the costume plot. The written plot indicates four costumes for Xueyan: an embroidered *nüpi*, an embroidered *nüxuezi*, wedding garments, and a plain black *nüxuezi*. In the Beijing Jingju Company production, she entered in a pink *nüpi* with lovely floral embroidery of a design usually worn by a *qingyi* (Table 6.15.B). The National Jingju Company production had her dressed in a lavender *nüpi* with a maroon collar band, a color combination that not all would view as pleasing, but the embroidery was appealing and in the standard format for young lady roles (Table 6.15.N). Both productions gave her a second *nüpi*, rather than a *nüxuezi* for her change. In the Beijing Jingju Company production, the *nüpi* was salmon, or "old flesh color," with a black collar, a rather harsh color combination outside of the usual spectrum to indicate the unattract-

ive aspects of the character (Table 6.16.B). In the National Jingju Company version, the change was barely noticeable, for she wore another lavender *nüpi* that was only slightly bluer than the first (Table 6.16.N). Again, the collar band was an odd match, as it was white with blue flowers, and the lavender robe had silver butterflies on it. In both performances, for the wedding she wore a red *nüpi* with the traditional roundels and a white skirt (Table 6.17.B and 6.17.N). In the National Jingju Company version, the wedding *pi* of the bride and groom matched again, while the Beijing Jingju Company wedding costumes again did not. After the wedding, when her fortunes deteriorate, Xueyan appeared in a black *nüxuexi* with the center-front closing and blue borders and a plain white skirt with matching blue borders. Both productions followed the plot and dressed her in this traditional image for destitute women, although neither changed the hair ornaments to silver, as suggested in the costume plot (Table 6.18.B and 6.18.N). Instead, Xueyan added a blue scarf in one production and removed some of her sparkling ornaments in the other.

Mu Juyi is a young scholar and a *xiaosheng* role. The costume plot lists four images for him, but in each production, he wore five costumes. In both performances, he started with a black embroidered *xuezi*, as the written record indicates he should (Table 6.19.B and 6.19.N). The garments were remarkably similar; each one was plain except for gold and lavender embroidery on the collar band, a simple embroidery design indicating a very lowly scholar. Cheng Xue'e says about her prospective husband, "His clothing made me sigh; his family has fallen on such very hard times."[9] Although the plot lists him as wearing a *wenxiaosheng jin* (civil *xiaosheng* hat), he wore a black *qiaoliang jin* (bridge hat) in the Beijing Jingju Company version and a black *gao fangjin* in the National Jingju Company performance. His next change was not described in the plot, but both productions moved him into an embroidered *xuezi* of slightly higher status. In the Beijing Jingju production, he wore a lavender *xuezi* with a black embroidered collar band (Table 6.20.B), while in the National Jingju Company version he was dressed in a blue *xiaosheng hua xuezi* with embroidery typical for his role, flowers on and around the collar band and on the left hem (Table 6.20.N). The two garments send different messages of wealth and status, with the more embroidered costume giving him a higher position. In the Beijing Jingju Company version, he retained the same hat, but he changed to a matching *qiaoliang jin* in the National Jingju Company performance. The second costume change in the plot lists a *wusheng jin* (military crescent hat) and embroidered *xuezi*. In the Beijing Jingju Company production, which had kept his position lower, he moves up a notch by wearing a *xiaosheng hua xuezi,* similar to what the National Jingju Company character had already worn, with floral embroidery around the collar and the hem (Table 6.21.B). Since the National Jingju Company performance had to select a costume with yet a higher position, Mu Juyi changed to a white *wuxiaosheng hua xuezi* with formal embroidery of floral roundels and borders reserved for martial *xiaosheng,* representing his new post in the army (Table 6.21.N). His headdress was the *wusheng jin* from the costume plot in both versions. The costume plot indicates a change to another headdress, a *jiangjin* (fabric and filigree headdress for generals), but this change was not noted in either performance. Next, Mu Juyi changed to a *mang,* which the costume plot designates as pink. While he was dressed in pink in the Beijing Jingju Company production (Table 6.22.B), he wore a white *mang* in the National Jingju Company performance (Table 6.22.N). The costume plot mentions the matching collar for the *mang,* which would indicate his military status, though it was not worn in either production. In the final scene, when he marries, he is dressed in the traditional red *pi* with floral roundels in the plot and in both performances as well (Table 6.23.B and 6.23.N). In both

versions, his headdress with the *mang* and the wedding *pi* was a *zhongsha* with a jade plaque (*maozheng*), appropriate for young men with official appointments, but neither dresser added the flowers (*dinghua*) called for in the plot.

Xue'e's handmaids (*yahuan*) were dressed in variations of maids' garments, either a combination of jacket, skirt, and vest, or of jacket, trousers, and vest in pastel pink, blue, yellow, and green. They are dressed as described in the costume plot, except that only one of maids in the two productions wore a skirt. The other three wore trousers instead. Their hair appeared as described, although the *zhuaji* (hair coil) is not visible in the photographs of either production (Table 6.24–25.B and 6.24–25.N).

Military Supervisor Zhou Jianjun is a eunuch. He has a red *taijian lian* (eunuch face) and does not wear a beard. In the costume plot, he is described as dressed in a purple (maroon) *mang,* but in both performances, he instead wore a red *mang,* a common color for eunuchs (Table 6.26.B and 6.26.N). His headdress was listed in the plot as the eunuch helmet (*taijian kui*), and that is what he wore in each performance, with tassels over the ears. The long black strips visible on either side of his face in the Beijing Jingju Company image represent his hair from childhood, since he was castrated when he was young. Although a eunuch usually wears a small waist cord with the *mang,* in the plot and onstage, Zhou wore a jade belt instead, indicating his high rank.

Hong Gong is a marshal played by a *laosheng* actor, and according to the written costume plot he wears a red *mang.* The Beijing Jingju Company red *mang* had embroidery that was predominantly blue (Table 6.27.B), while the National Jingju Company red robe featured gold couching with fewer decorations (Table 6.27.N). Both garments represent the same range of characters, those of high social status who are honorable and gentle personalities. The plot lists his headdress as a *shuaikui* (marshal's helmet), seen in the National Jingju Company production, whereas the Beijing Jingju Company actor wore a *taiding*, a headdress for a noble with military functions. Hong Gong then changed to a *zhongsha* in both performances (Table 6.28.B and 6.28.N). His *heisan* (three-part beard) and makeup appeared in the performances as delineated in the plot.

Madam Cheng, as a mother of a certain age and status, is a *laodan* role. In the costume plot, she is described as wearing a purple (maroon) *nüpi* and a green skirt. Mature husbands and wives are often depicted in the same color garments. As Cheng Pu wore an olive green *pi* in the Beijing Jingju Company performance, his wife also appeared in an olive-green *nüpi* (Table 6.29.B). Her skirt was a blue reserved for older women. In the National Jingju Company version, Madam Cheng also mirrored the clothing her husband wore, starting in a maroon *pi* and then changing to olive green (Table 6.29.N a and b). With both of these robes, she wore a green skirt, the color called for in the costume plot, and one that is often used for older women. In the plot, the hairstyle described for her is typical for older women, a gray *wangzi* (skullcap), gray *binfa* (side hair), *laodan guan* (high-status bun, *leizi* (black velvet trim), with a purple (maroon) scarf. In the Beijing Jingju Company performance, she had an olive-green scarf wrapped around her head that matched her *nüpi*. The National Jingju Company actor started in a matching maroon scarf, but when she changed to the olive *nüpi*, she retained the maroon scarf, rather than changing to one that matched the new color of her *nüpi*. In both cases, her hair was dressed as described. Her fortunes fail along with those of her unattractive daughter when robbers overtake their home. The costume plot records her wearing a plain *xuezi* with a waist scarf, an image applied to older women in poor financial circumstances. She was dressed in a dark maroon *xuezi*, with a plain teal blue skirt, in the Beijing Jingju Company production (Table 6.30.B) and an olive-green satin *xuezi* with a white collar band in the National Jingju Company

version (Table 6.30.N). The National Jingju Company performer also wore an orange waist cord, projecting a more dire image than the other. Neither headscarf matched the final garment.

The *zhongjun* (military gatekeeper) is a *laosheng* character not covered in the synopsis, but mentioned in the costume plot as wearing a red *kai chang*. In both productions, he wore a gold filigree headdress named for his character, a *zhongjun kui*, with a tall, slightly pointed, round crown and narrow flat brim. The plot lists an alternative headdress, the *da banjin* (flat board hat), perhaps an alternative for companies not having the hat unique to this character. In the Beijing Jingju Company production, his *kai chang* robe had large raging beasts embroidered on it, a style suited for strong military men (Table 6.31.B). In the National Jingju Company performance, he wore a more sedate *kai chang* robe, with gold couched roundels and border, which indicates a high-ranking civilian official (Table 6.31.N). As this character is a military man, the second costume, for a civilian, could be considered questionable. In the Beijing Jingju Company production, he had no beard, while in the National Jingju Company version, he did, but the age of this character is not significant.[10]

A *chefu* (cartman), played by a *za* (supporting role), guides a cart in which Madam Cheng rides. He is described as wearing a cotton *jianyi* and felt hat. This role was dressed more or less as prescribed in both performances; one *jianyi* was made of cotton with black trim, while the other was satin with red trim (Table 6.32.B and 6.32.N). Each garment was within the range of costumes for servants. Both wore the white felt hat with upturned brim listed in the costume plot.

The plot describes two sets of *longtao* attendants in red and white. One set of *longtao* attendants was wearing red *longtao yi and* red *da banjin* (big board soft hat) in both performances (Table 6.33.B and 6.33.N). Neither the white *longtao* set, nor the *binxiang* (*chou* wedding officials) mentioned in the costume plot, were recorded in either performance. An additional set of four guards in *longtao* (entourage) roles wearing red *dakai* (big armor) appeared in scene 7 in the National Jingju Company presentation (Table 6.34.N). They wore the *guanzi kui* (lit. "bucket-shaped helmet") with a diadem over the forehead and a peaked crown with a stem and a tuft of fur coming out of the point. Their trousers were likely to be red and worn with thin-soled ankle boots.

The cross-referencing of three sources of information for the costumes of a single play demonstrates both the concept of conventions and how they operate in the actual selection of costumes. The distinctions between the productions were slight and were far outweighed by the similarities. In all the comparisons, the convention of images assigned to each role was used as a guideline in the selection process, with the form of the garments identical and the variations occurring at the levels of color and embroidery. Colors were specified in the written costume plot for only a portion of the costumes, leaving much to the dresser's decision. When the color was indicated in the plot, that color, or a near relative, was reflected in actual usage, and in all cases, the color selected was appropriate for the conventions of the role. Generally, the embroidery fell within the standard patterns for the role. The plot describes garments as either embroidered or plain, leaving the details of the imagery to the dresser. A similar level of adherence to the principles of clothing selection can be expected in most performances of this or any play.

Dressing Techniques

Jobs. The jobs of dressing are typically divided among four personnel. The women's hairstyles and jewels are arranged by one person, while another is responsible for the men's head wraps and headdresses, as well as the *laodan* hair preparation. A third person takes responsibility for the outer clothing elements, and the fourth is in charge of the inner garments. The personnel involved in the dressing process need to be familiar with all facets of the process as the components are interlocking. For example, the headdress personnel must have an awareness of makeup so that they can place the headdress in the proper relation to the facial design. In addition, all dressers' efforts in preparing the performers for the stage need to be carefully coordinated in the proper sequence so that the pieces come together gracefully. In general, the makeup and hairstyles are completed first, then the costumes and headdresses are assembled. Sometimes the sequence of preparation requires that the actor go back and forth between the headdressing and wardrobe personnel. An actor preparing to play a general, for example, will apply his makeup, don the *kao* with help from the dresser, then have the headdress personnel arrange his headdress, and, finally, return to the dresser, who will tie on the flags.

Fastenings and Knots. Robes are closed with either loops and toggles or fabric ties that are knotted with a single sided bow. Trousers and skirts are tied on with a separate string. A few pieces use Velcro closings, including the matching sashes with some costumes and the gaiters worn on the legs of warriors.

For garments that are worn close to the body, waists are secured with sashes or belts. The scarf sashes are wrapped from front to back and around to the front again and tied either in the center or on the right side. The knots used are similar to a square knot, a single bow and a double bow, depending on the garments. The scarf sashes are made of lightweight silk and are embroidered on the ends. *Huadan*, *wuchou*, children, and prisoners can all wear a scarf, to mention a few characters (Fig. 6.33, Table 6. 24–25.B and 6.24–5.N).

The small cord belt comes in a variety of colors and has three tassels on it, one on each end and a third that attaches around the cord so that it can slide along the length of it. Male characters wear the tassel on the left and females on the right. The small cord belt wraps around the waist on the double and then ties in a bow.

The loops of the bow are pulled until the fringed ends are at the right length around mid calf. Then the ends of the loops are tucked behind the cords on either side forming a "W" shape with the ties hanging down the center. Eunuchs, old women, old men, children and nuns, among others, wear the cord belt (Figs. 6.3 and 6.42).

The wide firm sash *(luandai)* is worn by men connected with the military and by servants. It is about four inches wide and comes in either one or two long pieces. It can be tied in several knots, the most common being a flattened bow in the center front. The two-piece sash has a length with two fringed ends and another without. The piece with the fringe is placed at the center front at the waist so one fringed end just brushes the top of the shoes, while the other is flipped over the actor's left shoulder. The unfringed piece wraps around the waist from front to back and around to the center front and is tied in a square knot. The ends are folded into quarters and then tucked behind the outer wrap of the sash at forty-five degree angles from the center. Then the outer fringed end drops down over the knot, making a flat finish to the bow. If too long, then a tuck is made in this piece behind the sash (Fig. 8.5).

Silk cords *(si taozi)* are tied around the chest area of soldiers for a heroic look. These cords have two long tassels and two long loops of cording and are tied in two kinds of knots. When worn with the *kuaiyi* and the *jianyi*, the knot is placed at the center back of the neck and one of the loops goes around each arm. The tassels are lifted forward to the collarbone and each wraps twice around the cord on either side of the neck. The two loops are brought together in the center front and tied in a square knot. The ends of the loops are entwined to create a spoke-shaped pattern emanating in eight directions from the single knot in the front (Fig. 8.6). A more complicated knot with a honeycomb pattern may be used for the *baoyi*.

One of the most challenging aspects of dressing is securing the flags on the generals wearing the *yingkao*.

FIGURE 8.5. The wide firm sash holds the garments securely for military characters and is tied with a flat bow in front. ACTO, Beijing, China.

The four flag poles are mounted in a leather base in such a way that they can be stored parallel and fanned out when worn. Padding on the top of the inside of the leather base pitches the flags away from the back of the head. Four ropes on the leather base are placed so that two go over the shoulders and two under the arms. The actor holds the shoulder cords as the dresser adjusts the position of the flags, while holding on to the lower cords. The chest cords are tied first in a square knot and then the shoulder cords are lashed to the chest cords forming a harness. The excess ends are twisted together and concealed under the arm. The ropes are covered

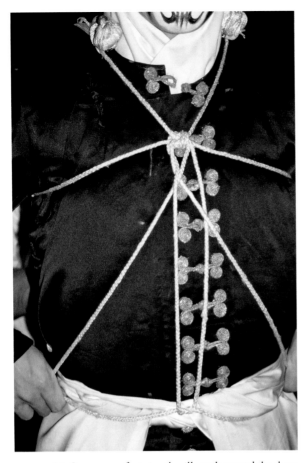

FIGURE 8.6. One pattern for tying the silk cords around the chest creates a spoke design. This configuration may be worn over the *kuaiyi* seen here, or the *jianyi*. ACTO, Beijing, China.

FIGURE 8.7. The *kao* flags are lashed around the chest to hold them securely. This performer's headdress is a *zhajin kui*. Character: Pei Yuanqing, actor: Wang Libo. *Attacking Pei Yuanqing with Fire (Huo shao Pei Yuanqing)*. ACTO, Beijing, China. May 31, 2002.

with a red silk sash attached to the base of the flags. The sash comes around both sides to the front, crosses over and twists around the knots on the opposite side. The ends of the sash hang down visibly on either side of the front of the *kao* (Fig. 1.4). The *kao* collar covers the ropes on the shoulders. The knots for this rigging are all slipknots and release quickly when the ends of the cords are pulled (Fig. 8.7).

Sizing to Fit. The factories generally make the garments in standard sizes unless instructed otherwise. The

dressers can adjust the fit of some of the costumes to the performer with folding and pleating techniques, and then secure them with strings or sashes. The women's skirts are mounted on a straight band and tied around the waist with the hem at the proper length. The trousers for both men and women are generally cut without any fitting, rather the waistband is a wide, flat circle of cotton. With the center front and back lined up on the actor's body, and the crotch seams at the desired height, the trousers are folded to fit in an inverted box pleat in the center front, and tied with a separate cord (Fig. 6.61). The cotton waistband helps to prevent slipping, particularly during acrobatics. The hems of the men's trousers are folded in an inverted box pleat to the back and tied with attached ties, while the women's hang straight.

Robes that fall straight from the shoulder to the hem obviously can't be adjusted by dressing and they are occasionally hemmed when necessary, but the results are not satisfactory, as this affects the placement of the embroidery and the way the fabric hangs. The *kao*, however, can be shortened by folding the front and back tabard pieces at the chest line. The folds are concealed by the flags in the back and the sashes for the flags across the chest. The *jianyi* is worn drawn in at the waist with a wide sash. The extra width of the garment can be pleated into a deep box pleat on the back of the waist and if the garment is too long, horizontal folds are made at the circumference of the waist, secured with a string, and concealed by the wide sash. When the wearer heads for battle, the front right side of the skirt of the *jianyi* is folded and tucked into the wide firm sash to give the impression of facilitating movement. The *jianyi* has slashes in the center front and back, and has an underwrap in the right, so the legs are still covered by the remaining skirt panels. The jackets of the *gailiang kao, baoyi, bingyi,* and *kuaiyi* are all pleated in the back for a smooth fit around the waist. The pleating and fitting techniques that change the size of the garments further support the convention of a stock wardrobe for all characters and all actors.

If the acrobats have additional decorative pieces, like a cloud collar, the pieces sometimes have tabs that can be secured into the waist sash (Fig. 2.12). Women warriors constrain their long hair when tying their sashes to prevent the hair from becoming entangled during quick fight movements. The hairline created with the dampened silk gauze wrapped around the forehead shrinks when it dries, creating a tight bond on the head. Then the headdresses are all tied tightly at the back of the head. Very few include additional ties under the chin, and given the energetic nature of the battles, a relatively small number are separated from their wearers onstage. Because of the extreme movements in the acrobatic scenes, the dressers are well trained in securing the garments and headdresses to allow for maximum movement, while maintaining the silhouette. To help in the complicated dressing and folding methods, the actors also learn how to assist in the dressing process.

Trunks and Storage

Most companies retain their own stock of costumes for use in their performances. In history, personal clothing was stored flat in chests or cupboards.[11] This technique conceivably contributed to the methodology that developed for the organization of costume storage into trunks, a practice that developed by the Ming era when most troupes didn't have their own performance venues. Now most companies store their costumes folded and in cabinets, using the same system of organization as was in place with the trunks. The costumes and accessories are divided into seven categories for storage. The primary set of costume trunks or cabinets contains the full-length clothing of principal players. There are two subsets within this category for the robes of the higher ranks and commoners. The upper trunk includes garments with water sleeves worn by the most important roles, the ceremonial, and formal robes including the *mang, pi, guanyi,* and the *kai chang.* Tradition requires the emperor's yellow *mang* robe to be third from the top under the red and green *mang* robes so that it does not become too self-important. The order of storage thereafter follows the sequence of the upper five colors.[12] The uppermost garment in the first trunk is the *fugui yi,* the patched garment that contains good wishes for a brighter future. The lower trunk stores the clothes with lesser rank, the *xuezi, xueshi yi, bagua yi,* and religious dress. The garments worn by warriors need to be stored separately from those of the scholars and civilians, therefore the second set of trunks or cabinets contains the garments for fighting men with generals also divided from the acrobat soldiers. In this set, the upper trunk stores the *kao*, the *jianyi* and *kuaiyi*, while the acrobats' *bingyi* go into the lower. The third trunk or cabinet contains the inner garments. These are the washable garments, including the water shirts, the white collars, and the padded vests. The four kinds of headdresses, ceremonial headdresses, helmets, official's hats, and soft hats are stored in the fourth trunk, along with the beards. The fifth trunk contains the fabric props, such as flags, curtains, tablecloths, and chair covers. The sixth trunk stores the boots and shoes and the seventh trunk contains the weapons.[13]

To prepare for a performance, the dressers select the costume pieces using only a list with the cast of characters and names of the actors playing the roles. The dressers managing the outer garments and headdresses may confer on their choices so that the colors match or blend correctly. The chosen costumes are placed in a touring trunk for transportation to the dressing room or the theatre where the performance will take place. Once they arrive at the performance venue, the dressers arrange all the garments and accessories backstage on tables and racks. The placement of the costumes in the dressing area depends on the production and which garments are required. Generally, like garments go together on shelves, sorted by male and female, military and civilian, still folded as they are in the storage cabinets. Some garments are hung on racks as well. The garments of the principal actors may be ironed, although the fold lines are usually visible onstage. Historical garments were not ironed as a matter of course, either.[14] The accessories and inner garments are arranged on a separate table. The small headdresses are stored on shelves and the larger ones are hung on specially designed racks. The beards are also hung on a rack.

Cleaning. Cotton and unadorned costumes are cleaned as needed. To preserve the multicolored and metallic threads, the embroidered costumes are not cleaned by emersion in water or chemicals. Instead, care is taken to avoid soiling as much as possible. The actors wear a water shirt or a T-shirt underneath the main garments to absorb moisture. A separate white cotton collar wraps around the neck providing a barrier between the makeup and the garments, as well as an attractive focal point for the face (Figs. 6.1, 6.3, and 8.7). These pieces can be laundered regularly. When action requires the white silk water sleeves to be held near the face, a simultaneous movement often holds the sleeve away to prevent it from actually coming into contact with the makeup. Performers are also trained to move and sit carefully in costume to avoid damage. If a costume does require cleaning, a spot remover is used, and they are sprayed with high proof, clear grain alcohol after use to freshen them. Each autumn, all the costumes are unfolded and placed in the sun to refresh them and then they are returned to the storage cabinets. With care, a garment may last between ten and twenty five years, depending on fabric and the frequency of use.

Folding. Between performances, the costumes are carefully folded inside out and stored on shelves in the cabinets. Besides following traditional practices, the folding protects the embroidery and prevents the shoulders from becoming distorted from hanging. The folding process is an important and meticulous part of the training. Each garment has a specific system for folding with a predominance of horizontal and vertical folds rather than diagonals. To fold a *mang*, for example, the shoulder and sleeves are straightened from wrist to wrist and the *mang* is placed flat on a table with the back panel facing up in the center of the garment. The left extension is straightened and placed vertically down the back, about one third in from the edge. Then the left sleeve is folded in from the wrist to the shoulder. Next, the left side of the garment is creased one third in along the line of the extension. The right sleeve and side of the garment are folded in the same way. Then the underwrap and overwrap are flipped inside out so that all the outer surfaces with embroidery are now protected on the inside. The length folds into thirds. Garments that have more than one piece like the *kao* or the jacket, skirt, and trousers sets are always folded as a single unit so that the pieces are stored together. After every performance, each costume is folded in the predetermined arrangement and returned to the proper place in the assigned cabinet. As the costumes are all lined with light blue, white, or yellow lining, they need to be placed in stacks in the right order so that they can be located again the next time they are needed.

Jingju costumes have evolved through the years under the influence of imperials bans, audience preferences, and actors' innovations. While the stage pictures give the impression of Chinese historical dress, in actuality, very little of what appears onstage replicates reality. The costumes developed specifically to suit the needs of the actors, enhancing movement and the nature of the characters and roles, and to create an image of utmost beauty. Without the position of costume designers, the management of the image falls to the dressers and the actors. In history, individual actors are often given credit for the invention, revision, or development of new costumes. On the other hand, as the dressers are well versed in both the costumes needed for productions and the costumes in the troupe's stock, they can be called upon to place orders for new costumes when they are needed. In this case, the choices might be to enhance the details of existing types of garments and

their patterns, unlike the innovative adjustments made by the actors. An order for new costumes might also be placed by a senior member of a troupe, an actor of considerable experience who has studied the patterns of usage of the costumes.

The person who makes these decisions about the costumes to be ordered and what they will look like performs the closest parallel to a designer in traditional Jingju costuming process. As the shapes of the garments are predetermined, the aesthetic is defined through choices of pattern and color within the acceptable range. One dresser consulted pursued the visual language of costuming through research into figures used in Chinese ornamentation and actual clothing, from which he prepared detailed sketches of the shared patterns. His notebooks contained countless versions of cloud designs, and pages of dragon eyes, noses, tails, and horns, along with graphs for the locations of the emblems on the surface. With these materials in hand, he negotiated with the factories on the surface details for new costumes to be made, sometimes determining the image down to the number of stitches required. While working within the prototypes for the use of color and pattern, he made selections that might be considered costume design. The repertoire of traditional Jingju costumes is the result of hundreds of anonymous people like this dresser, each making small decisions that shape the image onstage. Clothing from diverse sources and time periods, and different minds and purposes has been assimilated to create a unified and visually stunning whole. From brilliant colors, lavish silks, intricate embroidery, and glittering embellishment, a stage picture emerges that is opulent, elegant, and unforgettable.

TABLE 1. Character and Representative Costumes: Men

Character/Closet		*mang*	*kao*	*pi*	*xuezi*, rich	*xuezi*, poor	other
xiaosheng/ wuxiaosheng	Color	white, pink, red	white or pink with blue trim	yellow for emperor, red for wedding	pastels, pink, sky blue, turquoise, pale green	black, lavender	*guanyi*; red, blue, maroon for older characters
							kai chang
	Designs	round dragons	dragons or animals	round pattern	floral pattern around collar and on left hem	plain with embroidered collar band or *fugui yi*	*zuiyi*; red *jianyi* and *magua*
laosheng/ wulaosheng	Color	red, green, yellow; maroon, olive, beige, white for older	various colors, except black, blue	blue, maroon, beige, olive, yellow for emperor	rare, except as underclothing, maroon, brown	maroon, olive green, dark blue, off-white	
	Designs	round dragons	dragons or animals	round pattern	plain, or roundels	plain or *fugui yi*	
changkao/ wusheng	Color	red, green, blue, orange, pink, white*	white or colors	pastels for youth, darker colors for age*	upper colors, satin*	blue, black*	*gailiang kao*; upper colors *kai chang*; upper colors
	Designs	round or flying dragons	dragons or animals	roundels of animals or flowers	roundels	plain	
duanda/ wusheng	Color	red, green, blue, orange, pink, white*	n/a	pastels for youth, darker colors for age*	white, colors	light blue, black	*baoyi*; white, colors geometric or floral
							kuaiyi black, plain
	Designs	round or flying dragons	n/a	roundels of animals or orchids	geometric or floral	plain	

...d.

	mang	*kao*	*pi*	*xuezi*, rich	*xuezi*, poor	other
Color	red, black, blue, maroon	red, black, green, blue, maroon	rare, various colors	maroon, blue, orange	neutral colors	*kai chang, gailiang kao, jianyi*; red, green, black, maroon
Designs	large rampant dragons	dragons, tigers, dragon scales, geometric patterns	roundels of lucky symbols or animals	roundels of lucky symbols or animals	plain or scattered	*kuaiyi*: black
Color	red, olive green, blue, no black or pink*	n/a	pastels for youth, darker for age*	green, blue, black, purple	blue, black, brown	*guanyi*, eunuch robe
Designs	dragon roundels	n/a	roundels with patterned borders	scattered	plain	*jianyi* alone or with *magua* or *bufu*; big-sleeved robe; *chayi*
Color	red, olive green, blue, no black or pink*	rare, green, black, olive green	pastels for youth, darker for age*	maroon, olive green, green, red, no pink	light blue, black, off white	*kuaiyi*; black, colors; *kai chang*: butterflies or bees
Designs	dragon roundels	dragons	roundels with patterned borders	scattered	plain	
Color	n/a	n/a	copied from *qingyi*, pastels, odd colors	copied from *qingyi*	copied from *laodan*	*caipo ao* and trousers; long vest
Designs	n/a	n/a	flowers	copied from *qingyi*	copied from *laodan*	

a representative sample of costumes, colors, and designs worn by the role types. Characters and circumstances are fluid, and other ...ossible.

... wear this costume, color, or material in specific scenes, when the plot calls for it, but this style, color, or material is not typical for ... character

TABLE 2. Character and Representative Costumes: Women

Character/Costumes		*nümang*	*nükao*	*nüpi*	*nüxuezi,* rich	*nüxuezi,* poor	jacket and trousers	skirt	other
qingyi	Color	wavy or straight edge red, yellow	red, pink, white*	pastels and blended colors; red for wedding; yellow for royalty	center-front style, pastels	center-front style, *qing*, blue, gray, green	n/a	white, red for wedding	*gongzhuang*; multicolored *qipao*; white or pastels *qimang*; dragons and waves
	Design	phoenix and dragon can appear together or individually on wavy or straight edge	phoenixes and flowers	flower sprigs for younger; round flowers for marriage and after	sprigs or bordered flowers	plain-banded edges or *fugui yi*	n/a	pretty flower borders and in panels plain for poor	*zuiyi*; for prisoners, red with trim *guzhuang*: ancient clothing style
laodan	Color	straight edge in yellow, olive green, orange	olive green, maroon	maroon, olive green, blue	n/a	crossover style, olive green, maroon, beige, off white	olive green, maroon*	green, blue	*qimang*; olive green, yellow
	Design	dragons or dragon and phoenix combination	dragon	geometric roundel patterns	n/a	plain	plain or roundels	gold border, geometric	
huadan	Color	n/a	n/a	bright colors, not yellow	n/a	lake blue, pink, white	pastel colors	matches jacket	*guzhuang*; pieces in darker colors vests *gailiang kao, zhan'ao zhanqun*; pink, light blue, white
	Design	n/a	n/a	flowers or phoenix, birds	n/a	flowers	flowers	flowers	

Table 2 continued.

Character/ Costumes		*nümang*	*nükao*	*nüpi*	*nüxuezi,* rich	*nüxuezi,* poor	jacket and trousers	skirt	other
daoma dan	Color	wavy edge, red	red, pink, white, and pastels	pastels and blended colors*	center-front style pastels*	center-front style *qing*, blue, gray, green*	pastel colors*	white, red for wedding*	*gailiang nükao*, or *jianyi*, pastels flowers and geometrics
	Design	dragons	phoenix and flowers	flower sprigs for younger; round flowers after marriage	sprigs or bordered flowers	plain-banded edges or *fugui yi*	flowers	pretty flower borders and in panels; plain for poor	
wudan	Color	n/a	n/a	bright colors, not yellow*	n/a	lake blue, pink, white*	pastel colors	matches jacket*	*zhan'ao zhanqun*, pastels flowers and geometric
	Design	n/a	n/a	flowers or phoenix, birds	n/a	flowers	flowers	flowers	

This chart presents a representative sample of costumes, colors, and patterns worn by the role types. Characters and circumstances are fluid, and other combinations are possible.

*This role type may wear this costume, color, or material in specific scenes, when the plot calls for it, but this style, color, or material is not typical for the function of this character.

TABLE 3. Costumes by Rank, Role, and Event: Men

Role Type	Battle	Court	At home
jing, higher	*kao*	*kao, mang*	*kai chang*, large animals, *pi*
jing, lower	*gailiang kao, jianyi*		
wulaosheng	*kao*	*kao mang*	*kai chang*, round animals
laosheng	*ma gua/jianyi* traveling, *kao*	*mang, guanyi*	*pi*, roundels
wusheng, higher	*kao*	*kao, mang*	*kai chang*, round animals
wusheng, lower	*gailiang kao baoyi*	n/a	*xuezi*, or *kaichang*
wenxiaosheng, higher	n/a	*mang*	*xuezi* or *pi*
wenxiaosheng, lower	n/a	*guanyi*	*xuezi*
wuxiaosheng	*kao*	*mang* or *kao*, depending on rank	*xuezi*; border design
chou	*ma gua/jianyi* traveling, *kuaiyi*	*guanyi* or *mang*	*pi* or *xuezi*

This chart presents representative patterns of wear for male characters in common locations. Characters and circumstances are fluid, and other combinations are possible.

Table 4. Dressing Layers: Men

Male clothing	worn by	water shirt	padding	trousers	shoes	inner layer	collar	headdress	pieces	accessories
mang	*sheng, jing* high-ranking men at court	yes	*jing,* thick *sheng,* medium	yes	tall boots	*xuezi*	yes	*shamao,* helmet, or crown	robe, matching collar for military roles	jade belt
pi	*laosheng*	yes	yes	dark colors	tall boots	dark *xuezi*	yes	soft caps or *shamao*	robe	
pi	*xiaosheng*	yes	yes	red	tall boots	pink *xuezi*	yes	soft caps or *shamao*	robe	
kao	*sheng, jing* generals at battle	yes	yes	red, dark, plain or patterned	tall boots	dark blue shirt or *jianyi*	yes	helmet, could have feathers	tabard, leg flaps, flags, collar	red scarf
xuezi	all	yes	*jing,* thick *sheng,* medium	light for *xiaosheng,* bright for *chou,* dark for others	tall boots, medium soles for *chou*	no	yes	soft caps or helmets	robe	
kai chang	*sheng, jing* warriors, officials at home	yes	yes	red, dark plain or patterned	tall boots	*xuezi, jianyi,* or *kuaiyi*	yes	soft cap, helmet	robe	
guanyi	*sheng, chou* officials	yes	*sheng*	red or black	tall boots, medium for *chou*	no	yes	*shamao*	robe	jade belt
eunuch robe	eunuchs	yes	no	red or black	medium boots	no	yes	eunuch helmet	robe	cord belt
jianyi	*sheng, jing,* upper military	yes	yes	red	tall boots	no	yes	helmet	robe	collar, wide firm sash
jianyi and *magua*	travel	yes	some	red or other	tall boots	no	yes	*da banjin* and *ezi*	robe, jacket	collar of *magua,* wide firm sash

Table 4 continued.

Male clothing	worn by	water shirt	padding	trousers	shoes	inner layer	collar	headdress	pieces	accessories
longtao yi	attendants	yes	no	matching	martial boots	no	no	*da banjin*	robe, collar	sets of four men
dakai	attendants	yes	no	matching	martial boots	no	yes	*guanzi kui*	tabard, collar	
baoyi	*wusheng* independent fighters	yes	yes	matching	martial boots	no	yes	*luomao*	jacket, trousers	
kuaiyi	lower military	yes	yes	matching	martial boots	no	yes	*luomao*	jacket, trousers	wide firm sash
chayi	*chou* servants, boatmen	no	no	matching	straw sandals	no	no	various hats	jacket, trousers	pleated skirt
zuiyi	prisoners	yes	no	matching	flat slippers	no	no	head scarf	jacket, trousers	prisoner skirt, wide firm sash
bagua yi	Zhuge Liang and Daoists	yes	yes	maroon, dark blue, or *qing*	tall boots	*xuezi*	yes	*bagua jin*	robe	feather fan, beads
bufu	*chou* ethnic attendants	yes	no	dark	medium sole boots	*jianyi*, Manchu collar	no	*nuanmao* or *liangmao*	surcoat	beads, wide firm sash

This chart presents representative patterns of layering and accessories for key costumes. Characters and circumstances are fluid, and other combinations are possible.

TABLE 5. Dressing Layers: Women

Female clothing	worn by	water shirt	trousers	skirt	shoes	inner	headdress	pieces	accessories
nümang with wavy or straight edges	*qingyi* in young imperial women's roles	yes	pastel	white	flat slippers	no	phoenix, large, silver	cloud collar, robe	jade belt
nümang with straight edges	*laodan* in older imperial women's roles	yes	olive green	green or blue	*fuzi lü*	no	phoenix, small, gold	cloud collar, robe	jade belt and cloud collar, or white collar and cord belt
qimang	*qingyi* as ethnic royalty	yes	yes	no	*huapen di*	no	*liangba tou*	robe, collar with bib	beads, handkerchief
nüpi floral spray	*qingyi* young, dignified	yes	light	white	flat slippers	*xuezi*, center front	*datou* or *guzhuang tou*	robe	brooch at neck of *xuezi*
nüpi roundel pattern	*qingyi* married, dignified	yes	light	white	flat slippers	*xuezi*, center front	*datou* or *guzhuang tou*	robe	brooch at neck of *xuezi*
nüpi roundel pattern	*laodan* mature	yes	olive	green or blue	*fuzi lü*	crossover *xuezi*	*zongfa* scarf	robe	white collar
nükao	*daoma dan*	yes padding	pink, light blue, or green	white	martial boots or high sole boots for shorter women	no	*qixing ezi*	tabard, cloud collar, leg flaps, flags	scarf with rosette, feathers
gailiang nükao	*daoma dan, wudan*	yes	matching	no	martial boots	no	helmet, tassels, feathers	cloud collar, jacket, skirt panels, belt	scarf with rosette, feathers
nüxuezi, crossover style	*laodan*	yes	olive green	green	*fuzi lü*	no	*zongfa*	robe	white collar

Table 5 continued.

Female clothing	worn by	water shirt	trousers	skirt	shoes	inner	headdress	pieces	accessories
nüxuezi, center opening	*qingyi*, *gongnü*	yes	yes	white	flat slippers	no	may be simpler	robe	may be worn with vest, waist scarf, or cloud collar
gongzhuang	*qingyi* princesses and consorts	yes	yes	yes	flat slippers	no	phoenix headdress	cloud collar, dress	
aoqun	*huadan gongnü*	yes	yes	yes	flat slippers	no	*datou* or *guzhuang tou*	jacket, skirt, trousers	may be worn with vest, waist scarf
aoku	*huadan gongnü*	yes	yes	no	flat slippers	no	*datou* or *guzhuang tou*	jacket, trousers	may be worn with apron or vest and scarf
zhan'ao zhanqun	*wudan*	yes	matching	flaps	martial boots	no	*datou*, simpler	jacket, trousers, skirt flaps, belt	
zuiyi	*qingyi* prisoners	yes	matching	prisoner skirt	flat slippers	no	*datou* with scarf	jacket, trousers	waist scarf chains
qipao	*qingyi, laodan* ethnic roles	yes	yes	no	*huapen di*	no	*liangba tou*	robe	may be worn with vest

This chart presents representative patterns of layering and accessories for key costumes. Characters and circumstances are fluid, and other combinations are possible.

TABLE 6. *The Phoenix Returns to Its Nest:* Comparative Costume Plots

Character/ Role	A Galaxy of Character Images in Traditional Jingju	BEIJING JINGJU COMPANY July 9, 2000		NATIONAL JINGJU COMPANY October 3, 2001	
Cheng Pu *laosheng* father scene 1	HEADDRESS purple (maroon) *yuanwai jin*	HEADDRESS olive *yuanwai jin*		HEADDRESS maroon *yuanwai jin*	
	BEARD cansan	BEARD cansan		BEARD cansan	
	MAKEUP *junban*	MAKEUP *junban*		MAKEUP *junban*	
	CLOTHING purple plain *pi*	CLOTHING olive-green *pi/* roundels		CLOTHING maroon *pi/* roundels	
	su xuezi inside	maroon *su xuezi* inside		(*su xuezi* not visible)	
	olive trousers	(trousers not visible)		(trousers not visible)	
	SHOES tall, thick-soled boots	SHOES tall, thick-soled boots	1.B (actor, Qi Shijun)	SHOES (tall, thick-soled boots not visible)	1.N a (actor, Yan Shiqi)
	ACCESSORIES folding fan	ACCESSORIES folding fan		ACCESSORIES folding fan	
				Additional Change	
				HEADDRESS olive green *yuanwei jin*	
				CLOTHING olive green *pi*	1.N b (actor, Yan Shiqi)

NOTE: B stands for the Beijing Jingju Company; N stands for the National Jingju Company. Not visible = garment likely to be worn, but not visible in this image. Not evident = garment not in this image, but may have been used in another scene. Not recorded = garment not captured in photographs

Character/Role	A Galaxy of Character Images in Traditional Jingju	BEIJING JINGJU COMPANY July 9, 2000		NATIONAL JINGJU COMPANY October 3, 2001	
Cheng Pu change for scene 7	HEADDRESS *zhongsha* CLOTHING green *mang* ACCESSORIES jade belt horse whip	HEADDRESS *zhongsha* CLOTHING green *mang* ACCESSORIES jade belt (horse whip not evident)	 2.B	HEADDRESS *zhongsha* CLOTHING olive-green *mang* ACCESSORIES jade belt horse whip	 2.N
House Manager *laosheng*	HEADDRESS black *ruan luomao* yellow silk headscarf white hair BEARD white full beard MAKEUP *junban* CLOTHING black *su xuezi* SHOES thick-soled boots ACCESSORIES wide belt plain colored trousers	HEADDRESS black *ying luomao* no headscarf black hair BEARD black full beard MAKEUP *junban* CLOTHING black *su xuezi* SHOES thick soled boots ACCESSORIES orange wide belt (trousers not visible)	 3.B (actor unidentified)	HEADDRESS black *ying luomao* yellow silk headscarf black hair BEARD white full beard MAKEUP *junban* CLOTHING black *su xuezi* SHOES thick soled boots (not visible) ACCESSORIES yellow wide belt (trousers not visible)	 3.N (actor unidentified)

Character/Role	*A Galaxy of Character Images in Traditional Jingju*	BEIJING JINGJU COMPANY July 9, 2000		NATIONAL JINGJU COMPANY October 3, 2001	
Zhu Huanran suitor *chou* scene 2	HEADDRESS yellow *bangchui jin*	HEADDRESS orange *bangchui jin*		HEADDRESS yellow *bangchui jin*	
	BEARD N/A				
	MAKEUP *chou*	MAKEUP *chou*		MAKEUP *chou*	
	CLOTHING yellow *pi*	CLOTHING yellow *pi*		CLOTHING yellow *pi*	
	plain red *xuezi* inside	plain red *xuezi* inside		patterned red *xuezi* inside	
	SHOES *chaofang*	SHOES (*chaofang* not visible, see 6.6.B)		SHOES *chaofang*	
	ACCESSORIES waist cord	ACCESSORIES waist cord not worn	4.B (actor, Luan Zuxun)	ACCESSORIES waist cord not worn	4.N (actor, Zhang Yaning)
	red trousers	(red trousers not visible)		(trousers not visible)	
	folding fan	(folding fan not evident)		(folding fan not evident)	

Character/ Role	*A Galaxy of Character Images in Traditional Jingju*	BEIJING JINGJU COMPANY July 9, 2000		NATIONAL JINGJU COMPANY October 3, 2001	
Zhu Huanran scene 4 birthday	CLOTHING embroidered *xuezi*	CLOTHING purple embroidered *wenchou hua xuezi*	5.B	CLOTHING red embroidered *xuezi*	5.N
Zhu Huanran scene 4 birthday		Additional Change green *wenchou hua xuezi*	6.B	Additional change green *wenchou hua xuezi* (in servant's hands)	6.N

Character/ Role	*A Galaxy of Character Images in Traditional Jingju*	**BEIJING JINGJU COMPANY** July 9, 2000	**NATIONAL JINGJU COMPANY** October 3, 2001
Zhu Huanran scene 11 Zhu's wedding		Additional change HEADDRESS red *xueshi jin* CLOTHING red wedding *pi*  7.B	Additional change CLOTHING red wedding *pi*  7.N
Zhu Huanran scene 16 poor scene	HEADDRESS black *gao fangjin* CLOTHING black *xuezi* SHOES slippers ACCESSORIES small white pleated skirt, white big socks	HEADDRESS black *gao fangjin* CLOTHING black *xuezi* with velvet collar SHOES black thin soled high boots ACCESSORIES small white pleated skirt  8.B	HEADDRESS black *di fangjin* CLOTHING black *xuezi* with white collar SHOES (slippers not visible) ACCESSORIES small white pleated skirt (white big socks not evident)  8.N

Character/ Role	A Galaxy of Character Images in Traditional Jingju	BEIJING JINGJU COMPANY July 9, 2000	NATIONAL JINGJU COMPANY October 3, 2001
chou yuanzi (2) courtyard keepers chou	HEADDRESS black *ruan luomao* BEARD N/A MAKEUP *chou* CLOTHING black *xuezi* SHOES black slippers ACCESSORIES wide cloth belt black trousers white wide socks	HEADDRESS black *ruan luomao* MAKEUP *chou* CLOTHING black *xuezi* with blue piping SHOES (black slippers not visible) ACCESSORIES orange wide cloth belt (trousers not visible) (socks not evident) 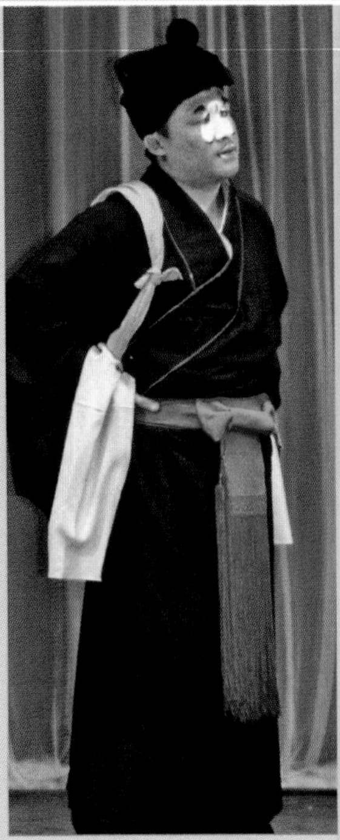	HEADDRESS black *ruan luomao* MAKEUP *junban* CLOTHING black *xuezi* with blue piping SHOES (black slippers not visible) ACCESSORIES orange wide cloth belt (trousers not visible) (socks not evident) 
qing pao (4) servants unimportant roles *(za)*	HEADDRESS black *su luomao* BEARD N/A MAKEUP *junban* CLOTHING black cotton *xuezi* SHOES thin-soled ankle boots ACCESSORIES red trousers	(not recorded)	(not recorded)

9.B (actor unidentified)

9.N (actor unidentified)

Character/ Role	A Galaxy of Character Images in Traditional Jingju	BEIJING JINGJU COMPANY July 9, 2000		NATIONAL JINGJU COMPANY October 3, 2001	
Cheng Xue'e younger daughter *qingyi*	HEADDRESS diamond and extra ornaments	HEADDRESS diamond and kingfisher ornaments		HEADDRESS diamond and kingfisher ornaments	
	HAIR *datou, xian lianzi*	HAIR *datou, xian lianzi*		HAIR *datou, xian lianzi*	
	MAKEUP *junban*	MAKEUP *junban*		MAKEUP *junban*	
	CLOTHING embroidered *nüpi*	CLOTHING green embroidered *nüpi*		CLOTHING blue embroidered *nüpi*	
	xuezi	blue *nüxuezi*		blue *nüxuezi*	
	white skirt	white skirt		white skirt	
	light trousers	(trousers not visible)	10.B (actor, Zhang Liwen)	(trousers not visible)	10.N (actor, Li Hongmei)
	SHOES embroidered slippers	SHOES (embroidered slippers not visible)		SHOES (embroidered slippers not visible)	
	ACCESSORIES handkerchief	ACCESSORIES (handkerchief not evident)		ACCESSORIES (handkerchief not evident)	

Character/Role	A Galaxy of Character Images in Traditional Jingju	BEIJING JINGJU COMPANY July 9, 2000	NATIONAL JINGJU COMPANY October 3, 2001
Cheng Xue'e younger daughter *qingyi* (continued)		Additional change red *nüpi* 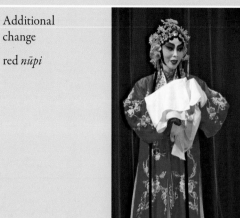 11.B	Additional change yellow *nüpi*  11.N
		Additional change blue *nüpi*  12.B	Additional change pink *nüpi*  12.N

Character/ Role	*A Galaxy of Character Images in Traditional Jingju*	**BEIJING JINGJU COMPANY** July 9, 2000		**NATIONAL JINGJU COMPANY** October 3, 2001	
Cheng Xue'e	HEADDRESS emerald ornaments CLOTHING *nüxuezi*	HEADDRESS no change CLOTHING blue *nüxuezi*	13.B	HEADDRESS no change CLOTHING lavender *nüxuezi*	13.N
Cheng Xue'e scene 17 wedding	HEADDRESS red velvet flowers red wedding veil CLOTHING red *nüpi*	HEADDRESS red velvet flowers red wedding veil (removed) CLOTHING red *nüpi* red skirt	14.B	HEADDRESS red velvet flowers red wedding veil (removed) CLOTHING red *nüpi* white skirt	14.N

Character/ Role	A Galaxy of Character Images in Traditional Jingju	BEIJING JINGJU COMPANY July 9, 2000		NATIONAL JINGJU COMPANY October 3, 2001	
Cheng Xueyan elder daughter *caidan*	HEADDRESS diamond ornaments	HEADDRESS diamond and flower ornaments		HEADDRESS diamond and flower ornaments	
	HAIR *datou* *xian lianzi*	HAIR *datou* *xian lianzi*		HAIR *datou* *xian lianzi*	
	MAKEUP *junban*	MAKEUP *junban*		MAKEUP *junban*	
	CLOTHING embroidered *nüpi*	CLOTHING pink embroidered *nüpi*		CLOTHING lavender embroidered *nüpi*	
	nüxuezi	pink *nüxuezi*		blue *nüxuezi*	
	embroidered white skirt	embroidered white skirt		embroidered white skirt	
	light trousers	(trousers not visible)		(trousers not visible)	
	SHOES embroidered slippers	SHOES (embroidered slippers not visible)	15.B (actor, Zhu Jinhua)	SHOES (embroidered slippers not visible)	15.N (actor, Lü Kunshan)
	ACCESSORIES handkerchief	ACCESSORIES (handkerchief not evident)		ACCESSORIES (handkerchief not evident)	

Character/ Role	A Galaxy of Character Images in Traditional Jingju	BEIJING JINGJU COMPANY July 9, 2000		NATIONAL JINGJU COMPANY October 3, 2001	
Cheng Xueyan	CLOTHING embroidered *nüxuezi*	CLOTHING salmon *nüpi*	16.B	CLOTHING lavender *nüpi*	16.N
Cheng Xueyan	HEADDRESS red velvet flowers CLOTHING *chou* wedding *nüpi*	HEADDRESS red velvet flowers (red wedding veil removed) CLOTHING red wedding *nüpi*	17.B	HEADDRESS red velvet flowers (red wedding veil removed) CLOTHING red wedding *nüpi*	17.N

Character/Role	A Galaxy of Character Images in Traditional Jingju	BEIJING JINGJU COMPANY July 9, 2000		NATIONAL JINGJU COMPANY October 3, 2001	
Cheng Xueyan	HEADDRESS silver ornaments CLOTHING black *nüxuezi* plain white skirt	HEADDRESS blue scarf CLOTHING black *nüxuezi* plain white skirt	 18.B	HEADDRESS fewer ornaments CLOTHING black *nüxuezi* (plain white skirt not visible)	 18.N
Mu Juyi scholar *xiaosheng*	HEADDRESS black *wenxiaosheng jin* BEARD N/A MAKEUP *junban* CLOTHING black embroidered *xuezi* inner *xuezi* light color trousers SHOES thick-soled boots ACCESSORIES cord belt	HEADDRESS black *qiaoliang jin* MAKEUP *junban* CLOTHING black embroidered *xuezi* (inner *xuezi* not visible) (trousers not visible) SHOES thick-soled boots ACCESSORIES not worn	 19.B	HEADDRESS black *gao fangjin* MAKEUP *junban* CLOTHING black embroidered *xuezi* (inner *xuezi* not visible) (trousers not visible) SHOES (thick-soled boots not visible) ACCESSORIES not worn	 19.N

Character/ Role	*A Galaxy of Character Images in Traditional Jingju*	BEIJING JINGJU COMPANY July 9, 2000		NATIONAL JINGJU COMPANY October 3, 2001	
Mu Juyi		Additional change CLOTHING lavender *xuezi*	20.B	HEADDRESS blue *qiaoliang jin* CLOTHING blue *xiaosheng hua xuezi*	20.N
Mu Juyi	HEADDRESS *wusheng jin* CLOTHING embroidered *xuezi*	HEADDRESS blue *wusheng jin* CLOTHING blue *xiaosheng hua xuezi*	21.B	HEADDRESS white *wusheng jin* CLOTHING white *wuxiaosheng hua xuezi*	21.N

Character/ Role	A Galaxy of Character Images in Traditional Jingju	BEIJING JINGJU COMPANY July 9, 2000		NATIONAL JINGJU COMPANY October 3, 2001	
Mu Juyi	HEADDRESS white embroidered *jiangjin*	HEADDRESS (not recorded)		HEADDRESS (not recorded)	
Mu Juyi	HEADDRESS *zhongsha* with jade plaque flowers CLOTHING pink *mang* matching collar ACCESSORIES jade belt	HEADDRESS *zhongsha* with jade plaque no flowers CLOTHING pink *mang* (no collar) ACCESSORIES jade belt	22.B	HEADDRESS *zhongsha* with jade plaque no flowers CLOTHING white *mang* (no collar) ACCESSORIES jade belt	22.N
Mu Juyi scene 17 wedding	CLOTHING red *pi* HEADDRESS *zhongsha* with jade plaque and flowers	CLOTHING red *pi* HEADDRESS *zhongsha* with jade plaque (no flowers)	23.B	CLOTHING red *pi* HEADDRESS *zhongsha* with jade plaque (no flowers)	23.N

Character/Role	A Galaxy of Character Images in Traditional Jingju	BEIJING JINGJU COMPANY July 9, 2000		NATIONAL JINGJU COMPANY October 3, 2001	
yahuan handmaid *dan* (one of two)	HEADDRESS diamond ornaments	HEADDRESS diamond ornaments		HEADDRESS diamond ornaments	
	HAIR *datou* *xian lianzi* *zhuaji*	HAIR *datou* *xian lianzi* (*zhuaji* not visible)		HAIR *datou* *xian lianzi* (*zhuaji* not visible)	
	MAKEUP *junban*	MAKEUP *junban*		MAKEUP *junban*	
	CLOTHING embroidered jacket and skirt	CLOTHING pink embroidered jacket and skirt		CLOTHING light green embroidered jacket (no skirt)	
	vest	blue vest		red vest	
	waist scarf	waist scarf		waist scarf	
	light color trousers	(trousers not visible)		light green trousers	
			24.B (actor unidentified)		24.N (actor unidentified)
	SHOES embroidered slippers	SHOES (embroidered slippers not visible)		SHOES embroidered slippers	
	ACCESSORIES handkerchief	ACCESSORIES red handkerchief		ACCESSORIES (handkerchief not evident)	

Character/ Role	A Galaxy of Character Images in Traditional Jingju	BEIJING JINGJU COMPANY July 9, 2000		NATIONAL JINGJU COMPANY October 3, 2001	
yahuan handmaid *dan* (two of two)	HEADDRESS diamond ornaments	HEADDRESS diamond ornaments		HEADDRESS diamond ornaments	
	HAIR *datou* *xian lianzi* *zhuaji*	HAIR *datou* *xian lianzi* (*zhuaji* not visible)		HAIR *datou* *xian lianzi* (*zhuaji* not visible)	
	MAKEUP *junban*	MAKEUP *junban*		MAKEUP *junban*	
	CLOTHING embroidered jacket and skirt	CLOTHING blue embroidered jacket (no skirt)		CLOTHING pink embroidered jacket (no skirt)	
	vest	red long vest		blue short vest	
	waist scarf	white waist scarf		blue waist scarf	
	light color trousers	blue trousers		pink trousers	
	SHOES embroidered slippers	SHOES embroidered slippers	25.B (actor unidentified)	SHOES embroidered slippers	25.N (actor unidentified)
	ACCESSORIES handkerchief	ACCESSORIES (handkerchief not evident)		ACCESSORIES (handkerchief not evident)	

Character/Role	A Galaxy of Character Images in Traditional Jingju	BEIJING JINGJU COMPANY July 9, 2000		NATIONAL JINGJU COMPANY October 3, 2001	
Zhou Jianjun military supervisor *jing*	HEADDRESS eunuch helmet tassels long black strips	HEADDRESS eunuch helmet tassels long black strips	26.B (actor, Zhang Runcheng)	HEADDRESS eunuch helmet tassels (long black strips not visible)	26.N (actor, Gu Qian)
	BEARD N/A				
	MAKEUP red *taijian lian*	MAKEUP red *taijian lian*		MAKEUP red *taijian lian*	
	CLOTHING purple *mang* red trousers	CLOTHING red *mang* (trousers not visible)		CLOTHING red *mang* (trousers not visible)	
	SHOES tall, thick-soled boots	SHOES tall, thick-soled boots		SHOES (tall, thick-soled boots not visible)	
	ACCESSORIES jade belt folding fan whip	ACCESSORIES jade belt (folding fan not evident) (whip not evident)		ACCESSORIES jade belt (folding fan not evident (whip not evident)	

Character/ Role	A Galaxy of Character Images in Traditional Jingju	BEIJING JINGJU COMPANY July 9, 2000		NATIONAL JINGJU COMPANY October 3, 2001	
Hong Gong marshal *laosheng*	HEADDRESS *shuaikui*	HEADDRESS *taiding*		HEADDRESS *shuaikui*	
	BEARD *heisan*	BEARD *heisan*		BEARD *heisan*	
	MAKEUP *junban*	MAKEUP *junban*		MAKEUP *junban*	
	CLOTHING red *mang*	CLOTHING red *mang*		CLOTHING red *mang*	
	matching collar	matching collar		matching collar	
	red trousers	(trousers not visible)		(trousers not visible)	
	SHOES tall, thick-soled boots	SHOES tall, thick-soled boots		SHOES (tall, thick-soled boots not visible)	
	ACCESSORIES jade belt	ACCESSORIES jade belt	27.B (actor, Kang Erming)	ACCESSORIES jade belt	27.N (actor, Li Wenlin)
	folding fan	(folding fan not evident)		(folding fan, see 6.28.N)	
	horse whip	(horse whip not evident)		(horse whip not evident	
Hong Gong	HEADDRESS *zhongsha*	HEADDRESS *zhongsha*		HEADDRESS *zhongsha*	
			28.B		28.N

Character/ Role	*A Galaxy of Character Images in Traditional Jingju*	**BEIJING JINGJU COMPANY** July 9, 2000		**NATIONAL JINGJU COMPANY** October 3, 2001	
Madam Cheng *laodan*	**HEADDRESS** gray *wangzi* gray *binfa* *laodan guan* *leizi* purple (maroon) scarf **MAKEUP** *junban* **CLOTHING** purple (maroon) *nüpi* plain green skirt light color trousers *su nüzuezi* **SHOES** *fuzi lü* ACCESSORIES N/A	**HEADDRESS** gray *wangzi* gray *binfa* *laodan guan* *leizi* olive scarf **MAKEUP** *junban* **CLOTHING** olive-green *nüpi* blue skirt (trousers not visible) (*nüzuezi* not visible) **SHOES** (*fuzi lü* not visible)	 29.B (actor, Shen Wenli)	**HEADDRESS** gray *wangzi* gray *binfa* *laodan guan* *leizi* maroon scarf **MAKEUP** *junban* **CLOTHING** maroon *nüpi* green skirt (trousers not visible) (*nüzuezi* not visible) **SHOES** (*fuzi lü* not visible)	 29.N a (actor, Lü Xin)
Madam Cheng				Additional change olive *nüpi*	 29.N b

Character/ Role	*A Galaxy of Character Images in Traditional Jingju*	BEIJING JINGJU COMPANY July 9, 2000	NATIONAL JINGJU COMPANY October 3, 2001
Madam Cheng scene 16 poor scene	CLOTHING plain *xuezi*	CLOTHING maroon *nüxuezi* with black velvet collar plain blue skirt	CLOTHING olive-green *nüxuezi* with white collar
	ACCESSORIES white scarf	ACCESSORIES green scarf	ACCESSORIES black scarf orange waist cord

30.B

30.N

zhongjun military gatekeeper *laosheng*	HEADDRESS *zhongjun kui* or *da banjin*	HEADDRESS *zhongjun kui*	HEADDRESS *zhongjun kui*
	BEARD *heisan*	BEARD no beard	BEARD *heisan*
	MAKEUP *junban*	MAKEUP *junban*	MAKEUP *junban*
	CLOTHING red *kaichang* red trousers	CLOTHING red *kaichang* (trousers not visible)	CLOTHING red *kaichang* (trousers not visible)
	SHOES tall, thick-soled boots	SHOES tall, thick-soled boots	SHOES (tall, thick-soled boots not visible)
	ACCESSORIES N/A		

31.B

31.N

Character/Role	A Galaxy of Character Images in Traditional Jingju	BEIJING JINGJU COMPANY July 9, 2000		NATIONAL JINGJU COMPANY October 3, 2001	
binxiang wedding officials *chou*	HEADDRESS green *heye jin* (lotus hat)	(not recorded)		(not recorded)	
	BEARD hanging black two piece moustache				
	MAKEUP old *chou* face				
	CLOTHING sapphire *xuezi*				
	SHOES big white cotton socks, black slippers				
	ACCESSORIES cord belt folding fan				
chefu cartman *za*	HEADDRESS felt hat, round crown, brim	HEADDRESS felt hat, round crown, brim	32.B (actor unidentified)	HEADDRESS felt hat, round crown, brim	32.n (actor unidentified)
	BEARD N/A				
	MAKEUP *junban*	MAKEUP *junban*		MAKEUP *junban*	
	CLOTHING cotton *jianyi* black trousers	CLOTHING blue satin *jianyi* (trousers not visible)		CLOTHING blue cotton *jianyi* (trousers not visible)	
	SHOES thin-soled ankle boots	SHOES (shoes not visible)		SHOES (shoes not visible)	
	ACCESSORIES wide stiff belt	ACCESSORIES orange wide stiff belt		ACCESSORIES orange wide stiff belt	
	flags for sedan chair	flags for sedan chair		flags for sedan chair	

Character/ Role	A Galaxy of Character Images in Traditional Jingju	BEIJING JINGJU COMPANY July 9, 2000	NATIONAL JINGJU COMPANY October 3, 2001
Red *longtao* retinue *za*	HEADDRESS red *da banjin* BEARD N/A MAKEUP *junban* CLOTHING red *longtao yi* red trousers SHOES thin-soled boots	HEADDRESS red *da banjin* MAKEUP *junban* CLOTHING red *longtao yi* (trousers not visible) SHOES (thin-soled boots not visible) 33.B (actor unidentified)	HEADDRESS red *da banjin* MAKEUP *junban* CLOTHING red *longtao yi* (trousers not visible) SHOES (thin-soled boots not visible) 33.N (actor unidentified)
White *longtao* retinue *za*	HEADDRESS white *da banjin* BEARD N/A MAKEUP *junban* CLOTHING white *longtao yi* red trousers SHOES thin-soled boots	(not recorded)	(not recorded)

Character/ Role	A Galaxy of Character Images in Traditional Jingju	BEIJING JINGJU COMPANY July 9, 2000	NATIONAL JINGJU COMPANY October 3, 2001
Four guards, *longtao* not in costume plot scene 7			HEADDRESS *guanzi kui* BEARD N/A MAKEUP *junban* CLOTHING *dakai* (red trousers not visible) SHOES (thin-soled short boots not visible) 34.N

Source: Zhang Yijuan et al., eds., *A Galaxy of Character Images*, 508–511 (translated for the author by Fan Yiqi).

Appendix 1. Costume Pattern Drafts

✺ The patterns were taken from specific costumes as representative of a garment style. When questions arose, other garments of the same style were examined or measured for comparison, however the garment patterns are generally standardized and variations are slight.

✺ The lines on the patterns are seam lines. If no collar or band is attached, then a single line indicates the cut line. Double lines indicate piping.

✺ On garments with added underlaps, the connecting seam on the right front is often concealed by the neck band. On asymmetrical closings with faced edges, a very small seam allowance is used to minimize the gap between the edge and the seam of the under lap.

✺ Both sides of asymmetrical garments are shown, while symmetrical patterns are indicated with half of the garment. Generally only one sleeve is indicated.

✺ The centerline is indicated with a dot-and-dash line; folds are long dashes; and placement and construction are shown with dotted lines. For example, long band collars are indicated in place with dotted lines on the garments and are also included as separate pattern pieces. Dotted shoulder sections are drawn to show how the under laps are attached.

✺ Appliqués, flat borders, and tabs are drawn in place with solid lines. Tabs are also indicated separately on the pattern grid.

✺ Edges of tabs, appliqués, collars, and collar bands are generally finished with bias binding, so no seam allowance is needed. Collars and collar bands are stiffened with interfacing.

✺ Shoulder-covering collars, in shapes other than standing bands as seen on the *mang* and *magua*, for example, are finished separately and not attached to the garments

✺ Notches on the side seams indicate that the seam is open below.

✺ The ties on openings indicate where the garment closings are.

✺ The water sleeves have not been drawn as they are rectangles of standard size. The measurements are indicated in the captions, and the lower edge of the water sleeve is cut on the selvedge.

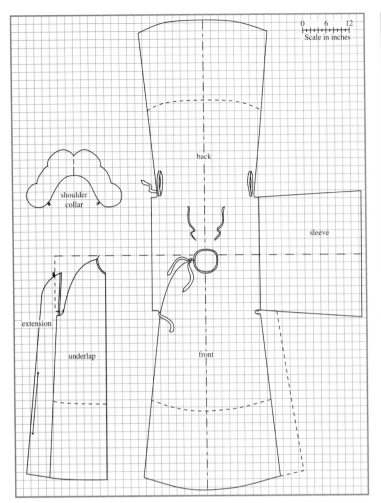

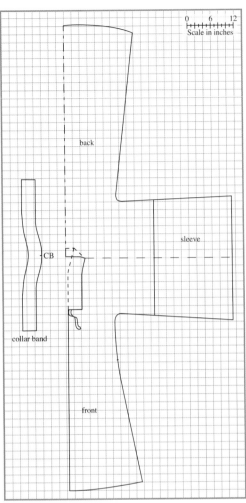

PATTERN I. *Mang.* The front overlap is narrower than the left side, and the under-lap is placed to extend the width on right side to match. The extension on the side fronts is shown stitched in place, with the true grain line indicated with an arrow. Canvas is used in the lower sections of the front and back, indicated by a horizontal dotted line, to support the wave embroidery on the hem. The neck edge is finished with covered 3/8-inch cording and facing. Cording is also inserted on the inside edge of the top of the extension to add support because the extensions are free from the main body of the garment. The ties on the back of the neck are laced through small loops on the top of the extensions to hold them in place. The loops at the underarms of the garment support the hooped jade belt. The collar is unattached. The *mang* is made from satin and lined with a coarse fabric to add volume. The water sleeve is 25 inches wide and 14 inches long (Figs. 6.1 and 6.2). From the author's collection.

PATTERN 2. *Pi.* The location of the seam between the body of the garment and the sleeve varies with the width of the fabric. The length of the collar piece may vary slightly to accommodate the embroidery pattern. Fig. 5.4 shows the folding of the collar band when attached. The *pi* is a soft robe made from crepe or satin, with a lightweight lining. The water sleeves are 28 inches wide and 14 inches long (Figs. 6.7 and 7.35). From the collection of DTD, UHM, Manoa, Hawai'i.

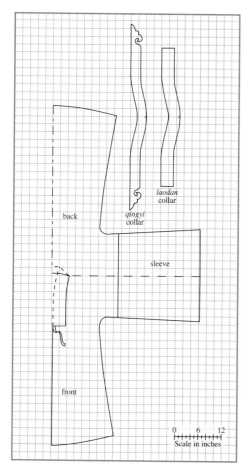

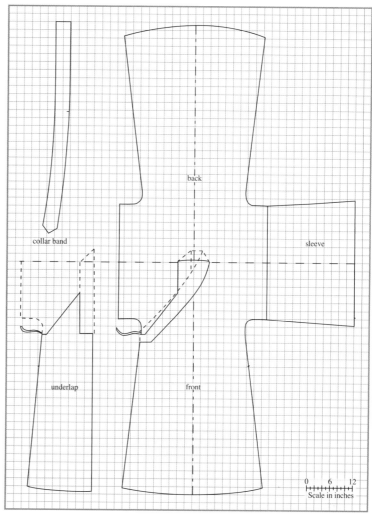

PATTERN 3. *Nüpi*. The base of the collar band usually has a straight edge for older women and an arabesque when worn by younger roles. The mature-style collar is also wider than the one for younger women. Both are indicated as separate pieces, and the style for the older woman's neckband is shown in place on the *pi* pattern piece. The neckline would be drafted narrower to fit the other collar. Fig. 5.4 shows the folding of the collar band after construction. The *nüpi* is made from satin or crepe, and a lightweight lining is used. The water sleeves are 20 inches wide and 25 inches long (Figs. 6.7–8). From the collection of DTD, UHM, Manoa, Hawai'i.

PATTERN 4. *Xuezi*. The collar band and closing are asymmetrical, as the right side of the front is curved and the left is straight. The width of the collar band conceals the seam for the underwrap. The mature woman's version of this garment is narrower and knee length. Crepe is used to make the *xuezi*. It has a soft lining, and the water sleeves are 28 inches wide and 14 inches long (Figs. 6.12–6.17). From the collection of DTD, UHM, Manoa, Hawai'i.

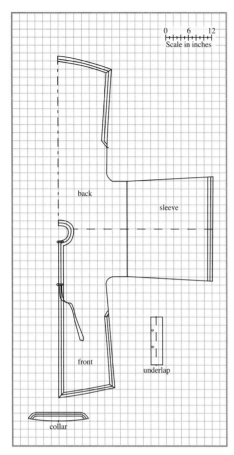

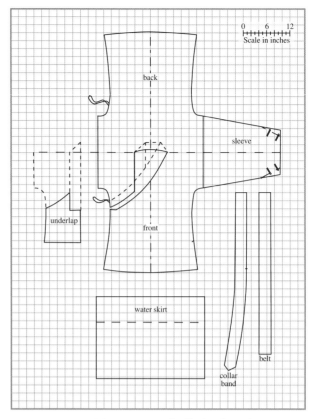

PATTERN 5. *Nüxuezi*. The *nüxuezi* has two forms, the asymmetrical closing that matches the men's garment, and this style with a center front closing. The sample pictured is the black cloth version with blue trim. The trim consists of two rows of 5/8-inch bias fabric with a white edging inserted in between, and binding on the inner edge. The placket is placed behind the closures and the standing band collar is set into the neckline. For plain or embroidered *nüxuezi,* the trim would not be included. The garment is crepe with a lightweight lining, and the water sleeves are 20 inches wide and 25 inches long (Fig. 6.18). From the collection of DTD, UHM, Manoa, Hawai'i.

PATTERN 6. *Baoyi*. The asymmetrical collar band stands up in the neckline, like that of the *xuezi*. The sides of the lower sleeves are folded in and closed with frogs to create the taper at the wrist. The belt is separate. The jacket is satin and lined with cotton. The moving-water skirts are made with two pieces of lightweight silk cut from a single layer of fabric 28 inches wide and 20 inches long, folded off center, and pleated to the bottom of the jacket to create the two layers of ruffles (Fig. 6.31). From the collection of DTD, UHM, Manoa, Hawai'i.

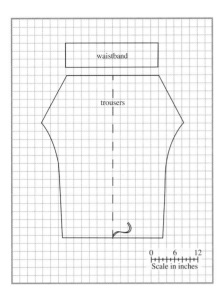

PATTERN 7. Trousers. The waistband is a single layer of muslin, shirttail hemmed at the top and flat-felled to the trousers. The trousers are generally crepe and unlined, so they are finished with double-stitched French seams (Figs. 6.33–35). Each leg is cut in one piece so there is no outer seam. From the collection of DTD, UHM, Manoa, Hawai'i.

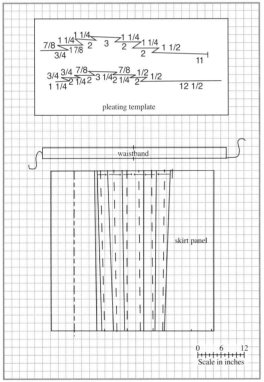

PATTERN 8. Skirt. The solid lines represent the outer folds of the pleats, while the dashed lines are the inside folds. The pleats are not on the grain line, which creates a slight flare to the skirt. They have been basted horizontally at 3-inch intervals to hold them in place. The two matching pleated sections have flat panels in the front, indicated by the dot-and-dash line. The front panels overlap, and the two sections are stitched onto a single cotton waistband. The other flat panels overlap in the back when worn. The strings are brought to the front and tied to secure the waist. This skirt is an example with relatively few pleats, such as for a *huadan*. The waistband is muslin, the skirt is made of crepe, and the lining is lightweight (Fig. 6.40). From the collection of DTD, UHM, Manoa, Hawai'i.

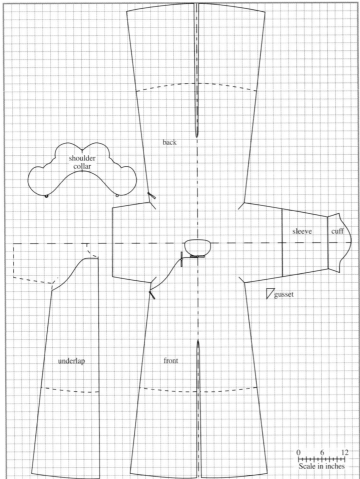

PATTERN 10. *Magua.* The *magua* is made from satin, with a heavy lining. The collar is unattached (Fig. 6.30). From the collection of DTD, UHM, Manoa, Hawai'i.

PATTERN 9. *Jianyi.* The *jianyi* may be constructed with or without a center seam to accommodate the slash in the lower part of the robe. With a center-front seam, the underlap is cut in one with the garment, using the same shape as the other side, whereas without that seam, the overwrap is cut with the body of the garment, as shown. A *jianyi* can be made of satin or cotton, depending on who will wear it. The satin *jianyi* for higher-status characters has a muslin lining in the top to the waist, and the lower half is finished with a lightweight fabric. The cuff is lined with a contrasting face fabric that is visible when turned back. A *long jianyi*, with waves on the hem, will have the lower 20 inches cut from canvas, embroidered, and then appliquéd onto the rest of the garment. The collar is unattached (Figs. 6.26–28). From the collection of DTD, UHM, Manoa, Hawai'i.

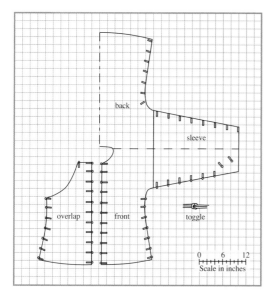

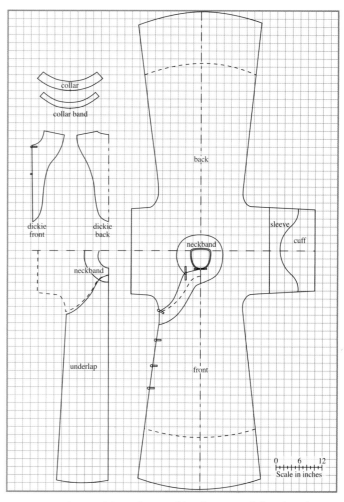

PATTERN 11. *Kuaiyi*. As the *kuaiyi* has a center-front seam, the left front and underlap are cut symmetrically, and the overwrap is cut from a separate piece. The toggles are decorative except for the wrists and the right side. A *kuaiyi* can be velvet or satin, with a stiff cotton lining (Fig. 6.32). The *bing* is cut without the center front seam. From the collection of DTD, UHM, Manoa, Hawai'i.

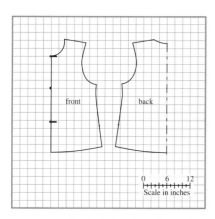

PATTERN 12. Soldier's Vest. One of several vest styles, this vest has bias binding around the neck, armholes, hem, side slashes, and center front below the lowest frog. This style vest is usually satin, with a cotton lining (Fig. 6.52). From the collection of DTD, UHM, Manoa, Hawai'i.

PATTERN 13. *Qimang*. The appliqué neckband is cut in a full circle and is seamed at the center front to continue the band on the overlap. The neck edge is finished with a piped facing, and the outer edge is bound. The band on the lap conceals the seam where the underlap is attached. The slight difference in the curves of this seam make the underlap swing out to match the side front edge. The cuffs and collar band are appliqués. The standing collar is attached to a separate dickie. The *qimang* is made from satin, with a lightweight lining. The lower section of the robe to about 13 inches above the hem is cut from canvas to support the rich embroidery (Fig. 6.5). From the collection of James Young, Honolulu, Hawai'i.

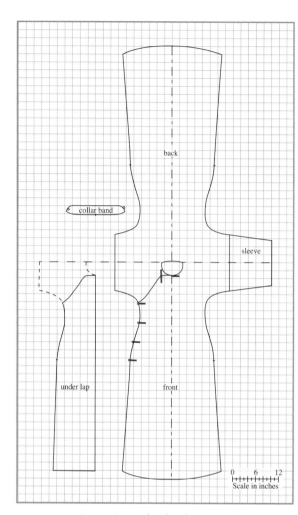

PATTERN 14. *Qipao*. The standing band collar is set into the neckline. The *qipao* is crepe and lined with a soft fabric (Fig. 6.52). From the collection of DTD, UHM, Manoa, Hawai'i.

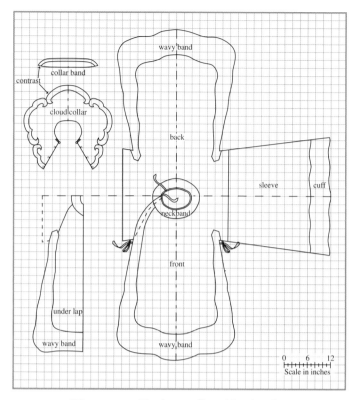

PATTERN 15. Wavy *nümang*. The sleeve cuffs, neckband, and contrasting edges on the cloud collar and garment are all bound with a contrasting color and appliquéd. A 3/8-inch piping is used to finish the garment neck with a ½-inch facing on the inside. The cut line for the underlap is indicated with a dotted line, and the seam is concealed by the applied band. The neckband is seamed on the right shoulder to accommodate the overlap. The loops on the underarm seam of the garment support the hooped jade belt. The cloud collar has knotted fringe, three snaps for closing, and is separate. The garment is crepe, with satin borders, and finished with a contrasting lightweight lining. The water sleeves are 28 inches wide and 25 inches long (Fig. 6.4). From the collection of James Young, Honolulu, Hawai'i.

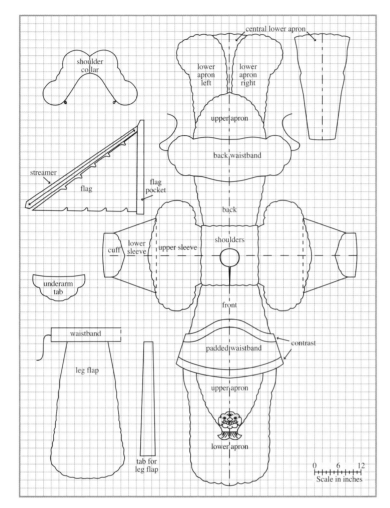

PATTERN 16. *Kao.* The opening is below the neckline at the center front, and then it cuts across to the right under the yoke. The lower sleeves are joined, while the upper sleeves are open flaps. At the front waist, the belt section is stiffened and padded to stand out from the body, while the back waist is softer and wraps around to tie in the center front. The apron pieces are stitched in layers to the waistbands. The underarm tabs may have frogs or be pinned in place to stabilize the tabard. The leg flaps and collar are separate pieces. The four flags are mounted on a harness with four poles, which is lashed onto the shoulders. The flag streamers have been drawn in place, but they are actually cut on the straight grain indicated. They are cut double and turned out. All the *kao* pieces are made from satin. The torso, sleeves, and waist sections are lined with cotton, and the flaps are finished with a lightweight fabric. The tabs on the leg flaps are made of a lighter-weight fabric and are unlined (Fig. 6.9). From the author's collection.

PATTERN 17. *Nūkao*. The fabrics, cut, and construction of the *nūkao* resemble that of the *kao,* without the underarm pieces. The closing is on the right shoulder, and is finished with an underlap. The decorative streamers are fringed on the lower edges, and the lower aprons, leg flaps, and separate cloud collar have knotted fringe. The torso, sleeves, and waist pieces have a cotton broadcloth lining, and the streamers are backed with a softer fabric (Fig 6.10). From the collection of James Young, Honolulu, Hawai'i.

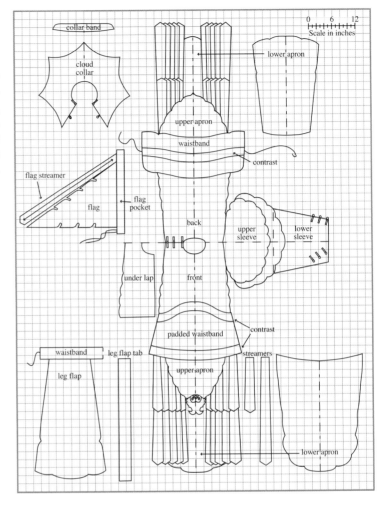

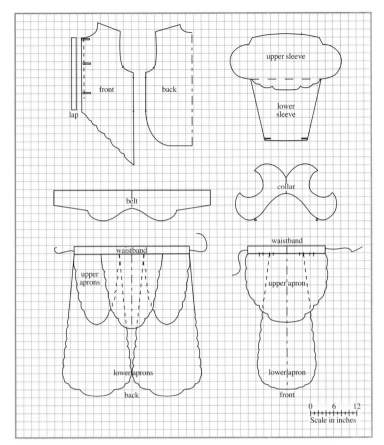

PATTERN 18. *Gailiang kao.* The upper sleeve flaps are set in over the cap to the underarm notches. The lower sleeves are joined, while the upper sleeves are open flaps. The side seams are open 1 ¼ inches below the underarm curve. The apron panels are in two sections, a single set of layered panels for the center front and three upper and two lower sets of panels for the sides and back. Both sets of panels are set onto a muslin waistband, covered by the separate fabric belt, which closes with Velcro. The collar is also unattached, and the women's version is edged with knotted fringe. The rest of the decorative edges have standard fringe. The garment is made from satin, with a cotton broadcloth lining in the jacket and a contrasting color fabric inside the leg flaps (Fig. 6.11). From the collection of ATCO, Beijing, China.

PATTERN 19. *Zhan'ao zhanqun.* The neck edge of the jacket collar is bound, and then collar is set into the neckline. A continuous bias strip is used to finish the top of the collar, center front, hem, and side slits. The skirt consists of two panels stitched onto a muslin waistband to meet in the front and overlap in the back. The separate cloud collar has a standing collar band. The trouser construction conforms to the methods used for the men's, and each leg is cut in a single piece. The pieces are made from crepe or satin and lined with a lightweight fabric, usually in a color similar to the garments (Fig. 1.10). From the collection of DTD, UHM, Manoa, Hawai'i.

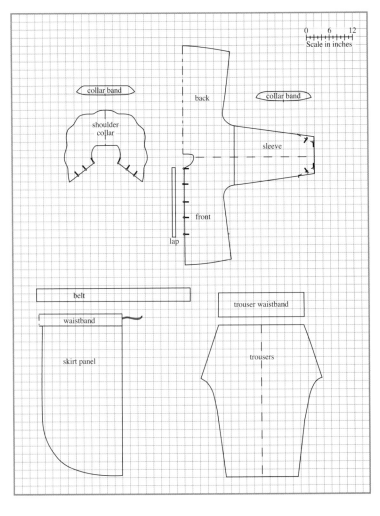

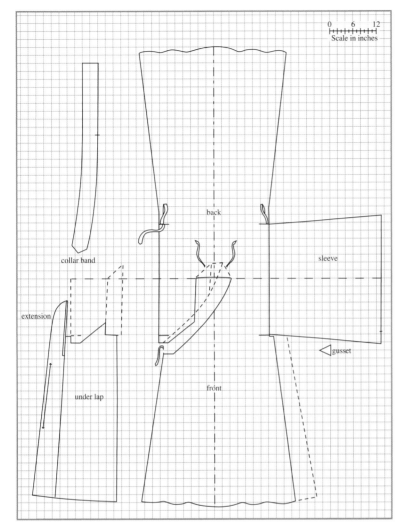

PATTERN 20. *Kai chang*. Construction of the *kai chang* is similar to that of the *mang*. The top of the extensions has rattan or cording on the inner edge and is secured to the back of the neck with loops and ties. The loops at the underarm of the garment support the hooped jade belt. This sample was all one color, but other versions have contrasting borders around the hem and overlap, matching the collar and extensions. The satin garment is lined with a medium-weight fabric, and the water sleeves are 27 inches wide and 14 inches long (Fig. 6.21). From the collection of DTD, UHM, Manoa, Hawai'i.

PATTERN 21. *Bagua yi*. The belt is applied, with the tabs stitched on behind it at their tops only, so they hang loose. The wavy bands are appliquéd on and have a flat braid top-stitched on the inner edges. The locations of the eight trigrams and the yin-yang symbol are indicated, but they are embroidered, rather than appliquéd. In this example, they are placed differently from the way they are described in Chapter Six. Made of satin, the *bagua yi* has a stiffer lining. The water sleeves are 36 inches wide and 14 inches long (Fig. 6.43). From the collection of DTD, UHM, Manoa, Hawai'i.

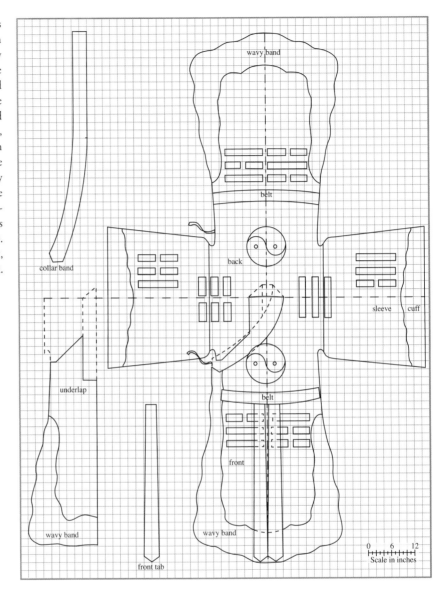

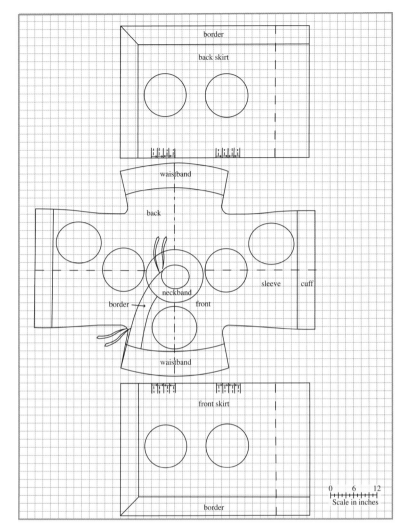

PATTERN 22. Eunuch robe. The borders on the skirt panels, circles, waistband, cuffs, neckband, and the overlap edge are all in a contrasting fabric. The skirt has ½-inch pleats facing out at the side fronts. An 8 ½-inch flap is folded under on the left side of the skirt, and the side seams are left open. This effect is reversed and repeated in the back skirt. There is no separate underlap for the bodice closing. The cutting line for the front opening coincides with the inner edge of the contrasting border, creating enough lap to mask the gap. The bodice and skirt are joined at the contrasting waistband, with a 5-inch knotted fringed inserted in the lower edge. The eunuch robes are made from satin, with the torso lined in cotton and faced with matching satin. The skirt lining is softer. The water sleeves are 26 inches wide and 17 inches long (Fig. 6.24). From the collection of DTD, UHM, Manoa, Hawai'i.

PATTERN 23. *Gongzhuang.* This example has extraordinary appliqué augmentation on the leaf tabs, aprons, and streamers, and notably, the unusual arabesque appliqué on the cloud collar. Each of these pieces is bound with a contrasting color, and the streamers and aprons have fringe added at the bottom. The cloud collar has a deep, knotted fringe. The sleeve stripes are also bound and stitched to the foundation sleeve. The lower apron is the same shape in the front and back, as are the upper and lower streamers. All of the outer pieces are cut from satin. The bodice is lined in white cotton, and the other pieces have a lightweight lining. The applied waistband closes with Velcro, lapping to the right the width of the upper apron. The *gongzhuang* is lined with a soft fabric, but the waistband is stiffened. A pleated inner skirt, not shown, is attached to the waistband. It consists of two 45-inch widths of lightweight silk crepe, with a ½-inch pleat every 2 inches. The unlined skirt is the same length as the longer tabs. The water sleeves have three layers, each 25 inches wide.

The outer blue sleeve is 8 inches long, the pink layer measures 17 inches long, and the inner white sleeve is 25 inches long (Figs. 3.6 and 6.29). From the collection of James Young, Honolulu, Hawai'i.

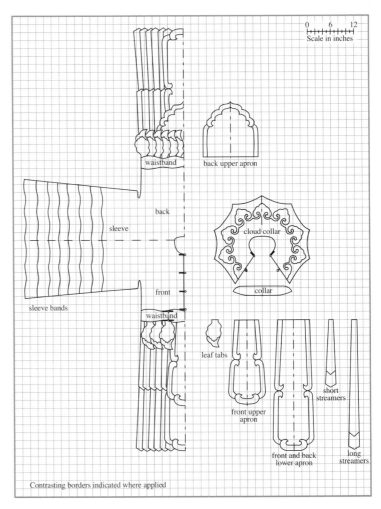

Appendix 2. Dictionary of Jingju Characters

Certain characters in the history and lore of China have become renowned for their bravery, beauty, valor, intelligence, or other outstanding characteristics. Their stories have mutated into the traditional Jingju canon, heightening their recognition. Some of these characters are referred to throughout the text to illuminate examples of dress patterns. To facilitate understanding of these characters and their place in the scripts, a brief description of their personalities and circumstances follows.

Bai Suzhen is the White Snake in *The Legend of the White Snake (Baishe zhuan)*. She takes on human form and falls in love with a young man named Xu Xian. They marry and have a child, although the monk Fahai challenges their relationship. When she is drawn into battle, she wears a distinctive headdress with snake imagery. *Qingyi* and *wudan* role.

Cao Cao is the ruthless warlord whom the sworn brothers Liu Bei, Guan Yu, and Zhang Fei are fighting to overcome in the Three Kingdoms period. Cao Cao's successor eventually prevails in the struggle for power. Cao Cao's face is flat white, the most treacherous of makeup colors. *The Gathering of Heroes (Qunying hui)* and *The Carefree Ford (Xiaoyao jin)* are two of the plays adapted from the novel in which he appears. *Jing* role.

Dou Erdun, a hero in *Stealing the Imperial Horse (Dao yu ma)*, has a blue face and wears a red beard. He steals the horse to gain revenge over a rival charged with guarding the emperor's horses. *Jing* role.

Guan Yu is one of the three sworn brothers from the Three Kingdoms story. He is so admired that he has been deified, onstage and off. His green costumes are specially designed for him to go with his red face makeup. He is among the characters in *Zhuge Liang Leaves His Thatched Roof Study for the First Time (Chuchu maolu)*, as well as other plays adapted from the novel. *Hongsheng* role.

Hongniang is a matchmaker and the title character in *Hongniang*. She arranges secret meetings between her mistress and her mistress's suitor. Her name has become synonymous with matchmaker. *Huadan* role.

Judge Bao is a character based on the historical Bao Zheng, who lived in the eleventh century during the Northern Song era (960–1127). A stern, capable judge, he is a model of justice and truth and appears in many scripts, including *Judge Bao and the Case of Qin Xianglian (Qin Xianglian)* and *The Beating of the Dragon Robe (Da longpao)*. *Jing* role.

Lady Diaochan is said to have been one of the four great beauties in Chinese history. Initially a slave girl, she is adopted by a high minister, Wang Yun. Together they plot discord between the evil Prime Minister Dong Zhuo and his adoptive son, Lü Bu, in the course of which Lady Diaochan seduces both men in *Lü Bu and Diaochan (Lü Bu yu Diaochan)*. *Qingyi* and *huadan* role.

Lady Yu is a concubine to Xiang Yu, the king in *The Hegemon King Says Farewell to His Concubine (Bawang bie ji)*. When he faces sure defeat in an upcoming battle, Lady Yu performs a sword dance to distract him and then commits suicide to prevent his worrying about her during combat. *Qingyi* role.

Liu Bei is the eldest of the three sworn brothers in the Three Kingdoms saga. The leader of Shu-han, he is known for his cleverness and his organizational ability. He appears with Guan Yu and Zhang Fei in *Zhuge Liang Leaves His Thatched Roof Study for the First Time (Chuchu maolu)*, and is the last of the three sworn brothers alive in *The City of Baidi (Baidi cheng)*. *Laosheng* role.

Liu Lihua is the innkeeper in *Fight at Crossroads Inn (Sancha kou)*, where a famous night fighting scene is staged in full light but the action is pantomimed as though it occurs in darkness. Lin Lihua mistakenly believes Ren Tanghui to be an enemy of one of his guests and steals into Ren's room at night, armed for a struggle. *Wuchou* role.

Lü Bu is a brilliant young general in the Three Kingdoms story, but he has a weakness for women. He is seduced and outsmarted by Lady Diaochan, who also flirts with Lü Bu's adoptive father, Dong Zhuo, thereby pitting them against each other in *Lü Bu and Diaochan*. *Xiaosheng* and *wusheng* role.

Mu Guiying, a woman warrior, takes over her husband's command after his death and leads the emperor's army along with other war widows in *Women Generals of the Yang Family (Yang men nü jiang)*. She also appears in *Mu Guiying Takes Command (Mu Guiying gua shuai)*. *Qingyi* role.

Ren Tanghui is the hero in *Fight at Crossroads Inn (Sancha kou)*. He has been secretly following Jiao Zan, to protect him, but is thought to be an adversary by the innkeeper, Liu Lihua. They accidentally meet at night and pantomime a vigorous fight as though it were in darkness when the stage is actually fully lit. *Duanda wusheng* role.

Su San appears in *Yutang Chun Unjustly Accused*. Under the name Yutang Chun, she is a courtesan who falls in love with a young scholar and helps him to go to the capital to take his examinations. She is bought by another man, whose main wife prepares poisoned noodles for Su San, but her husband eats them by mistake. Su San is accused of killing him and is sentenced to death. Her young scholar is the judge at her trial and finds that she has been wrongly accused. *Qingyi* role.

Sun Wukong, the Monkey King, appears in scripts based on *Journey to the West (Xiyou ji)*. He joins the monk Xuanzhuang in his travels from China to India to collect the sutras of Buddhism and bring them back to China. Favorite sections of this tale include *Causing an Uproar in the Dragon King's Palace (Nao longgong)* and *Stealing the Magic Peaches (Dao xiandan)* from *Causing an Uproar in the Heavenly Palace (Nao tian gong)*. *Wusheng* role.

Tiejing Gongzhu, Princess Iron Mirror, is married to the Han general Yang Silang, in *Silang Visits His Mother (Si-*

lang tan mu). She is from the non-Chinese Liao dynasty (916–1125) and wears Qing dynasty style clothing to represent her foreign birth. *Qingyi* role.

Xiang Yu, in *The Hegemon King Says Farewell to His Concubine*, takes the title of Hegemon King of Western Chu at the end of the Qin dynasty. His favorite consort accompanies him to battle, and when the king is faced with certain defeat, she commits suicide to prevent his worrying about her. He is defeated in battle, the Chu are annihilated, and Xiang Yu cuts his own throat. *Jing* role.

Xiao Qing, also called Qing'er, is a companion to the White Snake in *The Legend of the White Snake*. The "qing" in her name is the *qing* color, which is a dark blue-green black. She is also called Little Blue or Green Snake. She is a loyal, strong fighter, although she disapproves of Xu Xian as a mate for Bai Suzhen. *Wudan* role.

Yang Guifei, in *The Drunken Beauty (Guifei zuijiu)*, is the concubine who becomes intoxicated while pining for her emperor, Minghuang, when he chooses to turn his attentions to another. She dances her lament for herself, gradually getting more inebriated and performing more elaborate movements. *Huashan* role.

Yang Silang, alias **Yang Yanhui**, in *Silang Visits His Mother*, is a Han general who is captured by the Liao dynasty where he marries a daughter of the empress of the foreign dynasty. He confesses his origins to his wife in order to cross enemy lines to visit his own elderly mother. *Laosheng* role.

Zhang Fei is one of the three blood brothers from the Three Kingdoms epic. Brash and impetuous, he is also fiercely loyal and courageous. He appears in *Zhuge Liang Leaves His Thatched Roof Study for the First Time (Chuchu maolu)* and *The Battle at Reed Marshes (Luhua dang)*, among other stories from the epic. *Jing* role.

Zhuge Liang is a character from the Three Kingdoms epic. Zhuge Liang is the prime minister of Shu-han where Liu Bei is the leader. He combines Daoist knowledge with military strategy to cleverly outwit their enemies. He is the title character in *Zhuge Liang Leaves His Thatched Roof Study for the First Time (Chuchu maolu)* early in his life, and demonstrates his skills in *The Gathering of Heroes (Qunying hui)*. *Laosheng* role.

Notes

Chapter 1: The World of Traditional Jingju

1. William Dolby, "Early Chinese Plays," in Mackerras, ed., *Chinese Theatre*, 15.
2. William Dolby, "Yuan Drama," in Mackerras, ed., *Chinese Theatre*, 33.
3. Interested readers are referred to Mackerras's *Chinese Theatre from Its Origins to the Present Day* for additional information about the development of Chinese theatre.
4. For further information about the role types, as well as song and music, readers are referred to Wichmann, *Listening to Theatre*.
5. A. C. Scott, *Classical Theatre,* 29.
6. Huo, *Art of Peking Opera*, 21.
7. A. C. Scott, *Chinese Theatre*, 18.
8. Chuang, *Chinese Forms*, n. p.
9. Pang, *Dragon Emperor*, 7.
10. Teng, *Chinese Opera Costumes*, 13.
11. Tan Yuanjie, private communication, May 31, 2002.
12. Zhao Shaohua, ed., *Costumes of the Peking Opera*, 4.
13. Tan Yuanjie, private communication, May 31, 2002.
14. Wichmann, *Listening to Theatre*, 4.
15. Ibid., 4.
16. Ibid., 5–6.

Chapter 2: The World of Traditional Jingu Costumes

1. Lu Qing, *Peking Opera Stardom*, 94.
2. Dickenson and Wrigglesworth. *Imperial Wardrobe,* 29.
3. Pang, *Dragon Emperor*, 33–34.
4. More information about the sources of the garments can be found in Chapters Three and Six.
5. Dickenson and Wrigglesworth. *Imperial Wardrobe*, 63.
6. Tan Yuanjie, private communication, June 7, 2002.
7. Hsu, *Chinese Conception of Theatre*, 149.

8. Ibid., 147.
9. A. C. Scott, "Performance of Classical Theatre," in Mackerras, ed., *Chinese Theatre*, 131.
10. A. C. Scott, *Classical Theatre of China*, 133.
11. Wang Shiyin, private conversation, Oct. 9, 2001.
12. A. C. Scott, "Performance of Classical Theatre," 138.

Chapter 3: The Form and Historical Roots of Costumes

1. Vollmer, *Decoding Dragons*, 20.
2. Ma et al., *Pictorial Album of Costumes*, 4.
3. Burnham, *Cut My Cote*, 29.
4. Vollmer, *Presence of the Dragon Throne*, 16.
5. Burnham, *Cut My Cote*, 29.
6. Zhou Xun and Gao, *5000 Years of Chinese Costumes*, 13.
7. John E. Vollmer, email communication, May 23, 2001.
8. Burnham, *Cut My Cote*, 29.
9. Vollmer, *Decoding Dragons*, 20.
10. Tan Yuanjie, private communication, May 31, 2002.
11. Vollmer, *Presence of the Dragon Throne*, 21.
12. Vollmer, *Decoding Dragons*, 20.
13. Vollmer, *Ruling from the Dragon Throne*, 52–55.
14. Zhou Xun and Gao, *5000 Years of Chinese Costumes,* 123.
15. Tan Yuanjie, private communication, May 31, 2002.
16. Vollmer, *Presence of the Dragon Throne*, 24.
17. Vollmer, *Ruling from the Dragon Throne*, 114.
18. Vollmer, *Decoding Dragons*, 21.
19. Zhou Xun and Gao, *5000 Years of Chinese Costumes*, 210.
20. Tan Yuanjie, private communication, May 31, 2002.
21. Tan, *Zhongguo Jingju fuzhuang*, 70. Zhou's stage name was later changed to Qilin Tong, when he decided to exchange the "seven-year-old" reference for one to the mythical *qilin*, a composite animal sometimes called the

Chinese unicorn. The first character of his later stage
name is used to designate his school of acting, Qipai
(Qi school), rather than the number seven *(qi)* of his
initial stage name.

22. Jacobsen, *Imperial Silks,* vol. 1, 452.
23. John E. Vollmer, email communication, May 23, 2001.
24. A. C. Scott, *Chinese Costume in Transition,* 51.
25. Garrett, *Traditional Chinese Clothing,* 16.
26. The Chinese unit of measurement is the *cun,* which is
    longer than an inch. Ten *cun* equal one *chi,* the Chinese
    equivalent of the foot measurement, and ten *chi* make
    one *zhang,* which is significantly longer than a yard.
    Inches have been used here for clarity.
27. Garrett, *Traditional Chinese Clothing,* 12.
28. Vollmer, *Ruling from the Dragon Throne,* 11.
29. Ibid., 8.
30. Ibid., 11.
31. Garrett, *Traditional Chinese Clothing,* 5.
32. Vollmer, *Ruling from the Dragon Throne,* 7.
33. Anquetil, *Silk,* 14.
34. Gao, *Chinese Textile Designs,* 8.
35. Anquetil, *Silk,* 14.
36. Garrett, *Traditional Chinese Clothing,* 70.

Chapter 4: The Symbolism and Application of Color

1. Vollmer, *Five Colours,* 3–11.
2. Vollmer, *Decoding Dragons,* 59.
3. Gostelow, *Embroidery,* 248.
4. Gao, *Chinese Textile Designs,* 24.
5. Garrett, *Chinese Clothing,* 12.
6. Zhou Xun and Gao, *5000 Years of Chinese Costumes,* 107.
7. Gao, *Chinese Textile Designs,* 24.
8. Garrett, *Chinese Clothing,* 58.
9. Tan Yuanjie, private communication, May 29, 2002.
10. Chung, *Art of Oriental Embroidery,* 49.
11. Ibid., 50.

Chapter 5: The Aesthetics and Meanings of the Embroidered Imagery

1. Gao, *Chinese Textile Designs,* 10.
2. Ibid., 21.
3. Philippa Scott, *Book of Silk,* 23.
4. Chung, *Art of Oriental Embroidery,* 5.

5. Ibid., 11.
6. Jacobsen, *Imperial Silk of the Ch'ing Dynasty,* n. p.
7. Hu, *Traditional Chinese Culture,* 7.
8. Hong Kong Urban Council, *Heaven's Embroidered
   Cloths,* 61.
9. Wang Yarong, *Chinese Folk Embroidery,* 14.
10. Chung, *Art of Oriental Embroidery,* 6.
11. Tan Yuanjie, private communication, October 12, 2001.
12. Mailey, *Embroidery in Imperial China,* 50.
13. Wilson, *Chinese Dress,* 98.
14. Wang Yarong, *Chinese Folk Embroidery,* 133–134.
15. Vollmer, *Five Colours of the Universe,* 43.
16. Vollmer, *Decoding Dragons.,* 60.
17. Ibid., 115.
18. Long, *How to Paint,* 13.
19. Fong, *Beyond Representation,* 173.
20. Vollmer, *Decoding Dragons,* 59.
21. Ibid., 60.
22. Wilson, *Chinese Dress,* 106.
23. Barnhart, *Peach Blossom Spring,* 35.
24. Chung, *Art of Oriental Embroidery,* 22.
25. Yu, *Chinese Painting,* 3.
26. Long, *How to Paint,* 67.
27. Ibid., 34.
28. Ibid., 48.
29. The stitches used to create this effect are described in
    the section of this chapter on techniques.
30. Williams, *Outlines of Chinese Symbolism,* 317.
31. Ibid., 68.
32. A. C. Scott, *Chinese Costume in Transition,* 18.
33. Garrett, *Chinese Clothing,* 14.
34. Vollmer, *Five Colours of the Universe,* 25.
35. Chung, *Art of Oriental Embroidery,* 110.
36. Garrett, *Chinese Clothing,* 70.
37. In the late Qing dynasty, the military ranks were as fol-
    lows: (1) *qilin* (Chinese unicorn), (2) lion, (3) leopard, (4)
    tiger, (5) bear, (6) panther, (7) rhinoceros, (8) rhinoceros,
    and (9) seahorse. The civilian ranks were represented
    by: (1) crane, (2) golden pheasant, (3) peacock, (4) wild
    goose, (5) silver pheasant, (6) egret, (7) mandarin duck,
    (8) quail, and (9) paradise flycatcher. In some periods,
    adjacent ranks might be represented by the same crea-
    ture; see Vollmer, *Decoding Dragons,* 23.
38. A. C. Scott, *Chinese Costume in Transition,* 20.
39. The dragon, phoenix, tortoise, and *qilin* make up the

four supernatural creatures that represent the celestial empire. The dragon dominates among the scaly beasts, the phoenix leads the feathered creatures, the tortoise heads animals with shells, and the *qilin* rules among the hairy animals, despite being described as having scales. Man is number one among the naked animals. Williams, *Outlines of Chinese Symbolism*, 413–415.

40. Cammann, *China's Dragon Robes*, 4.
41. Tan, *Zhongguo Jingju fuzhuang*, 2–7.
42. Garrett, *Chinese Dragon Robes*, 51.
43. Williams, *Outlines of Chinese Symbolism*, 132.
44. Cammann, *China's Dragon Robes*, 131.
45. Ibid., 32.
46. Dickenson and Wrigglesworth. *Imperial Wardrobe*, 79.
47. Williams, *Outlines of Chinese Symbolism*, 323.
48. Vollmer, *Decoding Dragons*, 60.
49. Cammann, *China's Dragon Robes*, 94.
50. Williams, *Outlines of Chinese Symbolism*, various.
51. Eberhard, *Dictionary of Chinese Symbols.*, 52.
52. Williams, *Outlines of Chinese Symbolism*, various.
53. Cammann, *China's Dragon Robes*, 96.
54. Ibid., 97.
55. Ibid.
56. Chung, *Art of Oriental Embroidery*, 173.
57. Eberhard, *Dictionary of Chinese Symbols*, 32.
58. A. C. Scott, *Chinese Costume in Transition*, 51.

Chapter 6: The Costume Compendium

1. Garrett, *Chinese Dragon Robes*, 5.
2. Ibid., 8.
3. Dickenson and Wrigglesworth. *Imperial Wardrobe*, 197, plate 178.
4. Ibid., 197.
5. Chavannes, *Five Happinesses*, 31.
6. Zhan, *Xiju dianying meishu ziliao*, vol. 4, *Fushi*, 444.
7. Tan, *Zhongguo Jingju fuzhuang*, 70.
8. Ibid., 100
9. Pan, *Stagecraft of the Peking Opera*, 117.
10. Ma et al., *Pictorial Album of Costumes*, 171.
11. Tan Yuanjie, private communication, October 12, 2001.
12. Ibid.
13. Tan, *Zhongguo Jingju fuzhuang*, 134.
14. Garrett, *Chinese Clothing*, 12.

15. Zhang Weidong, private communication, August 24, 2002.
16. Garrett, *Chinese Clothing*, plate 5.
17. Tan Yuanjie, private communication, May 31, 2002.
18. Tan, *Zhongguo Jingju fuzhuang*, 150.
19. A. C. Scott, *Classical Theatre of China*, 157.
20. Liu Xiaoqing, private communication, August 2, 2000.
21. Tan Yuanjie, private communication, May 31, 2002.
22. Tan, *Zhongguo Jingju fuzhuang*, 128.
23. Ibid., 128.
24. Dickenson and Wrigglesworth. *Imperial Wardrobe*, 116.
25. Ma et al., *Pictorial Album of Costumes*, 153.
26. Yin Yongming, private communication, September 24, 2001.
27. Ma et al., *Pictorial Album of Costumes*, 157.
28. Teng, *Chinese Opera Costumes*, 39.
29. Zhang Jing, private communication, September 18, 2001.
30. Liu Xiaoqing, private communication, July 10, 2000.
31. Yin Yongming, private communication, September 10, 2001.
32. Tan, *Zhongguo Jingju fuzhuang*, 192.
33. Wu Zuguang, Huang, and Mei, *Peking Opera*, 81.
34. Liu Xiaoqing, private communication, July 10, 2000.
35. Ibid.
36. Tan, *Zhongguo Jingju fuzhuang*, 204.
37. Ma et al., *Pictorial Album of Costumes*, 113.
38. Liu Xiaoqing, private communication, July 10, 2000.
39. Williams, *Outlines of Chinese Symbolism*, 148.
40. Tan, *Zhongguo Jingju fuzhuang*, 210.
41. Ma et al., *Pictorial Album of Costumes*, 49.
42. Tan, *Zhongguo Jingju fuzhuang*, 214.
43. Tan Yuanjie, private communication, May 31, 2002.
44. Ma et al., *Pictorial Album of Costumes*, 105.
45. Priest and Simmons, *Chinese Textiles*, 88.
46. Zhang Weidong, private communication, August 27, 2002.
47. Tan, *Zhongguo Jingju fuzhuang*, 236.
48. Ibid., 286.
49. Zhou Xun and Gao, *5000 Years of Chinese Costumes*, 161.
50. Garrett, *Traditional Chinese Clothing*, 20.
51. Tan, *Zhongguo Jingju fuzhuang*, 246.
52. Ibid., 266.

53. Garrett, *Chinese Clothing*, 37.

54. Ibid., 74.

55. Ibid., 75.

56. Ibid., 82.

57. Ibid., 12.

58. Ibid., 22.

59. Pan, *Stagecraft of the Peking Opera*, 129.

60. A. C. Scott, "Performance of Classical Theatre," in Mackerras, ed., *Chinese Theatre*, 131.

61. Zung, *Secrets of Chinese Drama*, 77.

62. Zhou Xun and Gao, *5000 Years of Chinese Costumes*, 45.

63. A. C. Scott, "Performance of Classical Theatre," 134.

Chapter 7: Makeup, Hair, and Headdresses

1. Wu Mingchi, *Facial Makeup*, 7.

2. Zhang Geng, *Art of Face Painting*, 25–26.

3. Ibid., 28.

4. John Hu, "Ming Dynasty Drama," in Mackerras, ed., *Chinese Theatre*, 87.

5. Zhang Geng, *Art of Face Painting*, 29.

6. Pan, *Stagecraft of Peking Opera*, 83.

7. Zhang Jing, private communication, September 14, 2001.

8. Zhang Geng, *Art of Face Painting*, 124.

9. T'sao, *Face of Chinese Opera*, 27–31.

10. Ibid., 25.

11. Zhao Menglin and Yan, *Peking Opera Painted Faces*, 19–20.

12. Ibid., 20.

13. Some animals are also portrayed with masks.

14. The delineation of the painted face categories is based on Wu Wenxue, private communication, July, 2002, and T'sao, *Face of Chinese Opera*, 23–25.

15. Additional details about the individual elements of the face and their meanings is available from books on face painting in the bibliography: Lu, *Face Painting in Chinese Opero*; T'sao, *The Face of Chinese Opera*; Wu Mingchi, *Facial Makeup in Beijing Opera*; Zhang Geng, *The Art of Face Painting in Chinese Music-Drama*; Zhao Menglin, and Yan Jiqing, *Peking Opera Painted Faces*.

16. Zhang Geng, *Art of Face Painting*, 7.

17. T'sao, *Face of Chinese Opera*, 57.

18. Zhang Geng, *Art of Face Painting*, 11.

19. T'sao, *Face of Chinese Opera*, 24.

20. Descriptions of the application of makeup are based on demonstrations by Wu Wenxue, who is a *lianpu* instructor, and on the author's observations of actors preparing for performance.

21. Zhou Xun and Gao, *5000 Years of Chinese Costumes*, 147.

22. Ibid., 173.

23. Zhang Jing, private communication, September 10, 2001.

24. Ibid., September 14, 2001.

25. Garrett, *Chinese Clothing*, 23, Figure 2.8.

26. Zhang Jing, private communication, September 12, 2001.

27. Ibid.

28. Garrett, *Chinese Clothing*, 13.

29. Li Shuo, private communication, September 19, 2001.

30. Dolby, "Yuan Drama," in Mackerras, ed., *Chinese Theatre*, 54.

31. A. C. Scott, *Introduction to Chinese Theatre*, 27.

32. Pan, *Stagecraft of the Peking Opera*, 151.

33. Ibid., 154.

34. Tan, *Zhongguo Jingju fuzhuang*, 220.

35. Garrett, *Chinese Clothing*, Plate 5.

36. Zhou Xun and Gao, *5000 Years of Chinese Costumes*, 111.

37. Arlington, *Chinese Drama*, 92.

38. Zhang Weidong, private communication, September 1, 2002.

39. Zhou Xibao, *Zhongguo gudai fushi shi*, 393, Figure 6.

40. Ibid., 403, Figure 2.

41. Ibid., Figure 1.

42. Lindqvist, *China, Empire of Living Symbols*, 104.

43. Zhou Xibao, *Zhongguo gudai fushi shi*, 480, Figure 12, shows executioners with feathers on either side of their helmets.

Chapter 8: Dressing Techniques and Costume Plots

1. Zhang Yijuan et al., eds. *Chuantong Jingju renwu zaoxing huicui*; and Wan Ruquan et al., eds. *Jingju renwu zhuang ban bai chu*.

2. Yin Yongming, private communication. September 10, 2001.

3. Zou Zhiqiang, private communication, April 25, 1996.

4. Li Wencai, private communication, July 18, 2000.

5. Wichmann, *Phoenix Returns to Nest*, 6–8.

6. Tan Yuanjie, private communication, May 29, 2002.

7. Wichmann, *Phoenix Returns to Nest*, 24.

8. Ibid., 24.

9. Ibid., 29.

10. Tan Yuanjie, private communication, June 7, 2002.

11. Wilson, *Chinese Dress*, 92.

12. Pan, *Stagecraft of the Peking Opera*, 110–111.

13. Ibid., 111.

14. Wilson, *Chinese Dress*, 92.

Glossary

an'anyi 安安衣   lit. "safe" clothing for small children

ao 袄   jacket

aoku 袄裤   jacket and trousers set, usually worn by *huadan* and maids

aoqun 袄裙   jacket and skirt set, usually worn by *huadan* and maids

armscye   the seam between the body of the garment and the sleeve

babao 八宝   eight symbols of good fortune of Buddhism, eight attributes of Daoist immortals, or the eight precious objects, embroidered on *mang* and *nümang*

bagua yi 八卦衣   eight trigrams Daoist robe for characters who combine Daoist practices with brilliant military strategy, has water sleeves

bagua jin 八卦巾   headdress worn with the *bagua yi* robe, made from the same color fabric with similar embroidery

bai 摆   extensions on the open side seams of the front of the *mang* and *guanyi* robes

bai wuzui 白五嘴   white five-part beard for *chou* characters

baibu dawa 白布大袜   white woven fabric socks fitting loosely around the mid-calf, for male servants and other lower-class characters

baise caiqiu 白色彩球   white fabric rosette, worn by women in mourning or in pure white costumes

baizhe qun 百褶裙   lit. "one-hundred-pleats skirt"; for *qingyi* characters

bamian wei 八面威   eight-sided filigree helmet, worn by powerful *jing* generals

bangchui jin 棒椎(槌)巾   lit. "wooden club"; soft hat with top folded together into a flap

bangtui 绑腿   gaiters, worn by soldiers

baodi xue 薄底靴   thin-soled ankle boots for martial men and women in a variety of styles and colors

baohua 刨花   wood shavings, soaked in boiling water until the resin makes the gel that is used for styling the hairpieces and affixing them to the face

baoyi 豹(抱)衣   lit. "leopard/panther" or "embracing" clothes; tight-fitting hero's clothing (*yingxiong yi*) or *dayi* (fighting clothes), consisting of trousers and a jacket with *zoushui* (moving water) pleated fabric layers at the hem of the jacket

beizi 褙子   historical symmetrical long robe with center-front closing, source for *pi* costume

bias   fabric cut on a 45-degree angle from the straight grain

binfa 鬓发   pieces of hair on either side of the *laodan* hairstyle

bingyi 兵衣   soldiers' clothing, martial jacket and trousers set for soldiers

bu 布   cotton or plain cloth, such as *bu jianyi*; also refers to objects made from plain cloth, such as hats

bufu 补服 — coat with a badge, Qing dynasty (1644–1911) black court surcoat with *buzi* rank badge, costume of same description

buzi 补子 — rank badge on the *guanyi* official's robe

caidan 彩旦 — lit. "colorful" female *chou* comic roles; also called *choudan*

caiku 彩裤 — colored trousers, inner unembroidered trousers

caipo ao 彩婆袄 — colorful jacket worn for some *choudan* old-woman roles

caiqiao 踩跷 — lit. "stepping on stilts"; also the devices for imitating bound feet onstage; two styles: *ruanqiao*, the soft version and *yingqiao*, hard stilts

caixie 彩鞋 — embroidered flat slippers for women

cansan 黪三 — gray three-part beard for *laosheng* characters

caomao quan 草帽圈 — straw hat brim with no crown, worn by fishermen, woodcutters, and other laborers

caowang kui 草王盔 — lit. "grass king" helmet; self-proclaimed king's helmet for illegitimate regional rulers, with two pompoms, decorated with pearls, and blue and metallic filigree

caoxie 草鞋 — straw sandals for some lower-status male roles

changkao wusheng 长靠武生 — "long armor" martial men, name for high-ranking younger warriors who generally wear the *kao* armor

chaofang 朝方 — high-topped boots with a thin-to-medium thickness sole for *chou* and other lower-ranking characters

chaogua 朝褂 — court vest for Qing dynasty women

chaozhu 朝珠 — Buddhist rosary beads, worn with *bagua yi, qimang*, and sometimes the straight-edged *nümang*

chayi 茶衣 — lit. "tea clothes"; jacket and trousers in tea colors, for boatmen and workers

chenqun 衬裙 — lit. "inside skirt"; wide pleated skirt for *laodan* characters, usually green or blue

chi 翅 — wings on the back of the *shamao* official's headdresses

Chinese knot — loops of thread created in embroidery by wrapping the thread around the needle two or three times before piercing the fabric

chou 丑 — lit. "ugly"; clown roles, foolish magistrates, nagging women, and servants; also called *xiao hualian*

chou yuanzi 丑院子 — courtyard keepers, played by *chou* actors

choudan 丑旦 — *chou* comic female roles; also called *caidan*

chousan 丑三 — clown three-part beard; a comic version of the *sanliu ran* three-part beard worn by *laosheng* characters

choutiao 绸条 — silk band worn around a hat or scarf, for *laodan*

chuanqi 传奇 — lit. "transmit the strange"; Ming dynasty (1368–1644) theatre form, developed from *nanxi*

consolidated — surface patterns with arrangements of circles, a single square, yokes, or bands

costume plot — a list or chart describing all the garments worn by each character in a play

couching — a thick thread, usually metallic, is placed on top of the fabric, and thinner threads are stitched around it to secure it in place; used both for outlining and filling in areas of design

da banjin 大板巾 — big-board soft hat; a fabric headdress with a large flat board on the crown and a flap over the nape of the neck, for servants, travelers, and executioners

da fandan 大饭单 — large apron

da kanjian 大坎肩 — long vest

dadai 大带	firm sash about three yards long, with long fringe on each end; can be one or two pieces; also called *luandai*	diaper	an interlocking geometric motif repeated across the surface of a garment
dafa 大发	a switch of human hair that is used to cover and fill out the *fadian* bun	*diao da* 吊搭	hanging, dangling beard for comic *chou* characters
dahong 大红	bright crimson or pinkish-red grease-based makeup	*dinghua* 顶花	lit. "top flower"; metal circlet and leaf decorations for the *zhongsha* hat
dakai 大铠	big armor; palace guard armor for military attendants of the emperor and high officials worn by the *liuhang* role type, similar to the *kao,* with square flaps in the lower skirts	dispersed	surface pattern in a grid or scattered scheme
		doufu 豆腐	bean curd or tofu; here used to describe the face makeup for the *chou* roles
damao 鞑帽	Mongolian hat sometimes worn by barbarian kings onstage	*doupeng* 斗蓬	cape worn for traveling
dan 旦	female roles	*duanda wusheng* 短打武生	lit. "quick fighting" or "short clothing" for lower-ranking soldiers, disenfranchised bandits, and supernatural characters who engage in combat
daogu jin 道姑巾	Daoist headdress for young nuns		
daogu kanjian 道姑坎肩	Daoist vest for nuns		
daoma dan 刀马旦	lit. "sword and horse" women; high-ranking female generals equivalent to the *changkao wusheng* male roles	*duantiao* 短跳	lit. "short and convenient for playing"; robe for children, with *xuezi*-style collar
daoying kui 倒缨盔	soldier's one- or two-piece tasseled helmet, with stiff diadem and neck flap; see also *xiao daoying kui*	*er maozi* 耳毛子	two small ear tufts; upright hair in front of the ears, worn with the *zharan* style of beard
datou 大头	complete hair; women's hairstyle with curls framing the face and long tresses behind, for young women's roles	*ezi* 额子	lit. "forehead," here meaning diadem; worn alone or with other headdress pieces
		fadian 发垫	bun covered with a hair net
dawan 大弯	big curls; wefts of human hair in black, about 2 inches wide and 18 inches long, used to shape the sideburns for women's hairstyles	*faji* 发髻	hair coil for top of men's or older character's hairstyles, also used to form the top loops or buns for the *guzhuang* or ancient style of hair, called *yunhuan* or cloud loops; also called *fajiu*
daxie 大鞋	slippers for low-ranking male roles; also called *zaoxie*		
daxiu 大袖	big-sleeved robe for waiters	*fandan* 饭单	apron
dazan 大簪	a metal hairpin used to secure the back of the *wangzi* skullcap on women's hairstyles	*fayi* 法衣	lit. "magic power clothing"; Daoist priest's chasuble
		fenbai 粉白	white powder makeup for painted faces
di fangjin 低方巾	low square hat shaped like a house, with straight sides and a peaked crown; see also *gao fangjin*	*fengguan* 凤冠	phoenix headdress with metallic filigree, pearls, and tassels, worn by royal women, large and silver for *qingyi* and smaller and gold for *laodan*

fenyang mao 汾阳帽	prime minister's hat; a double-crowned hat of golden filigree, with *yunchi* (S-shaped wings); also called *wenyang mao*
flat fell seam	after the seam is stitched, one seam allowance is cut shorter, the other folded around it and stitched flat to the face fabric
French seam	the fabric is stitched wrong sides together 1/4-inch from the edge, then folded around the seam allowance and stitched again 3/8-inch from the fold
frogs	decorative closings with loop and braided knot fastenings
fu 蝠(福)	bat (meaning good fortune); also a symbol of power on historical emperor's robes
fuchen 抚尘	horsetail brush, carried by eunuchs
fugui yi 富贵衣	garment of wealth and nobility; a black, patched *xuezi* robe worn by dignified characters who have fallen on hard times, it carries the wish for a better future for male characters
fujing 副净	secondary *jing* roles requiring dance and acting skills; also called *jiazi hualian* (posture-painted face) and *erhualian* (second-painted face)
fuma taozi 驸马套子	hat ornament for the imperial son-in-law, a circlet addition to the *zhongsha* headdress; also called *taochi*, wing cover
futou 幞头	official's hat; a historical double-crowned headdress with bent wings that evolved from the shape of a turban wrapped around the men's bun on the crown, source for *shamao* onstage
fuzhuang 服装	contemporary word for costumes and clothing
fuzi kui 夫子盔	helmet of respect worn by *jing* generals, Guan Yu, Xiang Yu, and others
fuzi lü 福字履	lit. "good fortune" shoes; embroidered with bats and with a slight lift, worn by *laodan*, *laosheng*, and *chou*
gailiang 改良	reformed, applied to costumes modified from the original form of costume
gailiang guanyi 改良官衣	reformed official's robe, with a round design at chest instead of rank badge, has water sleeves
gailiang kao 改良靠	reformed armor, without flags, narrower and fewer pieces than the standard *kao* armor, for lesser battles
gailiang mang 改良蟒	reformed court robe, with fewer decorations than the standard version, has water sleeves
gailiang nükao 改良 女靠	reformed armor for women, slimmer and with fewer pieces than the standard *kao* armor, for lesser battles, no flags
gaitou 盖头	lit. "to cover the head"; a red wedding veil that conceals the bride's face
gao fangjin 高方巾	high square hat shaped like a house, with straight sides and a peaked crown; see also *di fangjin*
gongnü 宫女	female maids or dancers in sets of four or more
gongzhuang 宫装	palace garment with elaborately embroidered streamers on the skirt and striped sleeves, worn by princesses and consorts, has water sleeves
goulian 勾脸	lit. "to outline the face"; makeup for the *chou* and *jing* roles
guan 冠	crowns for imperial characters or ceremonial headdresses for others, also a higher-status version of the hairstyle for *laodan* characters
Guan Gong ran 关公髯	beard for Guan Yu, made of human hair
guanyi 官衣	official's robe, floor length, with the *buzi* rank badge, has water sleeves

guanzi kui 罐子盔   lit. "bucket-shaped helmet"; headdress with diadem, peaked crown, and neck flap, worn with the *dakai* armor for attendants

gui suizi 鬼穗子   lit. "ghost fringe"; strips of white paper attached to the headdresses of ghost characters

guizishou yi 刽子手   executioner's clothes; red jacket and trousers, with peplum flaps

gusset   a fabric insert to add ease for movement, for example, under the arms

Guoju 国剧   national drama, an alternate name for Jingju

guzhuang 古装   lit. "ancient-style" dress; meaning pre-Qing dynasty, with fitted waist, designed by Mei Lanfang

guzhuang tou 古装头   lit. "ancient-style" hair for young women; with soft loops of hair on the crown and a ponytail in back, developed by Mei Lanfang; also the fall wig used for the back of *guzhuang tou* style of hairdressing

hai'er fa 孩儿发   children's wig

haiqing xuezi 海青褶子   black *xuezi* robe with black velvet collar band, unembroidered, has water sleeves

hechang 鹤氅   crane robe, a version of the *bagua yi* with crane roundels, has water sleeves

heisan 黑三   black three-part beard, one of the *sanliu ran* styles worn by *laosheng* dignified men

heye jin 荷叶巾   lotus-leaf square fabric hat, with square flap of cloth on top

hongsheng 红生   a *sheng* role with a red face, such as Guan Yu

hou luomao 猴罗帽   monkey *luomao* with tiger-fur trim

houdi xue 厚底靴   tall boots with high soles for men

houjia 猴甲   monkey armor with black castellated lines and tiger-fur trim

houmao 侯帽   filigree hat for a marquis, with broad fringed stiff flaps over the ears; also called *taiding* when a horn-shaped decoration is added to the top for military characters, nicknamed *er buwen*, or "unable to hear" because the flaps cover the ears

houyi 猴衣   monkey clothes, a variation of the *hua baoyi* (flowered hero set), with moving-water pleated fabric layers, in yellow, with stylized fur embroidery

hua 花   flower, also colorful; for garments with flowers embroidered on the surface, such as *wenchou hua xuezi, hua baoyi, hua jianyi, hua kuaiyi, hualian huaxuezi, wuxiaosheng hua xuezi, xiaosheng hua xuezi,* and for embellished face makeup, such as *hua sankuaiwa lian, hua yuanbao lian,* and so on

huadan 花旦   lit. "flower woman"; flirtatious, roguish, and lively young women in comic and lighthearted roles

hualian 花脸   lit. "flower" face or painted face; also another name for *jing* roles

huamian 花面   lit. "flower" face on the faces of the *jing* and the *chou* roles, historical

huang magua 黄马卦   yellow *magua* worn by court attendants in the presence of the emperor or the entourage of a high-ranking official, historical garment and costume

huangmao 皇帽   stage king's yellow-fabric and gold-filigree crown; see also *wangmao*

huapen di 花盆底   flowerpot-sole shoes with pedestal soles to imitate the look of bound feet, worn with Manchu clothing and costumes; also called *qixie* (Manchu shoes)

huashan 花衫   lit. "flower shirt"; a twentieth-century role category combining at least two of the four roles for young women, *qingyi, huadan, daoma dan,* and *wudan hudie kui* 蝴蝶盔 butterfly helmet for women warriors

huling 护领 white inner collar worn with many costumes to frame the face and protect the costumes from makeup

huliwei 狐狸尾 white fox tails attached to headdresses, indicates non-Han roles

hunpa 魂帕 spirit cloth; a black gauze shroud indicating characters who are spirits

huxin baojing 护心宝镜 lit. "heart protecting mirror"; a round disk worn on the chest of armor

integrated composition pattern with motifs covering the surface of a garment in a unified theme

jiangjin 将巾 a combination fabric and filigree helmet for generals

jiangya 江芽 the frothy bubbles at the top of the waves in the terrestrial compositions on the *mang* and *jianyi*, for example

jiansha 奸纱 lit. "sharp" or "pointed" *shamao*-style hat; with peach- or diamond-shaped wings, indicating sinister or corrupt officials

jianyi 箭衣 archer's robe; costume from the Manchu garment called a *jifu*, with fitted sleeves with horseshoe-shaped cuffs, crossover closing, and center-front and back slits in the skirt

jiaoling pao 绞领袍 crossover-collar-closing historical long robe

jiasha 袈裟 red cloak for head monks

jiegu 戒箍 lit. "to forbid desires" tight ring; a gold fillet with paired arabesques in front, worn by military monks as a sign of their abstinence

jiemian 洁面 smart face, using makeup to enhance the features for the male and female roles, historical

jifu 吉服 lit. "auspicious attire or coat"; the semiformal robe of the Manchus in the Qing dynasty, with horseshoe cuffs and crossover closing, source for *jianyi* costume

jiguan 吉冠 lit. "auspicious hat"; Qing dynasty hat, with upturned brim and red fringe, source for *nuanmao* onstage

jin 巾 soft fabric hats; also called *bu* referring to the fabric from which they may be constructed

jing 净 painted-face roles; men of great strength, with formidable physical or mental powers

jinghu 京胡 two-string spike fiddle to accompany singing

Jingju 京剧 capital drama, the Beijing style of *xiqu* performance combining music, speech, song, pantomime, dance, and acrobatics into a single unified presentation, name used after mid-twentieth century

Jingxi 京戏 capital theatre, nineteenth-century name for Jingju

jinhua 金花 upright metallic wing-like flowers added to the *zhongsha* hat to identify number-one scholars, a form of *dinghua*

junban 俊扮 lit. "handsome/ beautiful makeup"; a redder version of the makeup used for *xiaosheng*, *qingyi*, and younger and wealthier *laosheng* and *laodan* characters

kai chang 开氅 lit. "open robe"; officials' informal robe, with crossover closing, for private and informal wear, worn by high-ranking military and government officials, has water sleeves

kanjian 坎肩 vest

kao 靠 stage armor for generals and high-ranking military roles, *yingkao* means hard or complete armor when worn with the flags, also called *dakao* or big *kao*; *ruankao* indicates soft armor, worn without flags

kaodu 靠腿 broad padded waistband on the front of armor at waist height *kaoqi* 靠旗 — the four flags strapped to the back of stage armor

kaotui 靠腿 — leg flaps of armor

kesi 缂丝 — carved or cut silk, fabric produced through tapestry weaving

kuai xue 快靴 — lit. "fast boots"; for martial men and women, flat with a pointed, curled toe, embroidered or plain

kuaiyi 快衣 — lit. "fast clothes"; martial jacket and trousers set for unattached fighters, also means tight or simple

kuazi 侉子 — skirt panels, on the *yulin jia* armor, for example

kui 盔 — war helmets made of filigree, with pearl and pompom trim

Kunqu 昆曲 — lit. "songs of Kunshan"; performance style popular from the Ming to late Qing dynasties, slow and gentle melodies with literary scripts featuring domestic stories

kuzi 裤子 — trousers; see also *caiku*, colored trousers

laodan 老旦 — mature women roles, generally dignified and venerated

laodan guan 老旦冠 — higher-ranking *laodan* hairstyle, with a larger bun, wider headscarf, and a jade ornament on the *leizi*

laodou yi 老斗衣 — poor old man clothing, a cream-colored *xuezi* robe, has water sleeves

laosheng 老生 — mature male roles, often dignified scholars, statesmen, and members of the court or heads of household

leitoudai 勒头带 — lit. "tighten hair ribbon"; a small square of muslin fabric with long twill tape ties, used as a base for hairstyling and to lift the outer corner of the eyes

leizi 勒子 — lit. "to tighten"; a narrow black velvet piece with a single ornament at the center of the forehead, for *laodan* roles

liangmao 凉帽 — cool hat, conical rattan headdress with red fringe radiating from the peak

liangba tou 两把头 — lit. "two pieces of hair"; a large flat upright structure on the hairstyles of Qing women; also called "archway" or "big wings"

liangxiang 亮相 — lit. "to strike a pose"; pauses in the action to reveal a character's inner essence

lianhua guan 莲花冠 — lotus crown for Zhuge Liang to represent his religious, magical qualities, related to the lotus of Buddhism

lianpu 脸谱 — lit. "face chart"; face-painting designs that emerged in the Ming dynasty and continue in use today, for *jing* roles

lingyi 灵衣 — small collar with dickie, worn with Manchu-style garments

lingzhi 灵芝 — sacred fungus, a shape that is used to finish ends of collars and side seam slits; see also *ruyi tou*

lingzi 领子 — six-foot-long pheasant feathers attached to the war helmets

lingzi tao 翎子套 — lit. "feather covers"; decorative shafts trimmed in colored fur, for affixing the feathers to the helmets

lishui 立水 — standing water; diagonal water patterns on the hems of the *mang, nümang, long jianyi, long magua*, and so on

liufen lian 六分脸 — 60 percent face; the lower 60 percent of the face is one color, and the upper is white, for *jing* painted-face designs

liuhang 流行 — lit. "flowing role type," as they flow onstage like water; these are attendants in nonspeaking roles, now called *longtao*

liwo sanjiang shui 立卧三江水 — standing, lying three-rivers water pattern of the chevrons in the waves embroidered on the hem of a *mang* court robe

liwo wujiang shui 立卧五江水 — standing, lying five-rivers water pattern of the chevrons in the waves embroidered on the hem of a *mang* court robe

long 龙 — dragon with five claws, garments with this dragon embroidered on the surface, such as *long jianyi, long magua,* and so on

long and short stitch — short, close parallel stitches with staggered lengths to create a blend of colors

longpao 龙袍 — historical dragon robe, with a five-clawed dragon, worn by men and women for semiformal official dress

longtao 龙套 — entourage, attendant roles, formerly called *liuhang*

longtao yi 龙套衣 — robe worn by male attendants

luandai 鸾带 — lit. "phoenix tail belt"; a firm sash about three yards long, with long fringe on each end, can be one or two pieces; also called *dadai*

luohan 罗汉 — a Buddhist who has reached the highest state of peace and enlightenment; also called arhat, when powers are enhanced

luomao 罗帽 — six-sided cloth hat on a wide band, when hard and worn upright, called *ying luomao,* or soft and worn collapsed like a beret, called *ruan luomao*

mabian 马鞭 — horse whip decorated with colored tassels emblematic for the horse

magua 马褂 — lit. "horse jacket"; Qing garment source for stage garment of the same name, riding jacket worn over the *jianyi* for traveling scenes

mang 蟒 — dragon with four claws, also court robe costume for the emperor and highest-ranking courtiers and generals, with embroidery of dragons and waves, has water sleeves

mao 帽 — hat, category for firm headdresses

man rankou 满髯口 — long, full beards worn by *jing* characters

maozheng 帽正 — white jade rectangle on the center front of *zhongsha* when worn by *xiaosheng*

maxue 马靴 — lit. "horse boots"; historical boots with high soles for riding with stirrups

mianguan 面冠 — lit. "face crown"; historical emperor's crown, with flat board and strings of pearls hanging over the forehead

mocai 抹彩 — ink coloring, to paint the face in the style of the *sheng* and *dan* roles

nanxi 南戏 — southern drama popular in the Southern Song court (1127–1279)

nü 女 — woman or women's

nü laodou yi 女 老斗衣 — poor old woman clothing; a rice-colored *xuezi* robe, has water sleeves, often worn belted with a cord or sash

nuanmao 暖帽 — black warm winter hat with upturned brim and red fringe on the crown, based on Qing dynasty *jiguan*

nükao 女靠 — armor with skirt streamers for women generals

nümang 女蟒 — women's court robe for royal women in two forms, one with straight edges and one with a wavy border, has water sleeves

nüpi 女帔 — women's formal robe with a symmetrical opening with long collar band, has water sleeves

nüxuezi 女褶子 — women's informal robe; two versions: one with a center-front closing for higher-ranking characters and one with an asymmetrical closing for poor and elderly women, has water sleeves

pang'ao 胖袄 — lit. "fat jacket"; a vest that pads shoulders and chest, inner garment for some male roles

pao 袍 — robe

peplum — a short flared flap from the waist to the hip

pengtou 蓬头   a wig of human or yak hair worn long and black or white by Daoists, or short and colorful by spirit characters

pi 帔   formal robe with symmetrical opening, worn by *laosheng* for domestic scenes and *xiaosheng* for weddings, has water sleeves

pianzi 片子   small pieces; refers to the combination of *dawan* and *xaiowan*, wefts of hair used to create the sideburns and curls in women's headdresses

pifa 披发   hair spread in the back, black or white and long, for male Daoists

pihuang 皮黄   term created out of words *xipi* and *erhuang*, the modal systems from Hubei and Anhui provinces, combined in the musical system employed in early Jingju

pipa 琵琶 closing   asymmetrical closing with squared extension to the right resembling the *pipa* instrument; used on some vests

qi 旗   banner or flag; also a colloquial term for Manchu

qiaoliang jin 桥梁巾   bridge hat, soft hat with peaked crown

qilin 麒麟   a composite animal with one or two horns, sometimes referred to as the Chinese unicorn

qimang 旗蟒   Manchu court robe worn by non-Han women onstage

qing 青   color of the twilight sky, dark blue-green black

qing guanyi 青官衣   dark *guanyi* robe with or without a rank badge for those in service positions outside the ranking system; also called *qingsu*

qingjing zhuang 清静装   lit. "clean garment"; historical name for red monk cloak, called *jiasha* onstage

qingyi 青衣   lit. "black clothing"; here it refers to a role type for women, young to middle-aged, who have or have had

high social status and dignity; name comes from the garment worn by these characters when in destitute circumstances

qinjiao mao 秦椒帽   pepper-shaped soft felt hat with cuff and tall rounded crown with a pompom, worn compressed on top of the head

qipao 旗袍   Manchu dress with standing collar and asymmetrical closing, used onstage for ethnic female roles

qitou 旗头   Manchu hair style, with the archway or "big wings"-style construction, worn onstage by female characters from non-Han families

qiuran 虬髯   curly beard for *chou* and *jing* roles indicating coarseness

qixing ezi 七星额子   seven-star-diadem helmet for women warriors

qunzi 裙子   skirt

rankou 髯口   whiskers

rongqiu 绒球   pompoms

ruan 软   soft; as in *ruan luomao*, soft version of the six-sided *luomao*, the beret headdress worn by soldiers and heroes, and *ruankao*, worn without flags

ruyi guan 如意冠   lit. "sacred fungus crown"; with *ruyi* arabesque shapes trimmed with strings of pearls, worn by Lady Yu, the famous concubine in *The Hegemon King Says Farewell to His Concubine*; see also *lingzhi*

ruyi tou 如意头   an arabesque pattern of the sacred fungus used to finish contrasting borders and collar bands, carries the meaning "may things be as you wish," see also *lingzhi*

sankuaiwa lian 三块瓦脸   three-tiled *jing* painted-face pattern, with forehead, nose, and both cheeks in a single color, forming three areas

sanlan 三蓝   three shades of blue, a popular color combination for embroidery

sanliu ran 三绺髯 — long, thin beards that are divided into three sections for *laosheng* roles

sanse dao beixin 三色道背心 — three-color Daoist vest for young nuns and monks with martial skills; also called "paddy-field clothing" (*shuitian yi*)

satin stitch — short, close parallel stitches to fill an area

scattered composition — surface design with motifs distributed evenly across the fabric

seng kanjian 僧坎肩 — vest for military monks, with moving-water silk layers on the hem; also called *wuseng yi*

sengdao lian 僧道脸 — Buddhist and Daoist monk face pattern for *jing* painted-face designs

sengmao 僧帽 — Buddhist hat, shaped with a peak in the front, taller for abbots, and shorter for monks

sengyi 僧衣 — long Buddhist robe for abbots

shamao 纱帽 — lit. "gauze hat"; official's headdress with double crown, black, with two straight wings on the back

shang wuse 上五色 — upper colors; the higher-ranking colors for court and official clothing: red (*hong*), green (*lü*), yellow (*huang*), white (*bai*), and black (*hei*)

shanjian 苫肩 — shoulder-covering collar; separate piece for men's garments, such as the *mang, kao, magua, jianyi*, when worn by military characters

shaozi mao 艄子帽 — boatman's hat; a felt hat with a round crown and upturned brim

sheng 生 — standard male roles with intrinsic dignity

shenguai lian 神怪脸 — god or demon face; for roles of gods, spirits, demons and strange creatures, for *jing* painted-face designs

shinü 仕女 — women who take orders, name for maid servants in domestic scenes

shirttail hem — the edge of the fabric is folded under twice about 1/4 inch and machine-stitched in the inside fold

shizimen lian 十字门脸 — lit. "ten face"; a category of *jing* painted-face design with a Chinese number-ten cross shape intersecting at the bridge of the nose

shou 寿 — Chinese character for long life

shuaifa 甩发 — lit. "to toss the hair"; a ponytail on a 3-inch post, worn by characters in unfavorable conditions who twirl their hair to indicate their state of distress

shuaiban 衰扮 — makeup with less color for older people; used for *laosheng* and *laodan* roles in poor health and of low status

shuaikui 帅盔 — marshal's helmet, with a horn-shaped crown

shuiqun 水裙 — water skirt; white or blue double-layered pleated skirt worn by boatmen and waiters

shuisha 水纱 — water gauze; a piece of black silk gauze 4 inches long and 16 inches wide that is dampened and wrapped around the head to create the hairline

shuixiu 水袖 — water sleeves; white silk extensions to the cuff of the garment sleeves

shui yizi 水衣子 — water jacket worn under all costumes for absorbing sweat to protect the costumes; made of cotton broadcloth

si taozi 丝绦子 — silk cord or long cord knotted at the chest for a heroic look

su 素 — plain; refers to both unembroidered or cotton cloth, such as *su baoyi, su jianyi, su luomao, su xuezi*, and so on

suihua lian 碎花脸 — scattered-pattern face; a category of *jing* painted face designs with multiple colors in small pieces, for complicated characters

suoyi 蓑衣 — stage version of a straw cape

surcoat — overcoat

taiding 台顶	a variation of the *houmao* helmet of a marquis, with an additional horn decoration on the crown to indicate military status	*wudan* 武旦	women fighters parallel to the *duanda wusheng* roles
taijian kui 太监盔	eunuch helmet; filigree headdress for eunuchs	*wufo guan* 五佛官	five-Buddha headdress for the head monk
taijian lian 太监脸	eunuch design for *jing* painted-face designs	*wuhang* 武行	military roles trained in acrobatics and martial arts, lesser, unnamed roles
taijian yi 太监衣	eunuch's robe, with wide waistband and pleated skirt panels, has water sleeves	*wujing* 武净	martial painted faces; also called *shuaida hua*; divided into *changkao wujing* for those who wear the armor, and *duanda wujing* for the more active fighters
toubu ezi 头布额子	a scarf and diadem, the two pieces making up a soldier's headdress	*wulaosheng* 武老生	*laosheng* who are generals and have fighting skills, usually wear *kao*
tuanhua magua 团花马褂	a *magua* embroidered with flower roundels	*wusheng* 武生	martial male roles, divided into *changkao* and *duanda*
tumian 涂面	to smear the face; the precedent of applying the disguise directly to the face, historical	*wusheng jin* 武生巾	young military male's soft hat, with crescent-shaped crest, butterfly-shaped rosette at the peak, and tassels over each ear, see also *xiaosheng jin*
wailian 歪脸	an asymmetrical face to indicate either an ugly visage or a flawed character in *jing* painted-face designs	*wuxi* 武戏	martial/military plays, featuring actions that focus on battles and heroic struggles
wangmao 王帽	king's fabric and gold-filigree crown; yellow for legitimate emperors, red for nonlegitimate, and white during periods of mourning; see also *huangmao*	*wuxiaosheng* 武小生	*xiaosheng* who are valiant young generals, generally wear *kao,* and are trained in combat
wangzi 网子	a fitted skullcap of horsehair, about 4 inches wide and 20 inches around, for covering the head in hairstyles	*xia wuse* 下五色	lower colors; more commonly used for domestic scenes: maroon (*zi*), pink (*fen*), blue (*lan*), lake blue (*hulan*), and olive green (*qiuxiang*)
wenchou 文丑	civil clown roles, sometimes shortened to *chou*	*xiajia* 下甲	lit. "under armor"; two-panel skirt for the *zhan'ao zhanqun*
wenxi 文戏	civil scenes or plays with actions featuring domestic and civil scenes, and love stories	*xian lianzi* 线帘子	drape of hair; long, black cords tied to the back of the head to simulate long tresses to the knees; also called *xian weizi*, tail of hair
wenxiaosheng 文小生	civil young male roles of princes, scholars, dandies, and lovers, sometimes shortened to *xiaosheng*	*xiangdiao* 相貂	decorated prime minister's hat of gold filigree, squared double crown, and flat wings with dragons
woshui 卧水	semicircles of embroidery representing still water on the hems of the *mang* and *long jianyi*; also called *pingshui*	*xiangjin* 相巾	informal soft square hat for prime ministers
wuchou 武丑	martial clown roles		

xiangsha 相纱 — prime minister's hat; a trapezoidal version of the *shamao* double-crowned headdress

xiangxing lian 象形脸 — pictographic face; for animal spirits or deities, uses patterns to mimic their shape for painted-face designs

xiao daoying kui 小倒缨盔 — small version of soldier's one- or two-piece tasseled helmet, with stiff diadem and neck flap; see also *daoying kui*

xiao ezi 小额子 — small diadem headdress especially for Bai Suzhen, the White Snake, with snake-like projections, often made with pearls

xiao fandan 小饭单 — small apron

xiao houyi 小猴衣 — little monkey clothes; similar to the *kuaiyi* martial jacket and trousers, in yellow with stylized fur embroidery

xiao hualian 小花脸 — small painted face; another term for the *chou* roles

xiao kanjian 小坎肩 — short vest for ladies

xiao manxue 小蛮靴 — lit. small "barbarian" boots for female warriors; flat, ankle-high, embroidered, with pointed, curled toes

xiao sengyi 小僧衣 — young monk robe, with crossover closing, mid-calf length

xiao taozi 小绦子 — small cord used as a waist belt, with tassels on the ends and one in the middle

xiao xuezi 小褶子 — small *xuezi* for children's roles

xiaosheng 小生 — young dignified men; role type for those generally under thirty and unmarried

xiaosheng jin 小生巾 — young male's soft hat with crescent-shaped crest from ear to ear; see also *wusheng jin*

xiaowan 小弯 — small curls; wefts of human hair in black, about 3/4 inches wide and 14 inches long, used to create the flat loops across the forehead for women's hairstyles

xieling taijian yi 斜领太监衣 — court robe for eunuchs with a *xuezi*-style straight crossover closing and wide band at waist, with fringe beneath it

xiepi 斜帔 — lit. "to wear crookedly"; to wear garments asymmetrically to indicate a state of distress

xingtou 行头 — all pieces included in costumes and actor's paraphernalia

xiqu 戏曲 — Chinese indigenous drama, entertainment with song and music

Xu Xian jin 许仙巾 — smaller version of the *yawei jin* ducktail hat designed specifically for Xu Xian, the husband of White Snake

xuanwu 玄武 — a tortoise surrounded by a snake, the animal connected with the color black

xueshi jin 学士巾 — scholar's firm-fabric double-crowned headdress with curved wings

xueshi yi 学士衣 — scholar's robe, with round chest embroidery and band above the hem, has water sleeves

xuezi 褶子 — informal robe with asymmetrical opening for men, has water sleeves

yanwei 燕尾 — the swallowtail piece that is worn on the back of the head for the Manchu-style hairstyle, shaped like a fiddle

yaobao 腰包 — lit. "bloated" skirt; plain white pleated skirt, for ill or pregnant characters

yao jinzi 腰巾子 — scarf worn at the waist

yawei jin 鸭尾巾 — ducktail hat with crescent of fur

yi 衣 — clothing; generic term for all costumes beyond the major four: *mang, pi, kao, xuezi*

ying 硬 — hard; as in stiffened version of the six-sided *ying luomao* hat worn by household servants, and *yingkao* with flags on the back

youbai 油白   shiny, oil-based white makeup for painted faces

yuanbao lian 元宝脸   ingot face category for *jing* painted-face designs; the forehead is one color in the shape of old Chinese money

yuanling taijian yi 圆领太监衣   round-collar court robe for eunuchs, with a curved crossover closing and wide band at waist, with fringe beneath it

yuanwai jin 员外巾   square fabric hat for wealthy or retired gentry worn with the crease in the front

yuansha 圆纱   version of the *shamao* with rounded wings, indicates dishonest characters

yudai 玉带   jade belt, hoop-shaped belt with jade ornaments, worn with *mang* and *guanyi*, and sometimes with the straight-edged *nümang*

yulin jia 鱼鳞甲   fish-scale armor; also called *Yuji jia*; designed by Mei Lanfang for Lady Yu to wear in *The Hegemon King Says Farewell to His Concubine*

yunchi 云翅   S-shaped or cloud wings on the back of the *fenyang* prime minister's hat

yunjian 云肩   cloud collar for women's garment

yuntai zhuang 云台装   cloud terrace costume, with fitted waist; designed by Mei Lanfang for fairies who can fly

za 杂   unimportant roles; servants and handmaids

zaju 杂剧   lit. "variety drama"; emerged in the Yuan dynasty (1271–1368) and supported by the Mongol rulers

zase 杂色   complicated or mixed colors, also miscellaneous colors; for less significant characters than those in the upper and lower colors

zhajin ezi 扎巾额子   lit. "tied cloth" helmet and diadem; with diadem of pearls and pompoms, and four upright pompoms on the crown, for male warriors and courtiers

zhajin kui 扎巾盔   lit. "tied cloth" helmet; with four upright pompoms behind on the crown

zhan'ao zhanqun 战袄战裙   martial jacket, trousers, and skirt for *wudan* women warriors who are acrobatic fighters

zhanmao 毡帽   felt hat with upturned brim and rounded crown

zharan 扎髯   beard "with a fierce outlook"; with center suspended from the main wire to reveal the mouth, for *jing* roles of rough characters

zhenglian 整脸   whole face; oldest and the simplest style of painted face design, with the entire face in one color, for *jing* characters with integrity

zhengjing 正净   primary *jing* roles; principal actors requiring strong singing skills; also called *da hualian* (great painted face), *tongchui* (copper hammer), and *heitou* (black head)

zheshan 折扇   folding fan

zhiduyi 制度衣   combat clothes for the Monkey King, consisting of a robe similar to the *jianyi* and trousers

zhongjun kui 中军盔   headdress for military gatekeeper who delivers messages and issues edicts; resembles a top hat with a tall cylindrical crown and narrow flat brim

zhongsha 忠纱   loyal hat; a version of the *shamao*, with double crown in black fabric with gold *chi* on the back

zhuaji 抓髻   hair coil: used on the back of the head for the *datou* style

zhuhong 朱红   scarlet or orange-red makeup

zijin guan 紫金冠   lit. "purple gold headdress"; lower in rank than yellow gold, a helmet in gold or silver filigree with a diadem of pearls, pompoms, and a distinctive filigree ball on the top of the crown, for princes and young noblemen *zongfa* 棕发 | lit. "palm fiber" hair; gray or white bun made now made of horsehair, for *laodan*

zongmao 棕帽 | lit. "mane hat"; a tall tapered hat made of sheer black mesh

zoushui 走水 | lit. "moving water"; layers of pleated fabric on the *baoyi* hero's set

zu kan 卒坎 | short vest for low-ranking soldiers

zuantian kui 钻天盔 | lit. "to drill through the sky"; headdress for Monkey King, with pearls and yellow pompoms

zuiqun 罪裙 | white skirt for criminals and prisoners

zuiyi 罪衣 | prisoner jacket and trousers in red

List of Performances

The following is a list of plays the author attended in live performance. The names of the companies have been shortened to initials, as listed in the Abbreviations at the front of the book. The length and completeness of each performance is noted according to the following categories: Long plays that tell a complete story are labeled "sole item performed." "Short play" identifies a performance that consists of only a few scenes from a larger work, but the selection tells a reasonably complete story. Short plays often appear with other items in one program. "Single scene" is a scene extracted from a longer play but performed under a title specific to that scene, which differs from the title of the complete play. "Excerpt" indicates a shorter version of the first two categories and is performed under the same title as the longer version. In a small minority of cases, assignment to a category was not entirely straightforward.

At the Mouth of the River at Jiujiang (Jiu jiang kou). PRSCJ (sole item performed), Beijing, China. April 23, 1996.

Attacking Pei Yuanqing with Fire (Huo shao Pei Yuanqing). ATCO (short play), Beijing, China. May 31, 2002.

Autumn River (Qiu jiang). BJC (short play), Beijing, China. May, 1996. Also NJC, Beijing, China. October 7, 2001.

The Battle at Red Cliffs (Chibi aozhan). NKKCOC (sole item performed), Taipei, Taiwan. December 21, 1995.

The Battle at Reed Marshes (Luhua dang). ATCO (single scene), Beijing, China. June 2, 2002.

Beating Jiao Zan (Da Jiao Zan). NJC (short play), Beijing, China. April 26, 1996.

The Beating of the Dragon Robe (Da longpao). PRSCJ (excerpt), Beijing, China. April 19, 1996. Also Amateur players, Beijing, China. September 16, 2001. Also NJC, Beijing, China. October 9, 2001.

The Bet on Li Cunxiao at the Banquet in Yaguan Tower (Yaguan lou). ATCO (excerpt), Beijing, China. May 31, 2002.

Blocking the Horse (Dangma). BJC (short play), Beijing, China, September 9, 2001. Also Amateur players, Beijing, China. September 16, 2001.

The Broken Bridge (Duan qiao). BJC (single scene), Beijing, China. July 2, 2000, BJC, Beijing, China. September 9, 2001. Also ATCO, Beijing, China. June 1, 2002.

The Carefree Ford (Xiaoyao jin). NJC (excerpt), Beijing, China. October 4, 2001.

Causing an Uproar in the Dragon King's Palace (Nao long-gong). NFDAAPOT (short play), Taipei, Taiwan. December 16, 1995. Also Independent players, Beijing, China. September 8, 2001. Also NJC, Beijing, China. October 7, 2001.

The City of Baidi (Baidi cheng). PRSCJ (sole item performed), Beijing, China. April 22, 1996. Also NJC, Beijing, China. September 30, 2001.

The Cosmic Blade (Yuzhou feng). NJC (excerpt), Beijing, China. October 9, 2001.

Defending the State (Da bao guo). NJC (short play), Beijing, China. October 5, 2001.

The Eight Mallets (Ba da chui). ATCO (excerpt), Beijing, China. June 1, 2002.

Eighteen Luohans Fight Wukong (Shiba luohan dou Wukong). BJC (short play), Beijing, China. May, 1996.

Exchanging Sons at the Execution Ground (Fa chang huan zi). ATCO (excerpt), Beijing, China. May 31, 2002.

Execution of the Son at the Headquarter's Gate (Yuanmen zhan zi). NFDAAPOT (sole item performed), Taipei, Taiwan. December 16, 1995.

The Exile of Qin Qiong (Qin Qiong fapei). PRSCJ (short play), Beijing, China. April 20, 1996.

Fiery Infernal Judge (Huo pan). NJC (short play), Beijing, China. April 27, 1996.

Fifteen Strings of Cash (Shiwu guan). NKKCOC (sole item performed), Taipei, Taiwan. November 3, 1995.

Fight at Crossroads Inn (Sancha kou). ATCO (short play), Beijing, China. June 2, 2002.

The First Scholar as Matchmaker (Zhuangyuan mei). PRSCJ (excerpt), Beijing, China. April 24, 1996.

The Gathering of Heroes (Qunying hui). BJC (sole item performed), Beijing, China. July 23, 2000.

Giving Away and Finding Again the Precious Purse (Suolin nang). PRSCJ (sole item performed), Beijing, China. April 18, 1996.

The Goddess of the Green Ripples (Bibo xianzi). ATCO (sole item performed), Beijing, China. April 28, 1996.

The Heavenly Fairy Spreading Flowers (Tiannü sanhua). PRSCJ (excerpt), Beijing, China. April 24, 1996.

The Hegemon King Says Farewell to His Concubine (Bawang bie ji). BIBOAP (excerpt), Beijing, China. July 10, 2000.

Hongniang (Hongniang). NJC (sole item performed), Beijing, China. July 31, 2000. Also NJC, Beijing, China. October 5, 2001.

Hongniang (Hongniang). BTAS (excerpt), Beijing, China. April 13, 1996.

Jiang Gan Steals the Letter (Jiang Gan dao shu). NJC (single scene), Beijing, China. October 7, 2001.

Judge Bao and the Case of Qin Xianglian (Qin Xianglian). NFDAAPOT (sole item performed), Taipei, Taiwan, December 3, 1995. Also PRSCJ, Beijing, China. April 17, 1996. Also DTD, UHM, Manoa, Hawai'i. February 6-8, 2002.

The Legend of White Snake (Bai she zhuan). Guest artists with NKKCOC (excerpt), Taipei, Taiwan. November 5, 1995. Also NKKCOC, Taipei, Taiwan. December 20, 1995. Also BTAS, Beijing, China. April 13, 1996. Also Independent players, Beijing, China. May 1, 1996.

Li Kui Visits His Mother (Li Kui tan mu). NJC (excerpt), Beijing, China. April 27, 1996.

Li Yaxian (Li Yaxian). BJC (sole item performed), Beijing, China. May 26, 2002.

Lian Jinfeng Stabs the Giant Clam (Lian Jinfeng). ATCO (excerpt), Beijing, China. June 1, 2002.

The Long Slope (Changban po). PRSCJ (excerpt), Beijing, China. April 21, 1996.

Lü Bu and Diaochan (Lü Bu yu Diaochan). BJC (sole item performed), Beijing, China. July 15, 2000.

Lü Bu and Diaochan (Lü Bu yu Diaochan). NJC (excerpt), Beijing, China. April 27, 1996.

Lü Bu Shoots an Arrow (Yuanmen she ji). NJC (excerpt), Beijing, China. April 29, 1996.

Lu Wenlong (Lu Wenlong). NKKCOC (sole item performed), Taipei, Taiwan. October 14, 1995.

Luo Cheng Calls Out to be Admitted at the Gate (Luo Cheng jiaoguan). Amateur players (excerpt), Beijing, China. September 16, 2001.

The Magic Cistern (Ju dagang). ATCO (short play), Beijing, China. June 1, 2002.

Magic Lotus Lantern (Bao lian deng). NJC (sole item performed), Beijing, China. April 28, 1996.

The Matching Spears (Dui hua qiang). NJC (excerpt), Beijing, China. September 28, 2001.

Mu Guiying Takes Command (Mu Guiying gua shuai). BJC (sole item performed), Beijing, China. July 16, 2000.

Mu Ke Stockade (Mu Ke zhai). PRSCJ (excerpt), Beijing, China, April 19, 1996. Also ATCO, Beijing, China, June 1, 2002.

Mulian Saves His Mother (Mulian jiumu). ATCO (excerpt), Beijing, China. June 2, 2002.

Orphan of the Zhao Family (Zhaoshi gu'er). NFDAAPOT (sole item performed), Taipei, Taiwan. December 6, 1995.

The Phoenix Returns to Its Nest (Feng huan chao). BJC (sole item performed), Beijing, China. July 9, 2000. Also NJC, Beijing, China. October 3, 2001.

Picking Up the Jade Bracelet (Shi yuzhuo). Independent players (short play), Beijing, China. September 8, 2001.

Qin Qiong Examines the Battle Formation (Qin Qiong guanzhen). ATCO (excerpt), Beijing, China. June 1, 2002.

Qin Xianglian (Qin Xianglian). PRSCJ (excerpt), Beijing, China. April 21, 1996.

Reconciliation of the Prime Minister and the General (Jiang xiang he). PRSCJ (excerpt), Beijing, China, April 24, 1996. Also BJC, Beijing, China, July 2, 2000.

The Red-Maned Fiery Steed (Hongzong liema). BJC (sole item performed), Beijing, China. October 6, 2001.

The Revenge of the Fisherman(Dayu shajia). PRSCJ (excerpt), Beijing, China. April 24, 1996.

Roster of Incorrupt Officials (Qingguan ce). PRSCJ (excerpt), Beijing, China. April 24, 1996.

The Ruse of the Bamboo Forest (Zhulin ji). ATCO (excerpt), Beijing, China. May 31, 2002.

The Second Entry into the Palace (Er jingong). NJC (short play), Beijing, China. April 26, 1996. Also NJC, Beijing, China. October 5, 2001.

Selling Water (Mai shui). NJC (short play), Beijing, China. September 28, 2001.

Silang Visits His Mother (Silang tan mu). NFDAAPOT (sole item performed), Taipei, Taiwan. December 5, 1995. Also DTD, UHM, Manoa, Hawai'i. February 6–7, 1998. Also BJC, Beijing, China, October 7, 2001.

Silang Visits His Mother (Silang tan mu). NJC (excerpt), Beijing, China. October 7, 2001.

A Sorrow that Transcends Life and Death (Sheng si hen). BJC (sole item performed), Beijing, China. July 30, 2000.

The Story of the Gold Turtle (Jingui ji). PRSCJ (excerpt), Beijing, China. April 24, 1996.

Tears in the Wild Mountains (Huangshan lei). PRSCJ (excerpt), Beijing, China. April 24, 1996. Also NJC, Beijing, China. April 29, 1996.

Turning Aside the Iron Carts (Tiao huache). ATCO (excerpt), Beijing, China. June 2, 2002.

A Visit to the Family Grave (Xiao shangfen). ATCO (short play), Beijing, China. May 31, 2002.

A Visit to the Imperial Tomb (Tan huangling). NJC (short play), Beijing, China. October 5, 2001.

White Snake Steals the Immortal Herbs (Dao xiancao). NJC (short play), Beijing, China. October 4, 2001.

Wild Boar Forest (Yezhu lin). NKKCOC (sole item performed), Taipei, Taiwan. December 19, 1995.

Women Generals of the Yang Family (Yangmen nüjiang). NJC (sole item performed), Beijing, China. October 3, 2001.

Wu Song Causes a Ruckus in the Inn (Wu Song da dian). BJC (short play), Beijing, China. July 2, 2000.

Xi Shi (Xi Shi). ATCO (excerpt), Beijing, China. June 2, 2002.

Xiao Shang River (Xiao Shang he). PRSCJ (short play), Beijing, China. April 24, 1996.

Xie Yaohuan (Xie Yaohuan). ATCO (excerpt), Beijing, China. May 31, 2002.

Yandang Mountain (Yandang shan). BJC (excerpt), Beijing, China. September 9. 2001.

Yutang Chun Unjustly Accused (Yutang Chun). NFDAAPOT (sole item performed), Taipei, Taiwan. December 2, 1995.

Yutang Chun (Yutang Chun). PRSCJ (excerpt), Beijing, China. April 20, 1996.

Zhaojun Goes beyond the Great Wall (Zhaojun chusai). ATCO (excerpt), Beijing, China. June 1, 2002.

Zhuge Liang Leaves His Thatched Roof Study for the First Time (Chuchu maolu). NJC (sole item performed), Beijing, China. October 4, 2001.

Bibliography

Anquetil, Jacques. *Silk*. New York: Flammarion, 1995.

Arlington, L. C. *The Chinese Drama from the Earliest Times until Today*. Shanghai: Kelly and Walsh, [1939].

Barnhart, Richard M. *Peach Blossom Spring: Gardens and Flowers in Chinese Paintings*. New York: Metropolitan Museum of Art, 1983.

Brandon, James R., ed. *The Cambridge Guide to Asian Theatre*. Cambridge: Cambridge University Press, 1993.

Burnham, Dorothy K. *Cut My Cote*. Canada: MacKinnon-Moncur, 1973.

Cahill, James. *Treasures of Chinese Painting*. New York: Skira, Rizzoli, 1977.

Cammann, Schuyler. *China's Dragon Robes*. New York: The Ronald Press Company, 1952.

Chavannes, Edouard. *The Five Happinesses*. Elaine Spaulding Atwood, trans. New York: Weatherhill, 1973.

Chuang Po Ho. *Chinese Forms*. Peter Eberly, trans. Taiwan: Sinorama Magazine, 1989.

Chung, Young Yang. *The Art of Oriental Embroidery: History, Aesthetics and Techniques*. New York: Charles Scribner's Sons, 1979.

DeFrancis, John, ed. *ABC Chinese-English Comprehensive Dictionary*. Honolulu: University of Hawai'i Press, 1996.

Dickenson, Gary, and Linda Wrigglesworth. *Imperial Wardrobe*. London: Bamboo Publishing Ltd., 1990.

Dolby, William. *A History of Chinese Drama*. New York: Barnes and Noble Books, 1976.

Eberhard, Wolfram. *Dictionary of Chinese Symbols*. Singapore: Federal Publications, 1990.

Fong, Wen C. *Beyond Representation, Chinese Painting and Calligraphy 8th-14th Century*. New Haven: Yale University Press, 1992.

Gao Hanyu. *Chinese Textile Designs*. Rosemary Scott and Susan Whitfield, trans. London: Penguin Books/Viking, 1992.

Garrett, Valerie. *Chinese Clothing: An Illustrated Guide*. Hong Kong: Oxford University Press, 1994.

———. *Chinese Dragon Robes*. Oxford: Oxford University Press, 1998.

———. *A Collector's Guide to Chinese Dress Accessories*. Singapore: Times Editions, [c1997].

———. *Mandarin Squares: Mandarins and Their Insignia*. Hong Kong: Oxford University Press, 1990.

———. *Traditional Chinese Clothing*. Oxford: Oxford University Press, 1987.

Gostelow, Mary. *Embroidery, Traditional Design, Techniques and Patterns from all over the World*. London: Marshall Cavendish Editions, 1978.

Guy, Nancy A. "Peking Opera as "National Opera" in Taiwan: What's in a Name?" *Asian Theatre Journal* 12, no. 1 (Spring, 1995): 85–103.

He Jianguo, Zhang Yanying, and Guo Youming. *Hair Fashions of Tang Dynasty Women*. Ding Shen, and Wen Bo, trans. Hong Kong: Hair and Beauty Co., Ltd., 1987.

Hong Kong Urban Council. *Heaven's Embroidered Cloths: One Thousand Years of Chinese Textiles*. Hong Kong: Urban Council of Hong Kong, 1995. (organized by the Hong Kong Museum of Art).

Hsu, Tao-Ching. *The Chinese Conception of Theatre*. Seattle: University of Washington Press, 1985.

Hu, Jason C. *Traditional Chinese Culture in Taiwan*. Taiwan: Kwang Hwa Publishing Company, 1994.

Huo Jianying. *The Art of China's Peking Opera*. Zhang Jie, trans. Beijing: China Today Press, 1997.

Jacobsen, Robert D. *Imperial Silks: Ch'ing Dynasty Textiles in the Minneapolis Institute of Arts,* 2 vols. Minneapolis: Minneapolis Institute of Arts, 2000.

———. *Imperial Silk of the Ch'ing Dynasty*. Minneapolis: The Minneapolis Institute of Arts, 1991.

Kao Yu-chen, ed. *Dextrous and Colorful Chinese*

Embroidery. Taiwan: China Art Printing Works, 1989.

Li Nianpei, ed. and trans. *The Beating of the Dragon Robe.* Hong Kong: Joint Publishing (H. K.) Co., Ltd; Beijing: China Travel and Tourism Press, 1988.

Lindqvist, Cecilia. *China, Empire of Living Symbols.* Reading, Massachusetts: Addison-Wesley Publishing Company, Inc., 1991.

Long, Jean. *How to Paint the Chinese Way.* Poole, Dorset: Blandford Press, 1980.

Lu Qing, compiler. *Peking Opera Stardom, Celebrating 200 Years of Peking Opera.* Liu Zhiguang, trans. Beijing, China: Beijing Publishing House, 1991.

Lu, Steve. *Face Painting in Chinese Opera.* Singapore: MPH Publications, Sdn. Bhd, 1968.

Liu Yuemei. *Zhongguo Jingju yixiang (Beijing opera costume).* Shanghai: Shanghai cishu, 2002).

Ma Qiang, Yu Qiaolan, Wang Gangniu, Ma Kuan, and Ma Kui. *The Pictorial Album of Costumes in Chinese Traditional Opera.* Wang Zhunzhong, and Wang Zhuping, trans. Taiyuan, Shanxi, PRC: Shanxi Education Press, 1992.

Mackerras, Colin, ed. *Chinese Theatre from its Origins to the Present Day.* Honolulu: University of Hawai'i Press, 1983.

———. *The Chinese Theatre in Modern Times.* Amherst: University of Massachusetts Press, 1975.

Mailey, Jean. *Embroidery in Imperial China.* New York: China Institute of America, 1978.

———. *The Manchu Dragon. Costumes of the Ching Dynasty 1644–1912.* New York: The Metropolitan Museum of Art, 1980.

Pan Xiafeng. *The Stagecraft of the Peking Opera from its Origins to the Present Day.* Beijing: New World Press, 1995.

Pang, Mae Anna. *Dragon Emperor: Treasures from the Forbidden City.* Melbourne: National Gallery of Victoria, 1988.

Priest, Alan, and Pauline Simmons. *Chinese Textiles.* New York: Metropolitan Museum of Art, 1934.

Rowley, George. *Principles of Chinese Painting.* New Jersey: Princeton University Press, 1959.

Scott, A. C. *Actors Are Madmen: Notebook of a Theatregoer in China.* Wisconsin: University of Wisconsin Press, 1982.

———. *Chinese Costume in Transition.* New York: Theatre Arts Books, 1960.

———. *The Classical Theatre of China.* New York: The Macmillan Company, 1957.

———. *An Introduction to the Chinese Theatre.* New York: Theatre Arts Books, 1962.

———. *Traditional Chinese Plays.* 3 vols. Madison: University of Wisconsin Press, 1967–1975.

Scott, Philippa. *The Book of Silk.* London: Thames and Hudson, 1993.

Silbergeld, Jerome. *Chinese Painting Style: Media Methods, and Principles of Form.* Seattle: University of Washington Press, 1982.

Tan Yuanjie. *Zhongguo Jingju fuzhuang tupu (An illustrated guide to costume in Jingju).* Beijiing: Beijing Gongyi Meishu Chubanshe, 1999.

Teng Chang-Kuo. *Chinese Opera Costumes.* Ku Hsien-Liang, English editor. Taipei: National Taiwan Arts Center, 1961.

Trapido, Joel, ed. *An International Dictionary of Theatre Language.* Connecticut and England: Greenwood Press, 1985.

T'sao Kuo-lin. *The Face of Chinese Opera.* William Hoyle, trans. Taiwan: Hilit Publishing Co., Ltd., 1987.

Vollmer, John E. *Decoding Dragons.* Oregon: University of Oregon, 1983.

———. *Five Colours of the Universe: Symbolism in Clothes and Fabrics of the Ch'ing Dynasty (1644–1911).* Edmonton: Edmonton Art Gallery, 1980.

———. *In the Presence of the Dragon Throne. Ch'ing Dynasty Costume in the Royal Ontario Museum.* Toronto: Royal Ontario Museum, 1977.

———. *Ruling from the Dragon Throne: Costume of the Qing Dynasty (1644–1911).* Berkeley: Ten Speed Press, 2002.

Wan Ruquan, Wan Fengzhu, Bai Bingjun, and Wu Zedong, eds. *Jingju renwu zhuang ban bai chu (Costuming and makeup for the characters in 100 Jingju plays).* Revised by Chen Guoqing. Beijing: Wenhua Yishu Chubanshe, 1998.

Wang Yarong. *Chinese Folk Embroidery.* London: Thames and Hudson, 1987.

Wichmann, Elizabeth. *Listening to Theatre: The Aural Dimensions of Beijing Opera.* Honolulu: University of Hawai'i Press, 1991.

———, trans. *The Phoenix Returns to Its Nest*. Beijing: New World Press, 1986.

Williams, C. A. S. *Outlines of Chinese Symbolism and Art Motives*. Shanghai: Kelly and Walsh, Limited, 1932.

Wilson, Verity. *Chinese Dress*. (London): Victoria and Albert Museum, 1986.

Wrigglesworth, Linda. *The Badge of Rank: China*. England: Rustin Clark, 1990.

Wu Mingchi. *Facial Makeup in Beijing Opera*. Luo Changyan, trans. Taipei: Sing Kuang Bookstore, 1990.

Wu Zuguang, Huang Zuolin, and Mei Shaowu. *Peking Opera and Mei Lanfang*. Beijing: New World Press, 1984.

Yu, Leslie Tseng Tseng with Gail Schiller Tuchman. *Chinese Painting in Four Seasons: A Manual of Aesthetics and Techniques*. New Jersey: Prentice-Hall, Inc. 1981.

Zhan Huijuan, ed. *Xiju dianying meishu ziliao*, vol. 4, *Fushi (Documentation for theatre, film and fine arts, vol. 4, Costumes)*. Beijing: Renmin Meishu Chubanshe, 1997.

Zhang Geng. *The Art of Face Painting in Chinese Music-Drama*. Mao Xiaoyu, trans. Hong Kong: Jiangxi Art Publishing House, 1993.

Zhang Yijuan, Wu Zedong, Li Shuping, Lu Jianrong, and Wan Fengzhu, Shen Shihua, eds. *Chuantong Jingju renwu zaoxing huicui (A galaxy of character images in traditional Jingju)*. Beijing: Zhongguo Xiju Chubanshe, 2001.

Zhao Heng, Chen Xiansu, and Li Jianbo, ed. *Pictorial History of Beijing Opera*. Hu Dongsheng, trans. Beijing: Beijing Yanshan Publishing House, 1990.

Zhao Menglin, and Yan Jiqing. *Peking Opera Painted Faces*. Gong Lizeng, trans. Beijing: Morning Glory Publishers, 1992.

Zhao Shaohua, ed. *Costumes of the Peking Opera*. People's Republic of China: Intercontinental Press, 1999.

Zheng Dai, ed. *Zhongguo gudai fushi jianshi (A concise history of ancient Chinese clothing)*. Beijing: Zhongguo Qinggongye Chubanshe, 1999.

Zhou Xibao. *Zhongguo gudai fushi shi (A history of ancient Chinese clothing)* Beijing: Zhongguo Xiju Chubanshe, 1996.

Zhou Xun, and Gao Chunming. *5000 Years of Chinese Costumes*. Hong Kong: The Commercial Press, Ltd., 1988.

Zung, Cecilia. *Secrets of the Chinese Drama*. London: George G. Harrap and Co., Ltd., 1937.

Interviews

Li Shuo, Headdress Supervisor, September-October, 2001 and May-June, 2002, Academy of Traditional Chinese Opera (Zhongguo Xiqu Xueyuan), Beijing, China.

Li Wencai, Head of the Acting Department, July-August, 2000. Academy of Traditional Chinese Opera (Zhongguo Xiqu Xueyuan), Beijing, China.

Liu Xiaoqing, Costume Instructor, July, 2000, and September, 2001. Academy of Traditional Chinese Opera (Zhongguo Xiqu Xueyuan), Beijing, China.

Ma Jing, Makeup and Hairstyles Instructor, July-August, 2000 and May-June, 2002, Academy of Traditional Chinese Opera (Zhongguo Xiqu Xueyuan), Beijing, China.

Tan Yuanjie, Costume Instructor, September-October, 2001 and May-June, 2002, Academy of Traditional Chinese Opera (Zhongguo Xiqu Xueyuan), Beijing, China.

Wang Shiyin, Acting Instructor, September-October, 2001, Academy of Traditional Chinese Opera (Zhongguo Xiqu Xueyuan), Beijing, China.

Wu Wenxue, Painted-Face Instructor, July-August, 2000 and May-June, 2002, Academy of Traditional Chinese Opera (Zhongguo Xiqu Xueyuan), Beijing, China.

Yin Yongming, Wardrobe Supervisor, September-October, 2001 and May-June, 2002, Academy of Traditional Chinese Opera (Zhongguo Xiqu Xueyuan), Beijing, China.

Zhang Jing, Costume History Instructor, September-October, Academy of Traditional Chinese Opera (Zhongguo Xiqu Xueyuan), Beijing, China.

Zhang Weidong, actor, Northern Kunqu Company (Beifang Kunqu Juyuan), September, 2001, June, 2002. Beijing, China.

Zhao Zhenbang, Wardrobe Personnel, April-May, 1996. The Affiliated Middle School for Traditional Chinese Opera (Zhongguo Xiqu Xueyuan Fushu Zhongxue), Beijing, China.

Zou Zhiqiang, Costume Instructor, May, 1996. The Affiliated Middle School for Traditional Chinese Opera (Zhongguo Xiqu Xueyuan Fushu Zhongxue), Beijing, China.

Index

The names of items are listed in the language commonly used in the text. Words with the prefix *nü* are listed under the garment, such as *kao, mang, pi, xuezi*, etc. Numbers in **boldface** refer to illustrations.

ABOUT THE AUTHOR

Alexandra B. Bonds is Professor of Costume Design at the University of Oregon. Her passion for Beijing Opera costumes began when she received a Fulbright to teach at the National Institute for the Arts in Taiwan in 1990. She became the first foreigner to study costumes at the Academy for Traditional Chinese Opera in Beijing, China, where she conducted extensive research for this book. An award-winning designer, she provides a unique point of view into the costumes from both a theoretical and functional perspective. Her research in this area has been recognized for excellence in writing for the performing arts by the United States Institute for Theatre Technology.